BATGIRL
OLD ENEMIES

writer
MAIRGHREAD SCOTT

artists
PAUL PELLETIER
NORM RAPMUND
ELENA CASAGRANDE
SCOTT GODLEWSKI
JOSÉ MARZÁN JR.

colorist
JORDIE BELLAIRE
JOHN KALISZ
HI-FI

letterer
ANDWORLD DESIGN

collection cover artists
EMANUELA LUPACCHINO and
DAVE McCAIG

BATMAN created by BOB KANE with BILL FINGER

VOL.
6

WITHDRAWN

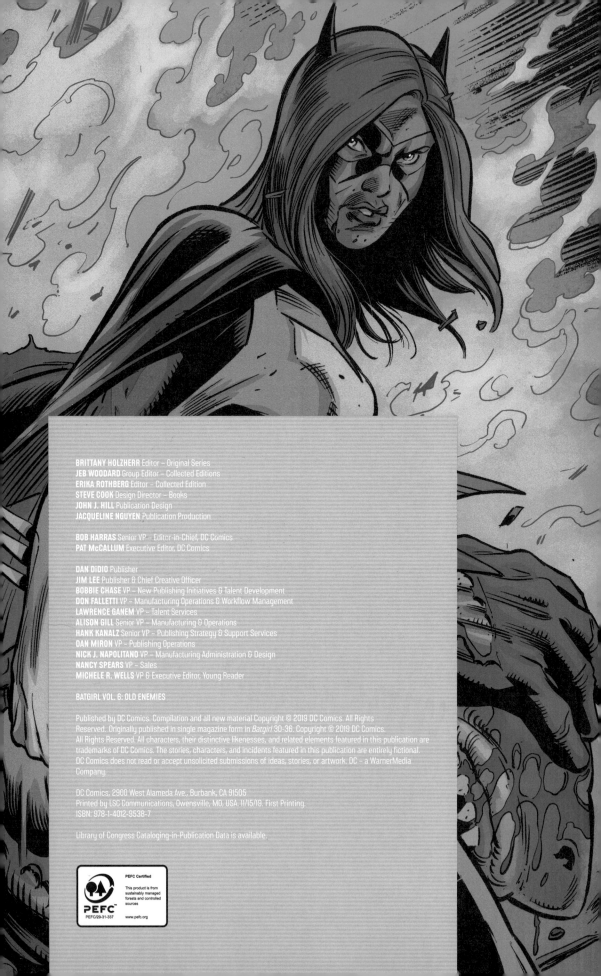

BRITTANY HOLZHERR Editor – Original Series
JEB WOODARD Group Editor – Collected Editions
ERIKA ROTHBERG Editor – Collected Edition
STEVE COOK Design Director – Books
JOHN J. HILL Publication Design
JACQUELINE NGUYEN Publication Production

BOB HARRAS Senior VP – Editor-in-Chief, DC Comics
PAT McCALLUM Executive Editor, DC Comics

DAN DiDIO Publisher
JIM LEE Publisher & Chief Creative Officer
BOBBIE CHASE VP – New Publishing Initiatives & Talent Development
DON FALLETTI VP – Manufacturing Operations & Workflow Management
LAWRENCE GANEM VP – Talent Services
ALISON GILL Senior VP – Manufacturing & Operations
HANK KANALZ Senior VP – Publishing Strategy & Support Services
DAN MIRON VP – Publishing Operations
NICK J. NAPOLITANO VP – Manufacturing Administration & Design
NANCY SPEARS VP – Sales
MICHELE R. WELLS VP & Executive Editor, Young Reader

BATGIRL VOL. 6: OLD ENEMIES

DC Comics, 2900 West Alameda Ave., Burbank, CA 91505
Printed by LSC Communications, Owensville, MO, USA. 11/15/19. First Printing.
ISBN: 978-1-4012-9538-7

Library of Congress Cataloging-in-Publication Data is available.

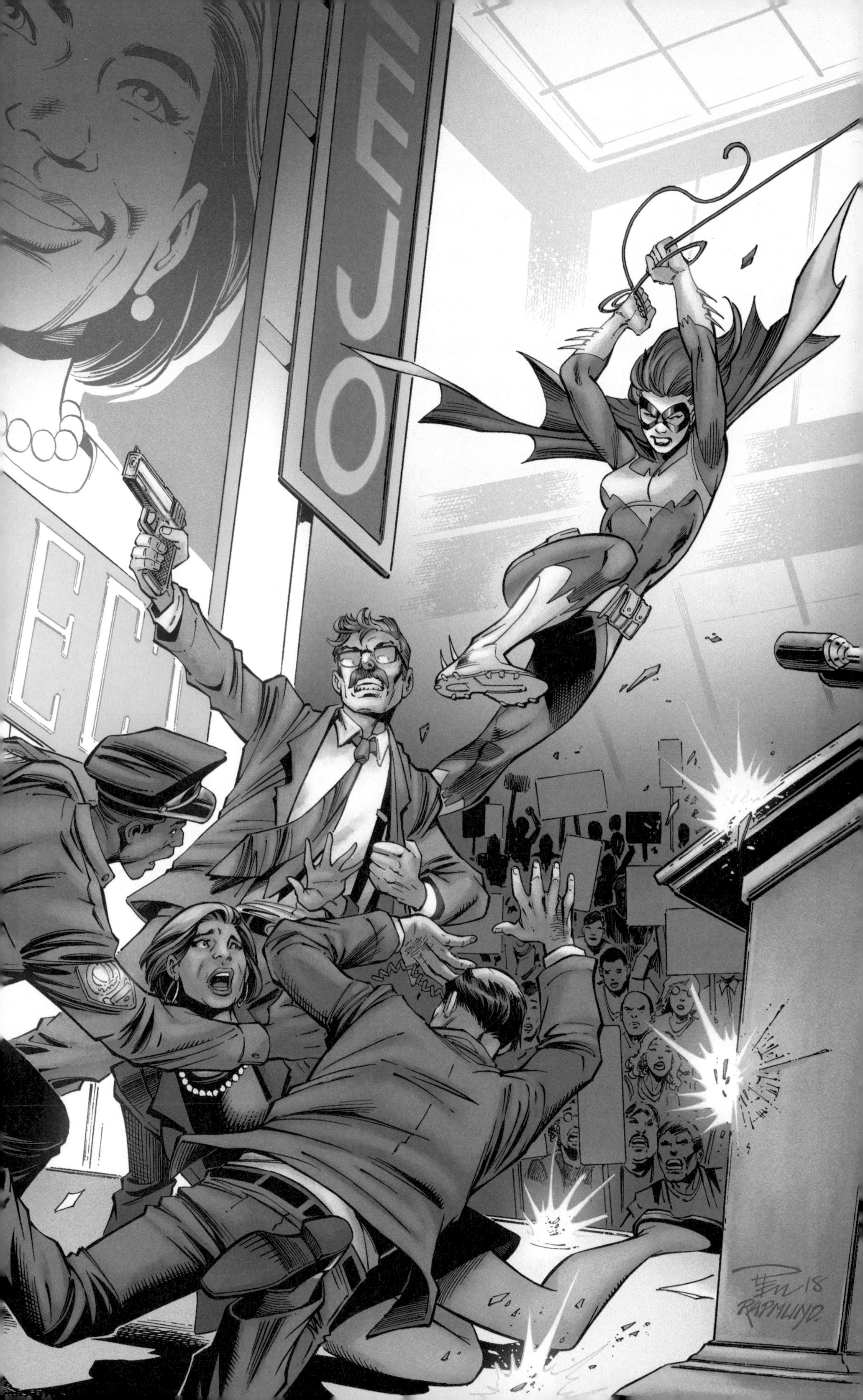
RAPMUND.

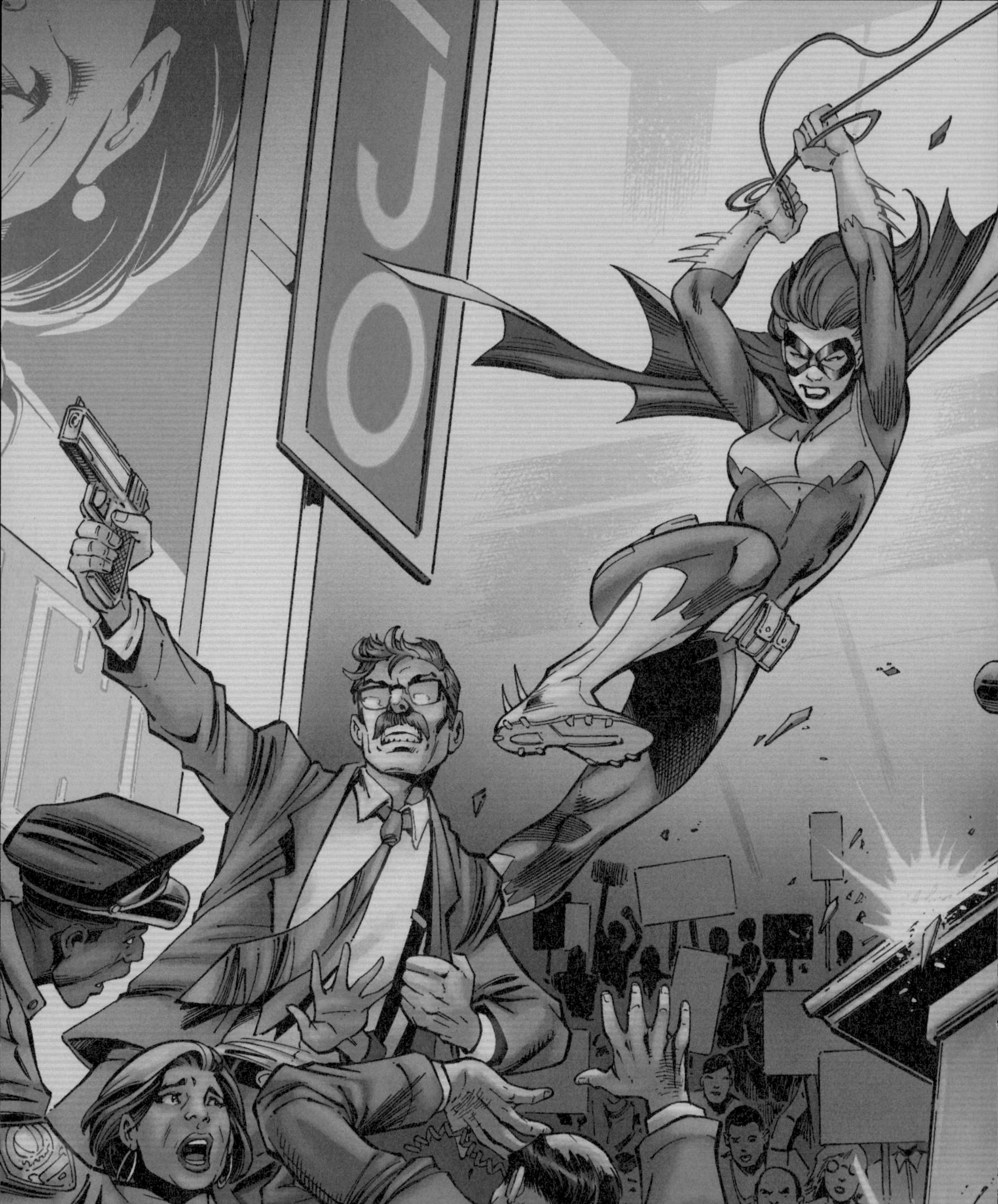

JO

BATGIRL

#30

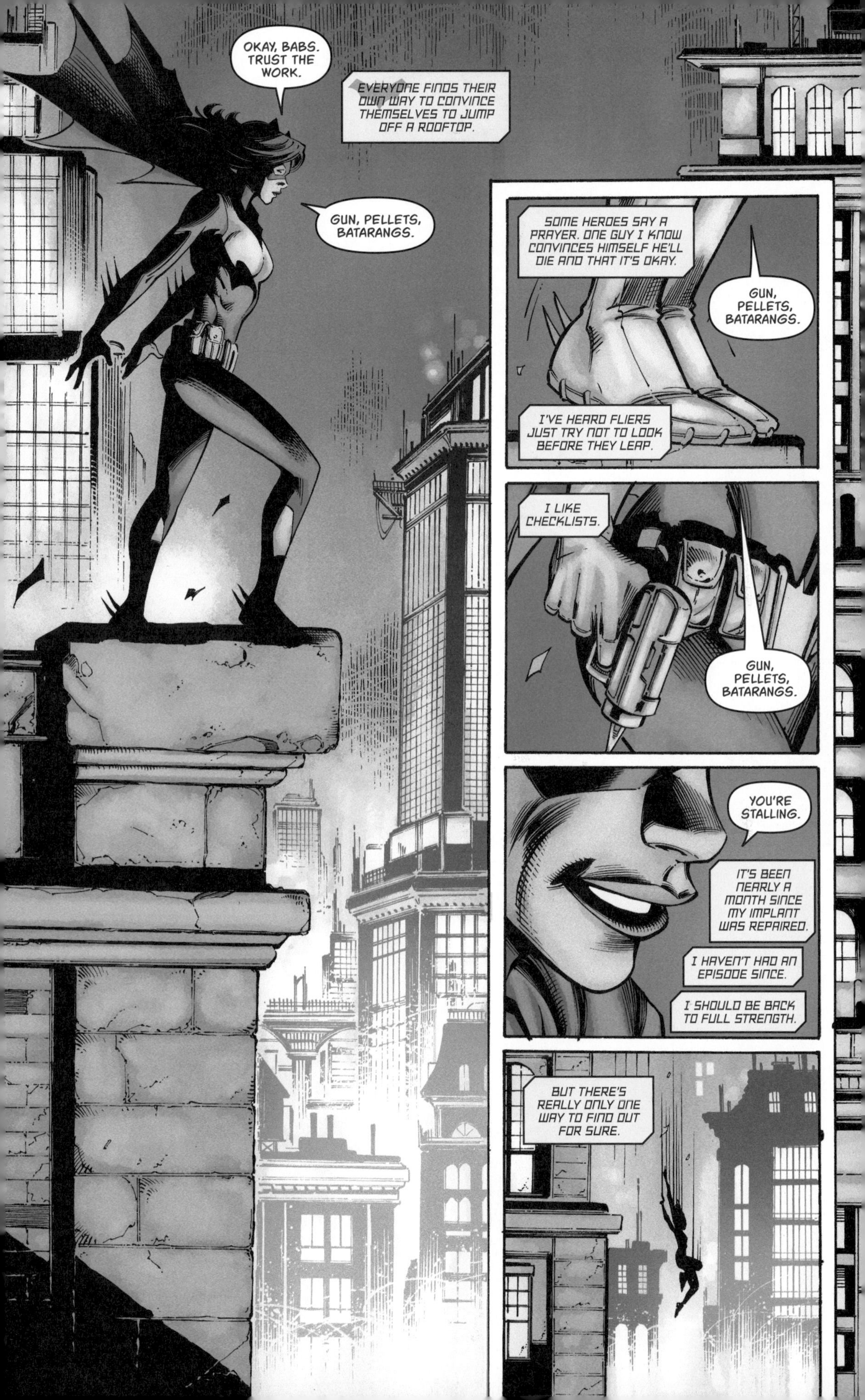
OKAY, BABS. TRUST THE WORK.
EVERYONE FINDS THEIR OWN WAY TO CONVINCE THEMSELVES TO JUMP OFF A ROOFTOP.
GUN, PELLETS, BATARANGS.
SOME HEROES SAY A PRAYER. ONE GUY I KNOW CONVINCES HIMSELF HE'LL DIE AND THAT IT'S OKAY.
GUN, PELLETS, BATARANGS.
I'VE HEARD FLIERS JUST TRY NOT TO LOOK BEFORE THEY LEAP.
I LIKE CHECKLISTS.
GUN, PELLETS, BATARANGS.
YOU'RE STALLING.
IT'S BEEN NEARLY A MONTH SINCE MY IMPLANT WAS REPAIRED.
I HAVEN'T HAD AN EPISODE SINCE.
I SHOULD BE BACK TO FULL STRENGTH.
BUT THERE'S REALLY ONLY ONE WAY TO FIND OUT FOR SURE.

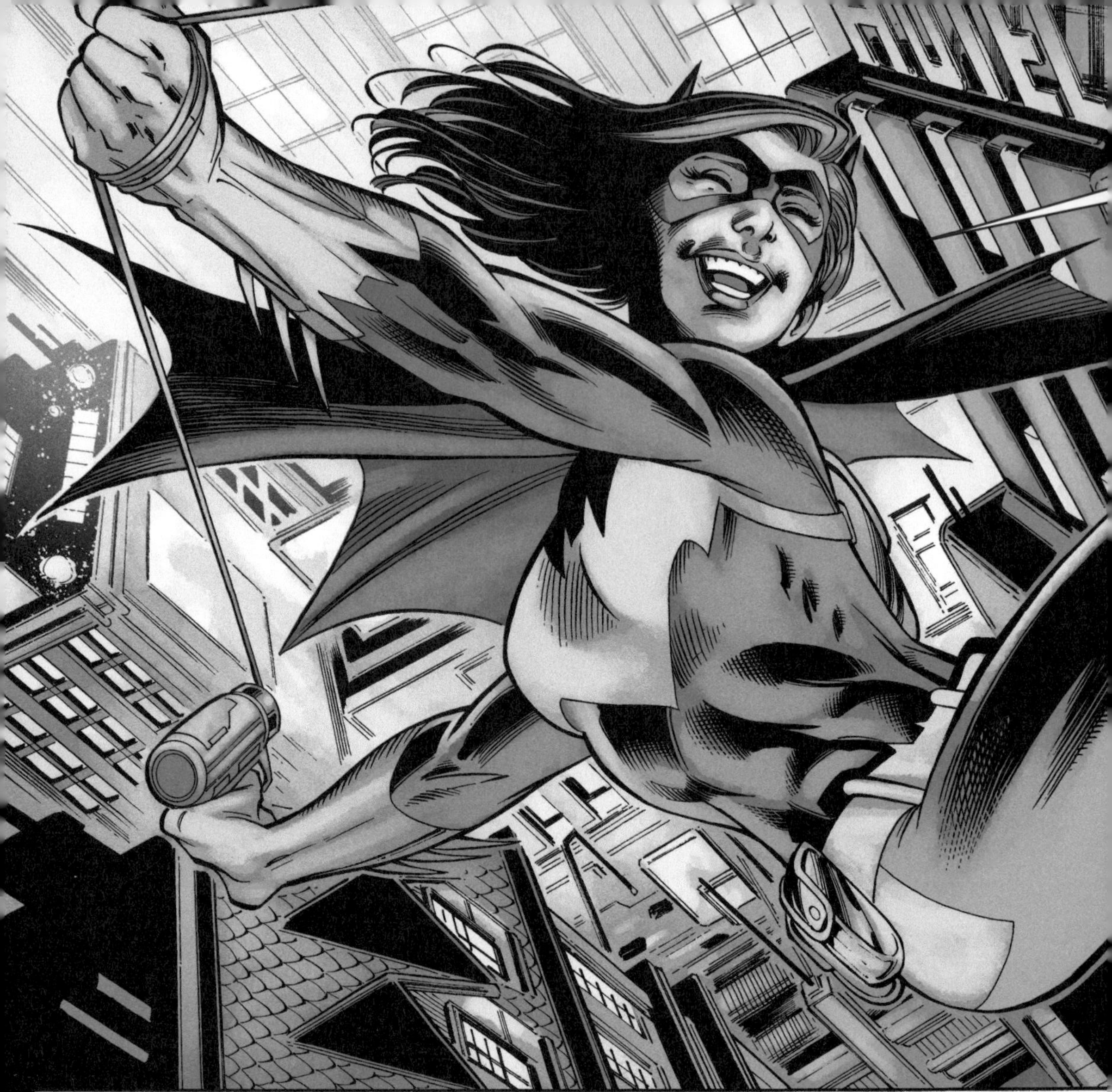

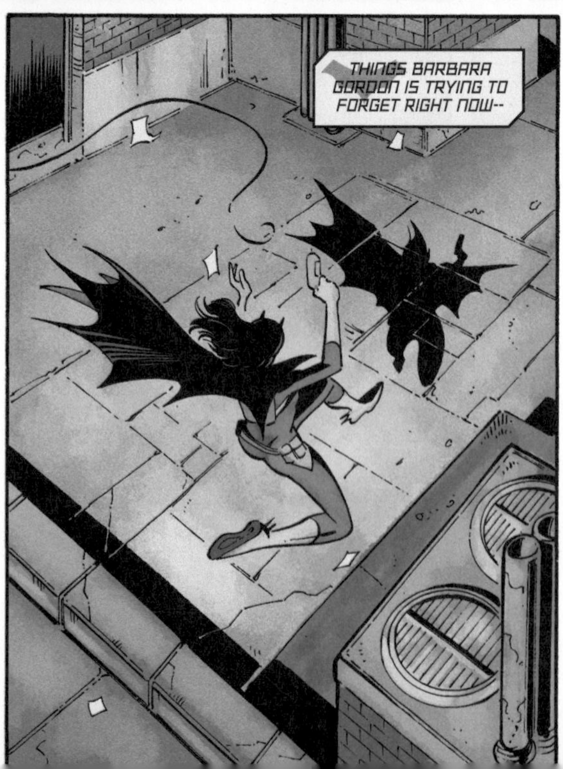
THINGS BARBARA GORDON IS TRYING TO FORGET RIGHT NOW--

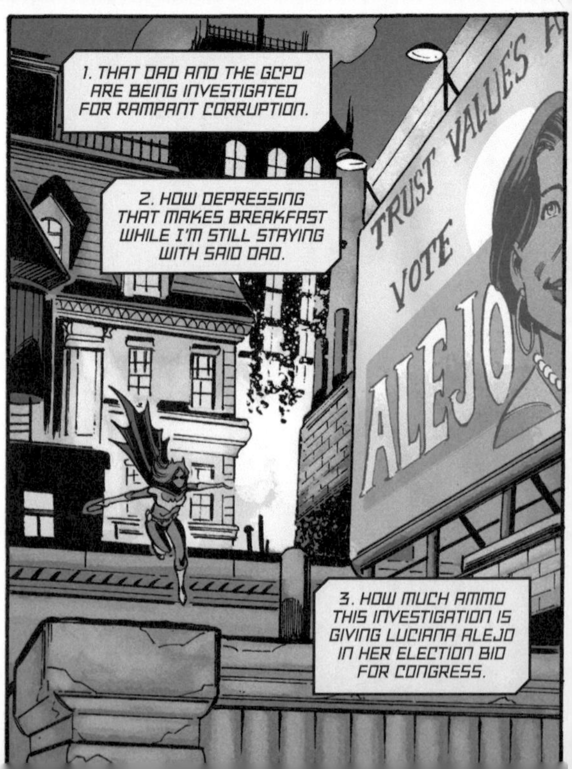
1. THAT DAD AND THE GCPD ARE BEING INVESTIGATED FOR RAMPANT CORRUPTION.
2. HOW DEPRESSING THAT MAKES BREAKFAST WHILE I'M STILL STAYING WITH SAID DAD.
TRUST VALUES
VOTE
ALEJO
3. HOW MUCH AMMO THIS INVESTIGATION IS GIVING LUCIANA ALEJO IN HER ELECTION BID FOR CONGRESS.

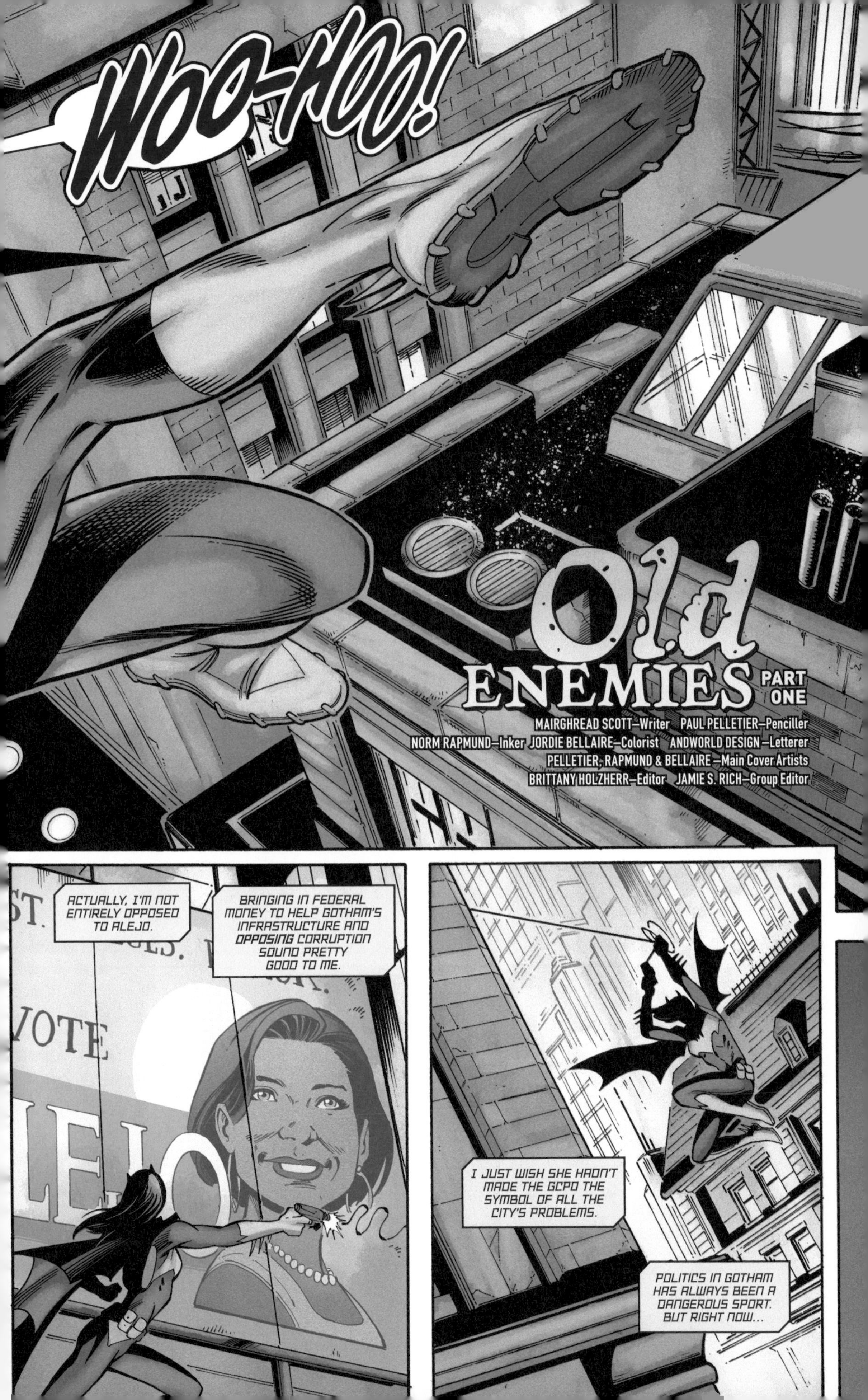
WOO-HOO!
Old ENEMIES PART ONE
MAIRGHREAD SCOTT—Writer PAUL PELLETIER—Penciller
NORM RAPMUND—Inker JORDIE BELLAIRE—Colorist ANDWORLD DESIGN—Letterer
PELLETIER, RAPMUND & BELLAIRE—Main Cover Artists
BRITTANY HOLZHERR—Editor JAMIE S. RICH—Group Editor
ACTUALLY, I'M NOT ENTIRELY OPPOSED TO ALEJO.
BRINGING IN FEDERAL MONEY TO HELP GOTHAM'S INFRASTRUCTURE AND OPPOSING CORRUPTION SOUND PRETTY GOOD TO ME.
VOTE
I JUST WISH SHE HADN'T MADE THE GCPD THE SYMBOL OF ALL THE CITY'S PROBLEMS.
POLITICS IN GOTHAM HAS ALWAYS BEEN A DANGEROUS SPORT. BUT RIGHT NOW...

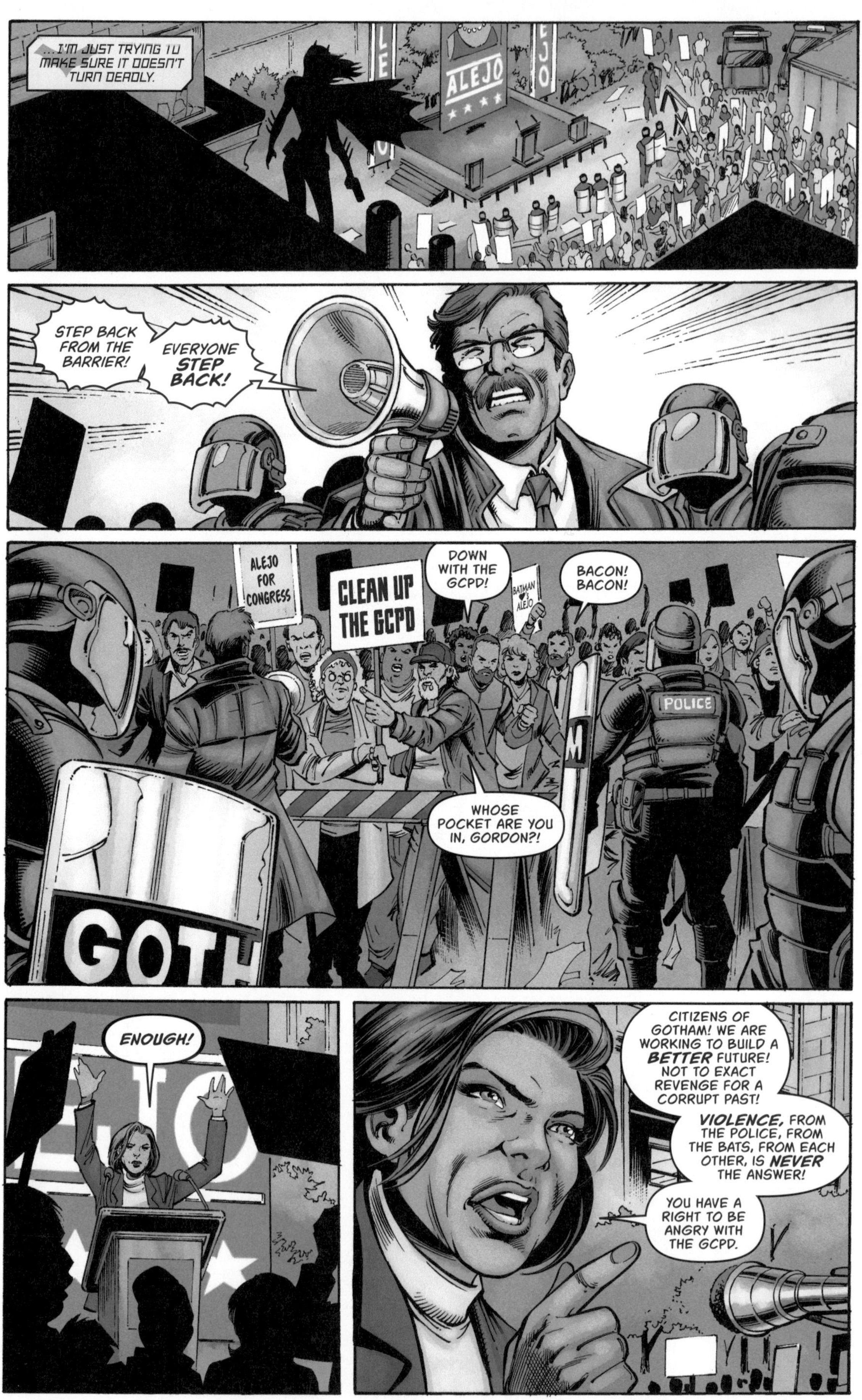
...I'M JUST TRYING TO MAKE SURE IT DOESN'T TURN DEADLY.
ALEJO
STEP BACK FROM THE BARRIER!
EVERYONE STEP BACK!
ALEJO FOR CONGRESS
CLEAN UP THE GCPD
DOWN WITH THE GCPD!
BATMAN ♥'s ALEJO
BACON! BACON!
POLICE
WHOSE POCKET ARE YOU IN, GORDON?!
GOTH
ENOUGH!
CITIZENS OF GOTHAM! WE ARE WORKING TO BUILD A BETTER FUTURE! NOT TO EXACT REVENGE FOR A CORRUPT PAST!
VIOLENCE, FROM THE POLICE, FROM THE BATS, FROM EACH OTHER, IS NEVER THE ANSWER!
YOU HAVE A RIGHT TO BE ANGRY WITH THE GCPD.

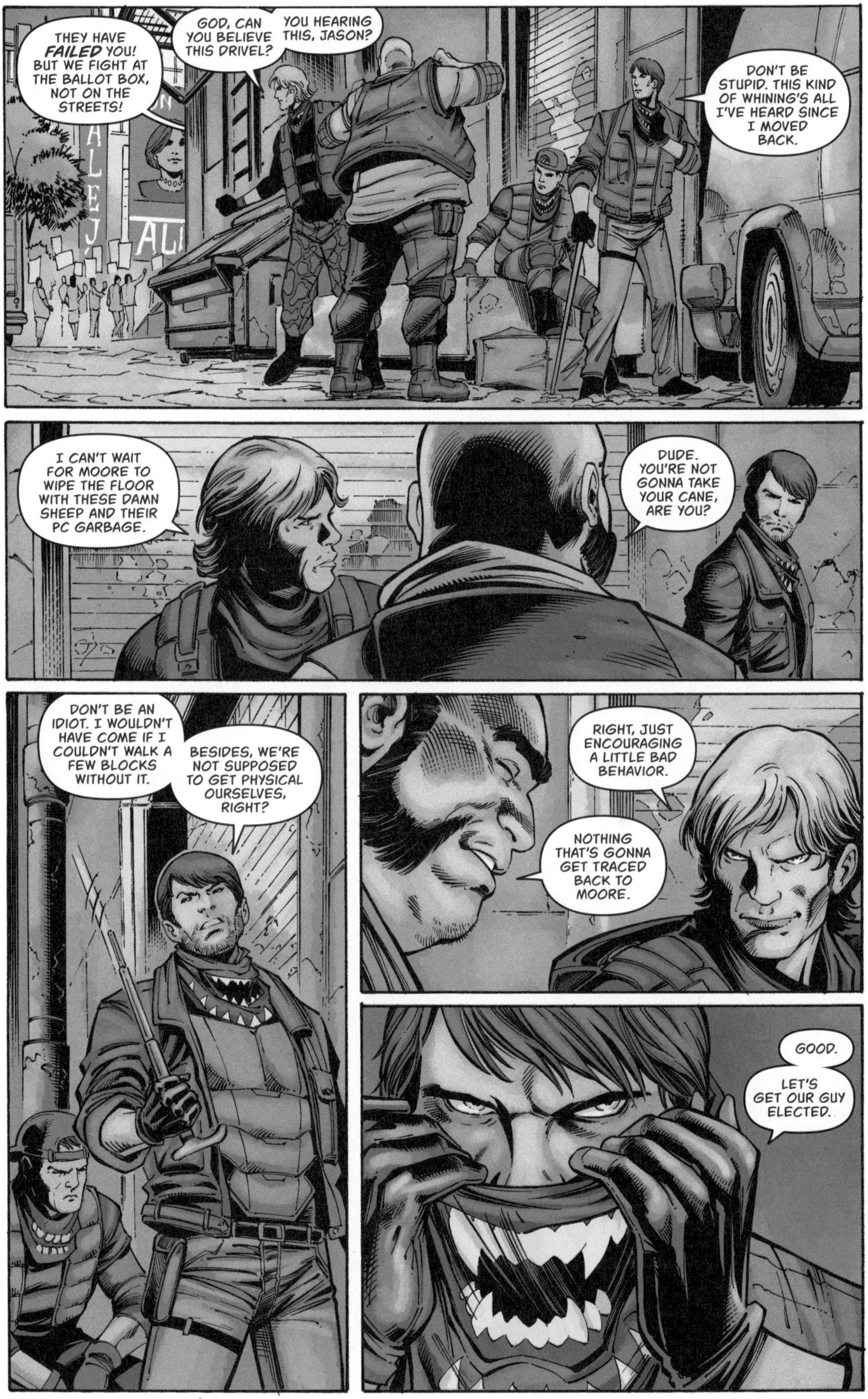
THEY HAVE FAILED YOU! BUT WE FIGHT AT THE BALLOT BOX, NOT ON THE STREETS!
GOD, CAN YOU BELIEVE THIS DRIVEL?
YOU HEARING THIS, JASON?
DON'T BE STUPID. THIS KIND OF WHINING'S ALL I'VE HEARD SINCE I MOVED BACK.
I CAN'T WAIT FOR MOORE TO WIPE THE FLOOR WITH THESE DAMN SHEEP AND THEIR PC GARBAGE.
DUDE. YOU'RE NOT GONNA TAKE YOUR CANE, ARE YOU?
DON'T BE AN IDIOT. I WOULDN'T HAVE COME IF I COULDN'T WALK A FEW BLOCKS WITHOUT IT.
BESIDES, WE'RE NOT SUPPOSED TO GET PHYSICAL OURSELVES, RIGHT?
RIGHT, JUST ENCOURAGING A LITTLE BAD BEHAVIOR.
NOTHING THAT'S GONNA GET TRACED BACK TO MOORE.
GOOD.
LET'S GET OUR GUY ELECTED.

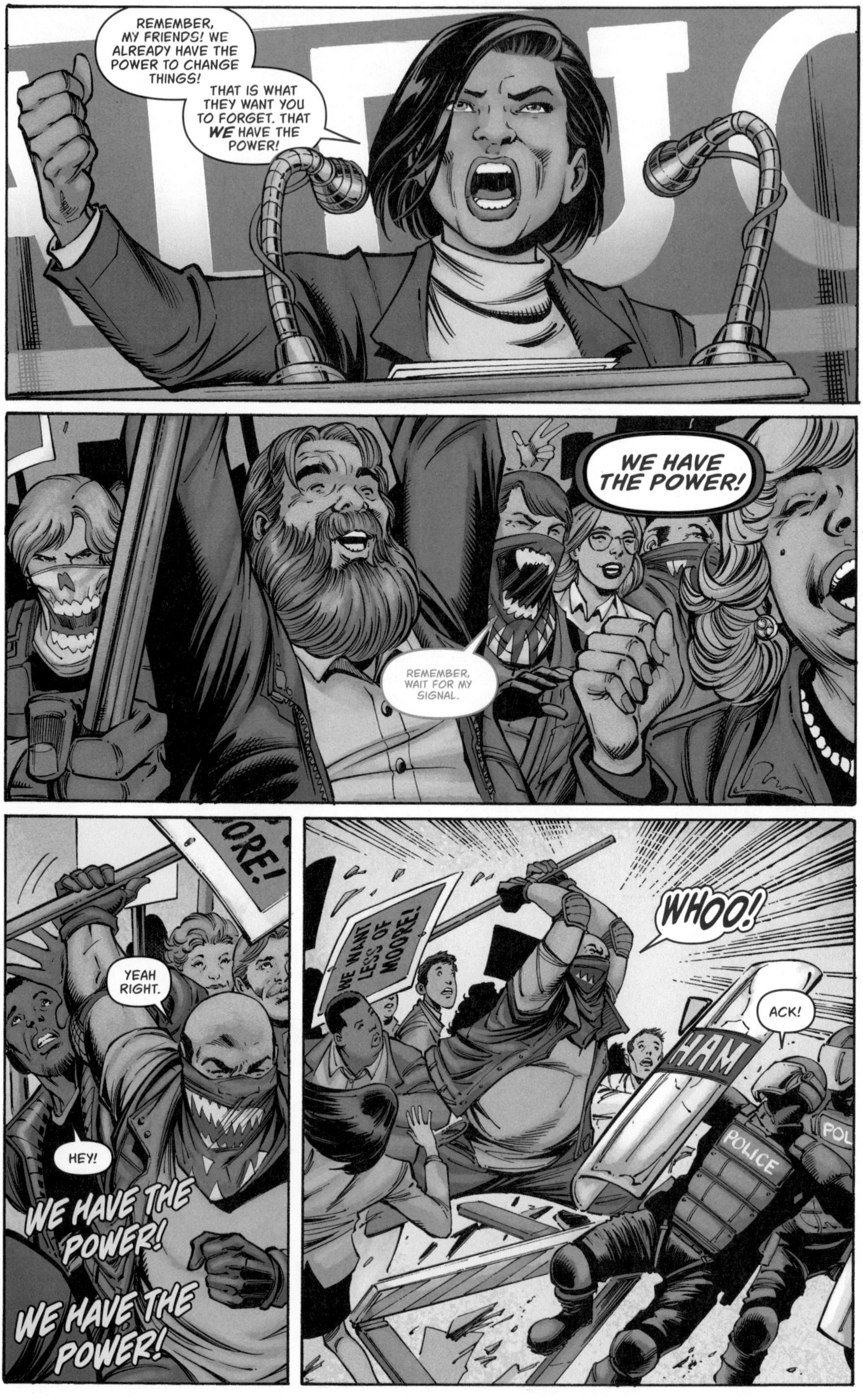
REMEMBER, MY FRIENDS! WE ALREADY HAVE THE POWER TO CHANGE THINGS!
THAT IS WHAT THEY WANT YOU TO FORGET. THAT WE HAVE THE POWER!
WE HAVE THE POWER!
REMEMBER, WAIT FOR MY SIGNAL.
ORE!
YEAH RIGHT.
HEY!
WE HAVE THE POWER!
WE HAVE THE POWER!
WE WANT LESS OF MOORE!
WHOO!
ACK!
HAM
POLICE
POL

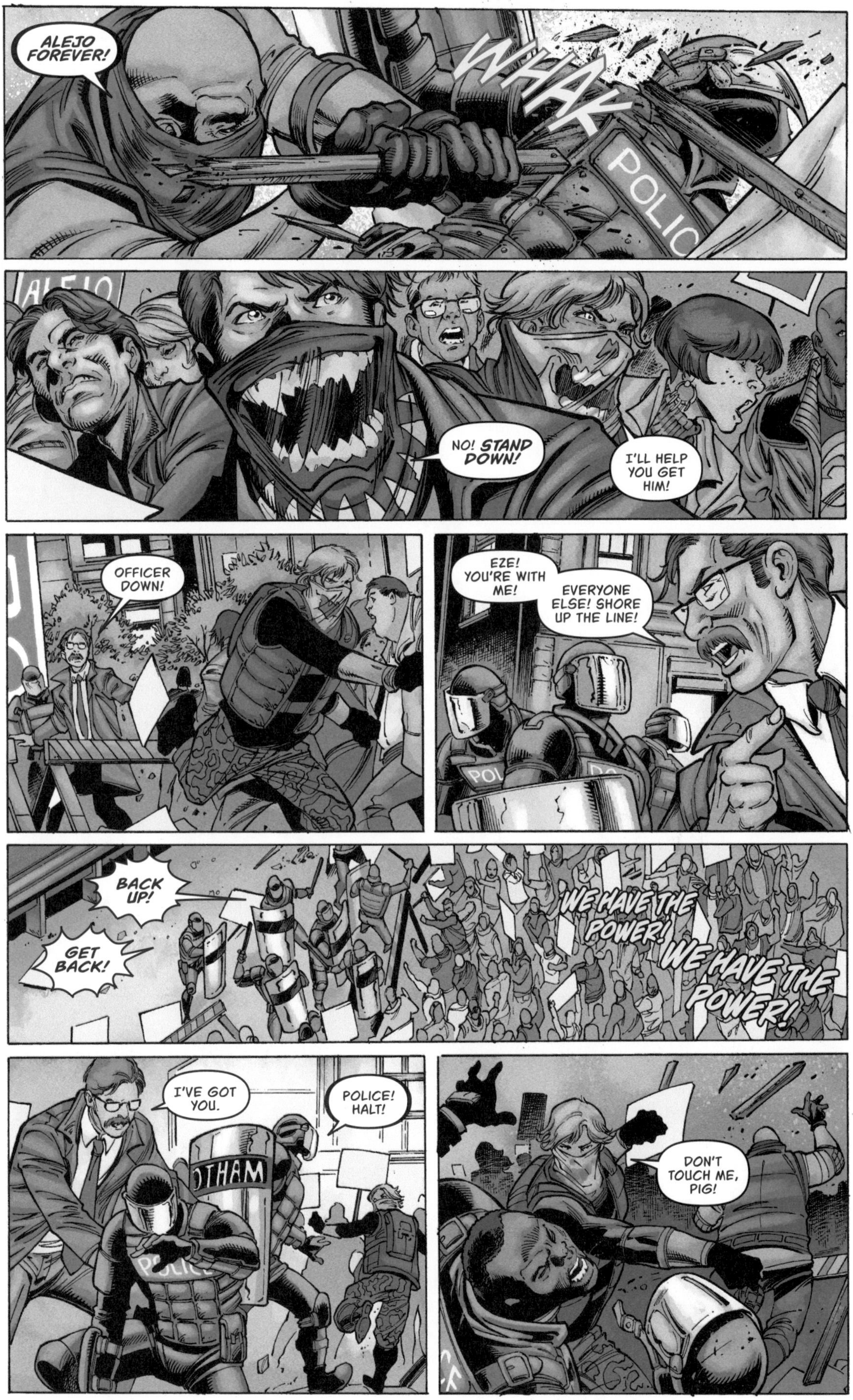
ALEJO FOREVER!
WHAK
POLIC
ALEJO
NO! STAND DOWN!
I'LL HELP YOU GET HIM!
OFFICER DOWN!
EZE! YOU'RE WITH ME!
EVERYONE ELSE! SHORE UP THE LINE!
BACK UP!
GET BACK!
WE HAVE THE POWER! WE HAVE THE POWER!
I'VE GOT YOU.
POLICE! HALT!
OTHAM
POLICE
DON'T TOUCH ME, PIG!

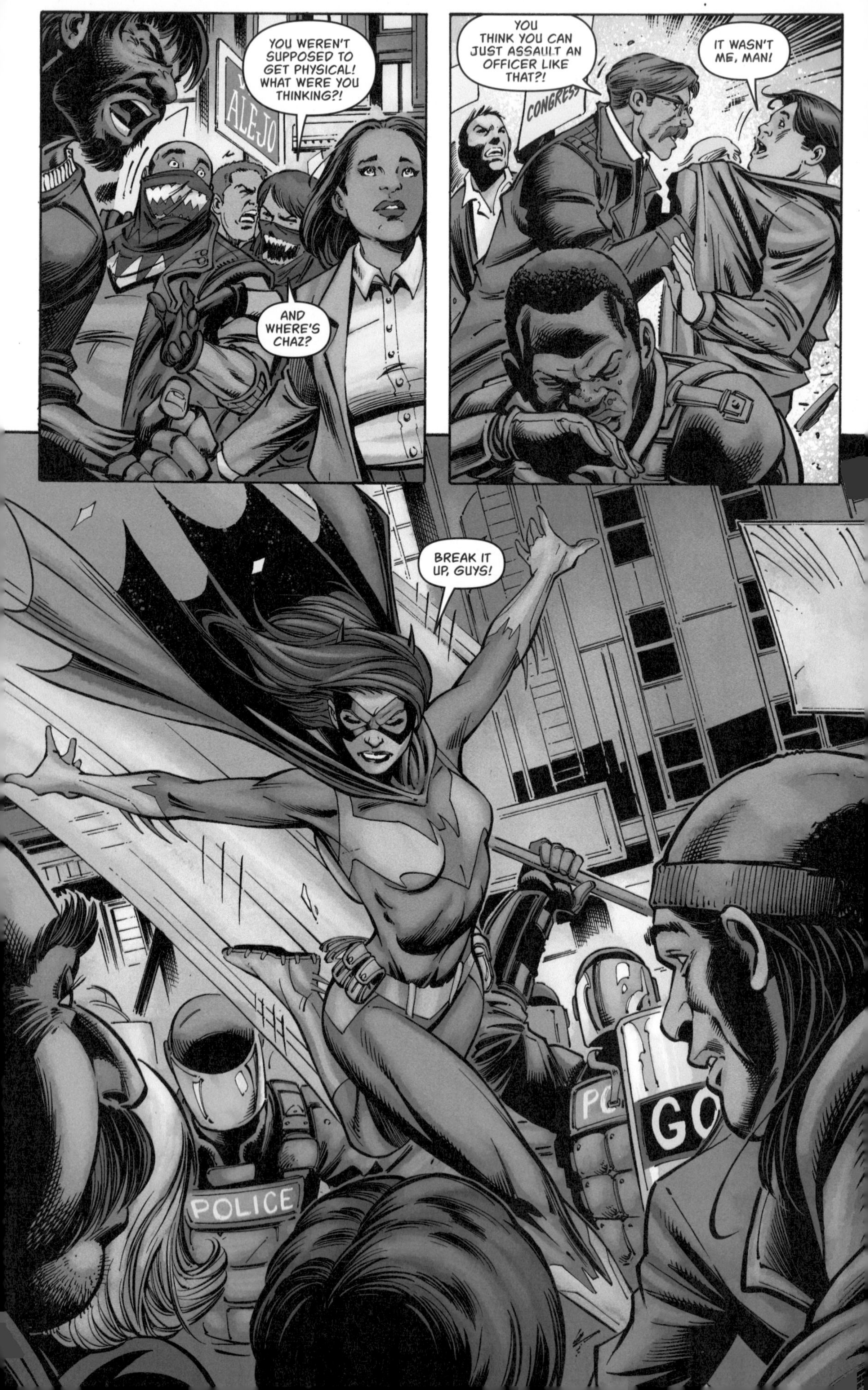
YOU WEREN'T SUPPOSED TO GET PHYSICAL! WHAT WERE YOU THINKING?!
AND WHERE'S CHAZ?
ALEJO
YOU THINK YOU CAN JUST ASSAULT AN OFFICER LIKE THAT?!
IT WASN'T ME, MAN!
CONGRESS
BREAK IT UP, GUYS!
POLICE
PO
GO

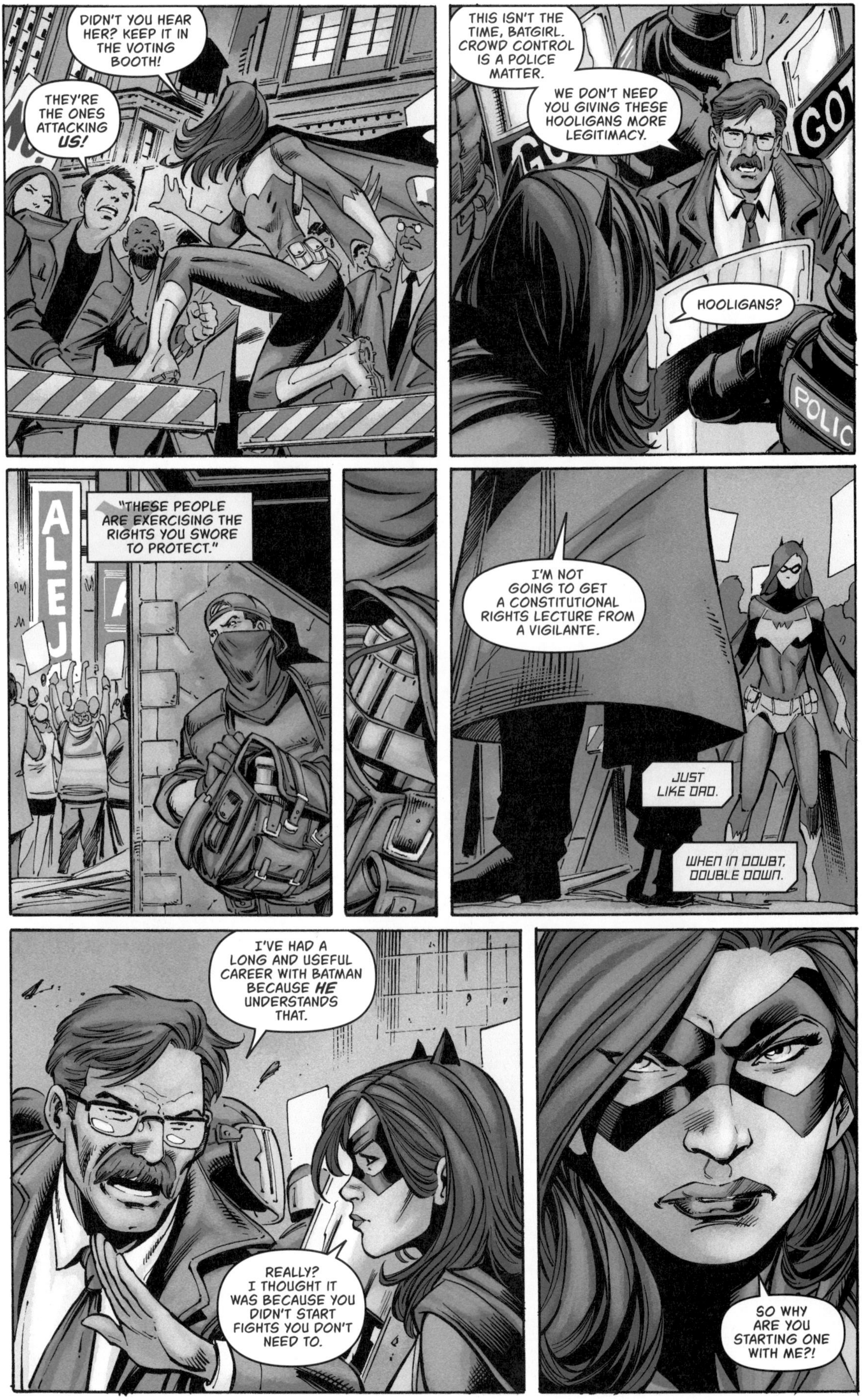
DIDN'T YOU HEAR HER? KEEP IT IN THE VOTING BOOTH!
THEY'RE THE ONES ATTACKING US!
THIS ISN'T THE TIME, BATGIRL. CROWD CONTROL IS A POLICE MATTER.
WE DON'T NEED YOU GIVING THESE HOOLIGANS MORE LEGITIMACY.
HOOLIGANS?
"THESE PEOPLE ARE EXERCISING THE RIGHTS YOU SWORE TO PROTECT."
I'M NOT GOING TO GET A CONSTITUTIONAL RIGHTS LECTURE FROM A VIGILANTE.
JUST LIKE DAD.
WHEN IN DOUBT, DOUBLE DOWN.
I'VE HAD A LONG AND USEFUL CAREER WITH BATMAN BECAUSE HE UNDERSTANDS THAT.
REALLY? I THOUGHT IT WAS BECAUSE YOU DIDN'T START FIGHTS YOU DON'T NEED TO.
SO WHY ARE YOU STARTING ONE WITH ME?!

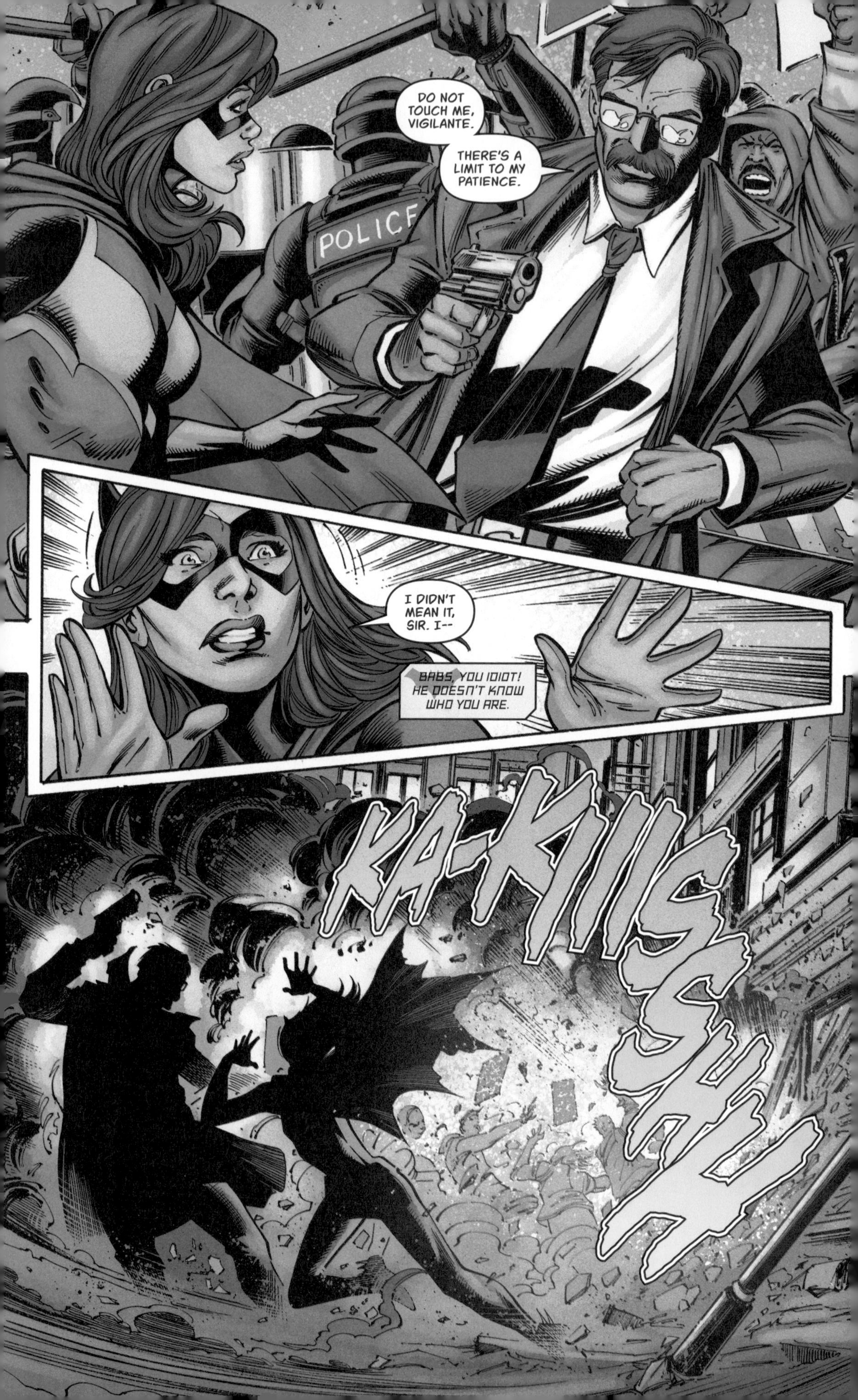
DO NOT TOUCH ME, VIGILANTE.
THERE'S A LIMIT TO MY PATIENCE.
I DIDN'T MEAN IT, SIR. I--
BABS, YOU IDIOT! HE DOESN'T KNOW WHO YOU ARE.
KA-KHSSHHH

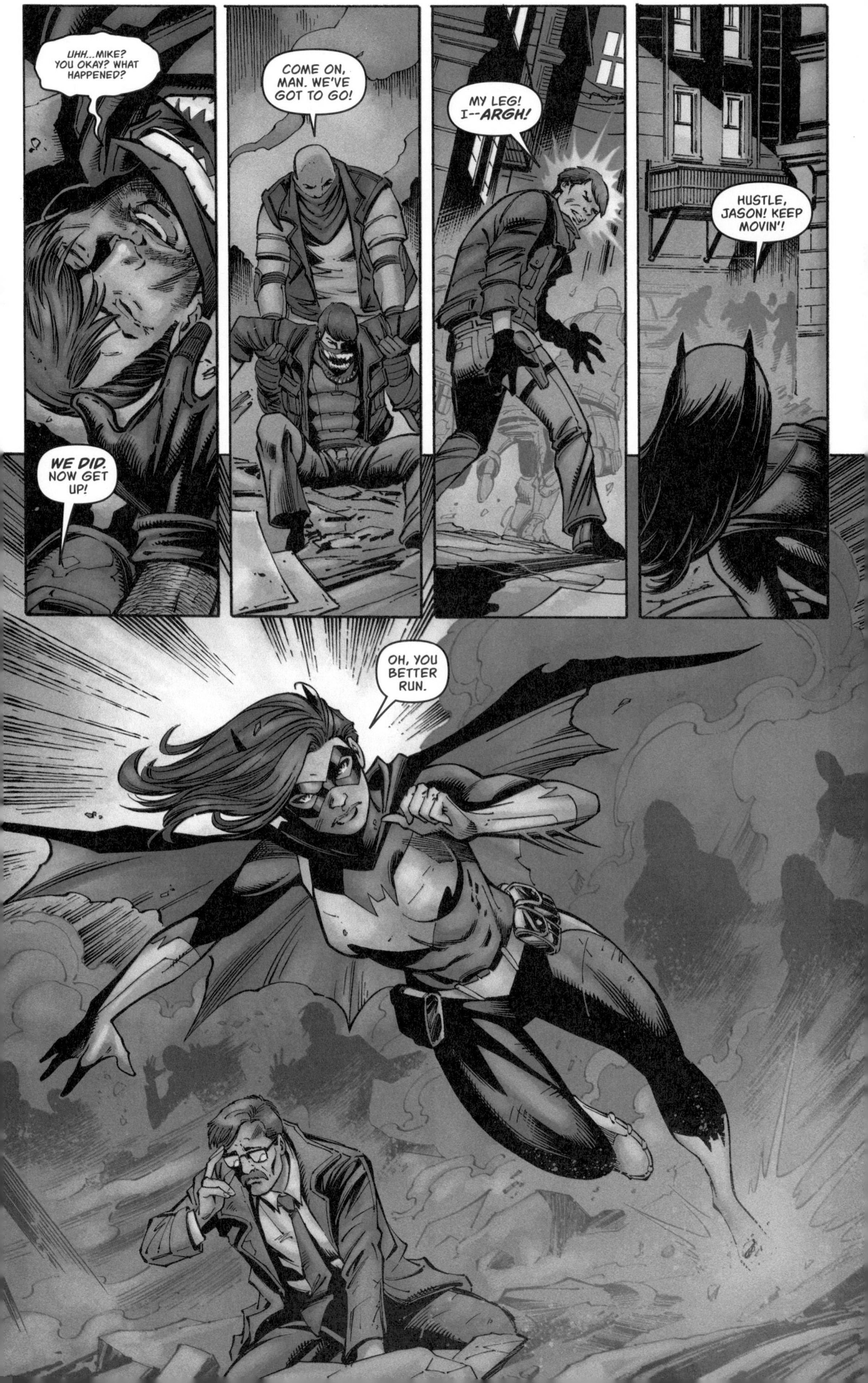

UHH...MIKE? YOU OKAY? WHAT HAPPENED?
WE DID. NOW GET UP!
COME ON, MAN. WE'VE GOT TO GO!
MY LEG! I--ARGH!
HUSTLE, JASON! KEEP MOVIN'!
OH, YOU BETTER RUN.

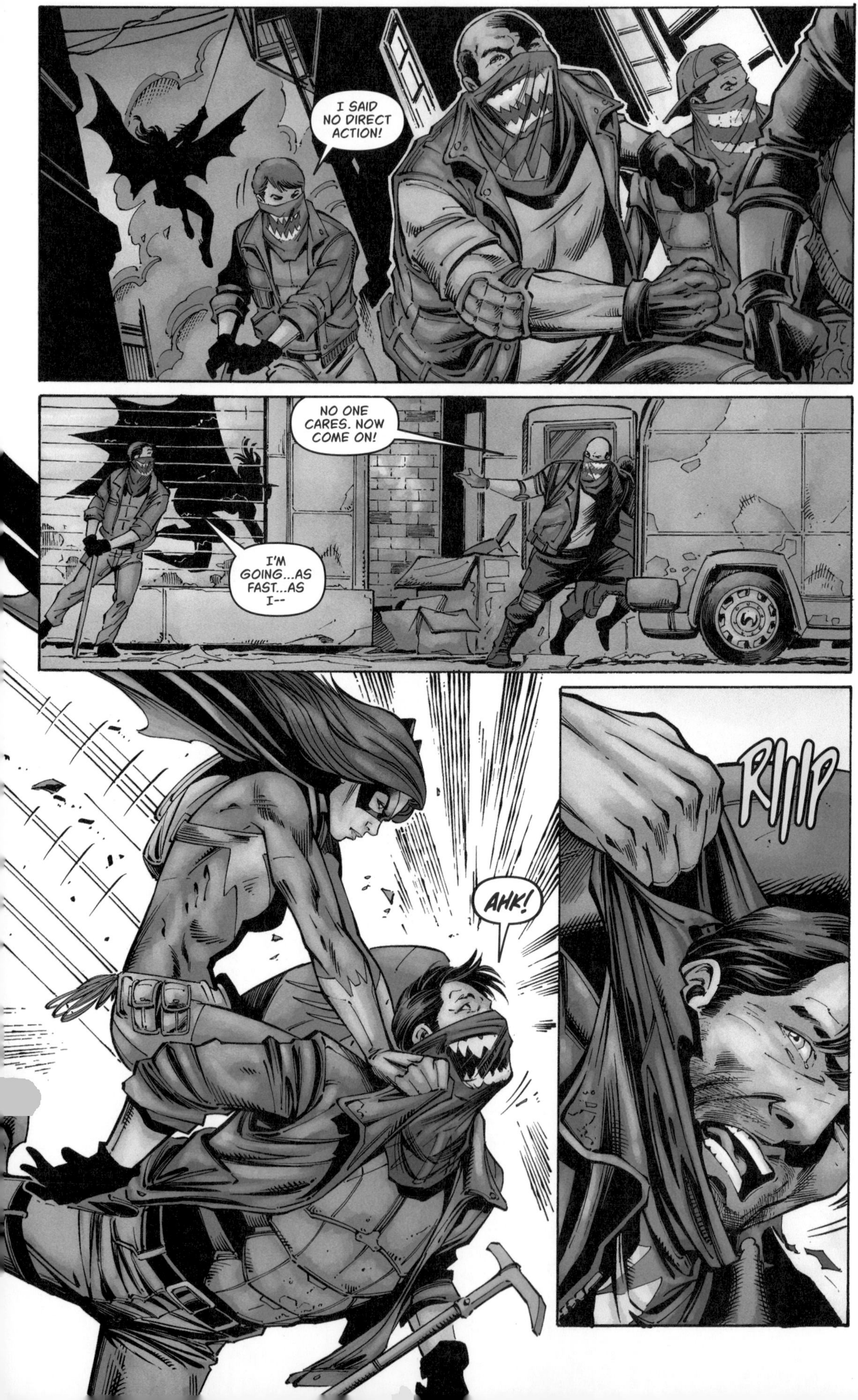
I SAID NO DIRECT ACTION!
NO ONE CARES. NOW COME ON!
I'M GOING...AS FAST...AS I--
AHK!
RIIIP

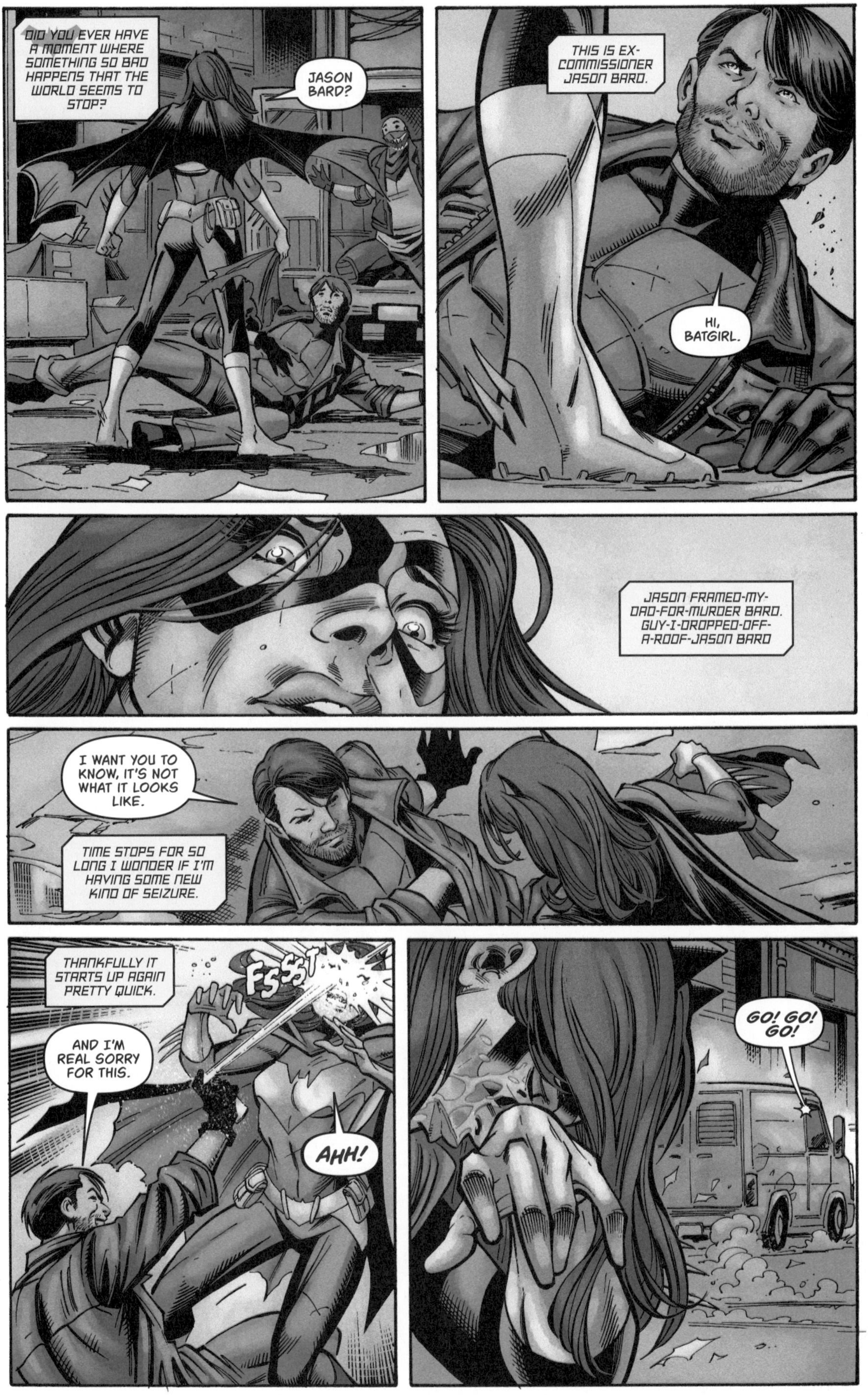

DID YOU EVER HAVE A MOMENT WHERE SOMETHING SO BAD HAPPENS THAT THE WORLD SEEMS TO STOP?
JASON BARD?
THIS IS EX-COMMISSIONER JASON BARD.
HI, BATGIRL.
JASON FRAMED-MY-DAD-FOR-MURDER BARD. GUY-I-DROPPED-OFF-A-ROOF-JASON BARD
I WANT YOU TO KNOW, IT'S NOT WHAT IT LOOKS LIKE.
TIME STOPS FOR SO LONG I WONDER IF I'M HAVING SOME NEW KIND OF SEIZURE.
THANKFULLY IT STARTS UP AGAIN PRETTY QUICK.
AND I'M REAL SORRY FOR THIS.
FSSST
AHH!
GO! GO! GO!

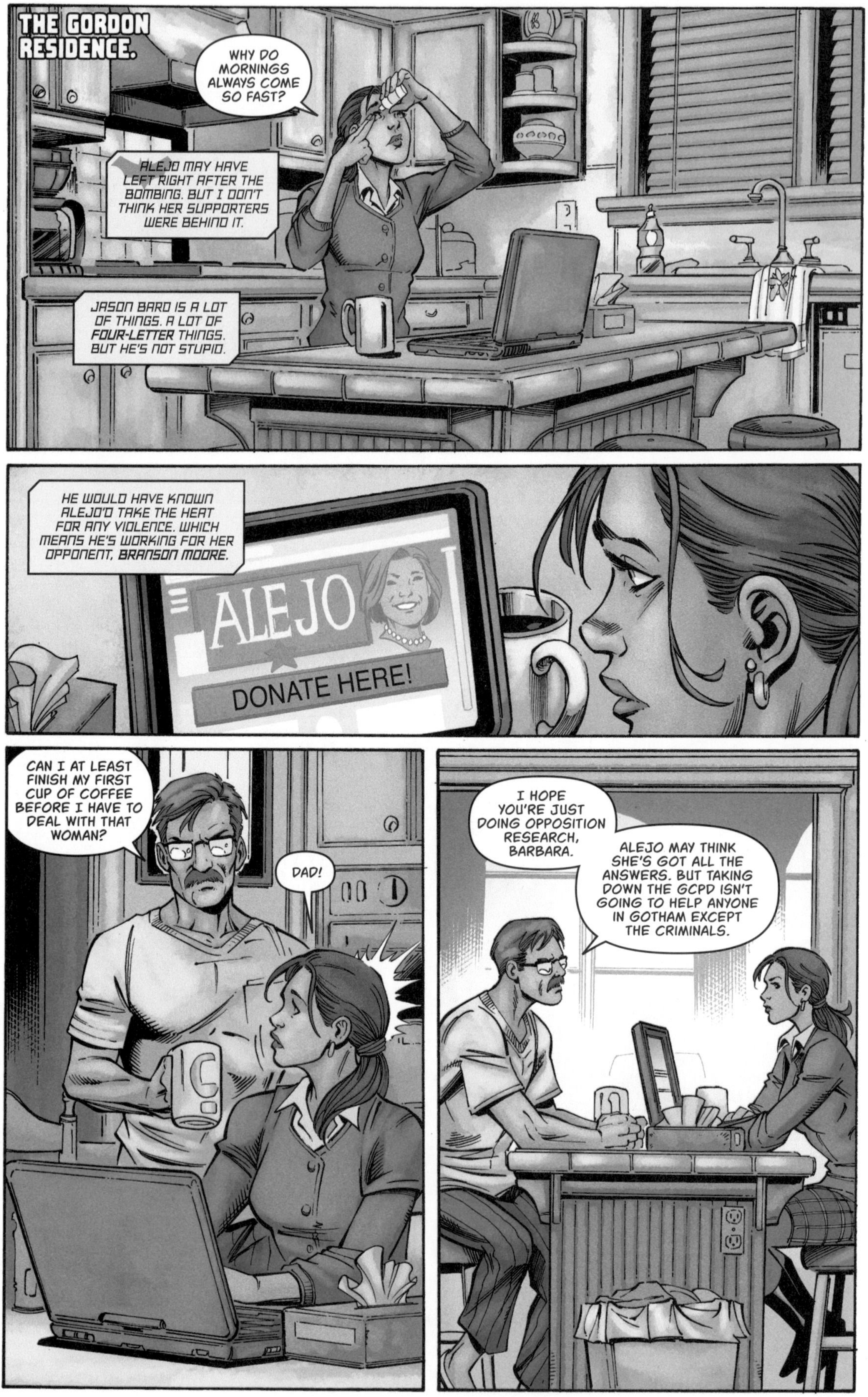
THE GORDON RESIDENCE.
WHY DO MORNINGS ALWAYS COME SO FAST?
ALEJO MAY HAVE LEFT RIGHT AFTER THE BOMBING. BUT I DON'T THINK HER SUPPORTERS WERE BEHIND IT.
JASON BARD IS A LOT OF THINGS. A LOT OF FOUR-LETTER THINGS. BUT HE'S NOT STUPID.
HE WOULD HAVE KNOWN ALEJO'D TAKE THE HEAT FOR ANY VIOLENCE. WHICH MEANS HE'S WORKING FOR HER OPPONENT, BRANSON MOORE.
ALEJO
DONATE HERE!
CAN I AT LEAST FINISH MY FIRST CUP OF COFFEE BEFORE I HAVE TO DEAL WITH THAT WOMAN?
DAD!
I HOPE YOU'RE JUST DOING OPPOSITION RESEARCH, BARBARA.
ALEJO MAY THINK SHE'S GOT ALL THE ANSWERS. BUT TAKING DOWN THE GCPD ISN'T GOING TO HELP ANYONE IN GOTHAM EXCEPT THE CRIMINALS.

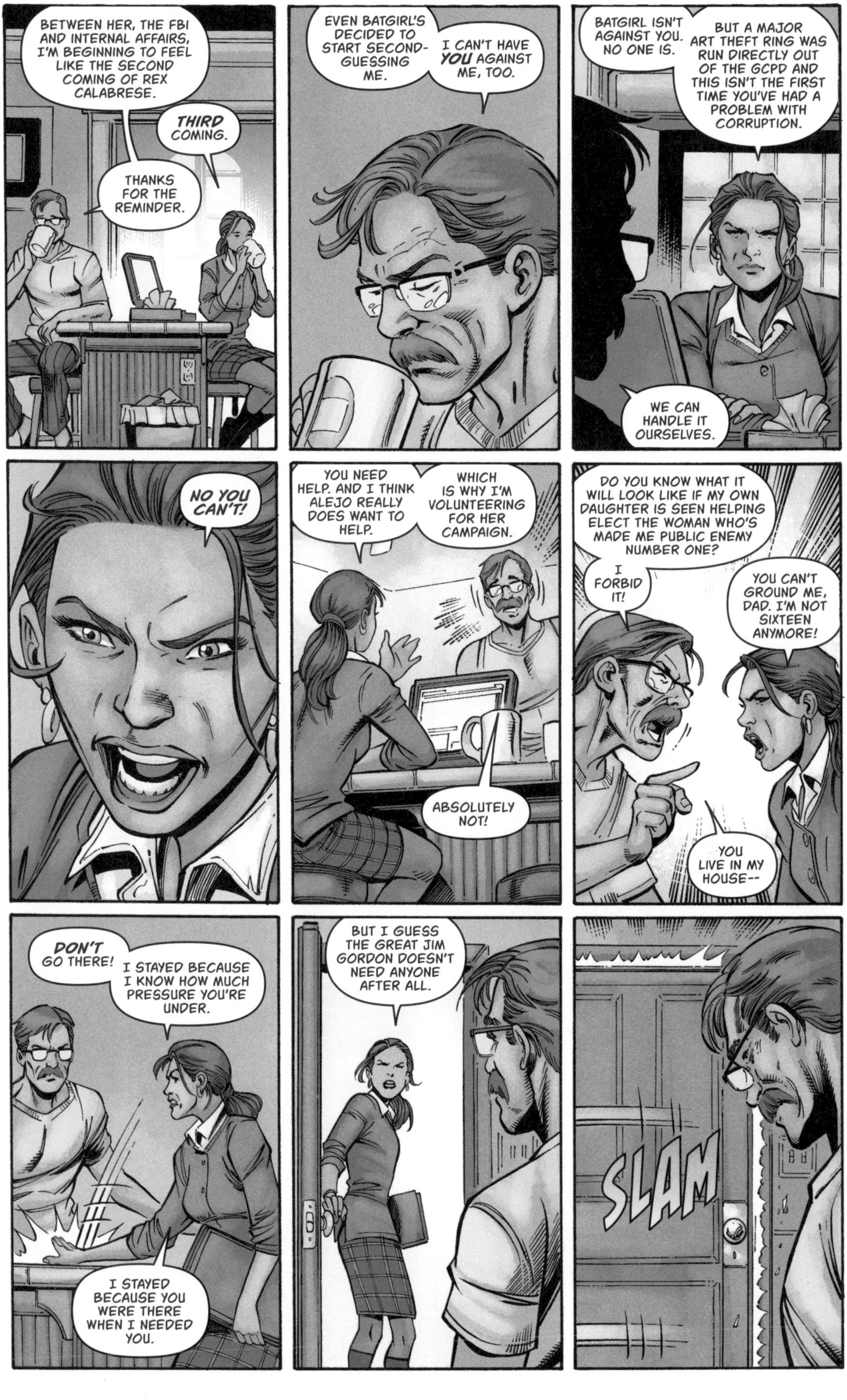
BETWEEN HER, THE FBI AND INTERNAL AFFAIRS, I'M BEGINNING TO FEEL LIKE THE SECOND COMING OF REX CALABRESE.
THIRD COMING.
THANKS FOR THE REMINDER.
EVEN BATGIRL'S DECIDED TO START SECOND-GUESSING ME.
I CAN'T HAVE YOU AGAINST ME, TOO.
BATGIRL ISN'T AGAINST YOU. NO ONE IS.
BUT A MAJOR ART THEFT RING WAS RUN DIRECTLY OUT OF THE GCPD AND THIS ISN'T THE FIRST TIME YOU'VE HAD A PROBLEM WITH CORRUPTION.
WE CAN HANDLE IT OURSELVES.
NO YOU CAN'T!
YOU NEED HELP. AND I THINK ALEJO REALLY DOES WANT TO HELP.
WHICH IS WHY I'M VOLUNTEERING FOR HER CAMPAIGN.
ABSOLUTELY NOT!
DO YOU KNOW WHAT IT WILL LOOK LIKE IF MY OWN DAUGHTER IS SEEN HELPING ELECT THE WOMAN WHO'S MADE ME PUBLIC ENEMY NUMBER ONE?
I FORBID IT!
YOU CAN'T GROUND ME, DAD. I'M NOT SIXTEEN ANYMORE!
YOU LIVE IN MY HOUSE--
DON'T GO THERE!
I STAYED BECAUSE I KNOW HOW MUCH PRESSURE YOU'RE UNDER.
I STAYED BECAUSE YOU WERE THERE WHEN I NEEDED YOU.
BUT I GUESS THE GREAT JIM GORDON DOESN'T NEED ANYONE AFTER ALL.
SLAM

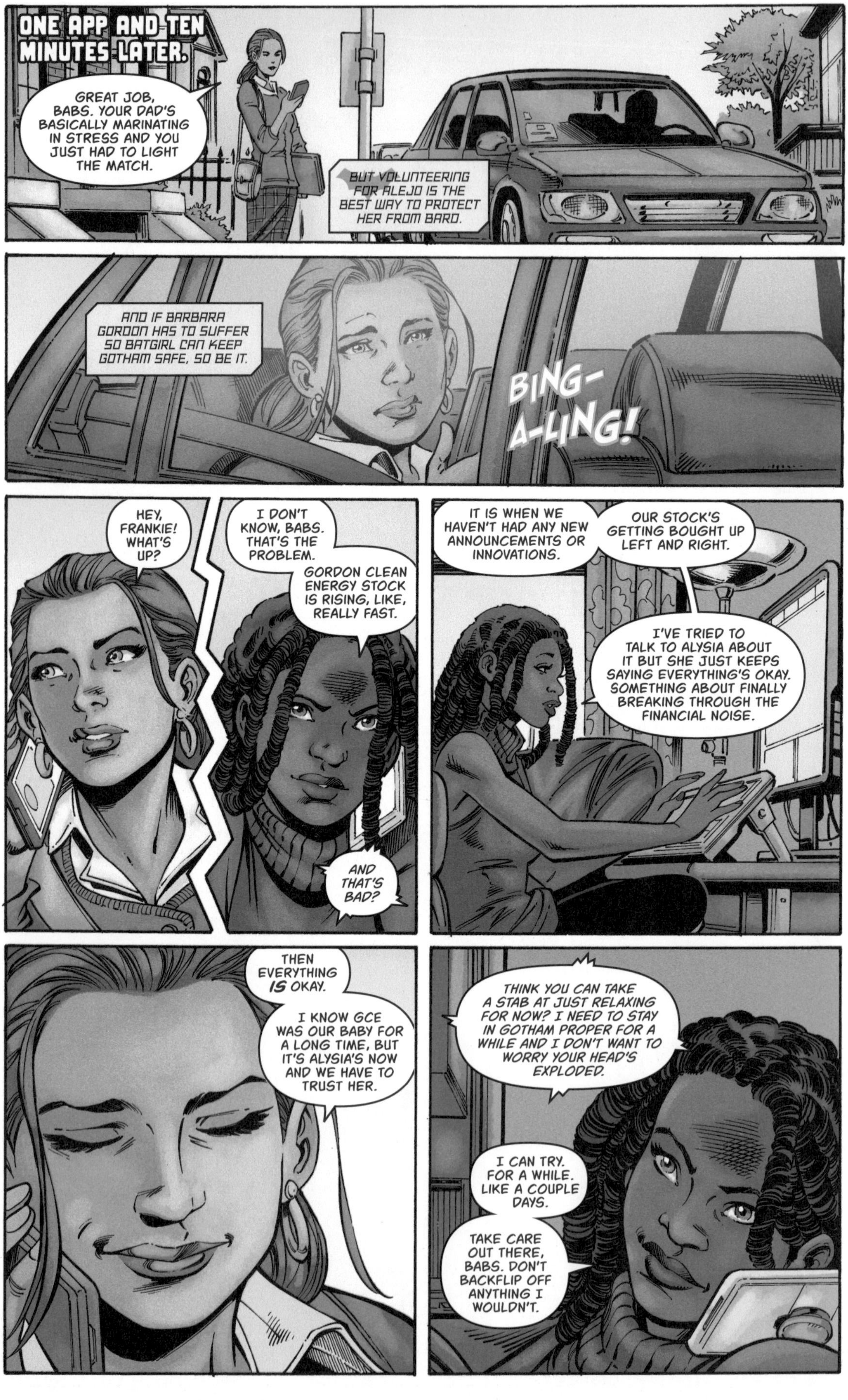
ONE APP AND TEN MINUTES LATER.
GREAT JOB, BABS. YOUR DAD'S BASICALLY MARINATING IN STRESS AND YOU JUST HAD TO LIGHT THE MATCH.
BUT VOLUNTEERING FOR ALEJO IS THE BEST WAY TO PROTECT HER FROM BARD.
AND IF BARBARA GORDON HAS TO SUFFER SO BATGIRL CAN KEEP GOTHAM SAFE, SO BE IT.
BING-A-LING!
HEY, FRANKIE! WHAT'S UP?
I DON'T KNOW, BABS. THAT'S THE PROBLEM.
GORDON CLEAN ENERGY STOCK IS RISING, LIKE, REALLY FAST.
AND THAT'S BAD?
IT IS WHEN WE HAVEN'T HAD ANY NEW ANNOUNCEMENTS OR INNOVATIONS.
OUR STOCK'S GETTING BOUGHT UP LEFT AND RIGHT.
I'VE TRIED TO TALK TO ALYSIA ABOUT IT BUT SHE JUST KEEPS SAYING EVERYTHING'S OKAY. SOMETHING ABOUT FINALLY BREAKING THROUGH THE FINANCIAL NOISE.
THEN EVERYTHING *IS* OKAY.
I KNOW GCE WAS OUR BABY FOR A LONG TIME, BUT IT'S ALYSIA'S NOW AND WE HAVE TO TRUST HER.
THINK YOU CAN TAKE A STAB AT JUST RELAXING FOR NOW? I NEED TO STAY IN GOTHAM PROPER FOR A WHILE AND I DON'T WANT TO WORRY YOUR HEAD'S EXPLODED.
I CAN TRY. FOR A WHILE. LIKE A COUPLE DAYS.
TAKE CARE OUT THERE, BABS. DON'T BACKFLIP OFF ANYTHING I WOULDN'T.

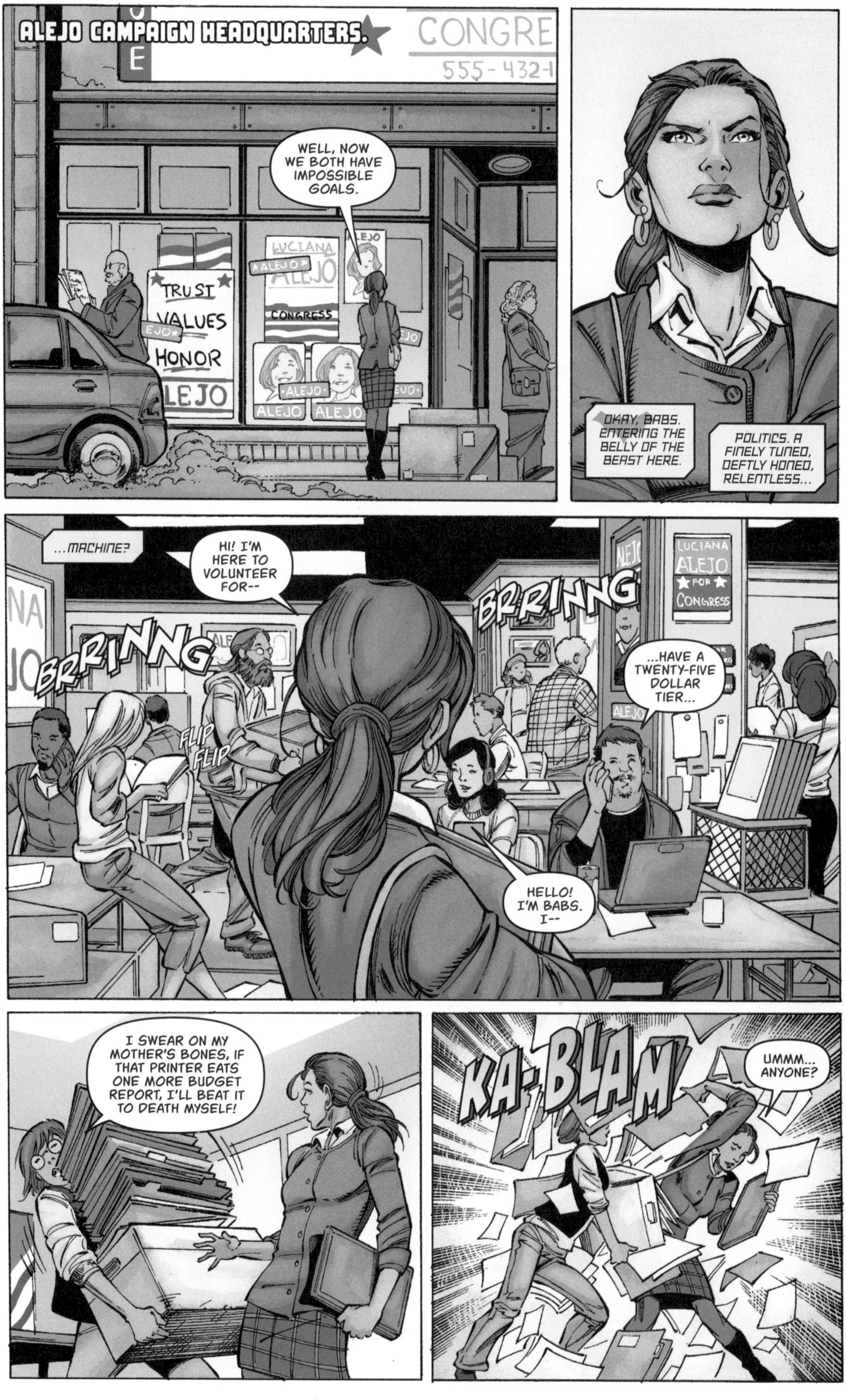
ALEJO CAMPAIGN HEADQUARTERS.
CONGRE
555-432-1
TRUST
VALUES
HONOR
ALEJO
LUCIANA
ALEJO
CONGRESS
WELL, NOW WE BOTH HAVE IMPOSSIBLE GOALS.
OKAY, BABS. ENTERING THE BELLY OF THE BEAST HERE.
POLITICS. A FINELY TUNED, DEFTLY HONED, RELENTLESS...
...MACHINE?
HI! I'M HERE TO VOLUNTEER FOR--
LUCIANA
ALEJO
FOR
CONGRESS
BRRINNG
BRRINNG
FLIP
FLIP
...HAVE A TWENTY-FIVE DOLLAR TIER...
HELLO! I'M BABS. I--
I SWEAR ON MY MOTHER'S BONES, IF THAT PRINTER EATS ONE MORE BUDGET REPORT, I'LL BEAT IT TO DEATH MYSELF!
KA-BLAM
UMMM... ANYONE?

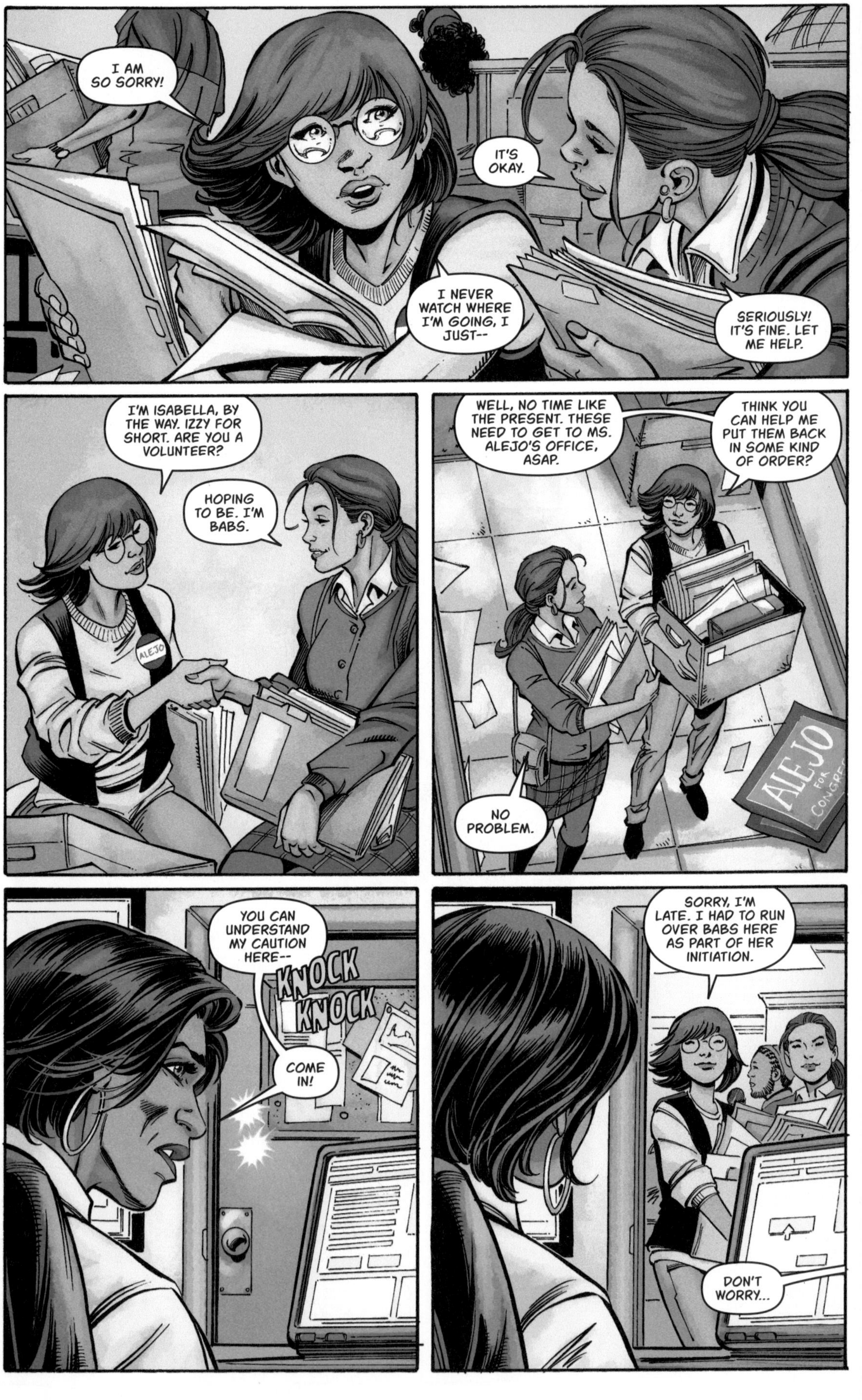
I AM SO SORRY!
IT'S OKAY.
I NEVER WATCH WHERE I'M GOING, I JUST--
SERIOUSLY! IT'S FINE. LET ME HELP.
I'M ISABELLA, BY THE WAY. IZZY FOR SHORT. ARE YOU A VOLUNTEER?
ALEJO
HOPING TO BE. I'M BABS.
WELL, NO TIME LIKE THE PRESENT. THESE NEED TO GET TO MS. ALEJO'S OFFICE, ASAP.
THINK YOU CAN HELP ME PUT THEM BACK IN SOME KIND OF ORDER?
NO PROBLEM.
ALEJO FOR CONGRE
YOU CAN UNDERSTAND MY CAUTION HERE--
KNOCK KNOCK
COME IN!
SORRY, I'M LATE. I HAD TO RUN OVER BABS HERE AS PART OF HER INITIATION.
DON'T WORRY...

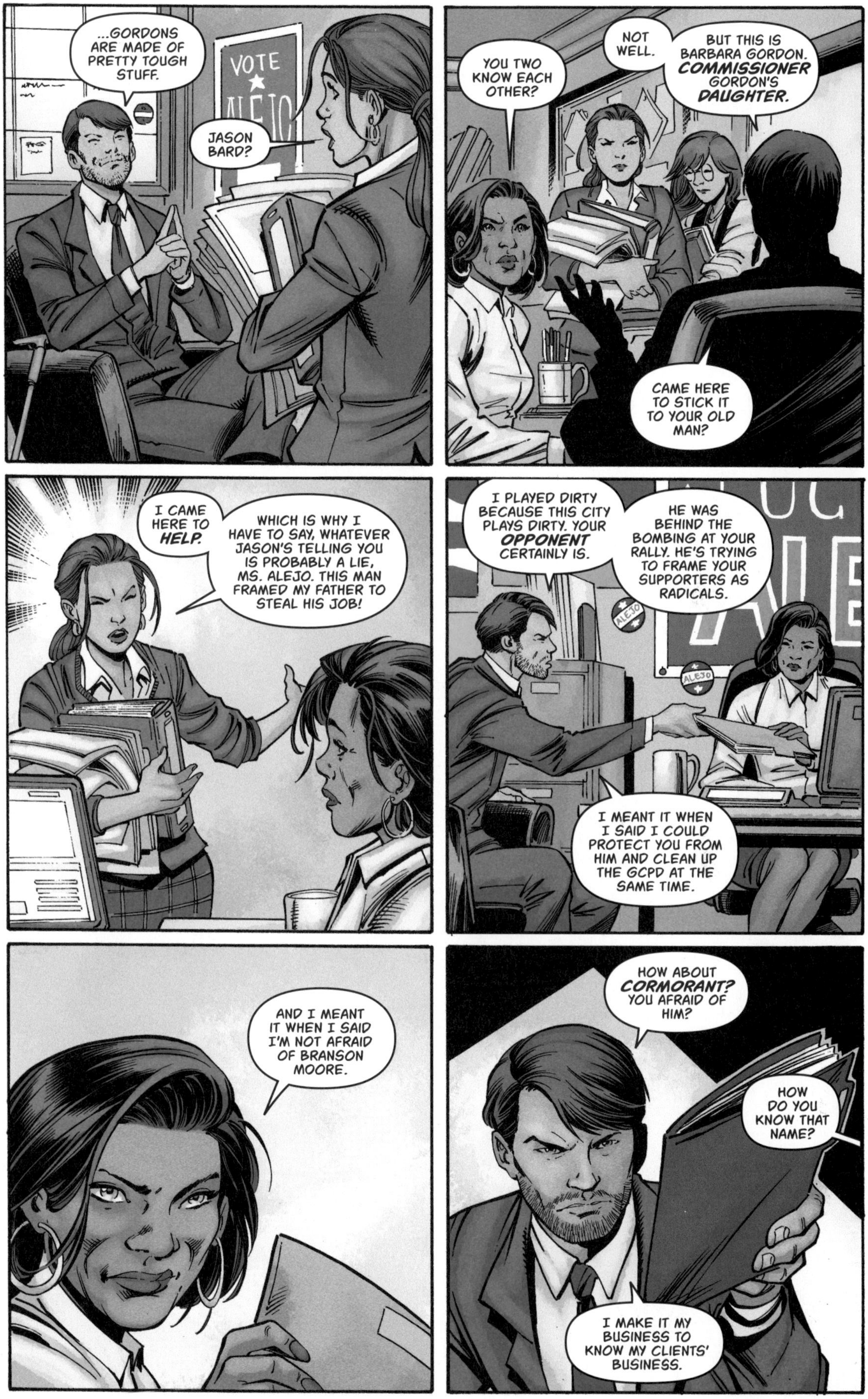
...GORDONS ARE MADE OF PRETTY TOUGH STUFF.
VOTE
JASON BARD?
YOU TWO KNOW EACH OTHER?
NOT WELL.
BUT THIS IS BARBARA GORDON. **COMMISSIONER** GORDON'S **DAUGHTER.**
CAME HERE TO STICK IT TO YOUR OLD MAN?
I CAME HERE TO **HELP.**
WHICH IS WHY I HAVE TO SAY, WHATEVER JASON'S TELLING YOU IS PROBABLY A LIE, MS. ALEJO. THIS MAN FRAMED MY FATHER TO STEAL HIS JOB!
I PLAYED DIRTY BECAUSE THIS CITY PLAYS DIRTY. YOUR **OPPONENT** CERTAINLY IS.
HE WAS BEHIND THE BOMBING AT YOUR RALLY. HE'S TRYING TO FRAME YOUR SUPPORTERS AS RADICALS.
ALEJO
ALEJO
I MEANT IT WHEN I SAID I COULD PROTECT YOU FROM HIM AND CLEAN UP THE GCPD AT THE SAME TIME.
AND I MEANT IT WHEN I SAID I'M NOT AFRAID OF BRANSON MOORE.
HOW ABOUT **CORMORANT?** YOU AFRAID OF HIM?
HOW DO YOU KNOW THAT NAME?
I MAKE IT MY BUSINESS TO KNOW MY CLIENTS' BUSINESS.

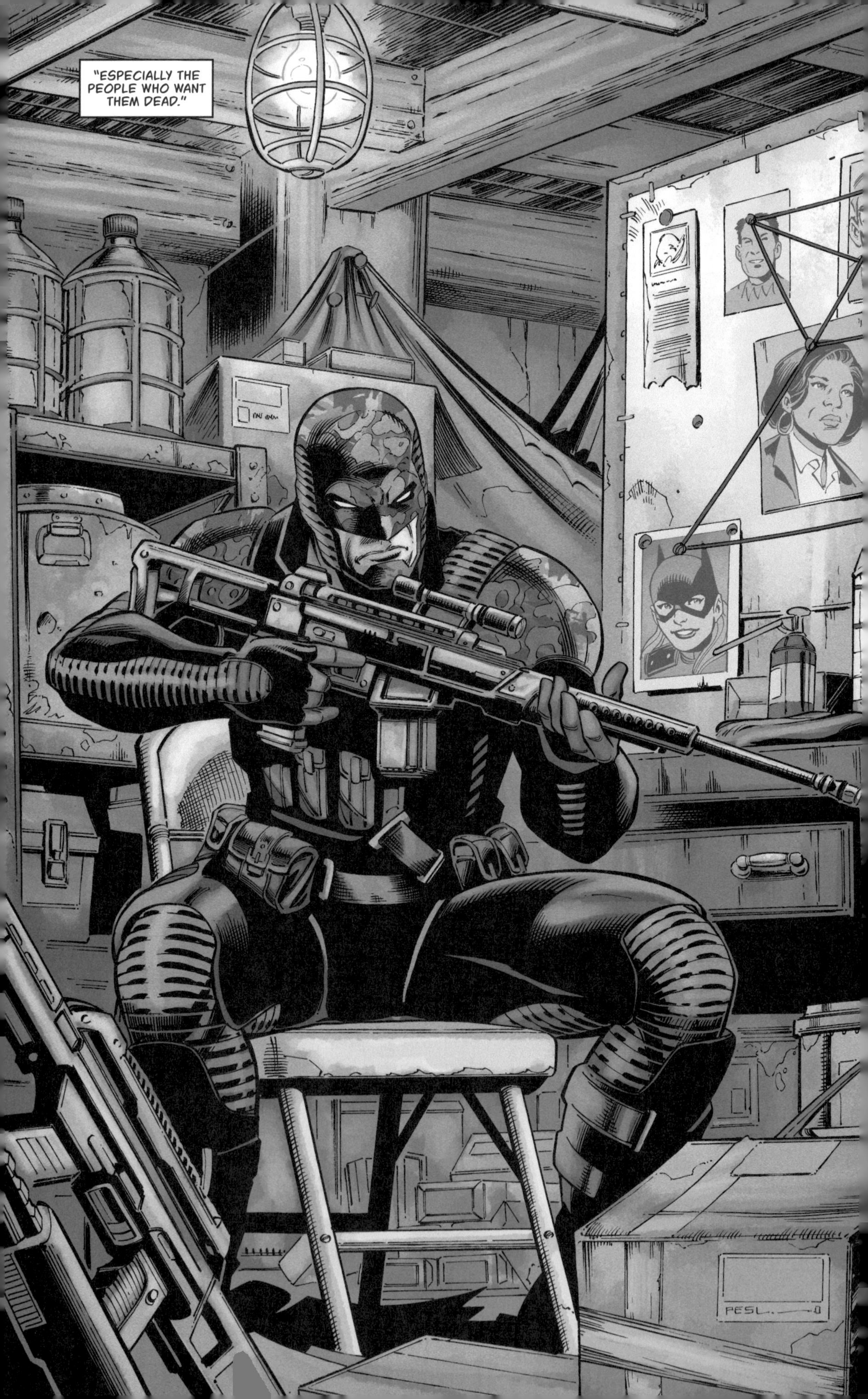
"ESPECIALLY THE PEOPLE WHO WANT THEM DEAD."
PESL.

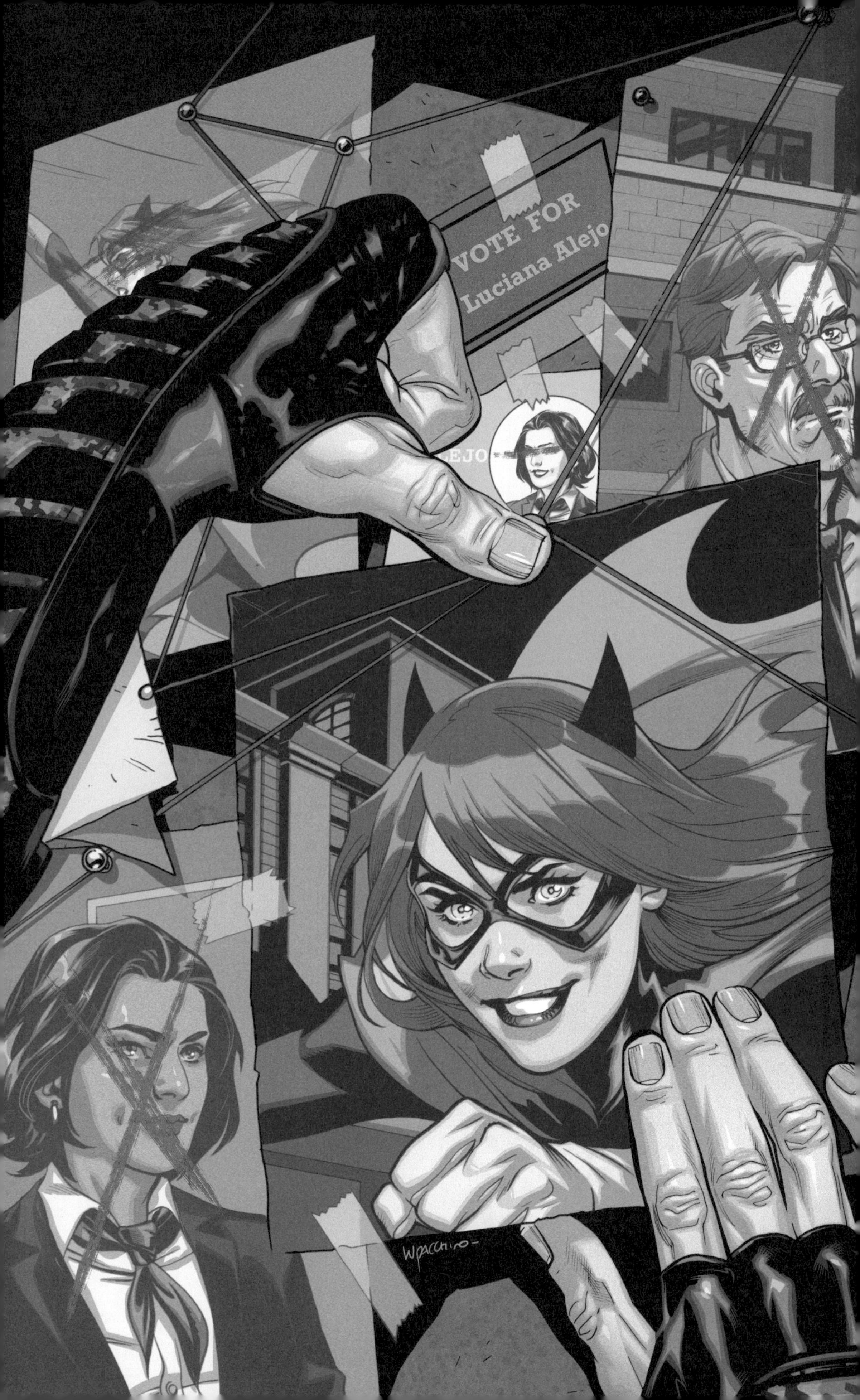
VOTE FOR
Luciana Alejo

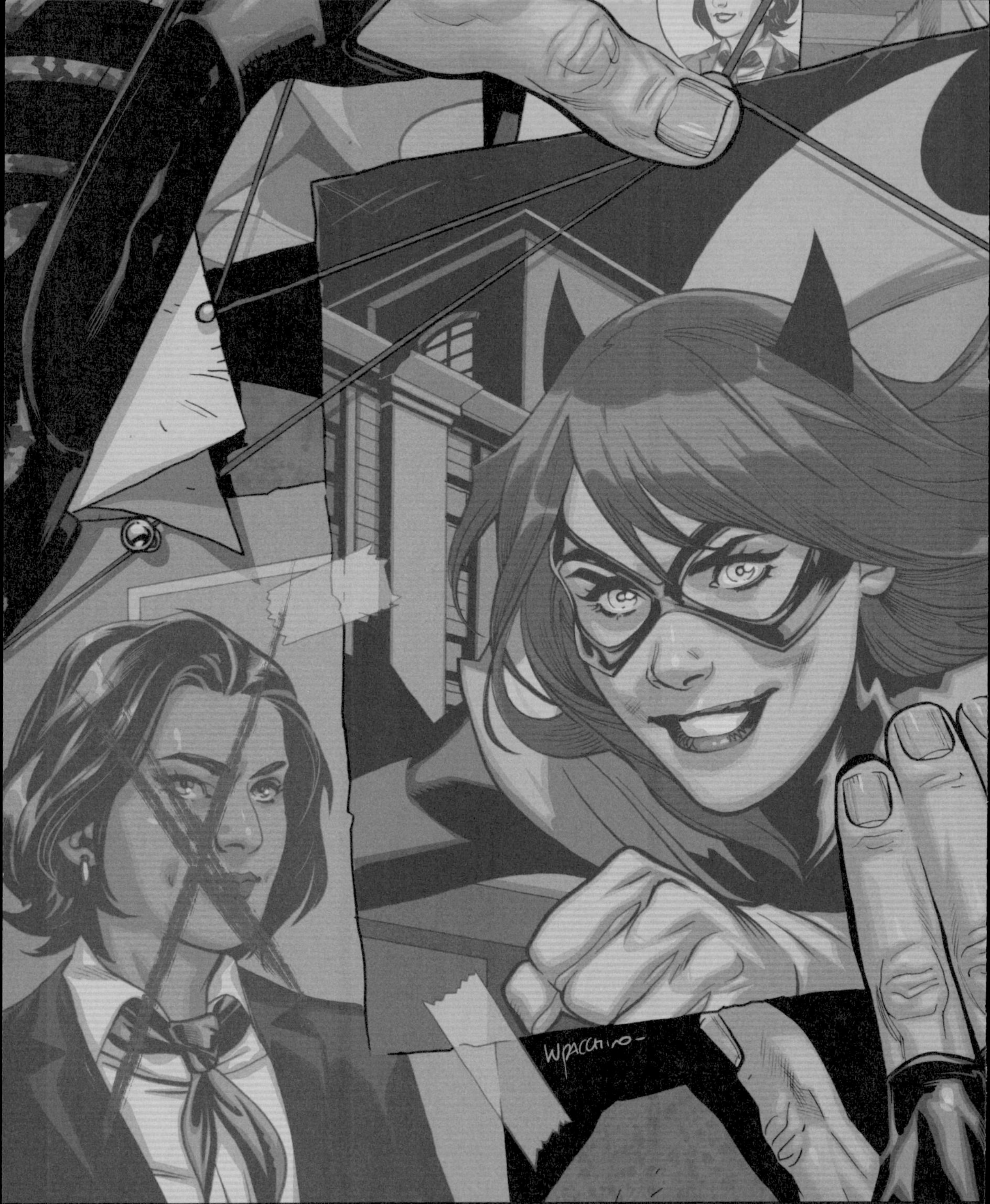

BATGIRL
#31

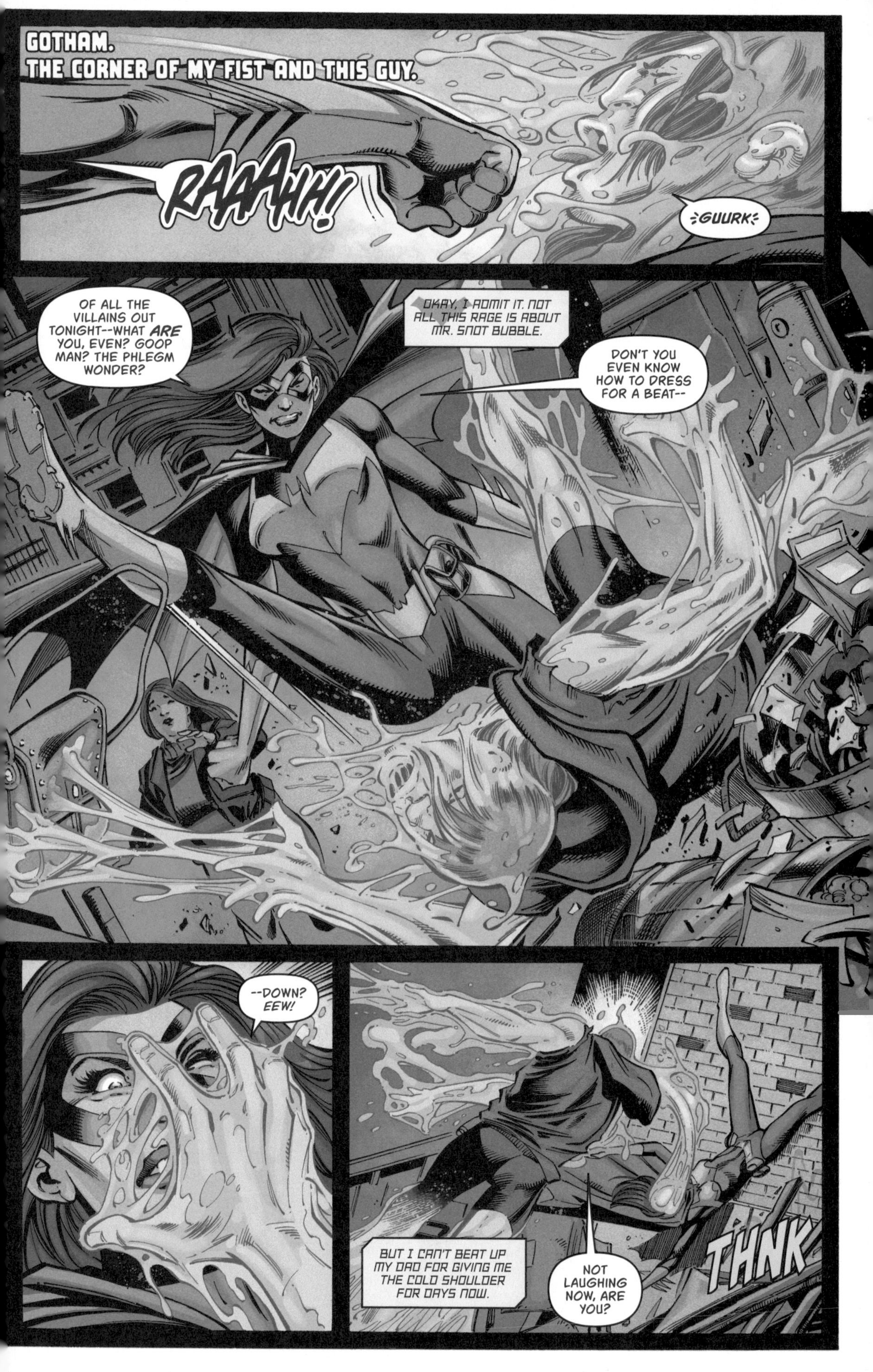

GOTHAM.
THE CORNER OF MY FIST AND THIS GUY.
RAAAHH!
GUURK
OF ALL THE VILLAINS OUT TONIGHT--WHAT ARE YOU, EVEN? GOOP MAN? THE PHLEGM WONDER?
OKAY, I ADMIT IT. NOT ALL THIS RAGE IS ABOUT MR. SNOT BUBBLE.
DON'T YOU EVEN KNOW HOW TO DRESS FOR A BEAT--
--DOWN? EEW!
BUT I CAN'T BEAT UP MY DAD FOR GIVING ME THE COLD SHOULDER FOR DAYS NOW.
NOT LAUGHING NOW, ARE YOU?
THNK

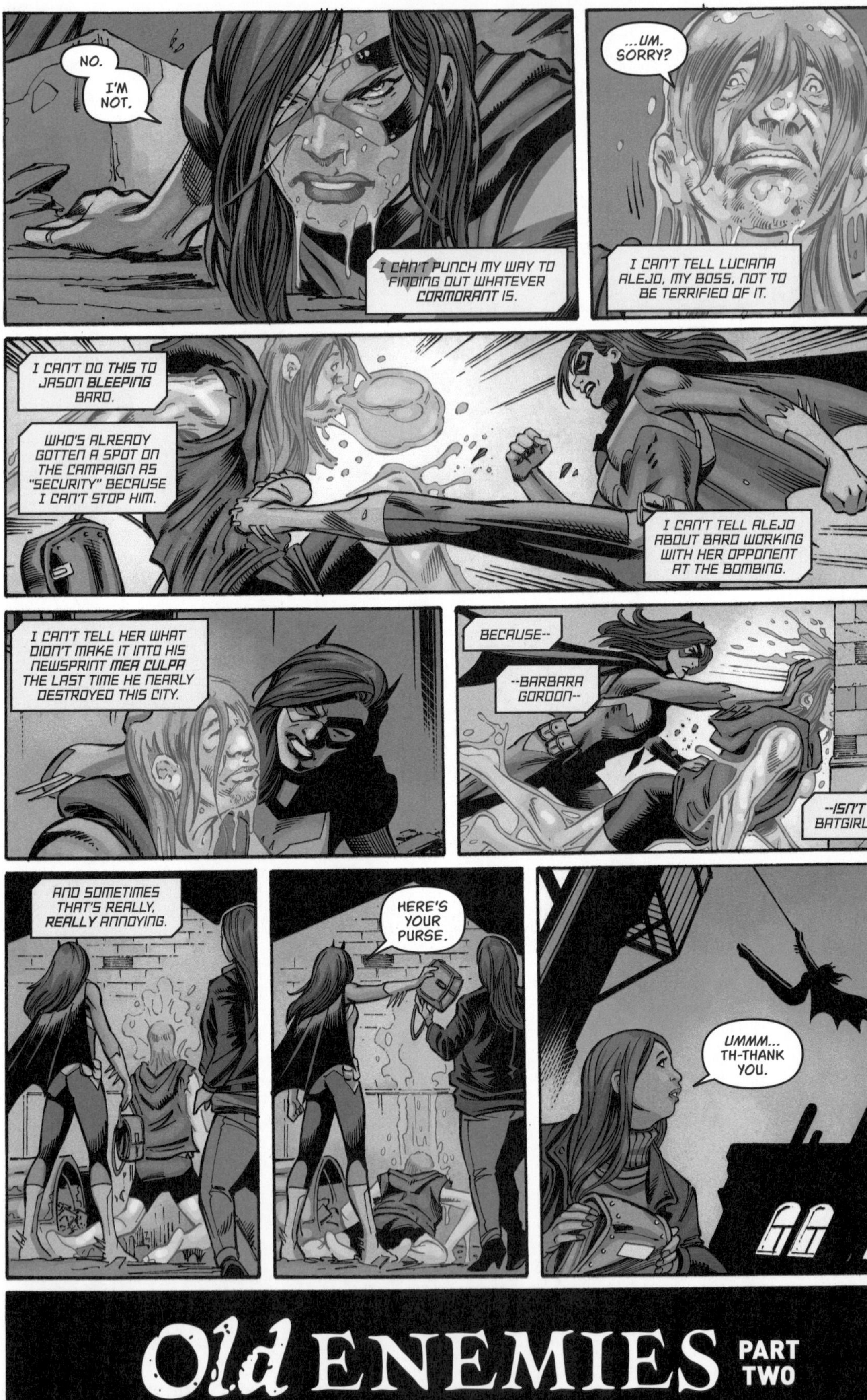
NO.
I'M NOT.
...UM. SORRY?
I CAN'T PUNCH MY WAY TO FINDING OUT WHATEVER CORMORANT IS.
I CAN'T TELL LUCIANA ALEJO, MY BOSS, NOT TO BE TERRIFIED OF IT.
I CAN'T DO THIS TO JASON BLEEPING BARD.
WHO'S ALREADY GOTTEN A SPOT ON THE CAMPAIGN AS "SECURITY" BECAUSE I CAN'T STOP HIM.
I CAN'T TELL ALEJO ABOUT BARD WORKING WITH HER OPPONENT AT THE BOMBING.
I CAN'T TELL HER WHAT DIDN'T MAKE IT INTO HIS NEWSPRINT MEA CULPA THE LAST TIME HE NEARLY DESTROYED THIS CITY.
BECAUSE--
--BARBARA GORDON--
--ISN'T BATGIRL!
AND SOMETIMES THAT'S REALLY, REALLY ANNOYING.
HERE'S YOUR PURSE.
UMMM... TH-THANK YOU.

Old ENEMIES PART TWO

MAIRGHREAD SCOTT—Writer PAUL PELLETIER—Penciller NORM RAPMUND—Inker JORDIE BELLAIRE—Colorist ANDWORLD DESIGN—Letterer
EMANUELA LUPACCHINO AND DAVE McCAIG—Main Cover Artists BRITTANY HOLZHERR—Editor JAMIE S. RICH—Group Editor

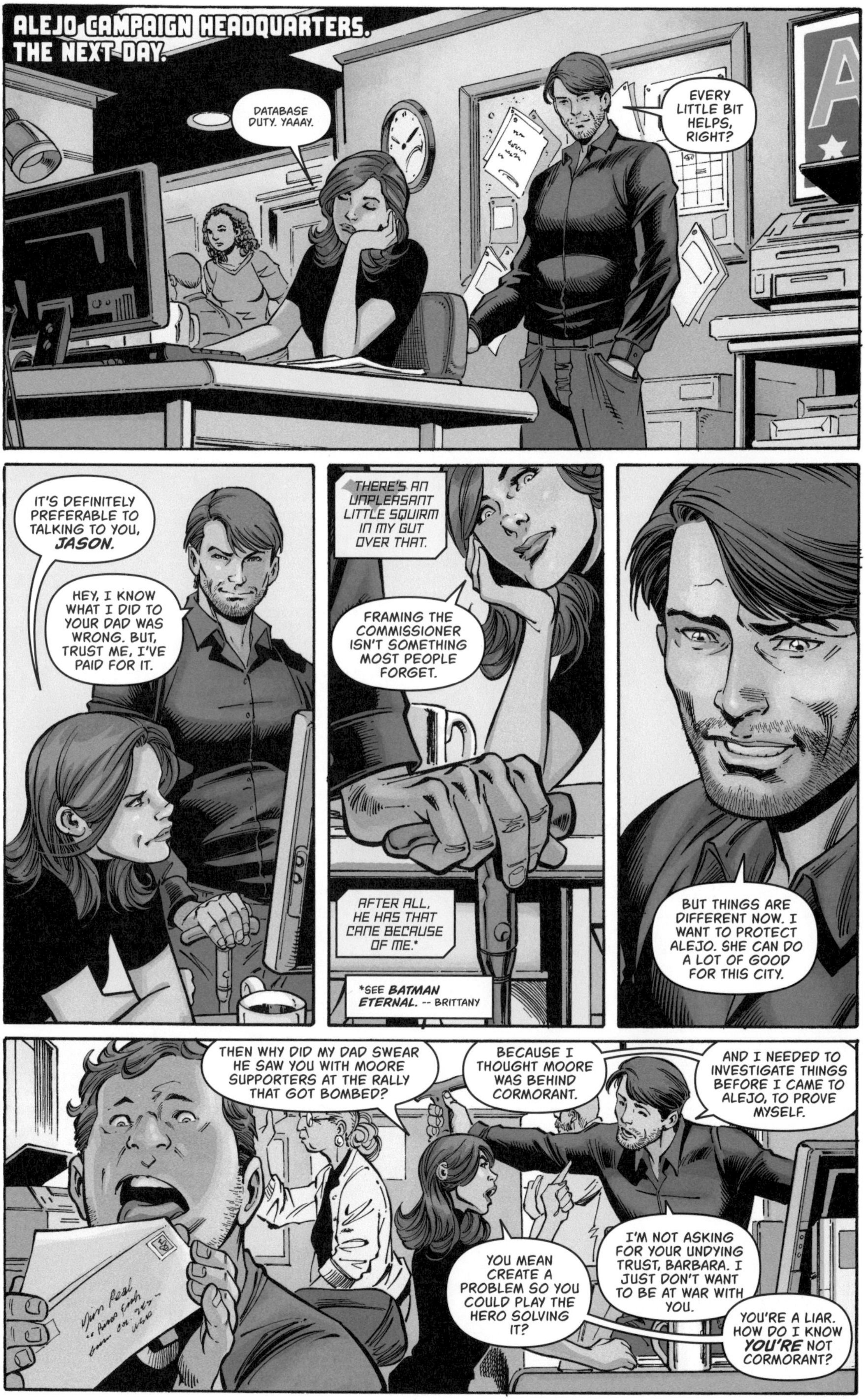
ALEJO CAMPAIGN HEADQUARTERS. THE NEXT DAY.
DATABASE DUTY. YAAAY.
EVERY LITTLE BIT HELPS, RIGHT?
IT'S DEFINITELY PREFERABLE TO TALKING TO YOU, JASON.
HEY, I KNOW WHAT I DID TO YOUR DAD WAS WRONG. BUT, TRUST ME, I'VE PAID FOR IT.
THERE'S AN UNPLEASANT LITTLE SQUIRM IN MY GUT OVER THAT.
FRAMING THE COMMISSIONER ISN'T SOMETHING MOST PEOPLE FORGET.
AFTER ALL, HE HAS THAT CANE BECAUSE OF ME.*
*SEE BATMAN ETERNAL. -- BRITTANY
BUT THINGS ARE DIFFERENT NOW. I WANT TO PROTECT ALEJO. SHE CAN DO A LOT OF GOOD FOR THIS CITY.
THEN WHY DID MY DAD SWEAR HE SAW YOU WITH MOORE SUPPORTERS AT THE RALLY THAT GOT BOMBED?
BECAUSE I THOUGHT MOORE WAS BEHIND CORMORANT.
AND I NEEDED TO INVESTIGATE THINGS BEFORE I CAME TO ALEJO, TO PROVE MYSELF.
YOU MEAN CREATE A PROBLEM SO YOU COULD PLAY THE HERO SOLVING IT?
I'M NOT ASKING FOR YOUR UNDYING TRUST, BARBARA. I JUST DON'T WANT TO BE AT WAR WITH YOU.
YOU'RE A LIAR. HOW DO I KNOW YOU'RE NOT CORMORANT?

WOULD *MY* WORD DO IT?

MS. ALEJO!

BARBARA, I KNOW A BIT ABOUT YOUR HISTORY WITH JASON. BUT YOU HAVE TO LET THAT GO NOW.

HE'S MY HEAD OF SECURITY AND YOU'RE THE BEST VOLUNTEER WE'VE HAD SINCE--*EVER*.

DON'T MAKE ME CHOOSE BETWEEN YOU.

OF COURSE NOT. I'M A TEAM PLAYER.

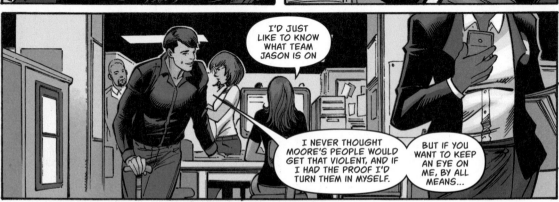

I'D JUST LIKE TO KNOW WHAT TEAM JASON IS ON

I NEVER THOUGHT MOORE'S PEOPLE WOULD GET THAT VIOLENT, AND IF I HAD THE PROOF I'D TURN THEM IN MYSELF.

BUT IF YOU WANT TO KEEP AN EYE ON ME, BY ALL MEANS...

IZZY! PUT BABS HERE ON THE LIST FOR TONIGHT'S FUNDRAISER. SHE CAN HELP YOU OUT.

SORRY. BUT VOLUNTEERS NEED TO WORK THREE MONTHS BEFORE--

JUST DO IT.

OF COURSE, *MR. BARD*.

GREAT. NOW ALEJO AND IZZY ARE MIFFED AT ME.

I BET HE DID THAT ON PURPOSE.

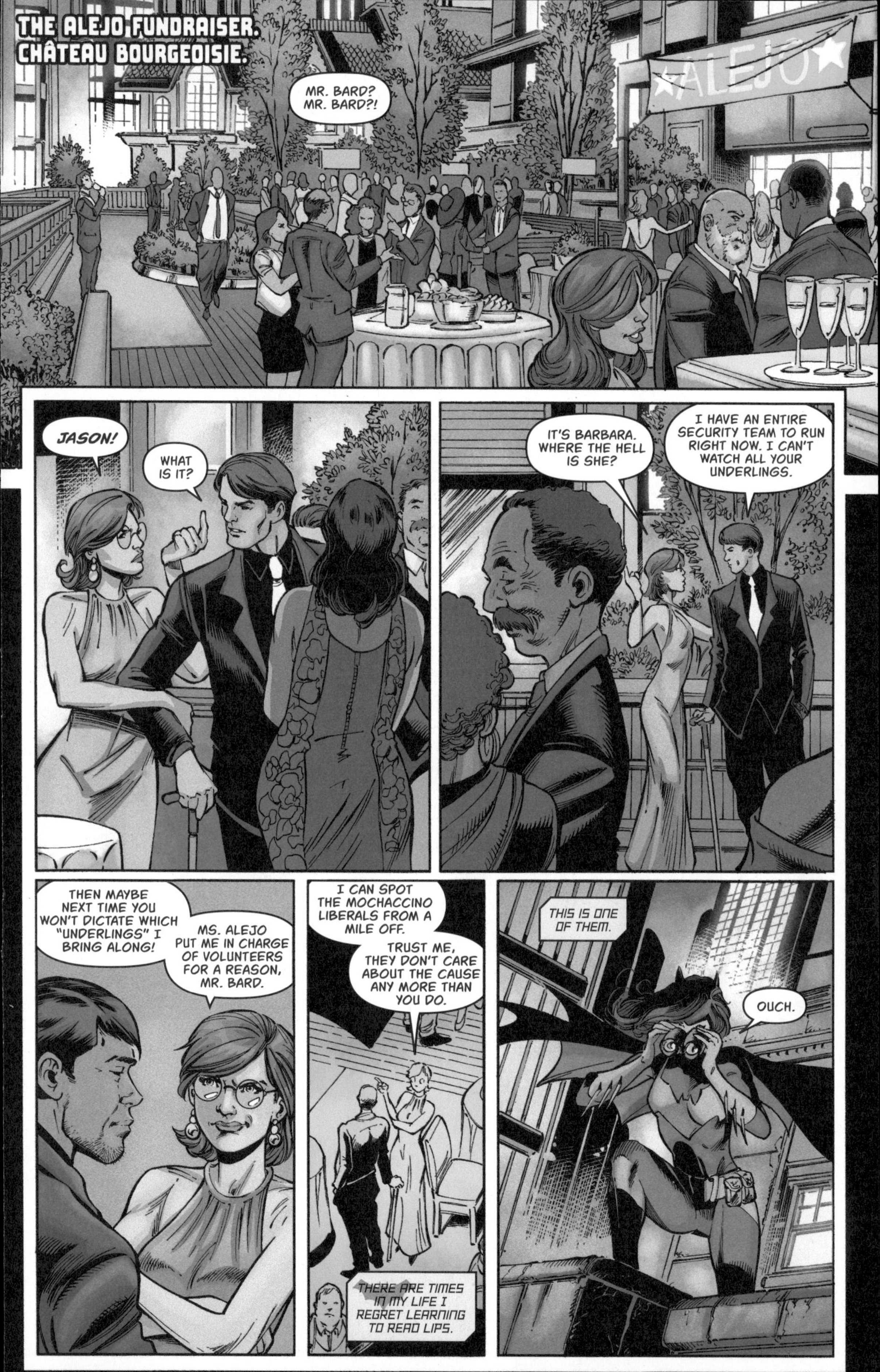
THE ALEJO FUNDRAISER. CHÂTEAU BOURGEOISIE.
MR. BARD? MR. BARD?!
ALEJO
JASON!
WHAT IS IT?
IT'S BARBARA. WHERE THE HELL IS SHE?
I HAVE AN ENTIRE SECURITY TEAM TO RUN RIGHT NOW. I CAN'T WATCH ALL YOUR UNDERLINGS.
THEN MAYBE NEXT TIME YOU WON'T DICTATE WHICH "UNDERLINGS" I BRING ALONG!
MS. ALEJO PUT ME IN CHARGE OF VOLUNTEERS FOR A REASON, MR. BARD.
I CAN SPOT THE MOCHACCINO LIBERALS FROM A MILE OFF.
TRUST ME, THEY DON'T CARE ABOUT THE CAUSE ANY MORE THAN YOU DO.
THERE ARE TIMES IN MY LIFE I REGRET LEARNING TO READ LIPS.
THIS IS ONE OF THEM.
OUCH.

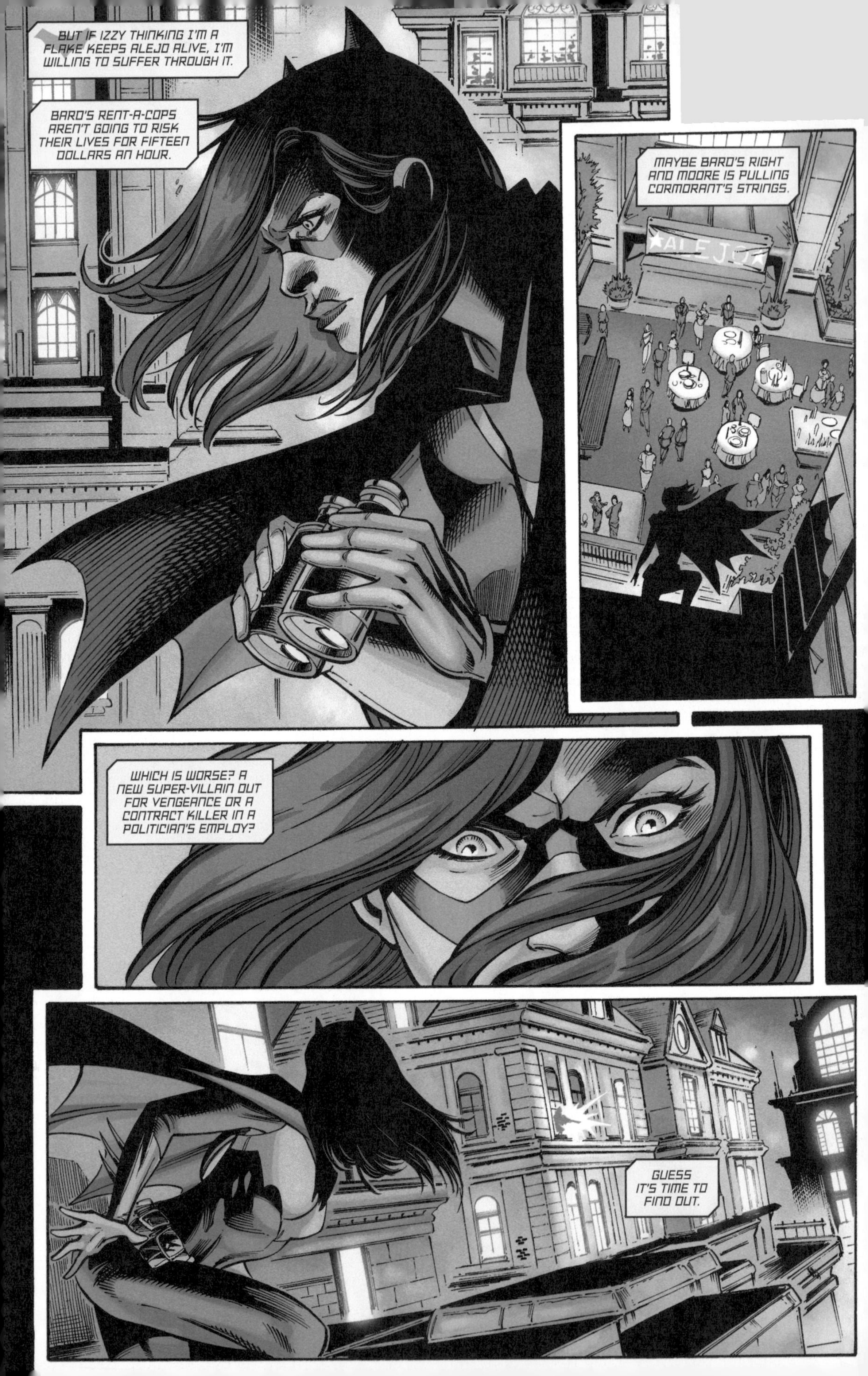
BUT IF IZZY THINKING I'M A FLAKE KEEPS ALEJO ALIVE, I'M WILLING TO SUFFER THROUGH IT.
BARD'S RENT-A-COPS AREN'T GOING TO RISK THEIR LIVES FOR FIFTEEN DOLLARS AN HOUR.
MAYBE BARD'S RIGHT AND MOORE IS PULLING CORMORANT'S STRINGS.
ALEJO
WHICH IS WORSE? A NEW SUPER-VILLAIN OUT FOR VENGEANCE OR A CONTRACT KILLER IN A POLITICIAN'S EMPLOY?
GUESS IT'S TIME TO FIND OUT.

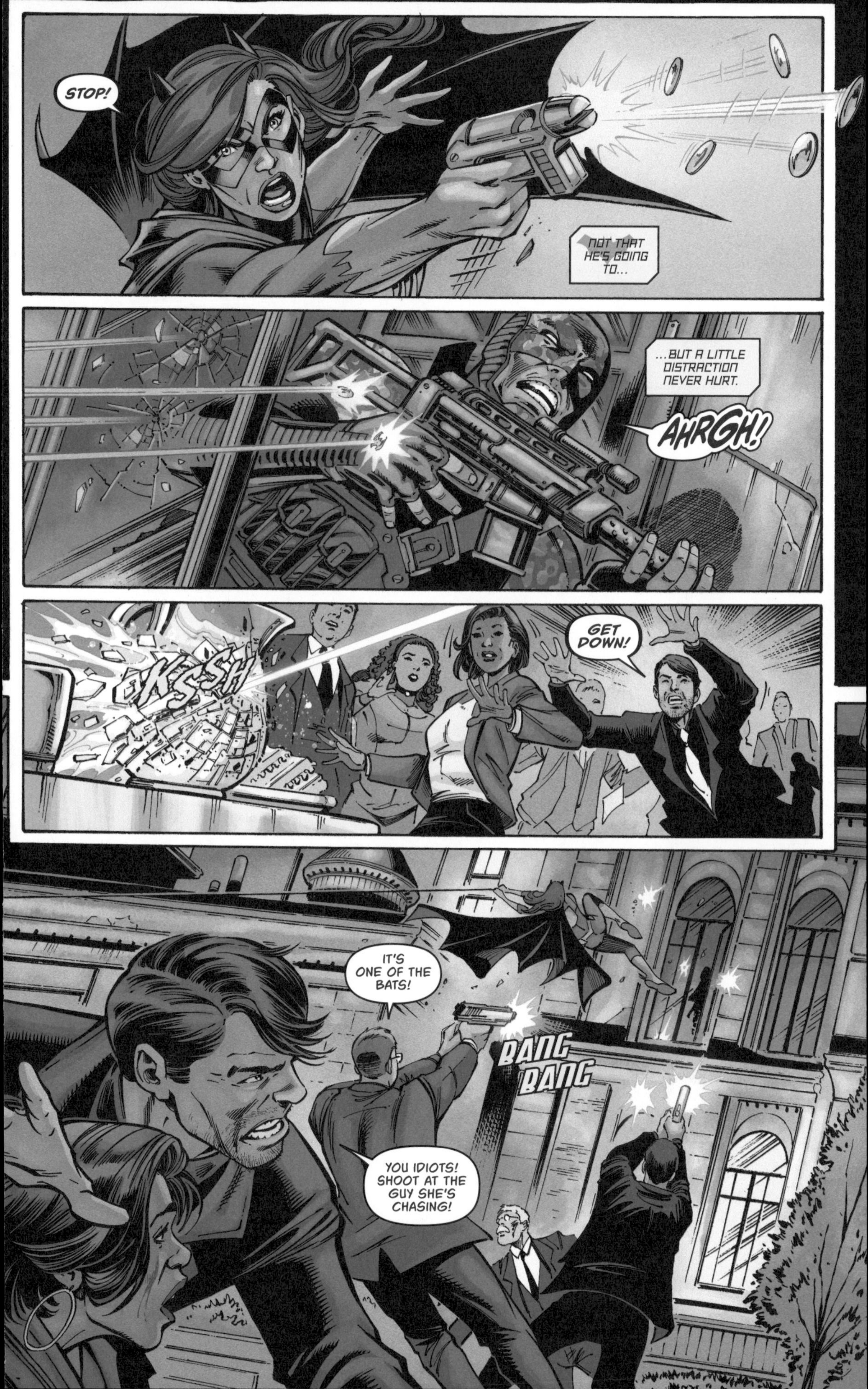
STOP!
NOT THAT HE'S GOING TO...
...BUT A LITTLE DISTRACTION NEVER HURT.
AHRGH!
KKSSH
GET DOWN!
IT'S ONE OF THE BATS!
BANG BANG
YOU IDIOTS! SHOOT AT THE GUY SHE'S CHASING!

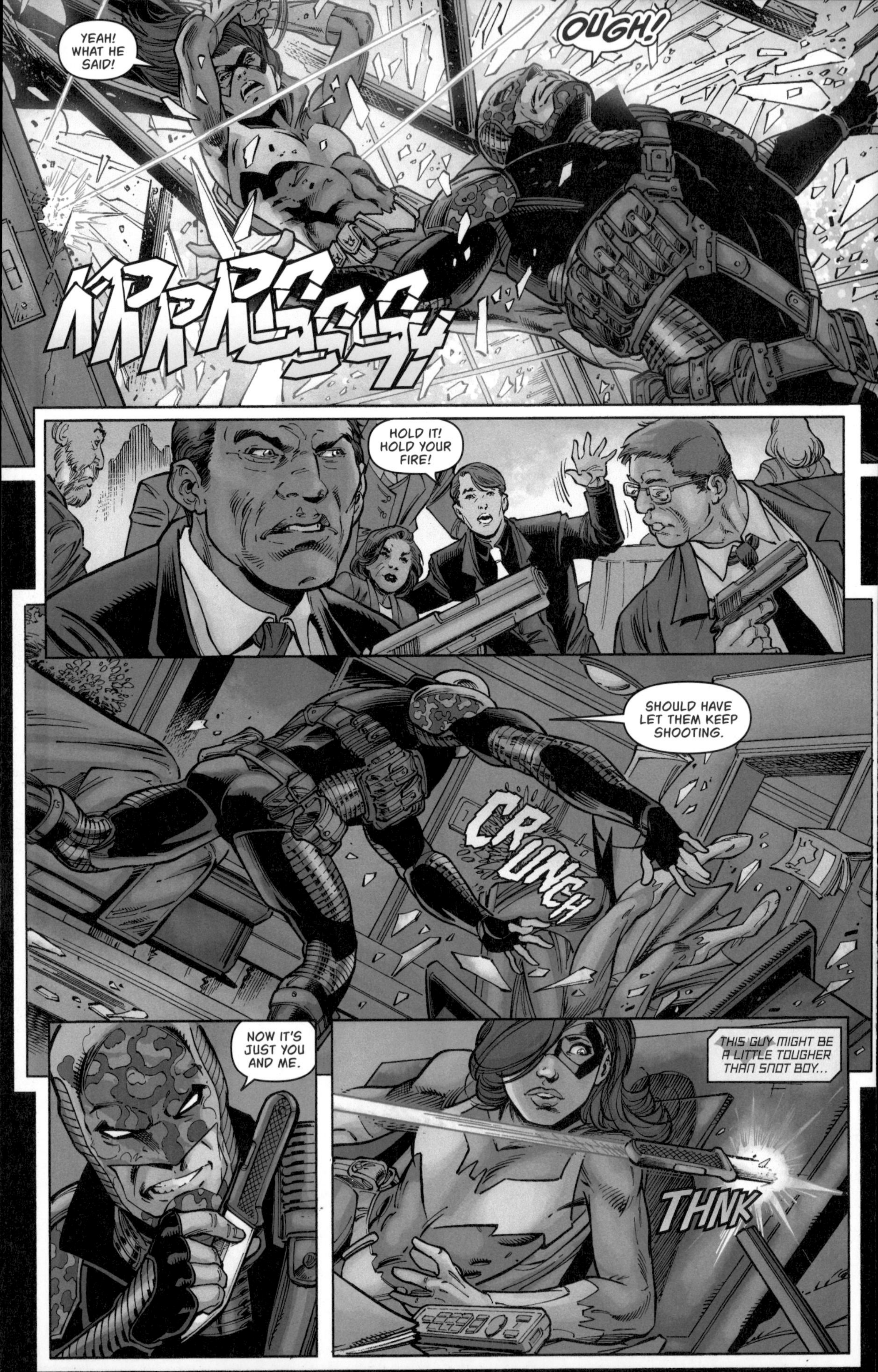
YEAH! WHAT HE SAID!
OUGH!
HOLD IT! HOLD YOUR FIRE!
SHOULD HAVE LET THEM KEEP SHOOTING.
CRUNCH
NOW IT'S JUST YOU AND ME.
THIS GUY MIGHT BE A LITTLE TOUGHER THAN SNOT BOY...
THNK

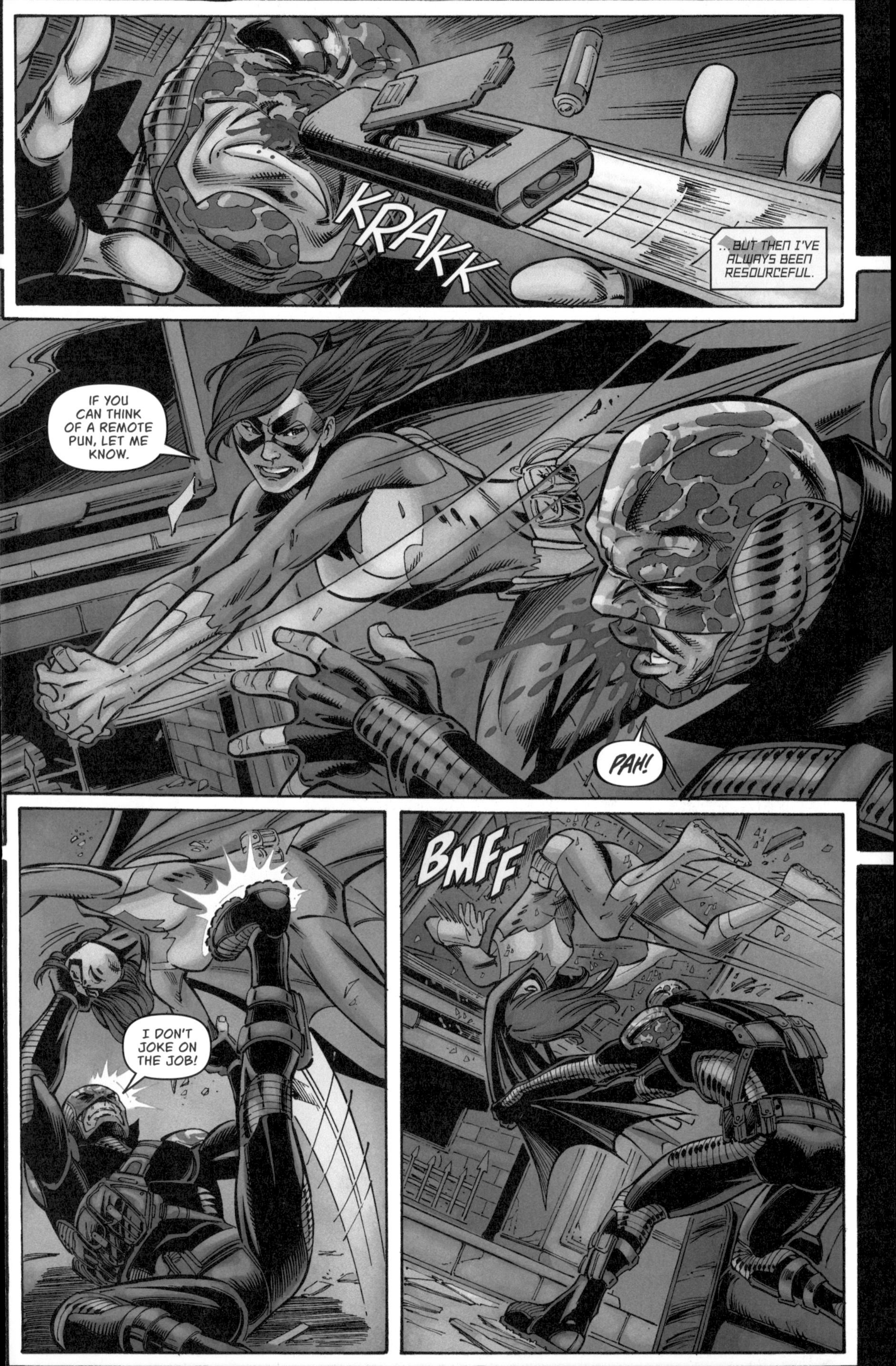
KRAKK
...BUT THEN I'VE ALWAYS BEEN RESOURCEFUL.
IF YOU CAN THINK OF A REMOTE PUN, LET ME KNOW.
PAH!
I DON'T JOKE ON THE JOB!
BMFF

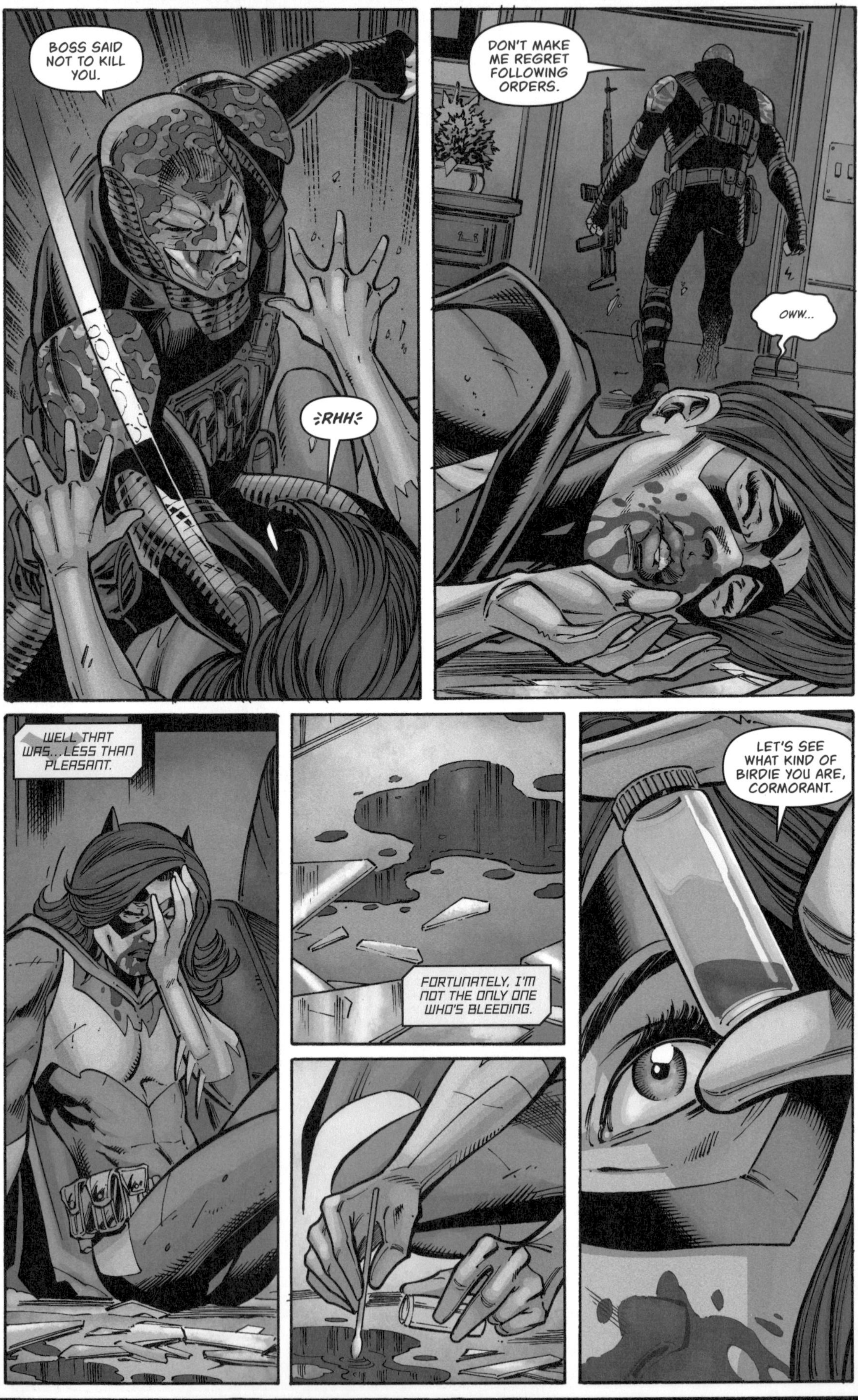
BOSS SAID NOT TO KILL YOU.
RHH
DON'T MAKE ME REGRET FOLLOWING ORDERS.
OWW...
WELL THAT WAS...LESS THAN PLEASANT.
FORTUNATELY, I'M NOT THE ONLY ONE WHO'S BLEEDING.
LET'S SEE WHAT KIND OF BIRDIE YOU ARE, CORMORANT.

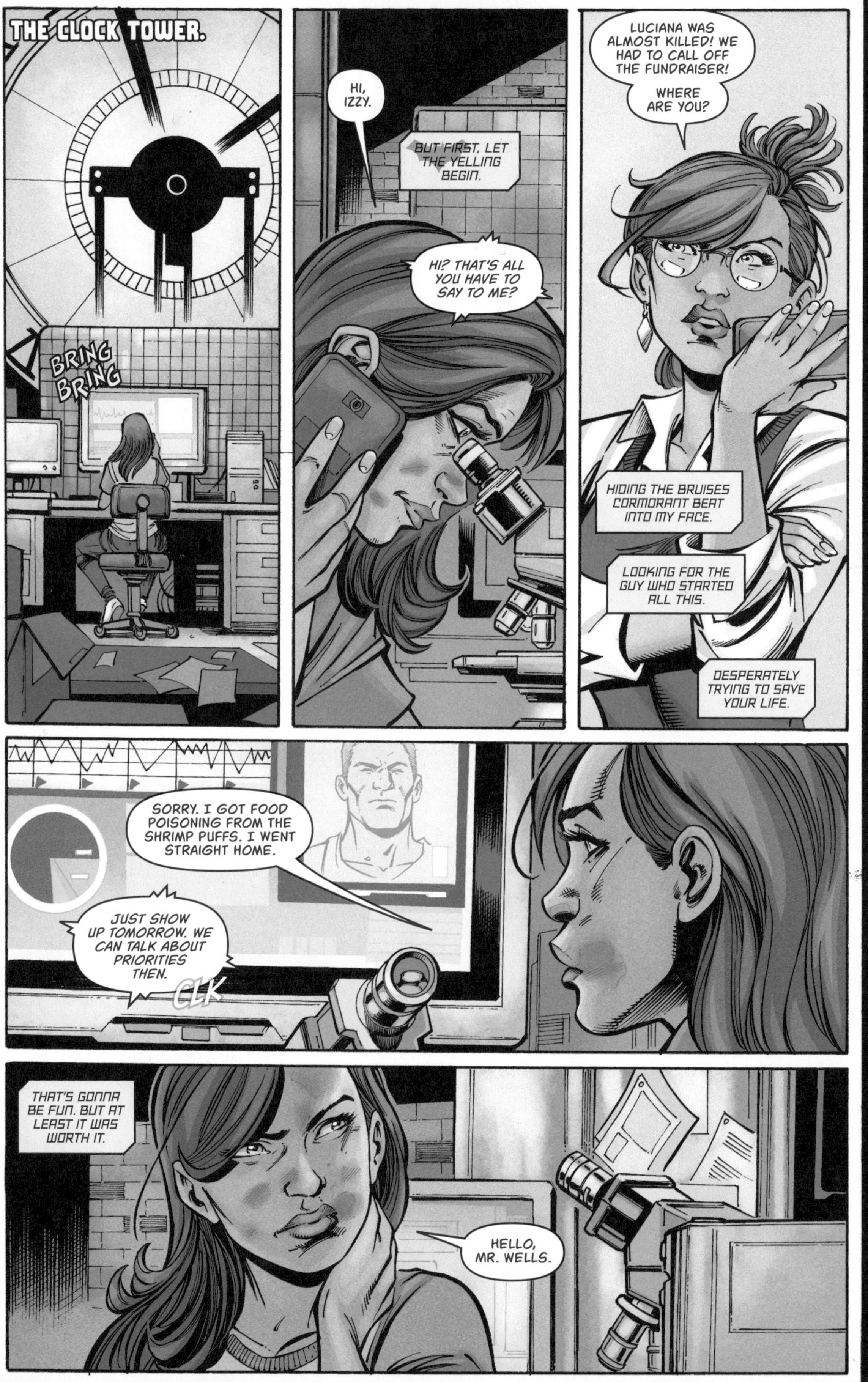
THE CLOCK TOWER.
BRING BRING
HI, IZZY.
BUT FIRST, LET THE YELLING BEGIN.
HI? THAT'S ALL YOU HAVE TO SAY TO ME?
LUCIANA WAS ALMOST KILLED! WE HAD TO CALL OFF THE FUNDRAISER!
WHERE ARE YOU?
HIDING THE BRUISES CORMORANT BEAT INTO MY FACE.
LOOKING FOR THE GUY WHO STARTED ALL THIS.
DESPERATELY TRYING TO SAVE YOUR LIFE.
SORRY. I GOT FOOD POISONING FROM THE SHRIMP PUFFS. I WENT STRAIGHT HOME.
JUST SHOW UP TOMORROW. WE CAN TALK ABOUT PRIORITIES THEN.
CLK
THAT'S GONNA BE FUN. BUT AT LEAST IT WAS WORTH IT.
HELLO, MR. WELLS.

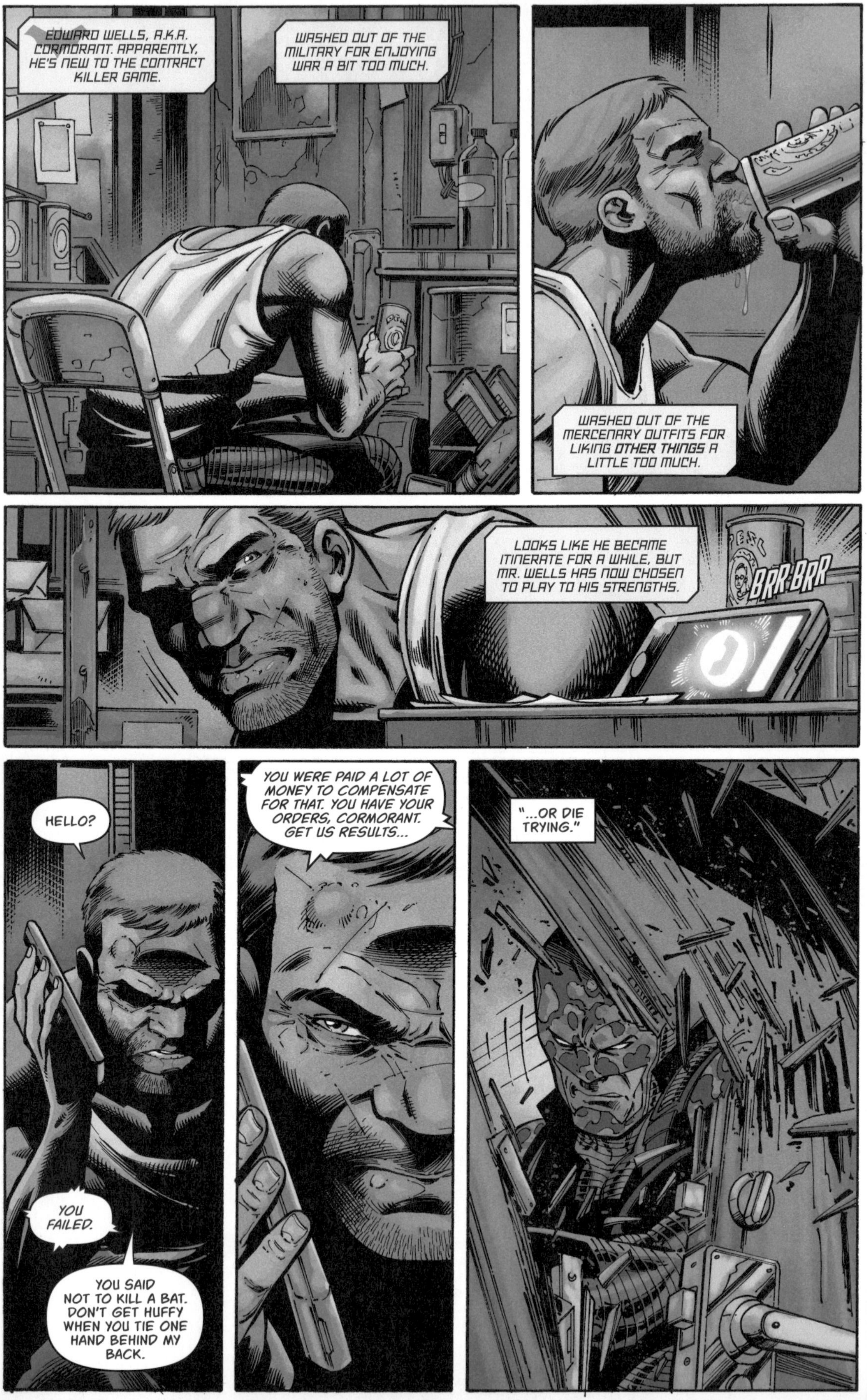
EDWARD WELLS, A.K.A. CORMORANT. APPARENTLY, HE'S NEW TO THE CONTRACT KILLER GAME.
WASHED OUT OF THE MILITARY FOR ENJOYING WAR A BIT TOO MUCH.
WASHED OUT OF THE MERCENARY OUTFITS FOR LIKING OTHER THINGS A LITTLE TOO MUCH.
LOOKS LIKE HE BECAME ITINERATE FOR A WHILE, BUT MR. WELLS HAS NOW CHOSEN TO PLAY TO HIS STRENGTHS.
BRR BRR
HELLO?
YOU FAILED.
YOU SAID NOT TO KILL A BAT. DON'T GET HUFFY WHEN YOU TIE ONE HAND BEHIND MY BACK.
YOU WERE PAID A LOT OF MONEY TO COMPENSATE FOR THAT. YOU HAVE YOUR ORDERS, CORMORANT. GET US RESULTS...
"...OR DIE TRYING."

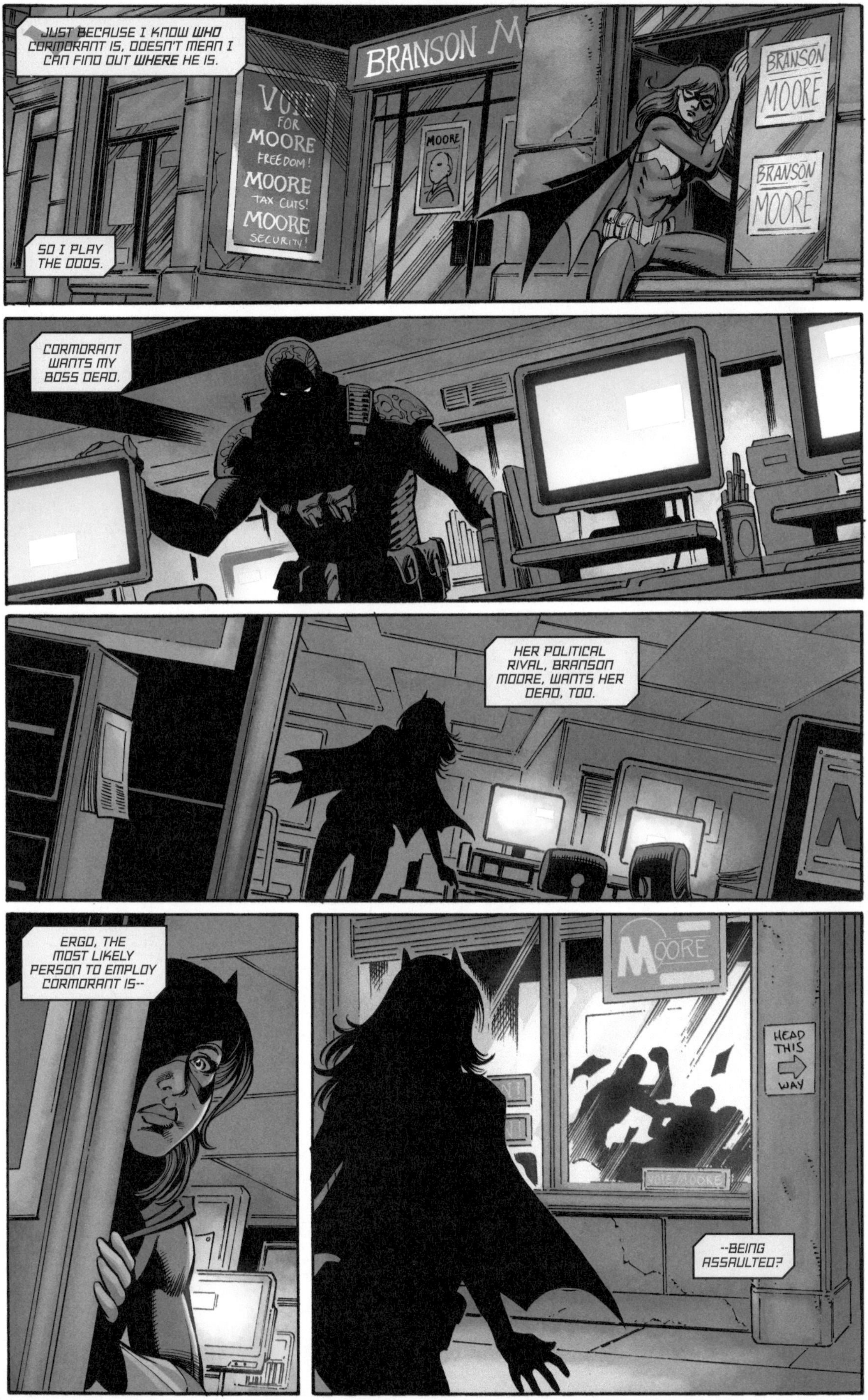

JUST BECAUSE I KNOW WHO CORMORANT IS, DOESN'T MEAN I CAN FIND OUT WHERE HE IS.
BRANSON M
VOTE FOR MOORE FREEDOM! MOORE TAX CUTS! MOORE SECURITY!
MOORE
BRANSON MOORE
BRANSON MOORE
SO I PLAY THE ODDS.
CORMORANT WANTS MY BOSS DEAD.
HER POLITICAL RIVAL, BRANSON MOORE, WANTS HER DEAD, TOO.
ERGO, THE MOST LIKELY PERSON TO EMPLOY CORMORANT IS--
MOORE
HEAD THIS WAY
VOTE MOORE
--BEING ASSAULTED?

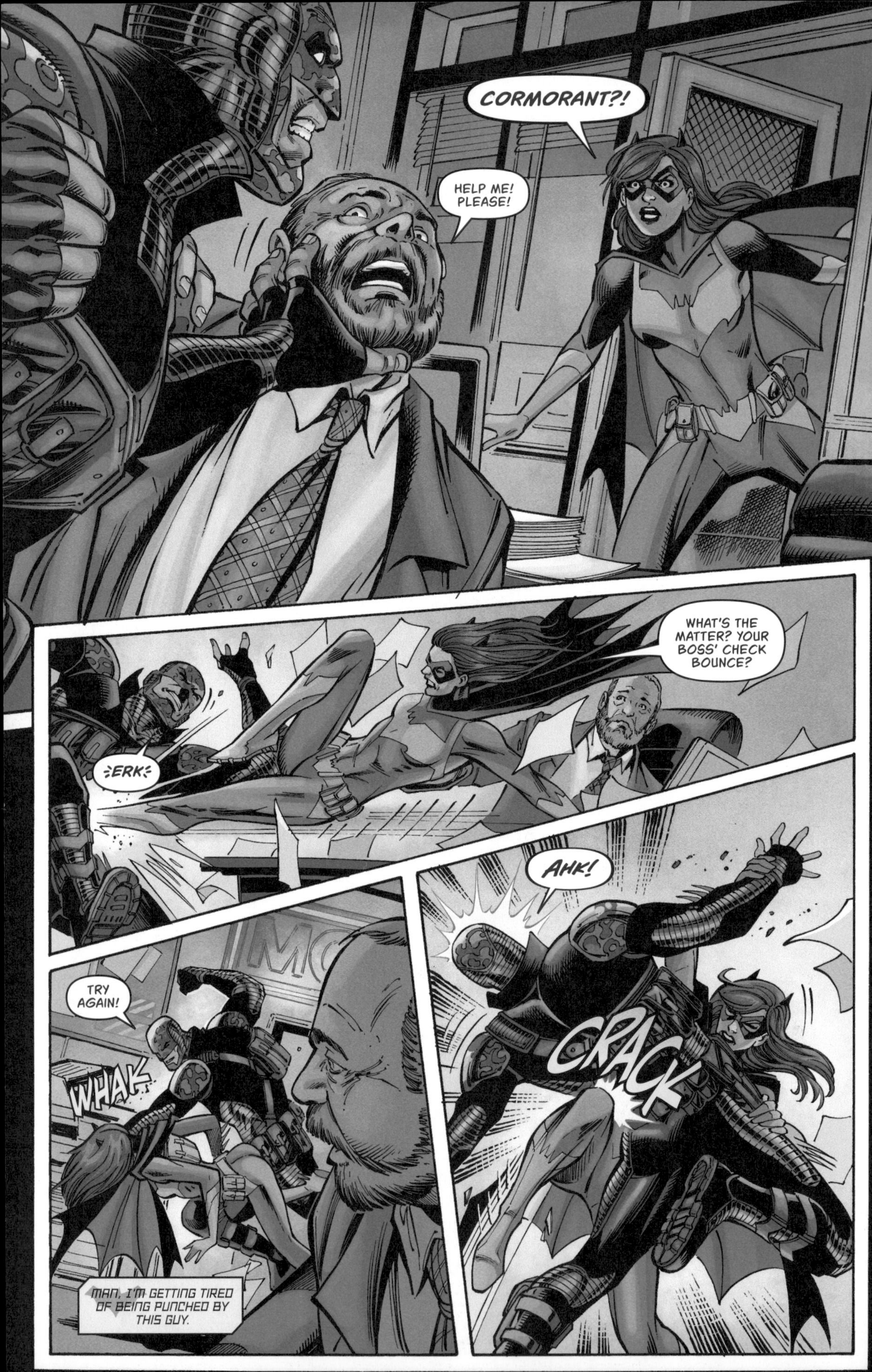
CORMORANT?!
HELP ME! PLEASE!
WHAT'S THE MATTER? YOUR BOSS' CHECK BOUNCE?
ERK
TRY AGAIN!
WHAK
MAN, I'M GETTING TIRED OF BEING PUNCHED BY THIS GUY.
AHK!
CRACK

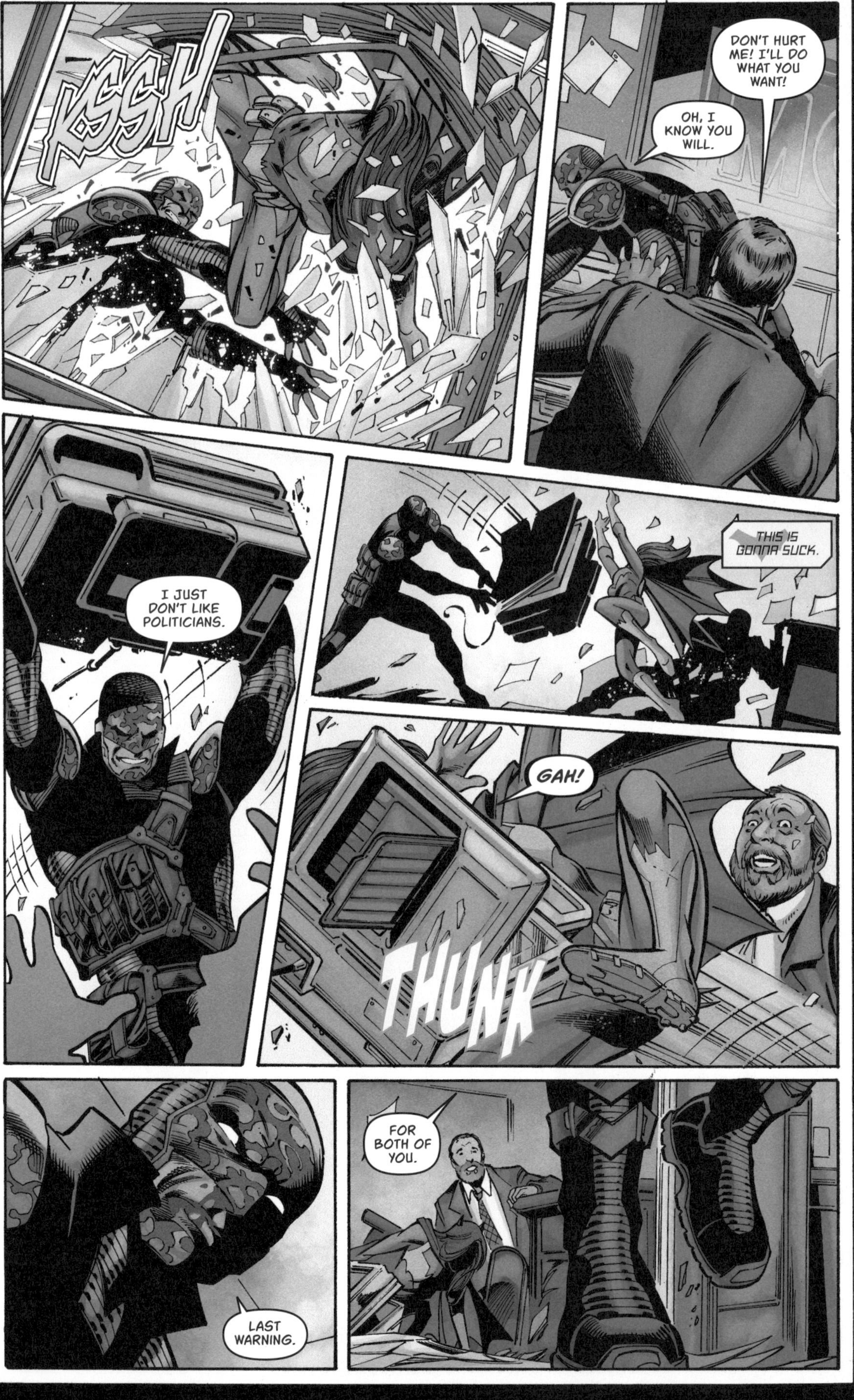
KSSH
DON'T HURT ME! I'LL DO WHAT YOU WANT!
OH, I KNOW YOU WILL.
I JUST DON'T LIKE POLITICIANS.
THIS IS GONNA SUCK.
GAH!
THUNK
LAST WARNING.
FOR BOTH OF YOU.

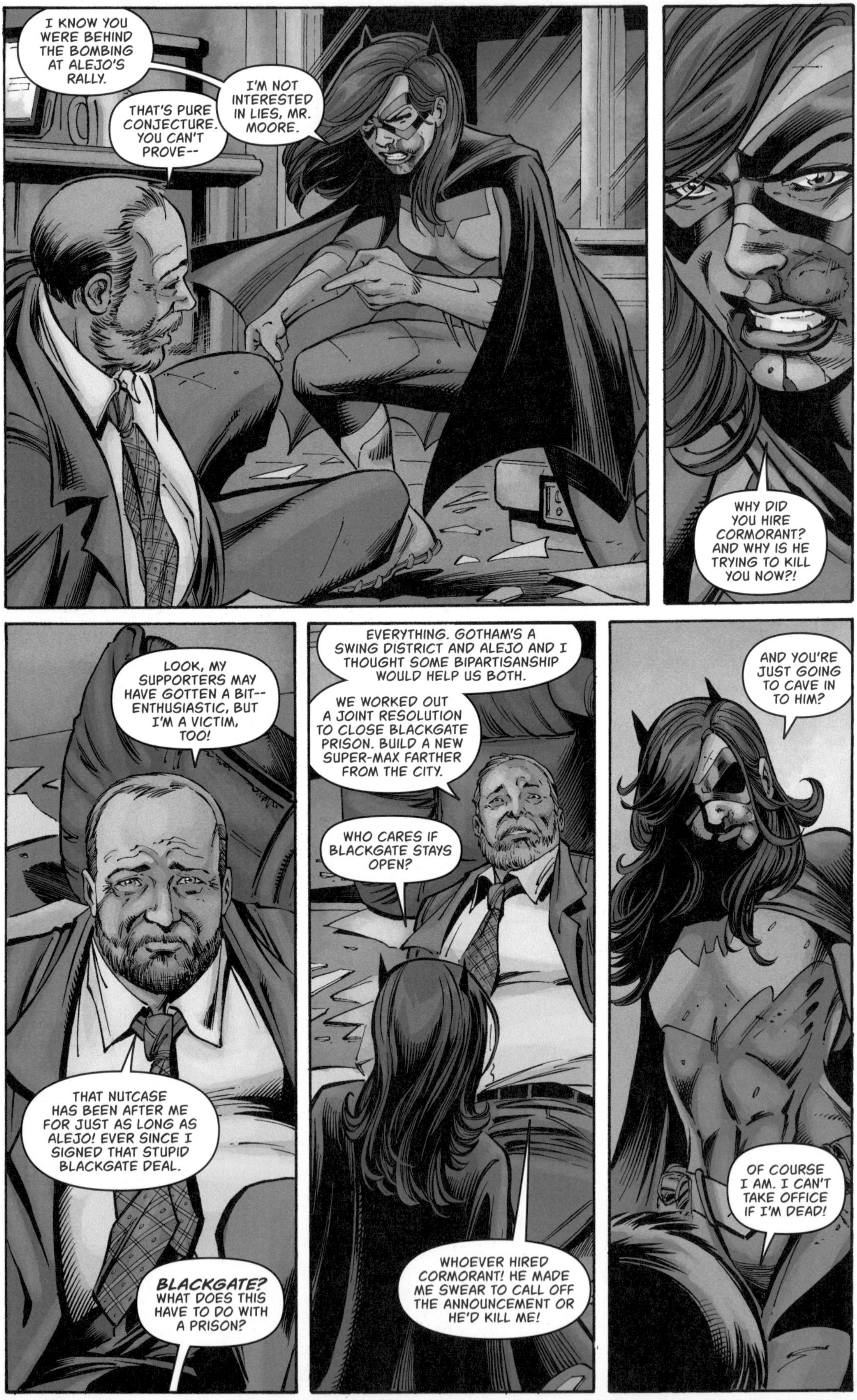
I KNOW YOU WERE BEHIND THE BOMBING AT ALEJO'S RALLY.
THAT'S PURE CONJECTURE. YOU CAN'T PROVE--
I'M NOT INTERESTED IN LIES, MR. MOORE.
WHY DID YOU HIRE CORMORANT? AND WHY IS HE TRYING TO KILL YOU NOW?!
LOOK, MY SUPPORTERS MAY HAVE GOTTEN A BIT--ENTHUSIASTIC, BUT I'M A VICTIM, TOO!
THAT NUTCASE HAS BEEN AFTER ME FOR JUST AS LONG AS ALEJO! EVER SINCE I SIGNED THAT STUPID BLACKGATE DEAL.
BLACKGATE? WHAT DOES THIS HAVE TO DO WITH A PRISON?
EVERYTHING. GOTHAM'S A SWING DISTRICT AND ALEJO AND I THOUGHT SOME BIPARTISANSHIP WOULD HELP US BOTH.
WE WORKED OUT A JOINT RESOLUTION TO CLOSE BLACKGATE PRISON. BUILD A NEW SUPER-MAX FARTHER FROM THE CITY.
WHO CARES IF BLACKGATE STAYS OPEN?
WHOEVER HIRED CORMORANT! HE MADE ME SWEAR TO CALL OFF THE ANNOUNCEMENT OR HE'D KILL ME!
AND YOU'RE JUST GOING TO CAVE IN TO HIM?
OF COURSE I AM. I CAN'T TAKE OFFICE IF I'M DEAD!

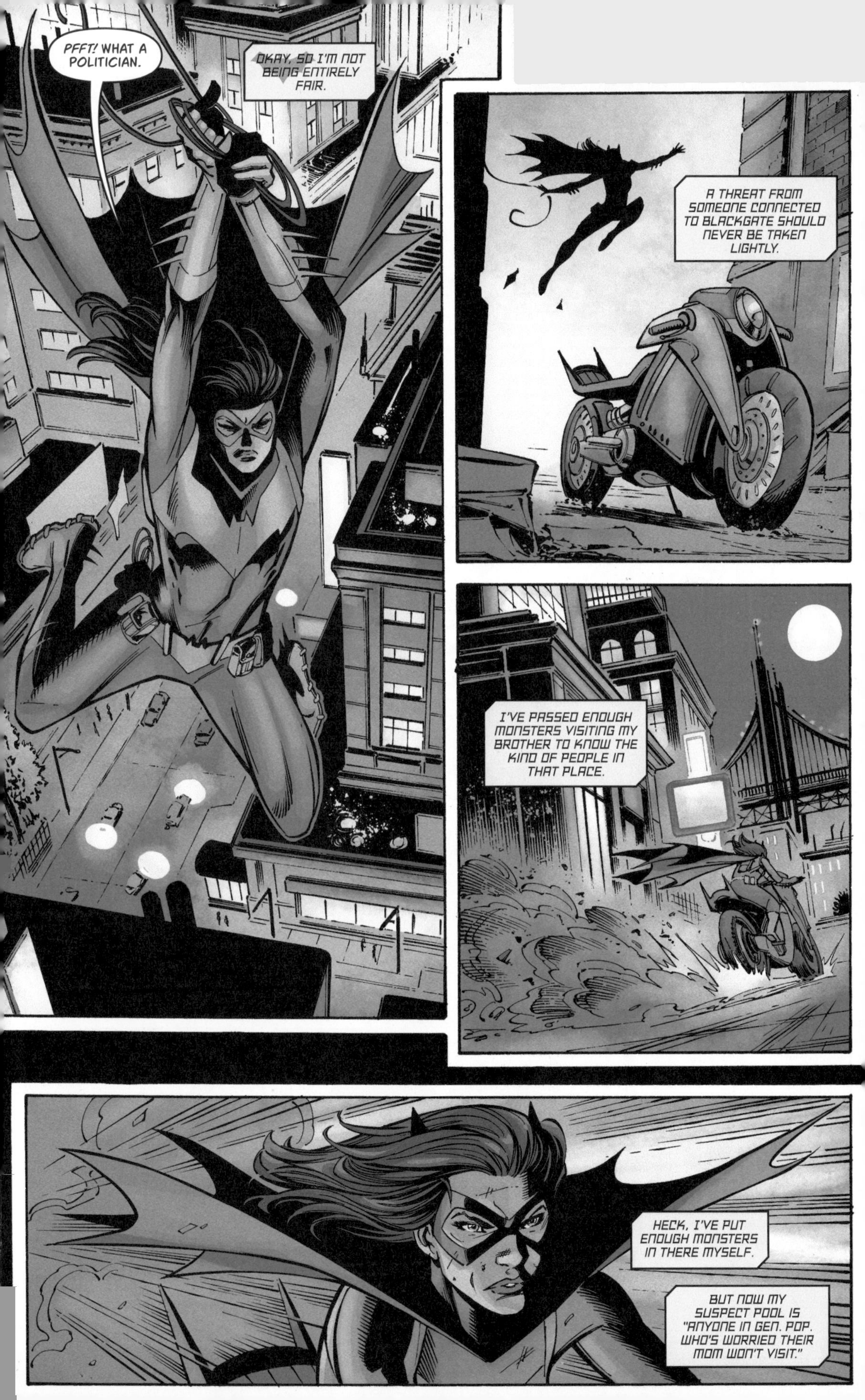
PFFT! WHAT A POLITICIAN.
OKAY, SO I'M NOT BEING ENTIRELY FAIR.
A THREAT FROM SOMEONE CONNECTED TO BLACKGATE SHOULD NEVER BE TAKEN LIGHTLY.
I'VE PASSED ENOUGH MONSTERS VISITING MY BROTHER TO KNOW THE KIND OF PEOPLE IN THAT PLACE.
HECK, I'VE PUT ENOUGH MONSTERS IN THERE MYSELF.
BUT NOW MY SUSPECT POOL IS "ANYONE IN GEN. POP. WHO'S WORRIED THEIR MOM WON'T VISIT."

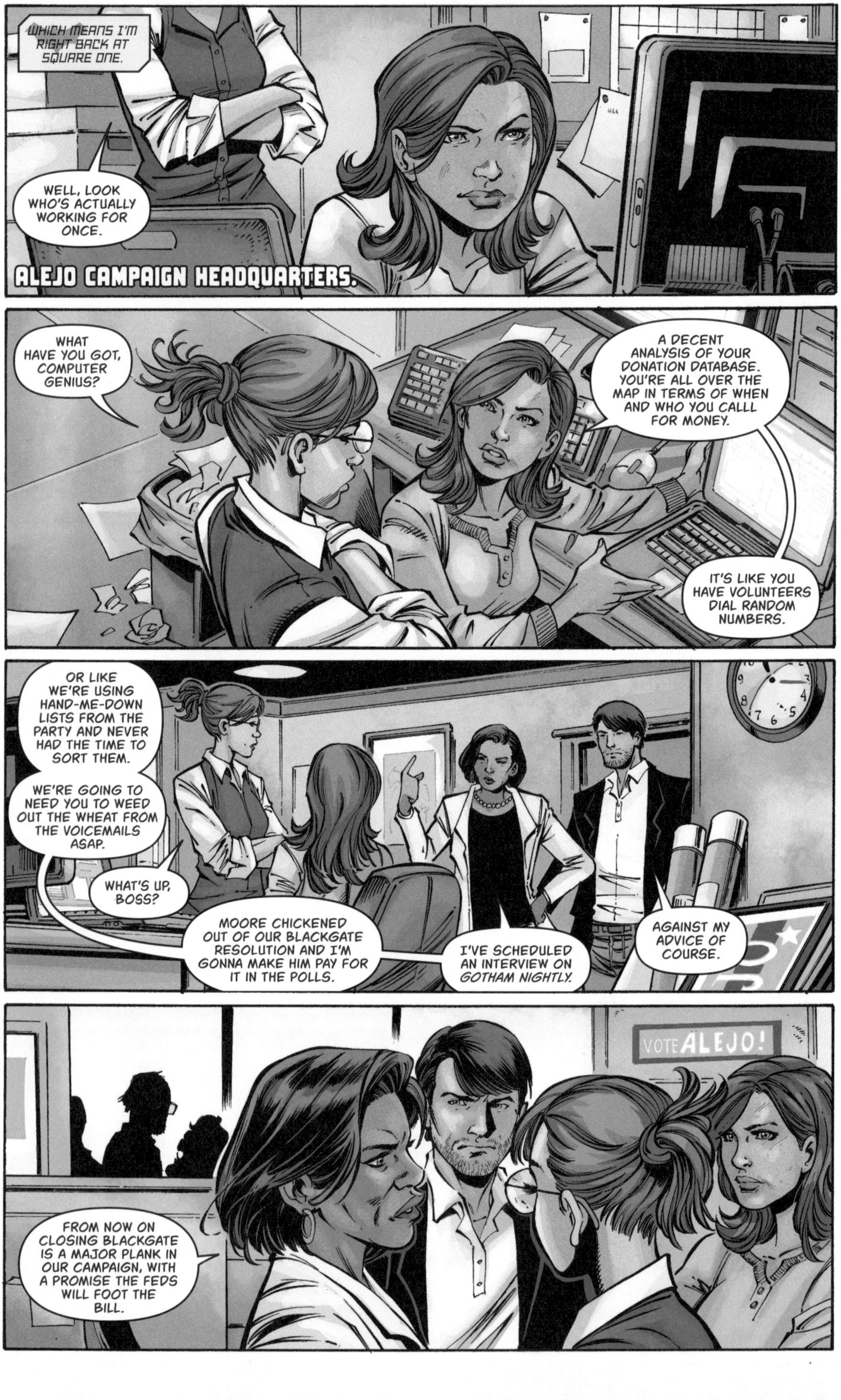
WHICH MEANS I'M RIGHT BACK AT SQUARE ONE.
WELL, LOOK WHO'S ACTUALLY WORKING FOR ONCE.
ALEJO CAMPAIGN HEADQUARTERS.
WHAT HAVE YOU GOT, COMPUTER GENIUS?
A DECENT ANALYSIS OF YOUR DONATION DATABASE. YOU'RE ALL OVER THE MAP IN TERMS OF WHEN AND WHO YOU CALLL FOR MONEY.
IT'S LIKE YOU HAVE VOLUNTEERS DIAL RANDOM NUMBERS.
OR LIKE WE'RE USING HAND-ME-DOWN LISTS FROM THE PARTY AND NEVER HAD THE TIME TO SORT THEM.
WE'RE GOING TO NEED YOU TO WEED OUT THE WHEAT FROM THE VOICEMAILS ASAP.
WHAT'S UP, BOSS?
MOORE CHICKENED OUT OF OUR BLACKGATE RESOLUTION AND I'M GONNA MAKE HIM PAY FOR IT IN THE POLLS.
I'VE SCHEDULED AN INTERVIEW ON *GOTHAM NIGHTLY.*
AGAINST MY ADVICE OF COURSE.
VOTE ALEJO!
FROM NOW ON CLOSING BLACKGATE IS A MAJOR PLANK IN OUR CAMPAIGN, WITH A PROMISE THE FEDS WILL FOOT THE BILL.

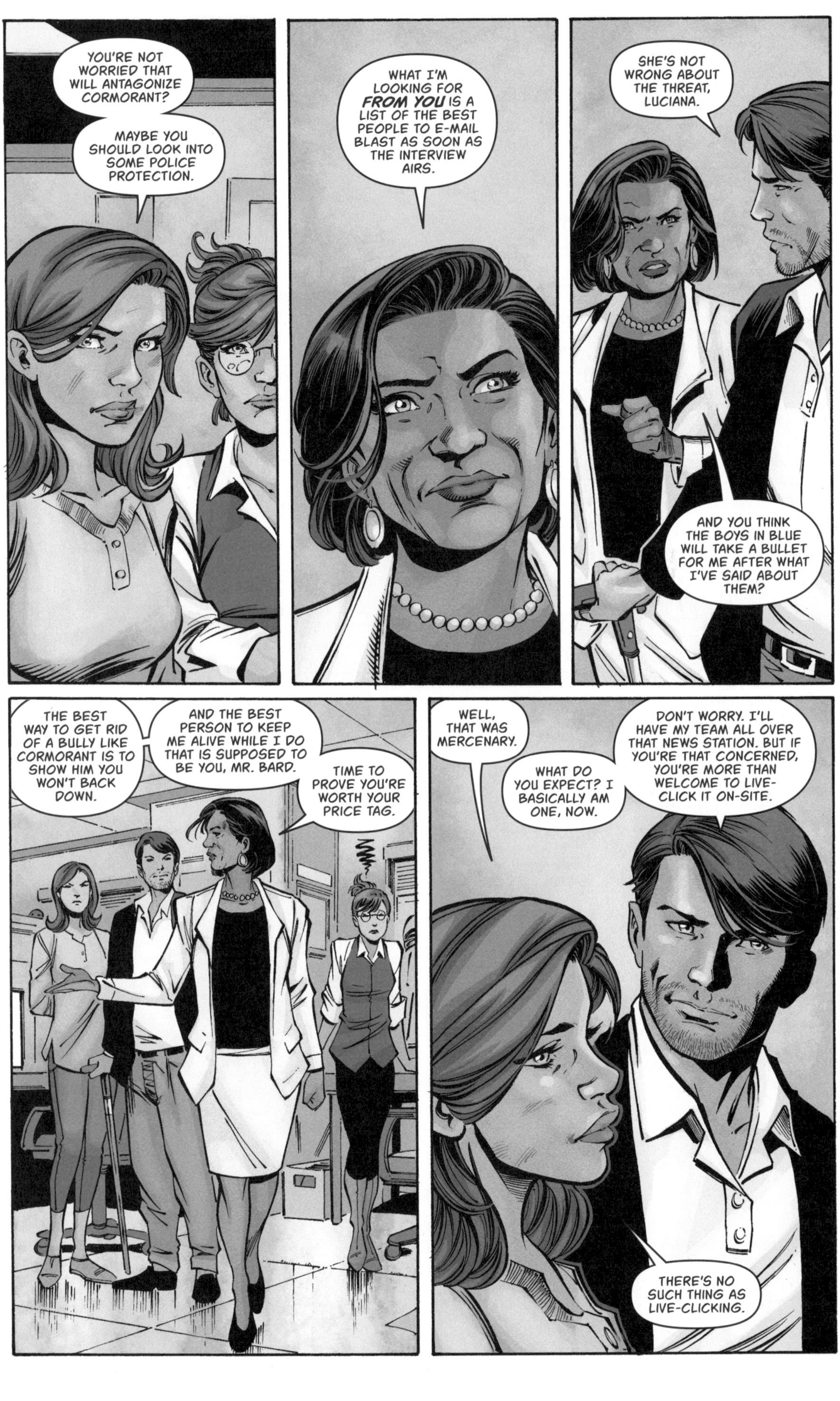
YOU'RE NOT WORRIED THAT WILL ANTAGONIZE CORMORANT?
MAYBE YOU SHOULD LOOK INTO SOME POLICE PROTECTION.
WHAT I'M LOOKING FOR **FROM YOU** IS A LIST OF THE BEST PEOPLE TO E-MAIL BLAST AS SOON AS THE INTERVIEW AIRS.
SHE'S NOT WRONG ABOUT THE THREAT, LUCIANA.
AND YOU THINK THE BOYS IN BLUE WILL TAKE A BULLET FOR ME AFTER WHAT I'VE SAID ABOUT THEM?
THE BEST WAY TO GET RID OF A BULLY LIKE CORMORANT IS TO SHOW HIM YOU WON'T BACK DOWN.
AND THE BEST PERSON TO KEEP ME ALIVE WHILE I DO THAT IS SUPPOSED TO BE YOU, MR. BARD.
TIME TO PROVE YOU'RE WORTH YOUR PRICE TAG.
WELL, THAT WAS MERCENARY.
WHAT DO YOU EXPECT? I BASICALLY AM ONE, NOW.
DON'T WORRY. I'LL HAVE MY TEAM ALL OVER THAT NEWS STATION. BUT IF YOU'RE THAT CONCERNED, YOU'RE MORE THAN WELCOME TO LIVE-CLICK IT ON-SITE.
THERE'S NO SUCH THING AS LIVE-CLICKING.

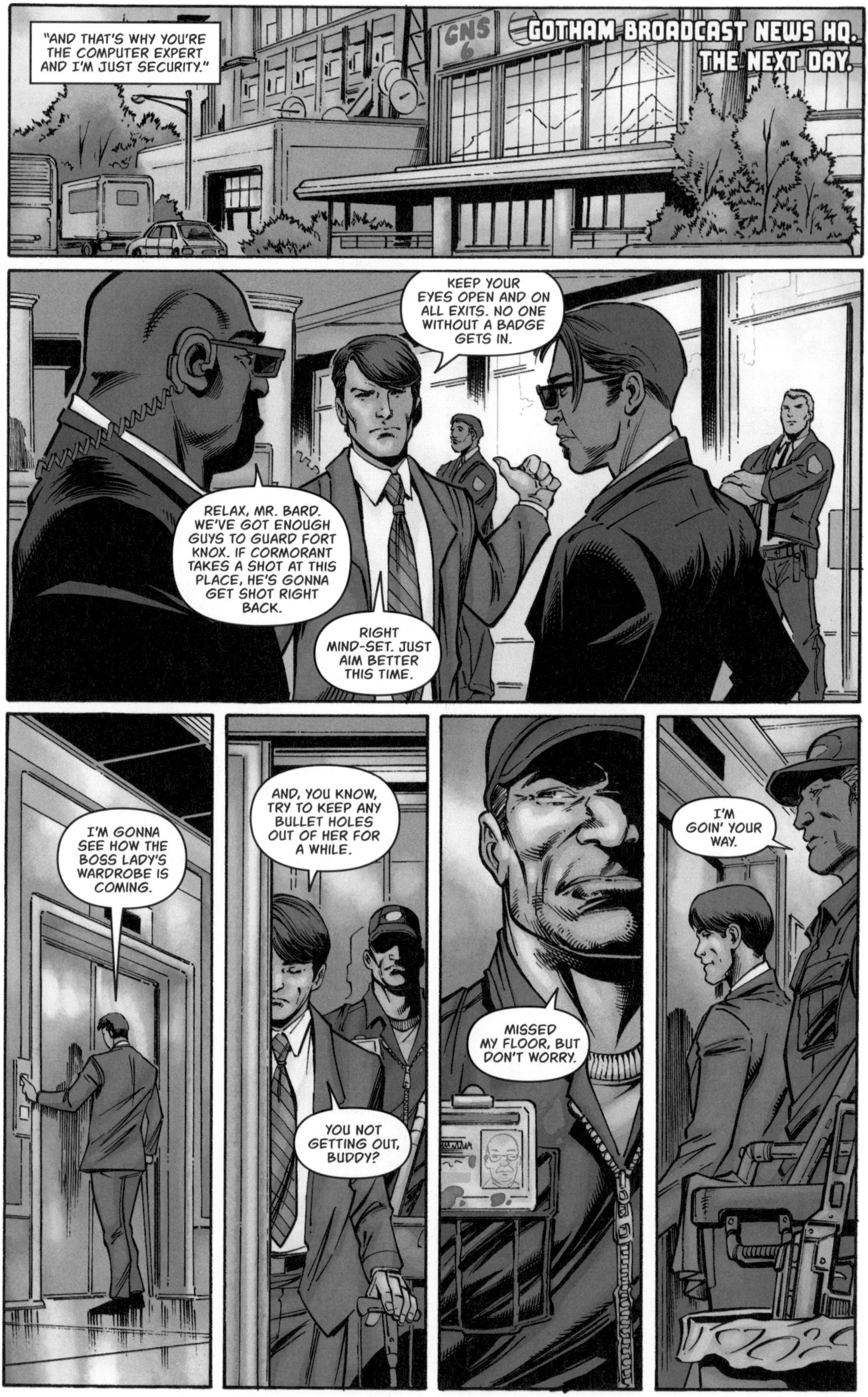
"AND THAT'S WHY YOU'RE THE COMPUTER EXPERT AND I'M JUST SECURITY."
GOTHAM BROADCAST NEWS HQ. THE NEXT DAY.
GNS 6
KEEP YOUR EYES OPEN AND ON ALL EXITS. NO ONE WITHOUT A BADGE GETS IN.
RELAX, MR. BARD. WE'VE GOT ENOUGH GUYS TO GUARD FORT KNOX. IF CORMORANT TAKES A SHOT AT THIS PLACE, HE'S GONNA GET SHOT RIGHT BACK.
RIGHT MIND-SET. JUST AIM BETTER THIS TIME.
I'M GONNA SEE HOW THE BOSS LADY'S WARDROBE IS COMING.
AND, YOU KNOW, TRY TO KEEP ANY BULLET HOLES OUT OF HER FOR A WHILE.
YOU NOT GETTING OUT, BUDDY?
MISSED MY FLOOR, BUT DON'T WORRY.
I'M GOIN' YOUR WAY.

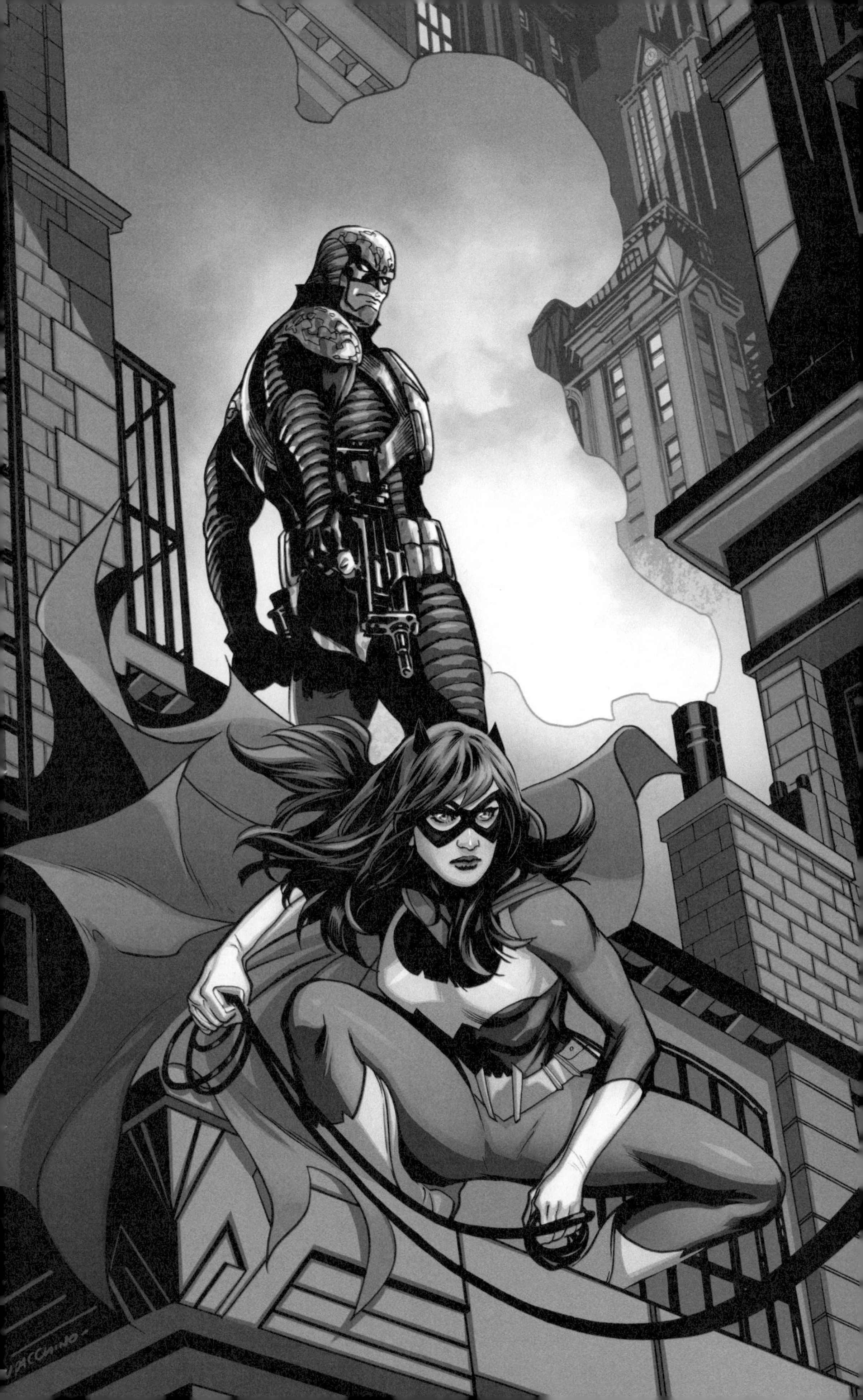

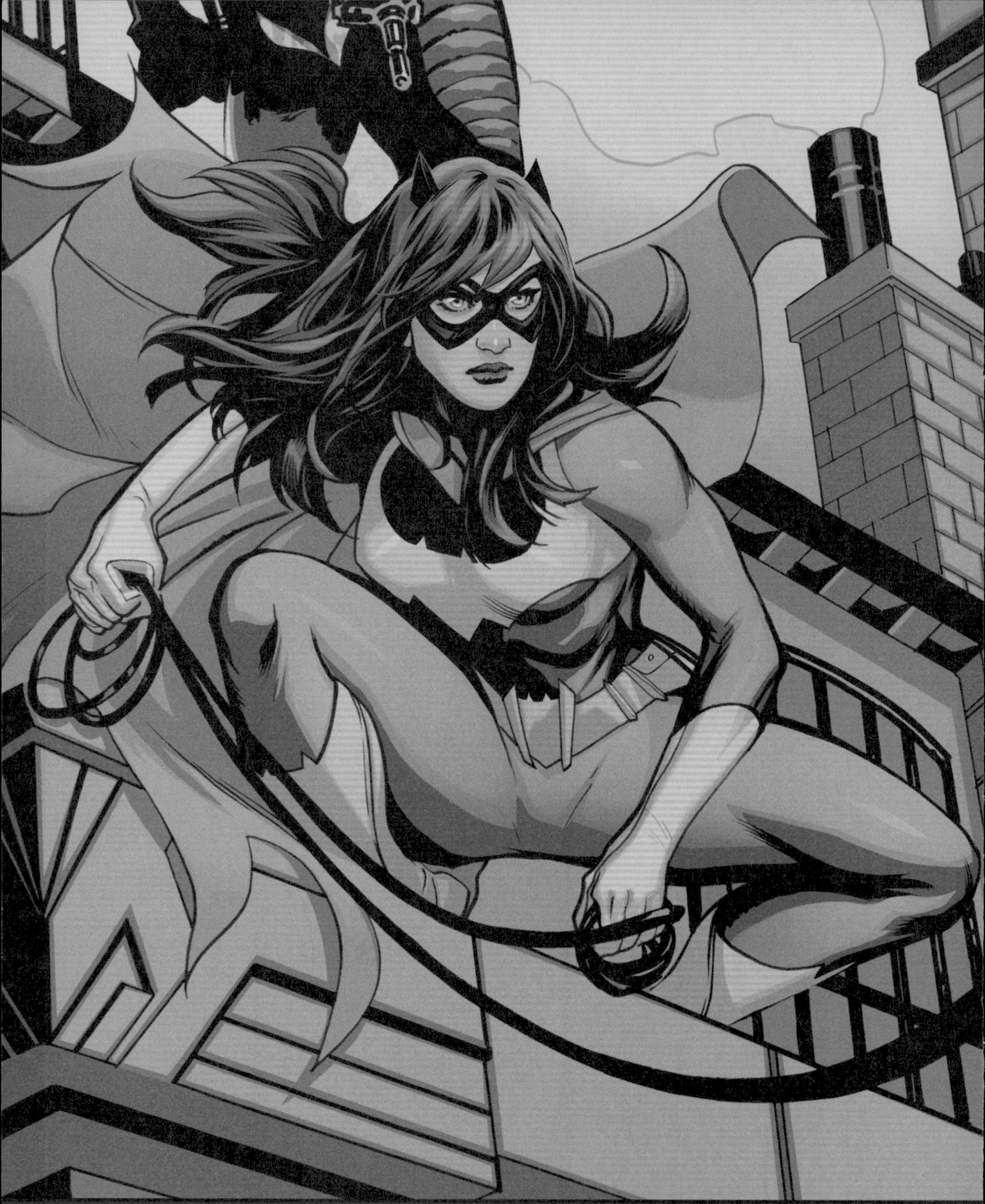

BATGIRL
#32

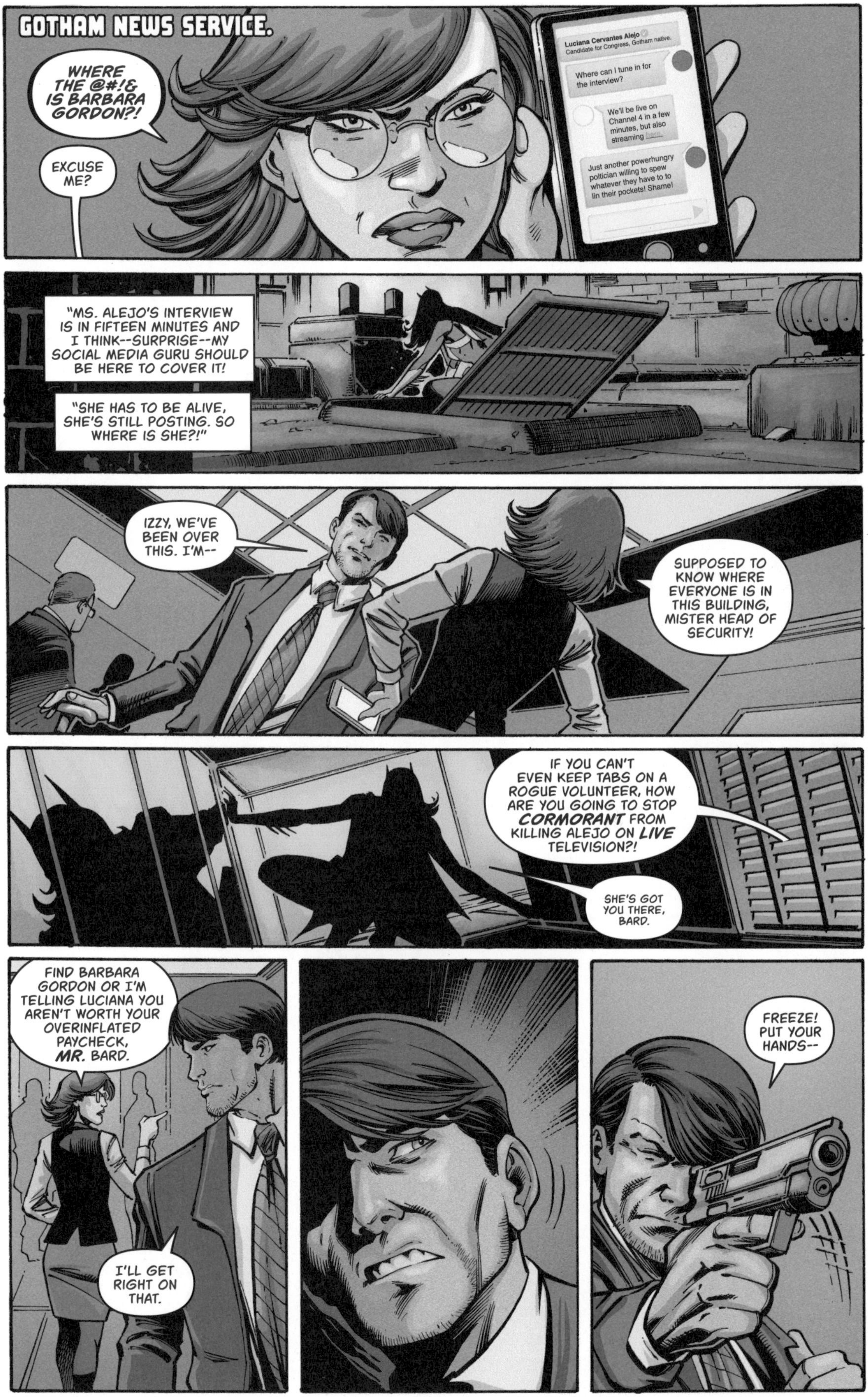
GOTHAM NEWS SERVICE.
WHERE THE @#!& IS BARBARA GORDON?!
EXCUSE ME?
Luciana Cervantes Alejo
Candidate for Congress, Gotham native.
Where can I tune in for the interview?
We'll be live on Channel 4 in a few minutes, but also streaming here.
Just another powerhungry politician willing to spew whatever they have to to lin their pockets! Shame!
"MS. ALEJO'S INTERVIEW IS IN FIFTEEN MINUTES AND I THINK--SURPRISE--MY SOCIAL MEDIA GURU SHOULD BE HERE TO COVER IT!
"SHE HAS TO BE ALIVE, SHE'S STILL POSTING. SO WHERE IS SHE?!"
IZZY, WE'VE BEEN OVER THIS. I'M--
SUPPOSED TO KNOW WHERE EVERYONE IS IN THIS BUILDING, MISTER HEAD OF SECURITY!
IF YOU CAN'T EVEN KEEP TABS ON A ROGUE VOLUNTEER, HOW ARE YOU GOING TO STOP CORMORANT FROM KILLING ALEJO ON LIVE TELEVISION?!
SHE'S GOT YOU THERE, BARD.
FIND BARBARA GORDON OR I'M TELLING LUCIANA YOU AREN'T WORTH YOUR OVERINFLATED PAYCHECK, MR. BARD.
I'LL GET RIGHT ON THAT.
FREEZE! PUT YOUR HANDS--

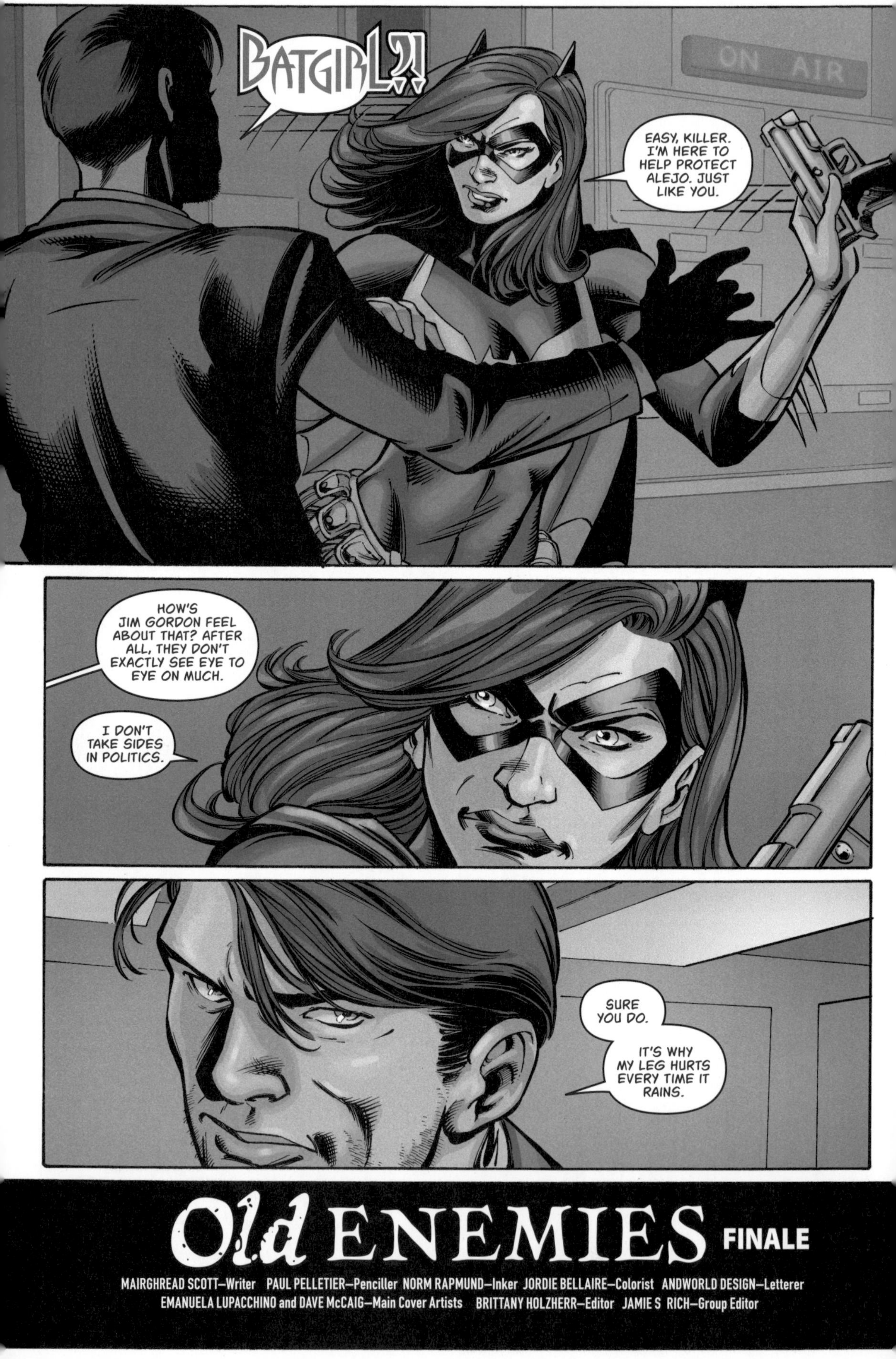
BATGIRL?!
EASY, KILLER. I'M HERE TO HELP PROTECT ALEJO. JUST LIKE YOU.
ON AIR
HOW'S JIM GORDON FEEL ABOUT THAT? AFTER ALL, THEY DON'T EXACTLY SEE EYE TO EYE ON MUCH.
I DON'T TAKE SIDES IN POLITICS.
SURE YOU DO.
IT'S WHY MY LEG HURTS EVERY TIME IT RAINS.

Old ENEMIES FINALE

MAIRGHREAD SCOTT—Writer PAUL PELLETIER—Penciller NORM RAPMUND—Inker JORDIE BELLAIRE—Colorist ANDWORLD DESIGN—Letterer
EMANUELA LUPACCHINO and DAVE McCAIG—Main Cover Artists BRITTANY HOLZHERR—Editor JAMIE S RICH—Group Editor

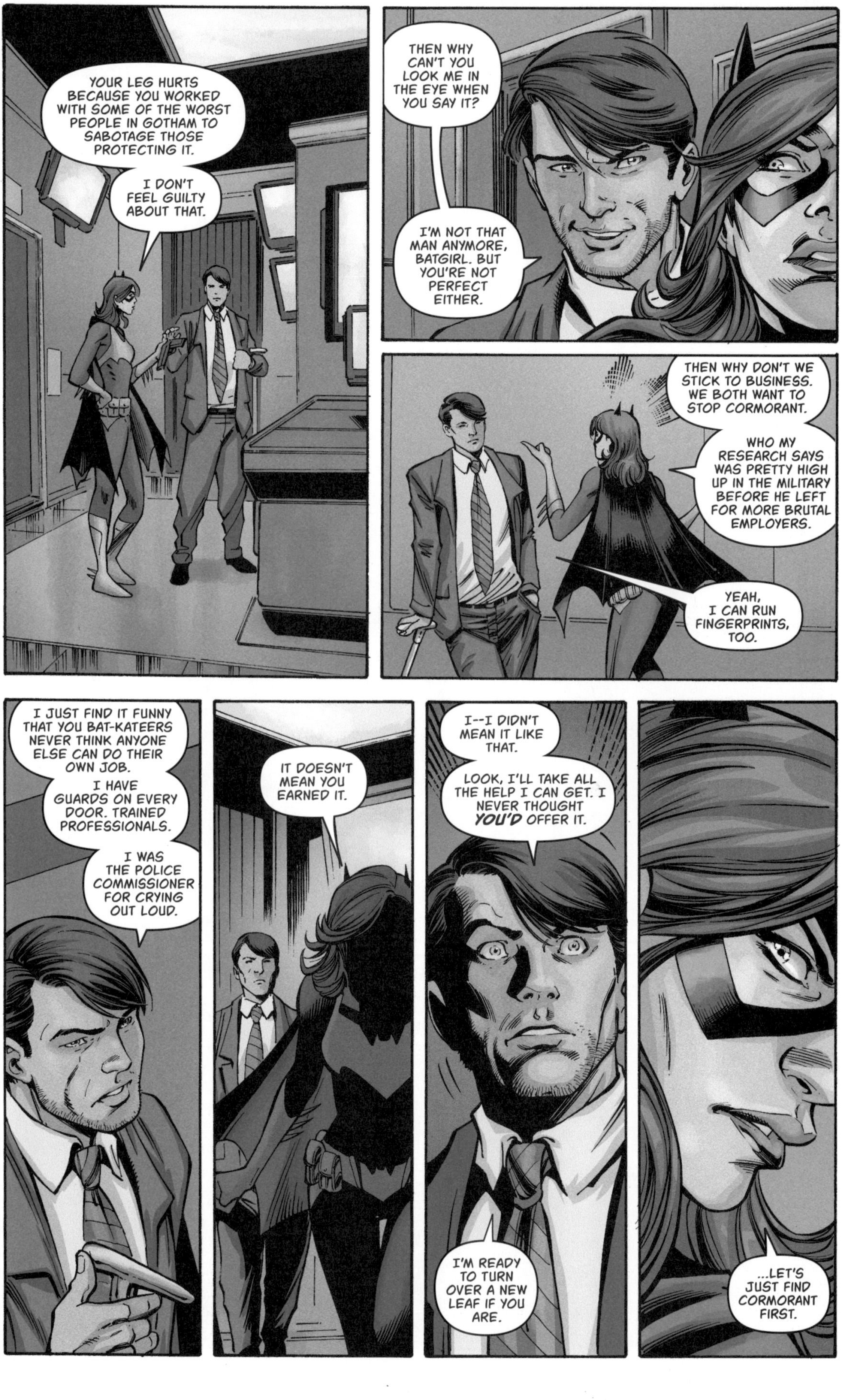
YOUR LEG HURTS BECAUSE YOU WORKED WITH SOME OF THE WORST PEOPLE IN GOTHAM TO SABOTAGE THOSE PROTECTING IT.
I DON'T FEEL GUILTY ABOUT THAT.
THEN WHY CAN'T YOU LOOK ME IN THE EYE WHEN YOU SAY IT?
I'M NOT THAT MAN ANYMORE, BATGIRL. BUT YOU'RE NOT PERFECT EITHER.
THEN WHY DON'T WE STICK TO BUSINESS. WE BOTH WANT TO STOP CORMORANT.
WHO MY RESEARCH SAYS WAS PRETTY HIGH UP IN THE MILITARY BEFORE HE LEFT FOR MORE BRUTAL EMPLOYERS.
YEAH, I CAN RUN FINGERPRINTS, TOO.
I JUST FIND IT FUNNY THAT YOU BAT-KATEERS NEVER THINK ANYONE ELSE CAN DO THEIR OWN JOB.
I HAVE GUARDS ON EVERY DOOR. TRAINED PROFESSIONALS.
I WAS THE POLICE COMMISSIONER FOR CRYING OUT LOUD.
IT DOESN'T MEAN YOU EARNED IT.
I--I DIDN'T MEAN IT LIKE THAT.
LOOK, I'LL TAKE ALL THE HELP I CAN GET. I NEVER THOUGHT ***YOU'D*** OFFER IT.
I'M READY TO TURN OVER A NEW LEAF IF YOU ARE.
...LET'S JUST FIND CORMORANT FIRST.

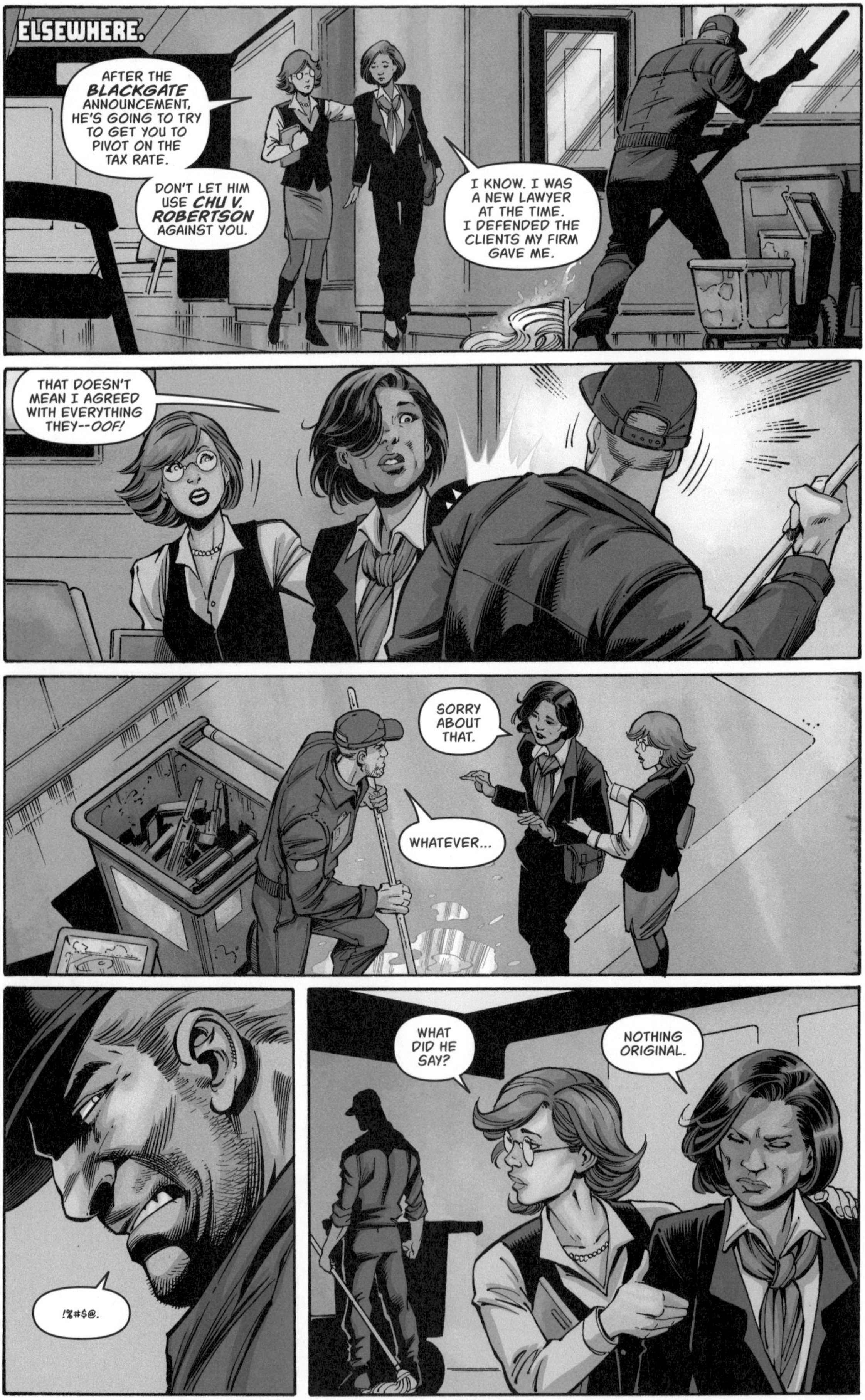
ELSEWHERE.
AFTER THE BLACKGATE ANNOUNCEMENT, HE'S GOING TO TRY TO GET YOU TO PIVOT ON THE TAX RATE.
DON'T LET HIM USE CHU V. ROBERTSON AGAINST YOU.
I KNOW. I WAS A NEW LAWYER AT THE TIME. I DEFENDED THE CLIENTS MY FIRM GAVE ME.
THAT DOESN'T MEAN I AGREED WITH EVERYTHING THEY--OOF!
SORRY ABOUT THAT.
WHATEVER...
!%#$@.
WHAT DID HE SAY?
NOTHING ORIGINAL.

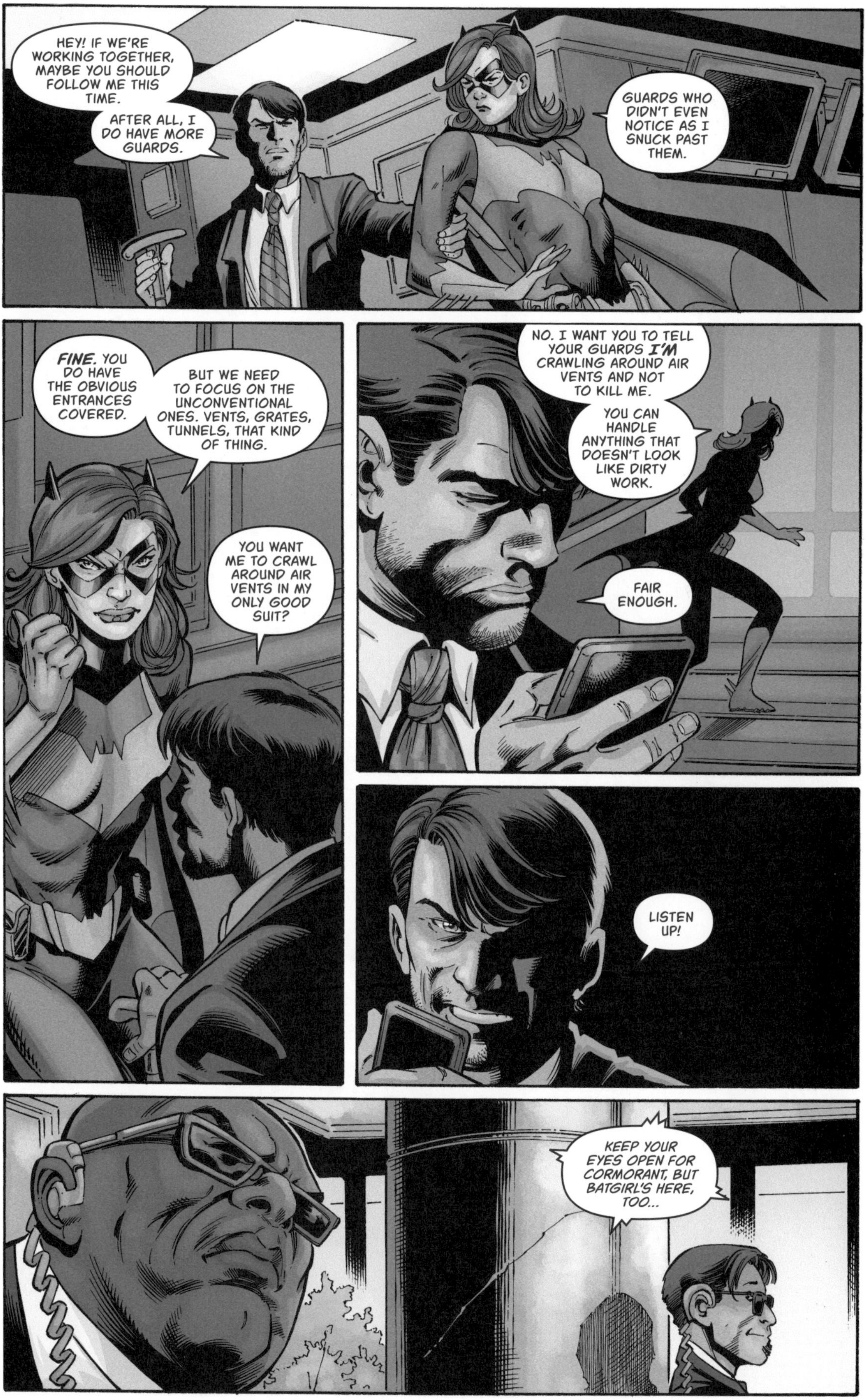
HEY! IF WE'RE WORKING TOGETHER, MAYBE YOU SHOULD FOLLOW ME THIS TIME.
AFTER ALL, I DO HAVE MORE GUARDS.
GUARDS WHO DIDN'T EVEN NOTICE AS I SNUCK PAST THEM.
FINE. YOU DO HAVE THE OBVIOUS ENTRANCES COVERED.
BUT WE NEED TO FOCUS ON THE UNCONVENTIONAL ONES. VENTS, GRATES, TUNNELS, THAT KIND OF THING.
YOU WANT ME TO CRAWL AROUND AIR VENTS IN MY ONLY GOOD SUIT?
NO. I WANT YOU TO TELL YOUR GUARDS I'M CRAWLING AROUND AIR VENTS AND NOT TO KILL ME.
YOU CAN HANDLE ANYTHING THAT DOESN'T LOOK LIKE DIRTY WORK.
FAIR ENOUGH.
LISTEN UP!
KEEP YOUR EYES OPEN FOR CORMORANT, BUT BATGIRL'S HERE, TOO...

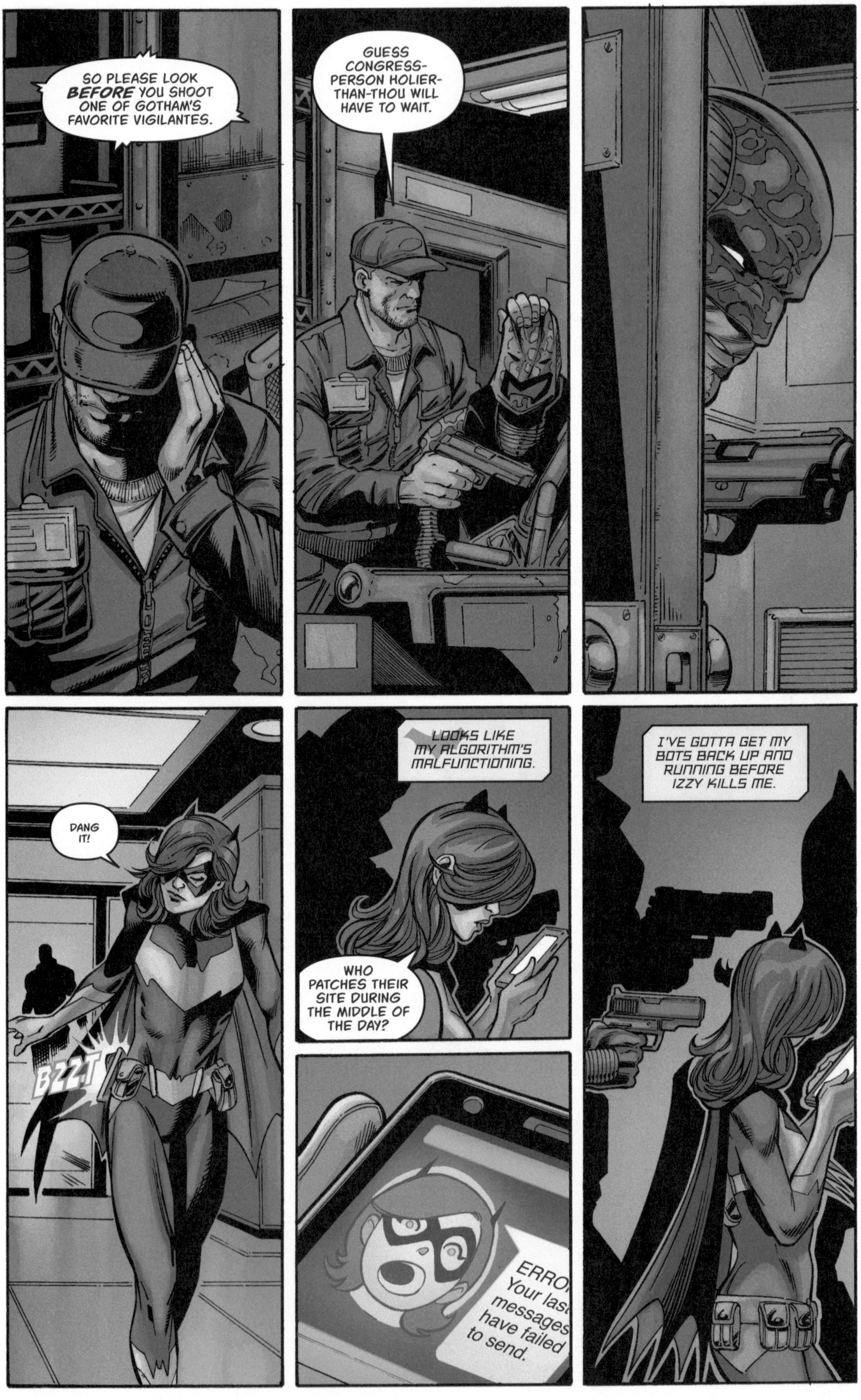
SO PLEASE LOOK BEFORE YOU SHOOT ONE OF GOTHAM'S FAVORITE VIGILANTES.
GUESS CONGRESS-PERSON HOLIER-THAN-THOU WILL HAVE TO WAIT.
DANG IT!
BZZT
LOOKS LIKE MY ALGORITHM'S MALFUNCTIONING.
WHO PATCHES THEIR SITE DURING THE MIDDLE OF THE DAY?
ERRO
Your las
message
have failed
to send.
I'VE GOTTA GET MY BOTS BACK UP AND RUNNING BEFORE IZZY KILLS ME.

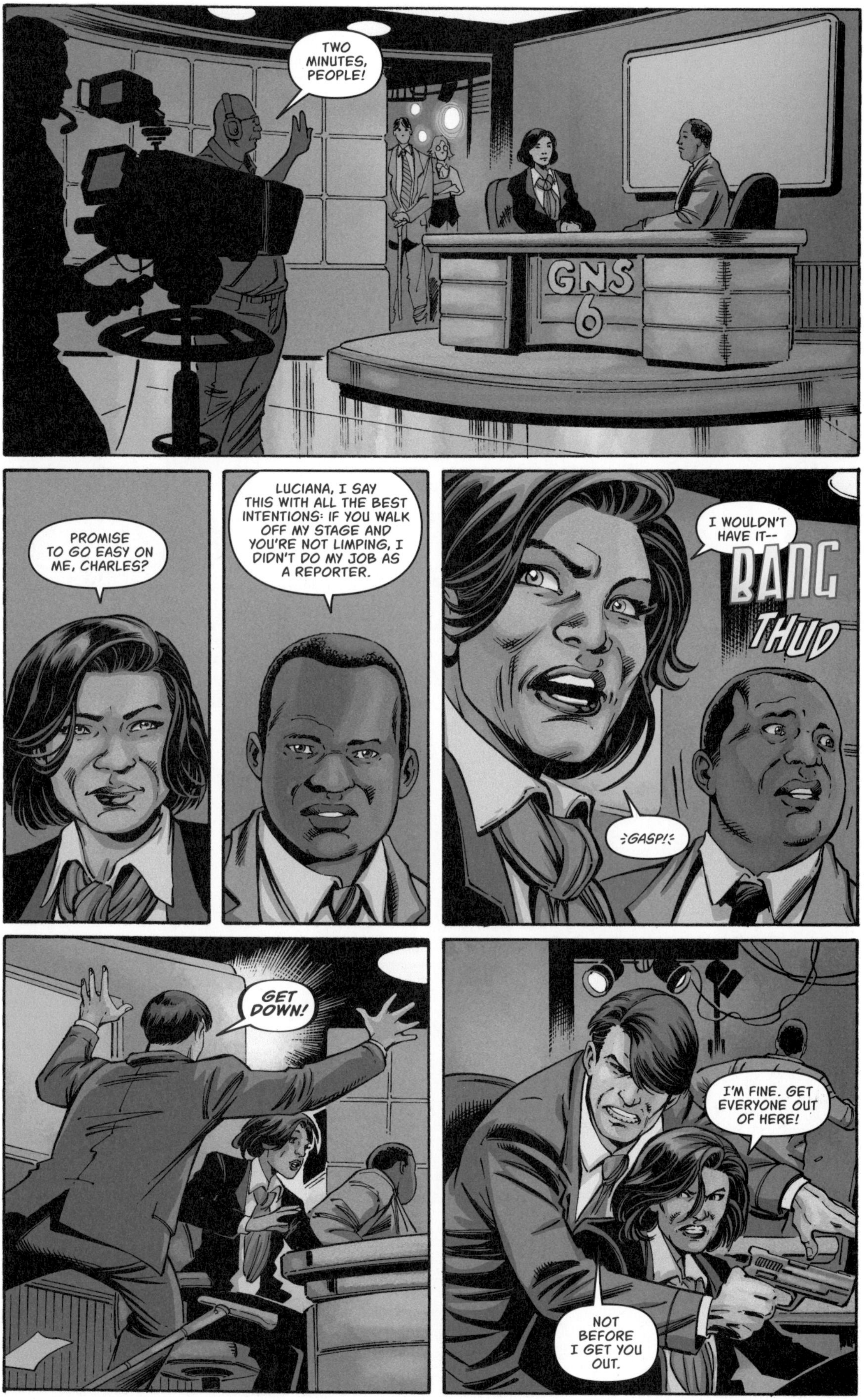
TWO MINUTES, PEOPLE!
GNS 6
PROMISE TO GO EASY ON ME, CHARLES?
LUCIANA, I SAY THIS WITH ALL THE BEST INTENTIONS: IF YOU WALK OFF MY STAGE AND YOU'RE NOT LIMPING, I DIDN'T DO MY JOB AS A REPORTER.
I WOULDN'T HAVE IT--
BANG
THUD
GASP!
GET DOWN!
I'M FINE. GET EVERYONE OUT OF HERE!
NOT BEFORE I GET YOU OUT.

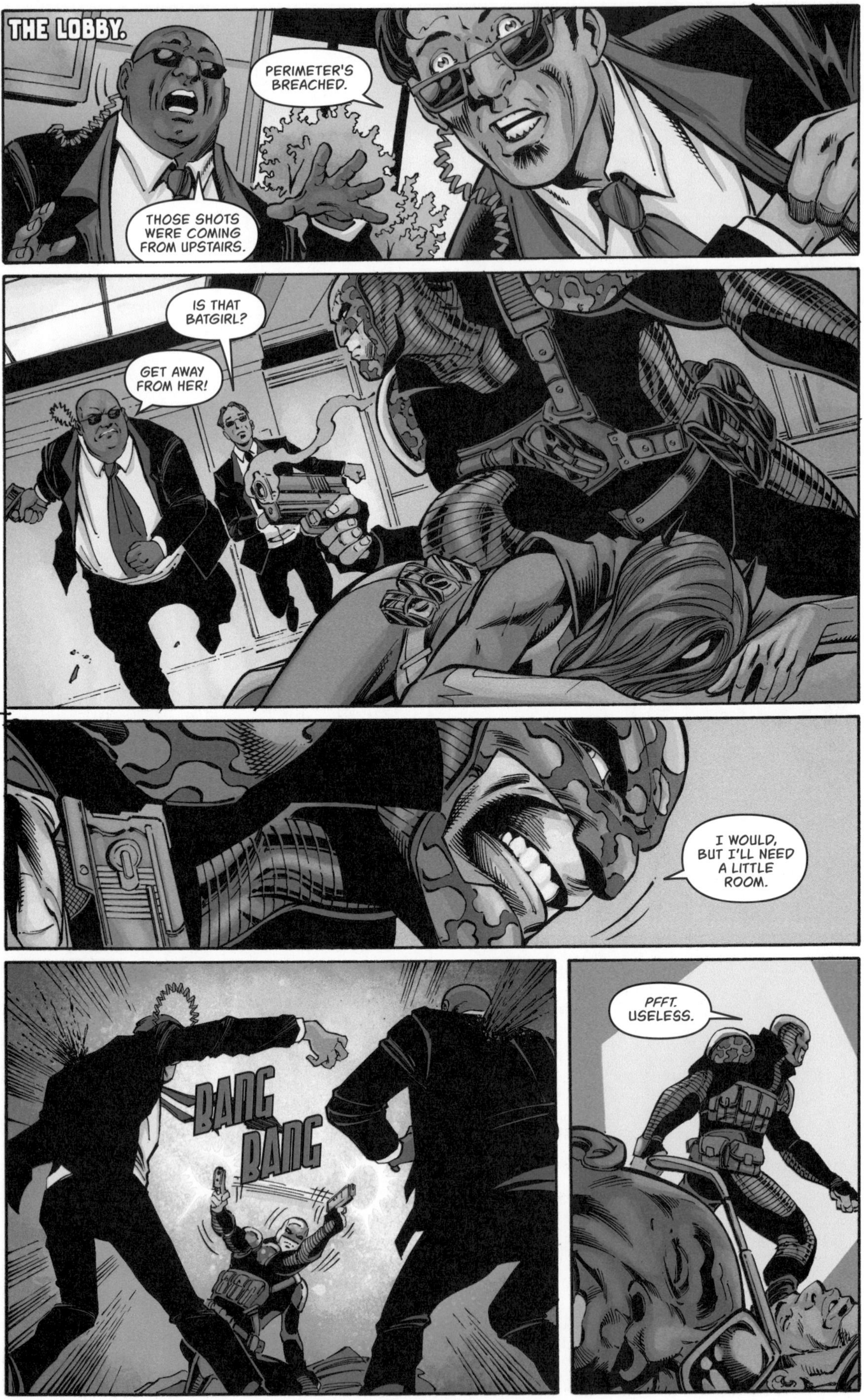
THE LOBBY.
PERIMETER'S BREACHED.
THOSE SHOTS WERE COMING FROM UPSTAIRS.
IS THAT BATGIRL?
GET AWAY FROM HER!
I WOULD, BUT I'LL NEED A LITTLE ROOM.
BANG
BANG
PFFT. USELESS.

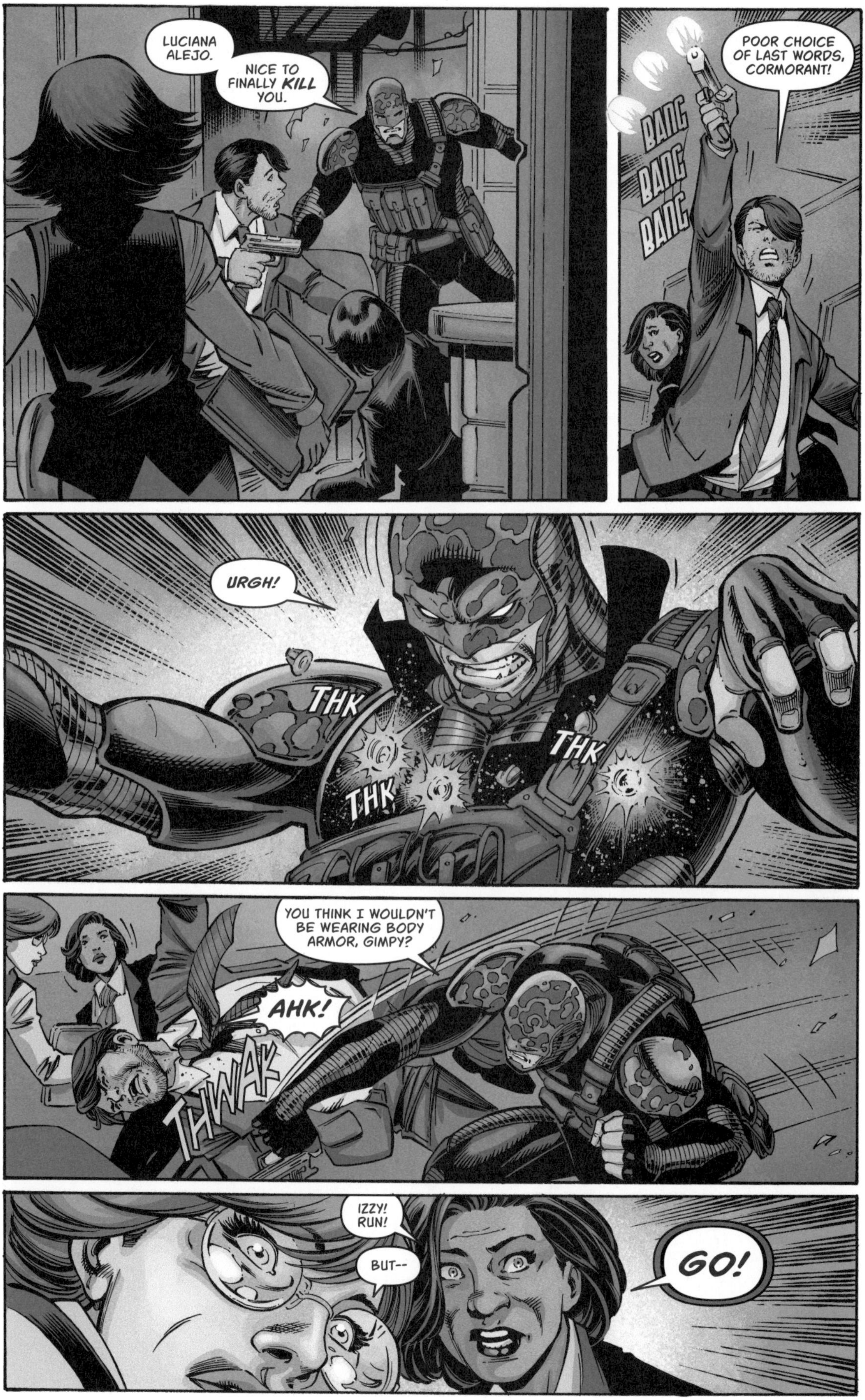
LUCIANA ALEJO.
NICE TO FINALLY KILL YOU.
POOR CHOICE OF LAST WORDS, CORMORANT!
BANG BANG BANG
URGH!
THK
THK
THK
YOU THINK I WOULDN'T BE WEARING BODY ARMOR, GIMPY?
AHK!
THWAK
IZZY! RUN!
BUT--
GO!

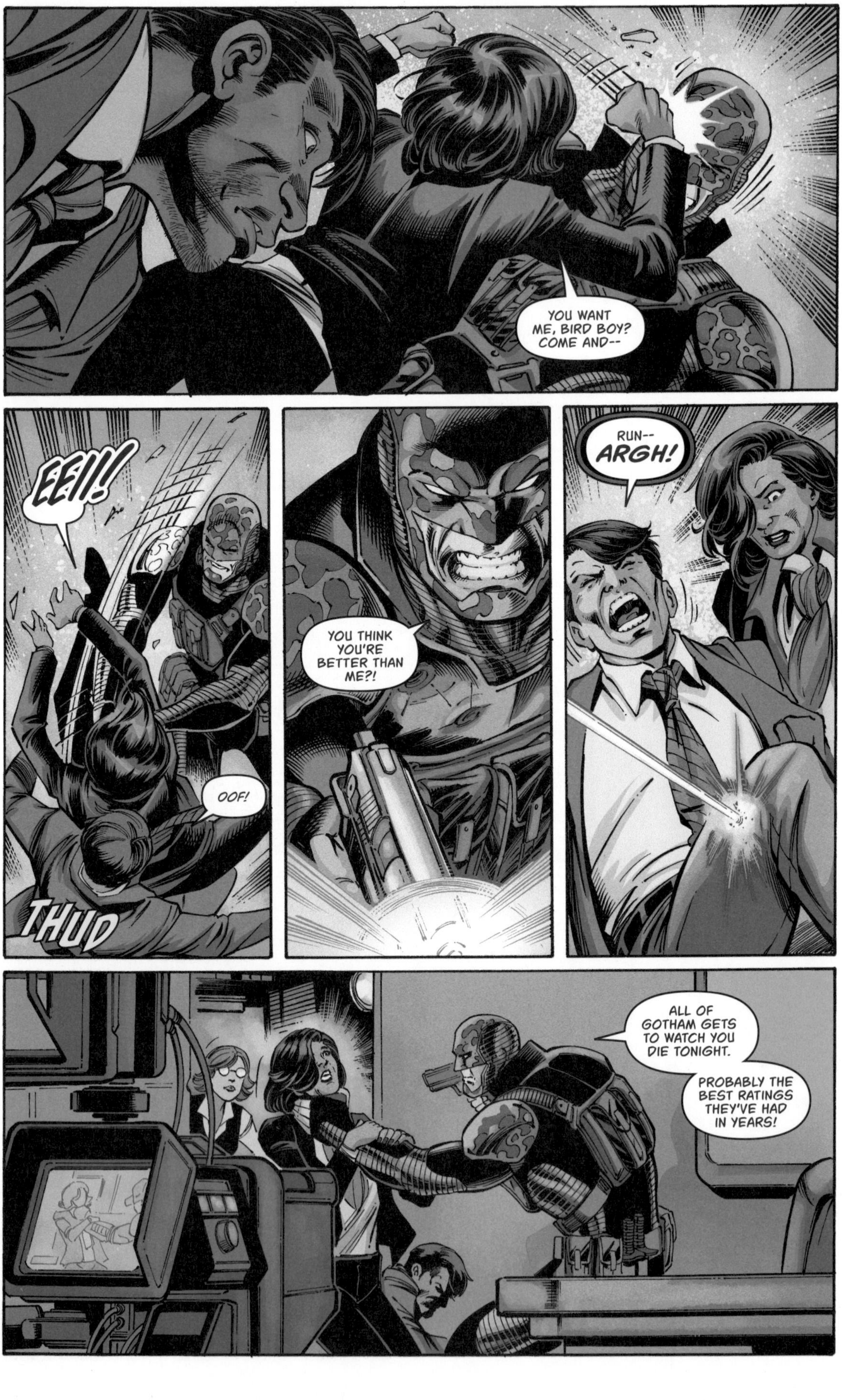
YOU WANT ME, BIRD BOY? COME AND--
EEII!
OOF!
THUD
YOU THINK YOU'RE BETTER THAN ME?!
RUN-- ARGH!
ALL OF GOTHAM GETS TO WATCH YOU DIE TONIGHT.
PROBABLY THE BEST RATINGS THEY'VE HAD IN YEARS!

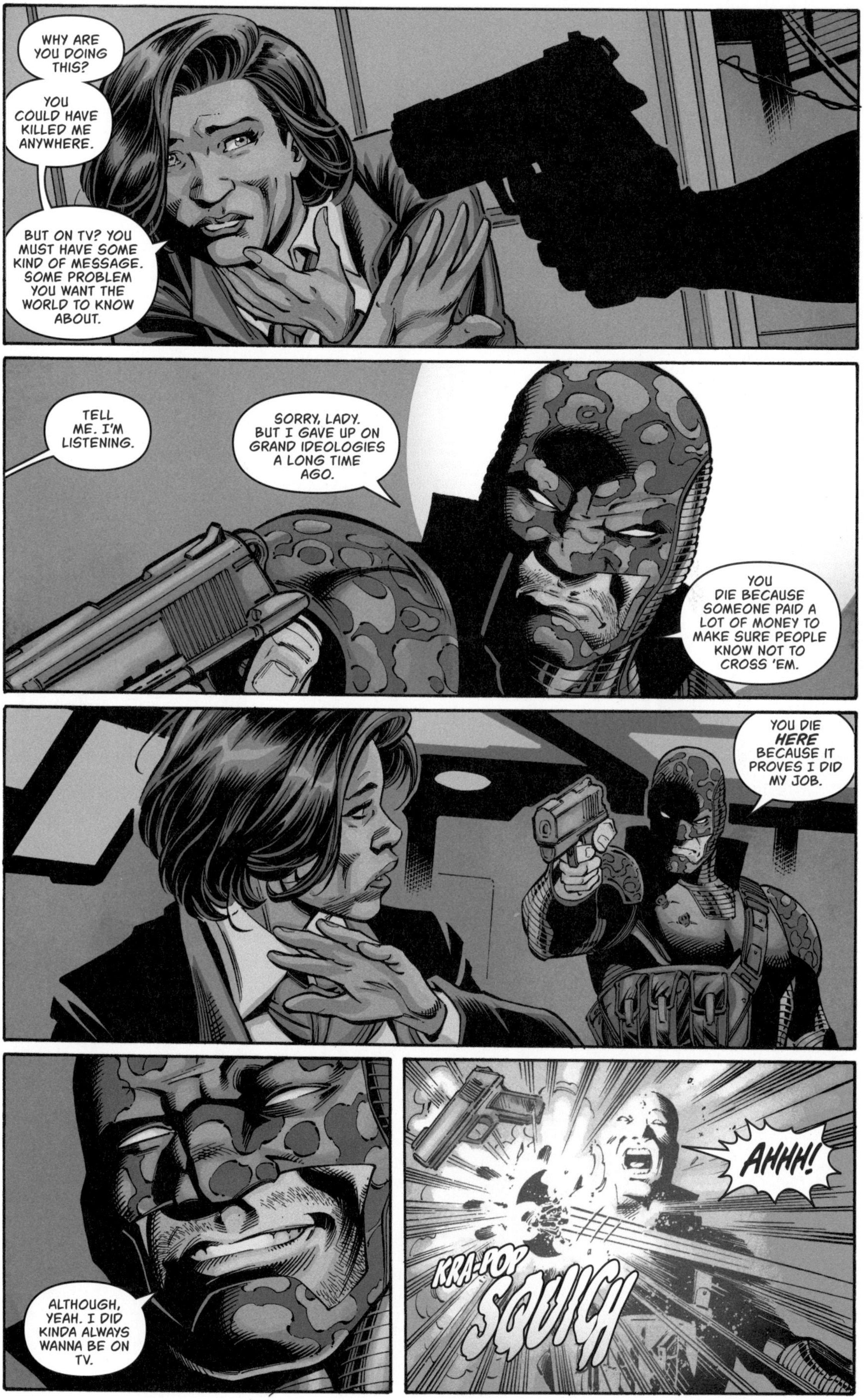
WHY ARE YOU DOING THIS?
YOU COULD HAVE KILLED ME ANYWHERE.
BUT ON TV? YOU MUST HAVE SOME KIND OF MESSAGE. SOME PROBLEM YOU WANT THE WORLD TO KNOW ABOUT.
TELL ME. I'M LISTENING.
SORRY, LADY. BUT I GAVE UP ON GRAND IDEOLOGIES A LONG TIME AGO.
YOU DIE BECAUSE SOMEONE PAID A LOT OF MONEY TO MAKE SURE PEOPLE KNOW NOT TO CROSS 'EM.
YOU DIE HERE BECAUSE IT PROVES I DID MY JOB.
ALTHOUGH, YEAH. I DID KINDA ALWAYS WANNA BE ON TV.
AHHH!
KRA-POP
SQUICH

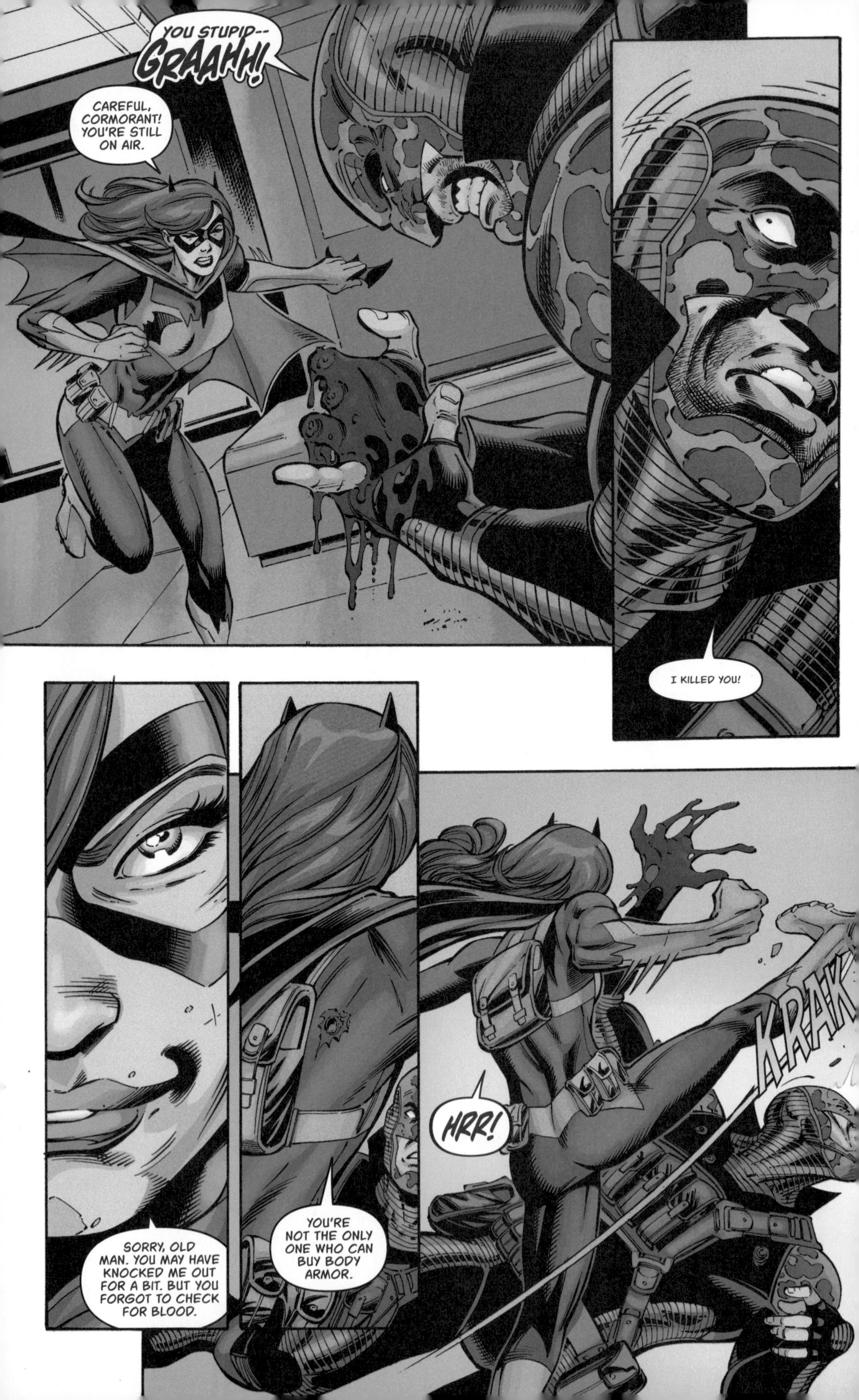
YOU STUPID-- GRAAHH!
CAREFUL, CORMORANT! YOU'RE STILL ON AIR.
I KILLED YOU!
SORRY, OLD MAN. YOU MAY HAVE KNOCKED ME OUT FOR A BIT. BUT YOU FORGOT TO CHECK FOR BLOOD.
YOU'RE NOT THE ONLY ONE WHO CAN BUY BODY ARMOR.
HRR!
KRAK

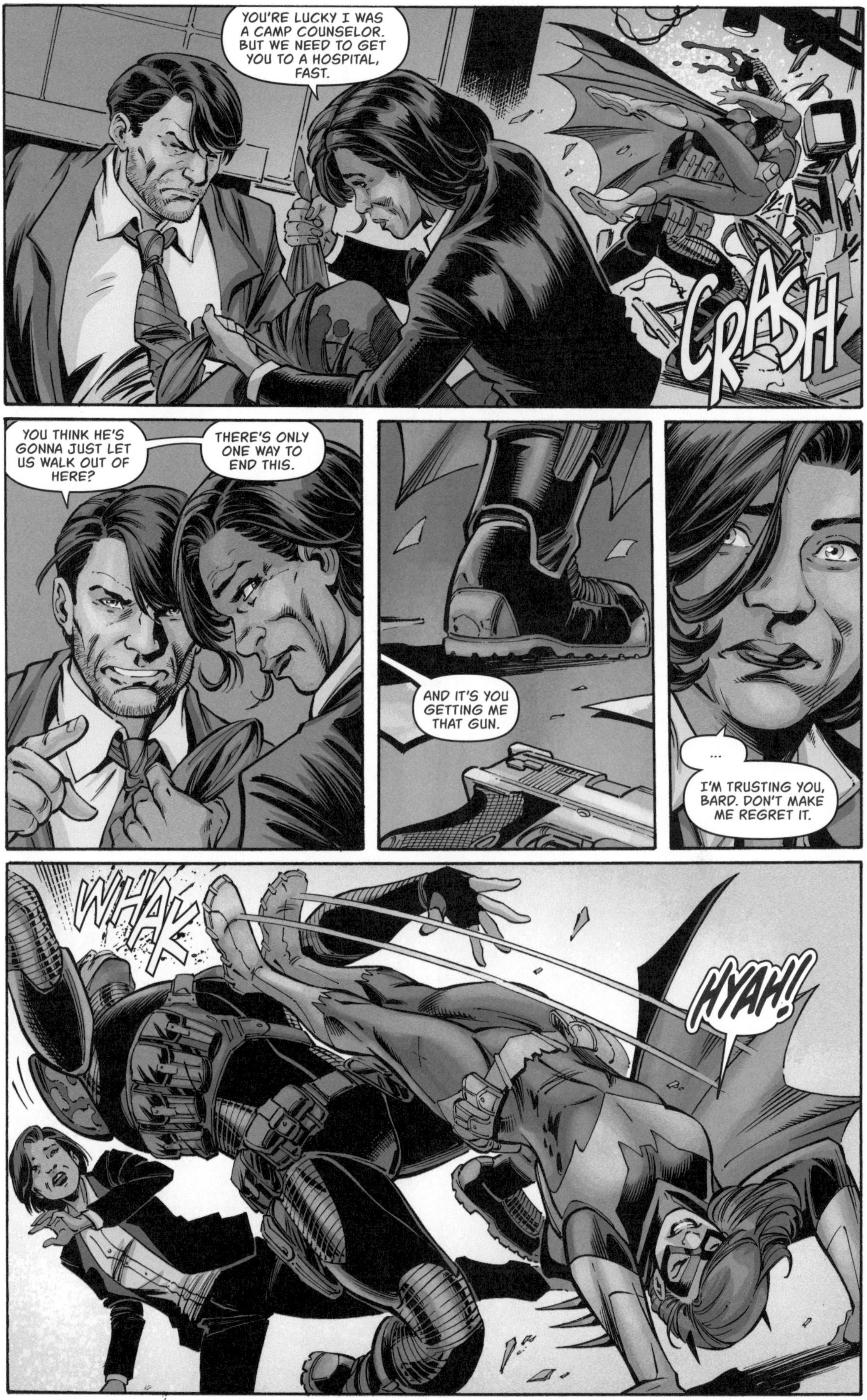
YOU'RE LUCKY I WAS A CAMP COUNSELOR. BUT WE NEED TO GET YOU TO A HOSPITAL, FAST.
CRASH
YOU THINK HE'S GONNA JUST LET US WALK OUT OF HERE?
THERE'S ONLY ONE WAY TO END THIS.
AND IT'S YOU GETTING ME THAT GUN.
...
I'M TRUSTING YOU, BARD. DON'T MAKE ME REGRET IT.
WHAK
HYAH!!

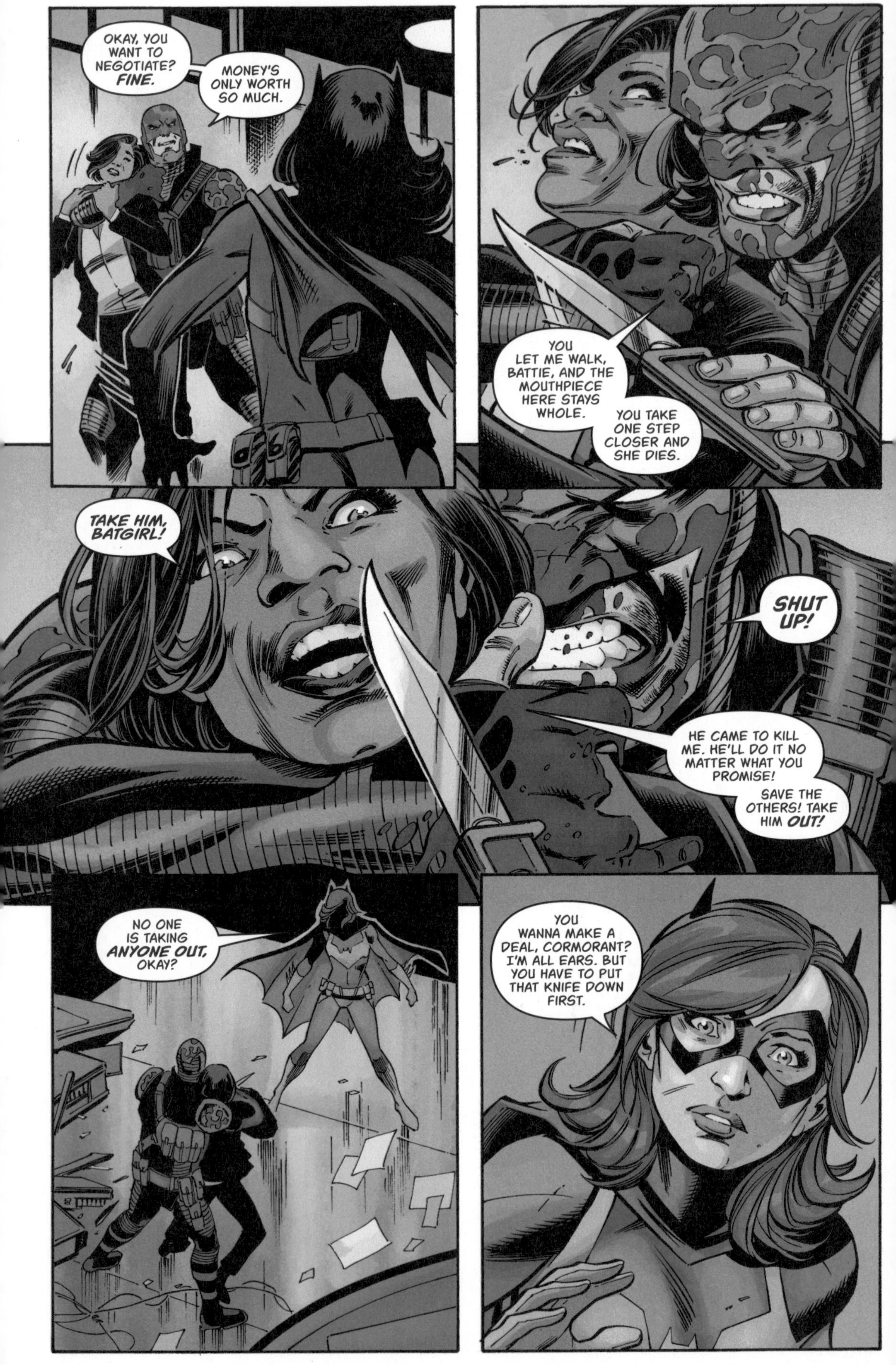
OKAY, YOU WANT TO NEGOTIATE? FINE.
MONEY'S ONLY WORTH SO MUCH.
YOU LET ME WALK, BATTIE, AND THE MOUTHPIECE HERE STAYS WHOLE.
YOU TAKE ONE STEP CLOSER AND SHE DIES.
TAKE HIM, BATGIRL!
SHUT UP!
HE CAME TO KILL ME. HE'LL DO IT NO MATTER WHAT YOU PROMISE!
SAVE THE OTHERS! TAKE HIM OUT!
NO ONE IS TAKING ANYONE OUT, OKAY?
YOU WANNA MAKE A DEAL, CORMORANT? I'M ALL EARS. BUT YOU HAVE TO PUT THAT KNIFE DOWN FIRST.

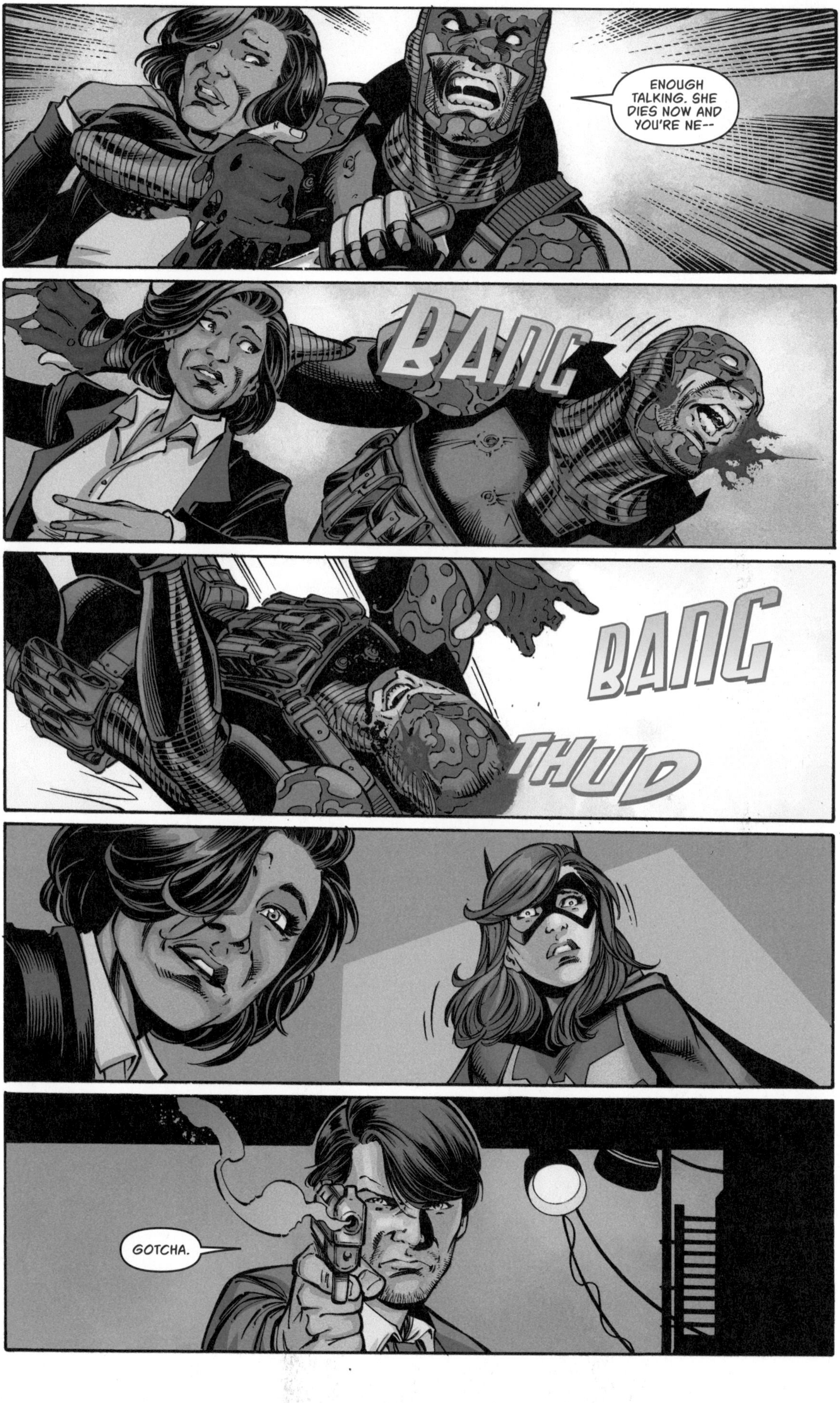
ENOUGH TALKING. SHE DIES NOW AND YOU'RE NE--
BANG
BANG
THUD
GOTCHA.

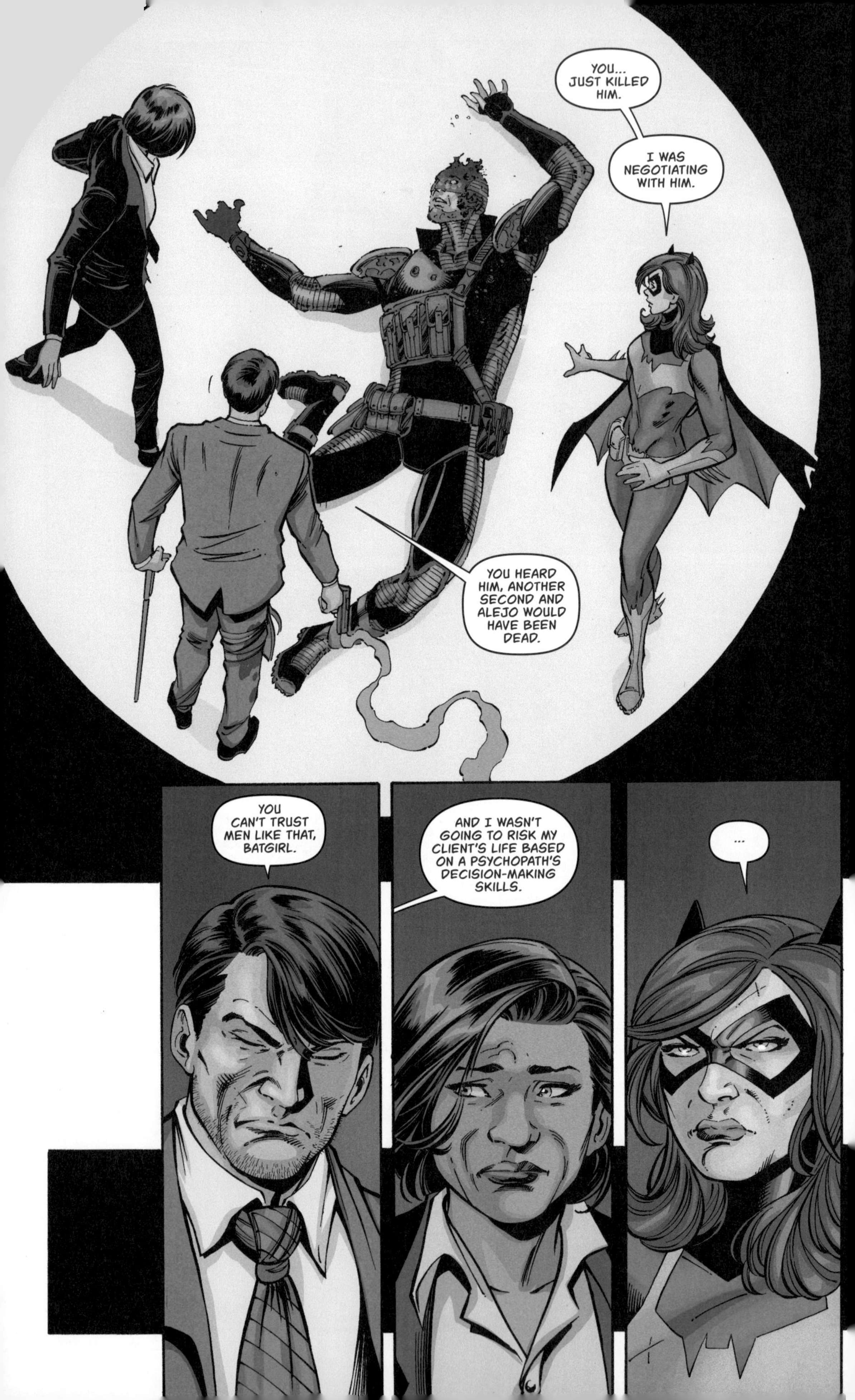
YOU... JUST KILLED HIM.
I WAS NEGOTIATING WITH HIM.
YOU HEARD HIM, ANOTHER SECOND AND ALEJO WOULD HAVE BEEN DEAD.
YOU CAN'T TRUST MEN LIKE THAT, BATGIRL.
AND I WASN'T GOING TO RISK MY CLIENT'S LIFE BASED ON A PSYCHOPATH'S DECISION-MAKING SKILLS.
...

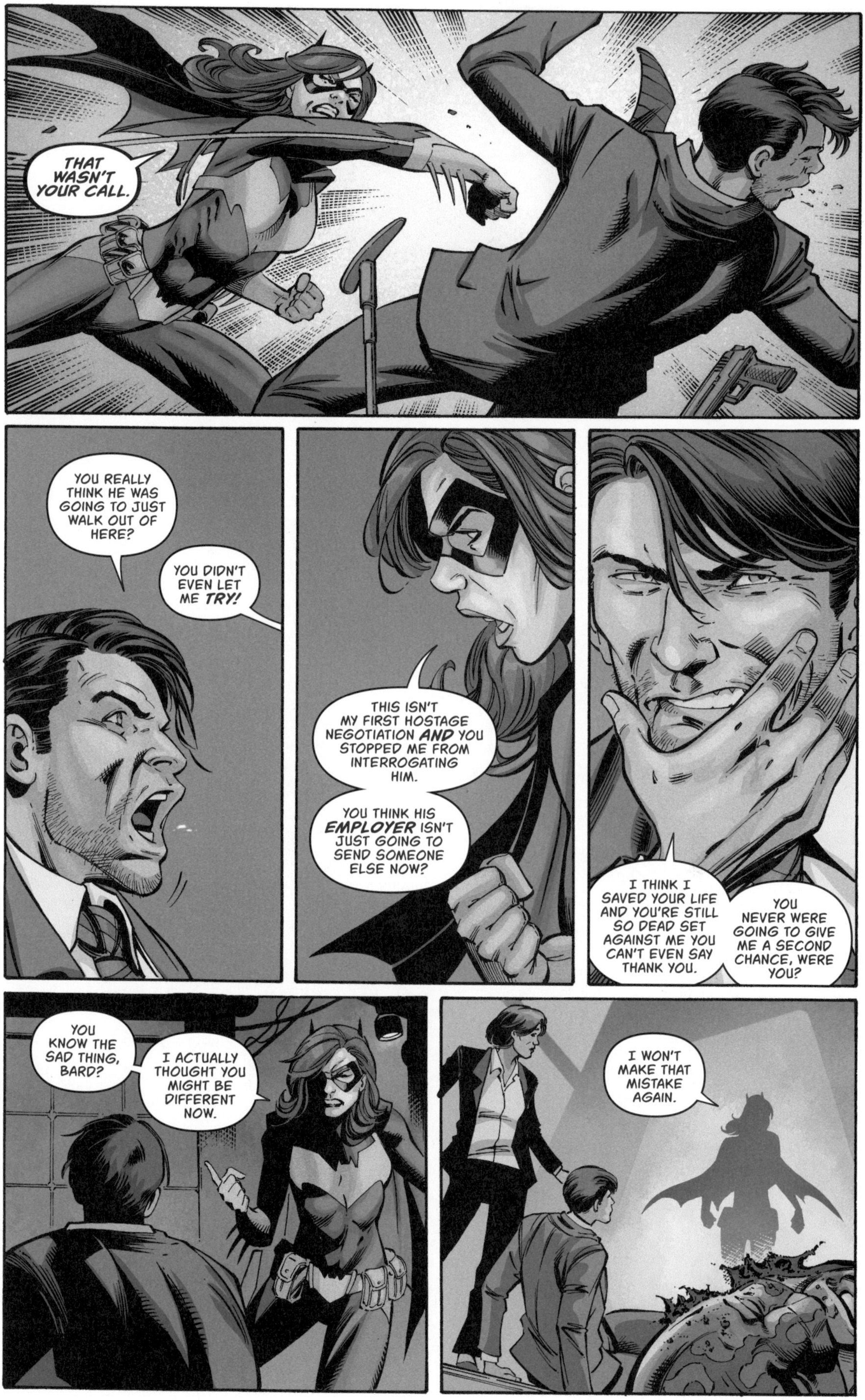
THAT WASN'T YOUR CALL.
YOU REALLY THINK HE WAS GOING TO JUST WALK OUT OF HERE?
YOU DIDN'T EVEN LET ME TRY!
THIS ISN'T MY FIRST HOSTAGE NEGOTIATION AND YOU STOPPED ME FROM INTERROGATING HIM.
YOU THINK HIS EMPLOYER ISN'T JUST GOING TO SEND SOMEONE ELSE NOW?
I THINK I SAVED YOUR LIFE AND YOU'RE STILL SO DEAD SET AGAINST ME YOU CAN'T EVEN SAY THANK YOU.
YOU NEVER WERE GOING TO GIVE ME A SECOND CHANCE, WERE YOU?
YOU KNOW THE SAD THING, BARD?
I ACTUALLY THOUGHT YOU MIGHT BE DIFFERENT NOW.
I WON'T MAKE THAT MISTAKE AGAIN.

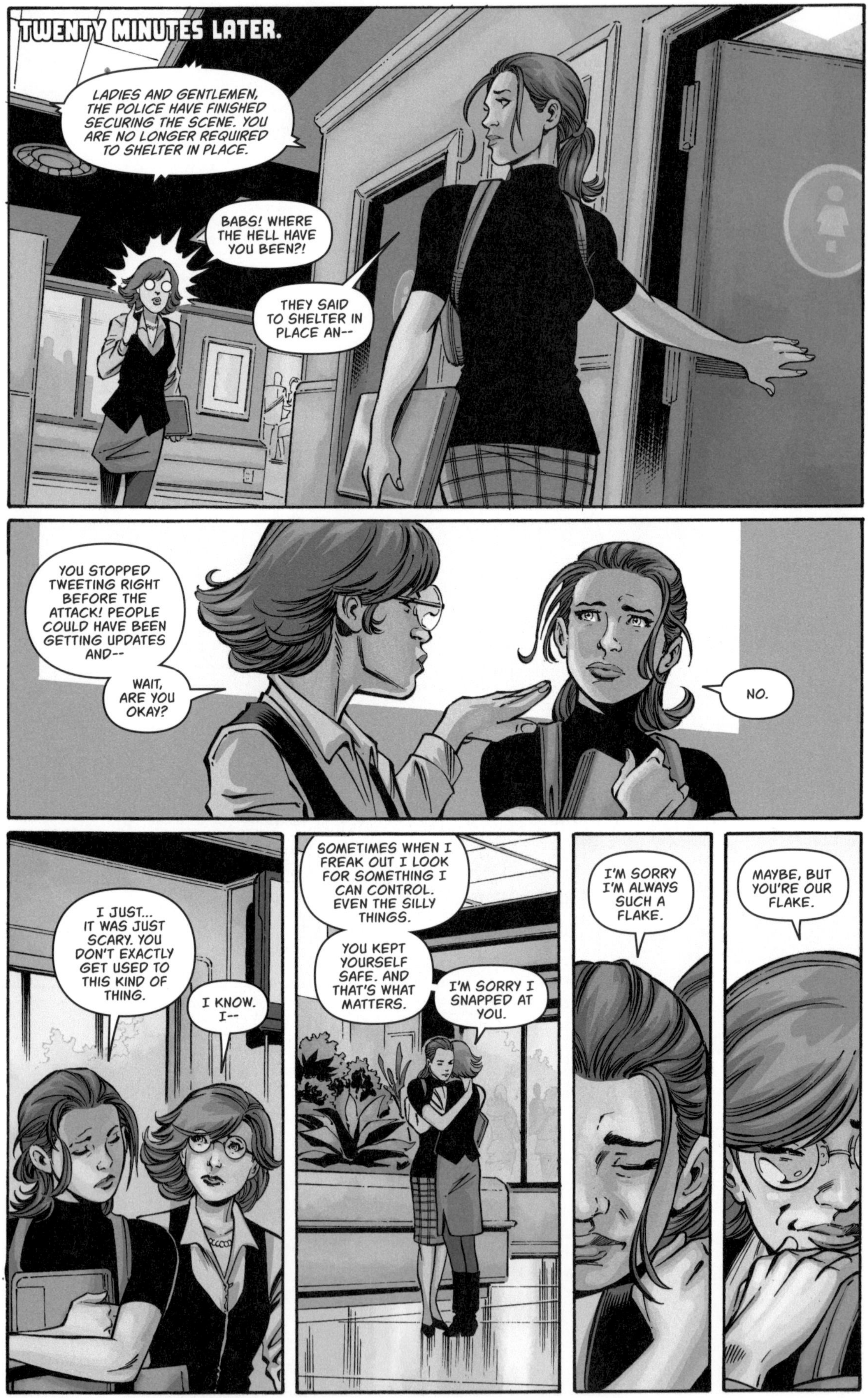
TWENTY MINUTES LATER.
LADIES AND GENTLEMEN, THE POLICE HAVE FINISHED SECURING THE SCENE. YOU ARE NO LONGER REQUIRED TO SHELTER IN PLACE.
BABS! WHERE THE HELL HAVE YOU BEEN?!
THEY SAID TO SHELTER IN PLACE AN--
YOU STOPPED TWEETING RIGHT BEFORE THE ATTACK! PEOPLE COULD HAVE BEEN GETTING UPDATES AND--
WAIT, ARE YOU OKAY?
NO.
I JUST... IT WAS JUST SCARY. YOU DON'T EXACTLY GET USED TO THIS KIND OF THING.
I KNOW. I--
SOMETIMES WHEN I FREAK OUT I LOOK FOR SOMETHING I CAN CONTROL. EVEN THE SILLY THINGS.
YOU KEPT YOURSELF SAFE. AND THAT'S WHAT MATTERS.
I'M SORRY I SNAPPED AT YOU.
I'M SORRY I'M ALWAYS SUCH A FLAKE.
MAYBE, BUT YOU'RE OUR FLAKE.

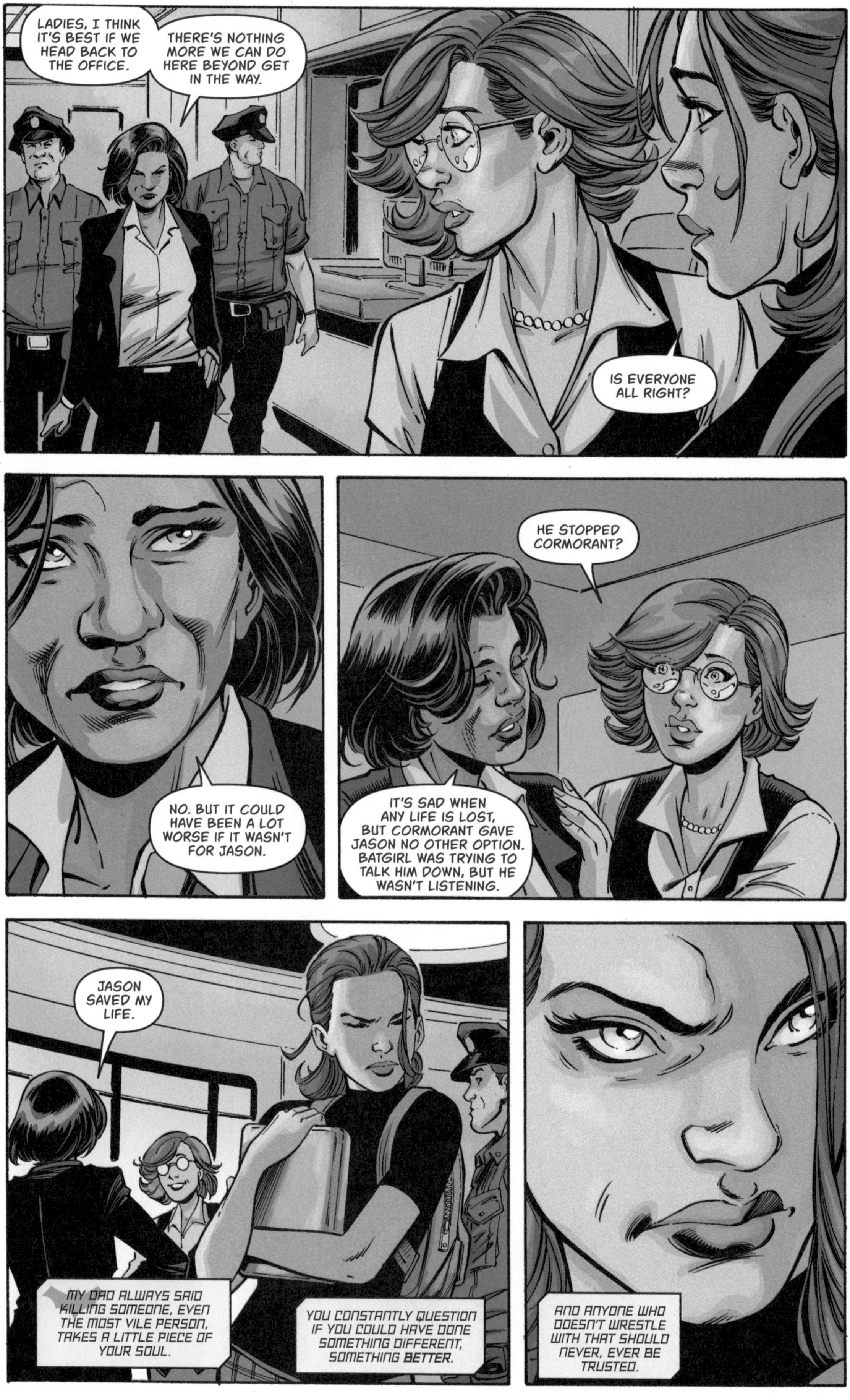

LADIES, I THINK IT'S BEST IF WE HEAD BACK TO THE OFFICE.
THERE'S NOTHING MORE WE CAN DO HERE BEYOND GET IN THE WAY.
IS EVERYONE ALL RIGHT?
NO. BUT IT COULD HAVE BEEN A LOT WORSE IF IT WASN'T FOR JASON.
HE STOPPED CORMORANT?
IT'S SAD WHEN ANY LIFE IS LOST, BUT CORMORANT GAVE JASON NO OTHER OPTION. BATGIRL WAS TRYING TO TALK HIM DOWN, BUT HE WASN'T LISTENING.
JASON SAVED MY LIFE.
MY DAD ALWAYS SAID KILLING SOMEONE, EVEN THE MOST VILE PERSON, TAKES A LITTLE PIECE OF YOUR SOUL.
YOU CONSTANTLY QUESTION IF YOU COULD HAVE DONE SOMETHING DIFFERENT, SOMETHING BETTER.
AND ANYONE WHO DOESN'T WRESTLE WITH THAT SHOULD NEVER, EVER BE TRUSTED.

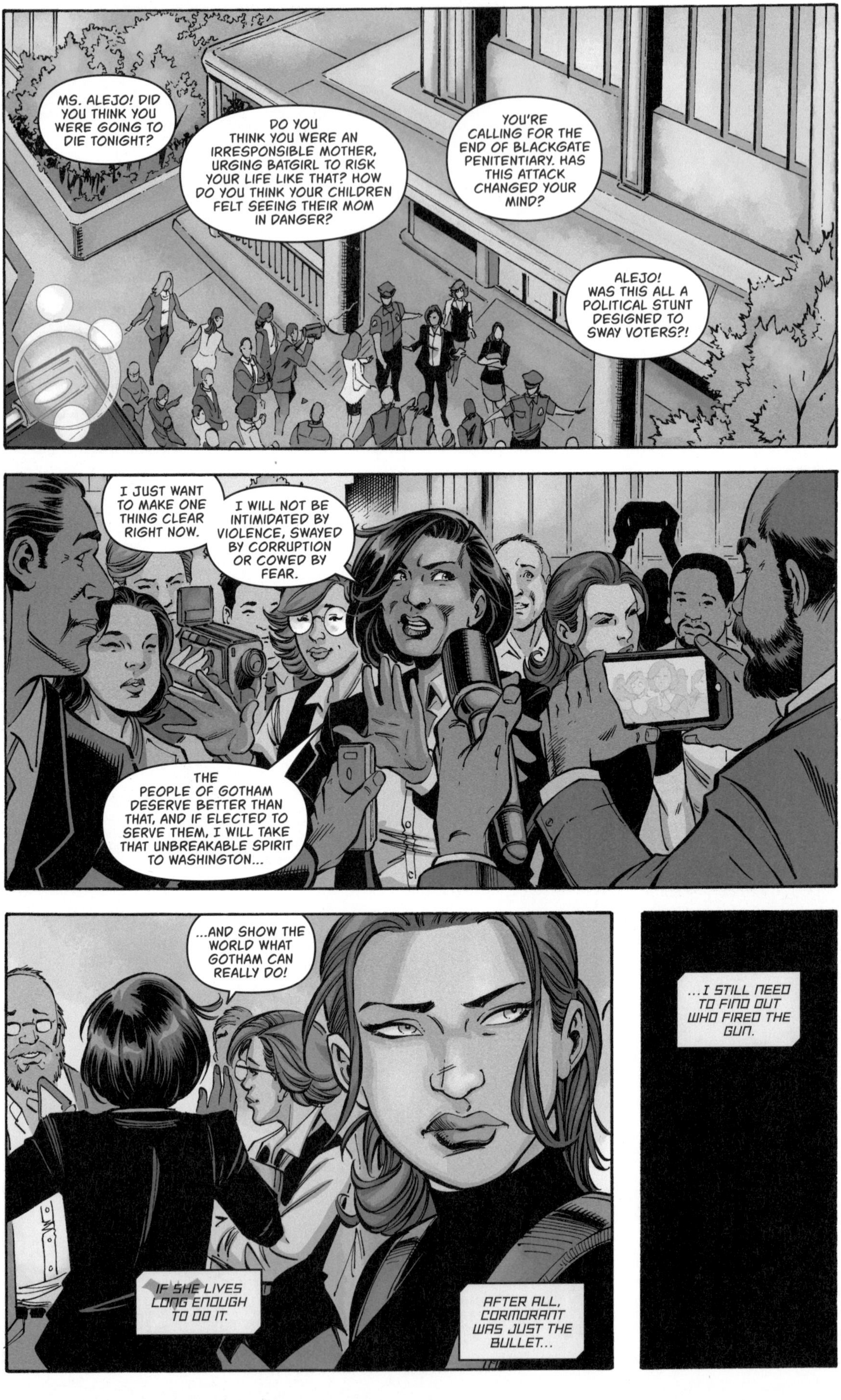
MS. ALEJO! DID YOU THINK YOU WERE GOING TO DIE TONIGHT?
DO YOU THINK YOU WERE AN IRRESPONSIBLE MOTHER, URGING BATGIRL TO RISK YOUR LIFE LIKE THAT? HOW DO YOU THINK YOUR CHILDREN FELT SEEING THEIR MOM IN DANGER?
YOU'RE CALLING FOR THE END OF BLACKGATE PENITENTIARY. HAS THIS ATTACK CHANGED YOUR MIND?
ALEJO! WAS THIS ALL A POLITICAL STUNT DESIGNED TO SWAY VOTERS?!
I JUST WANT TO MAKE ONE THING CLEAR RIGHT NOW.
I WILL NOT BE INTIMIDATED BY VIOLENCE, SWAYED BY CORRUPTION OR COWED BY FEAR.
THE PEOPLE OF GOTHAM DESERVE BETTER THAN THAT, AND IF ELECTED TO SERVE THEM, I WILL TAKE THAT UNBREAKABLE SPIRIT TO WASHINGTON...
...AND SHOW THE WORLD WHAT GOTHAM CAN REALLY DO!
IF SHE LIVES LONG ENOUGH TO DO IT.
AFTER ALL, CORMORANT WAS JUST THE BULLET...
...I STILL NEED TO FIND OUT WHO FIRED THE GUN.

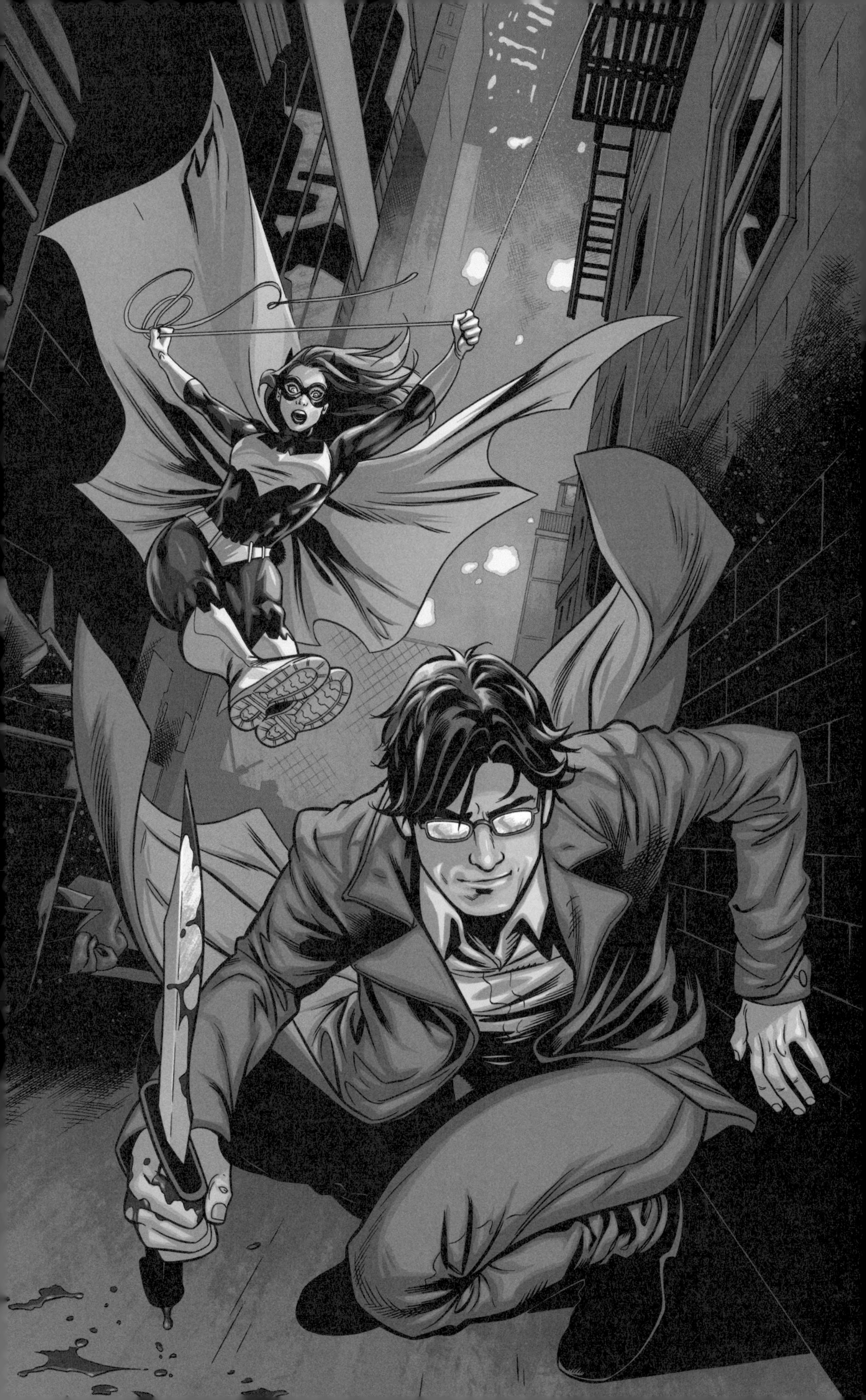

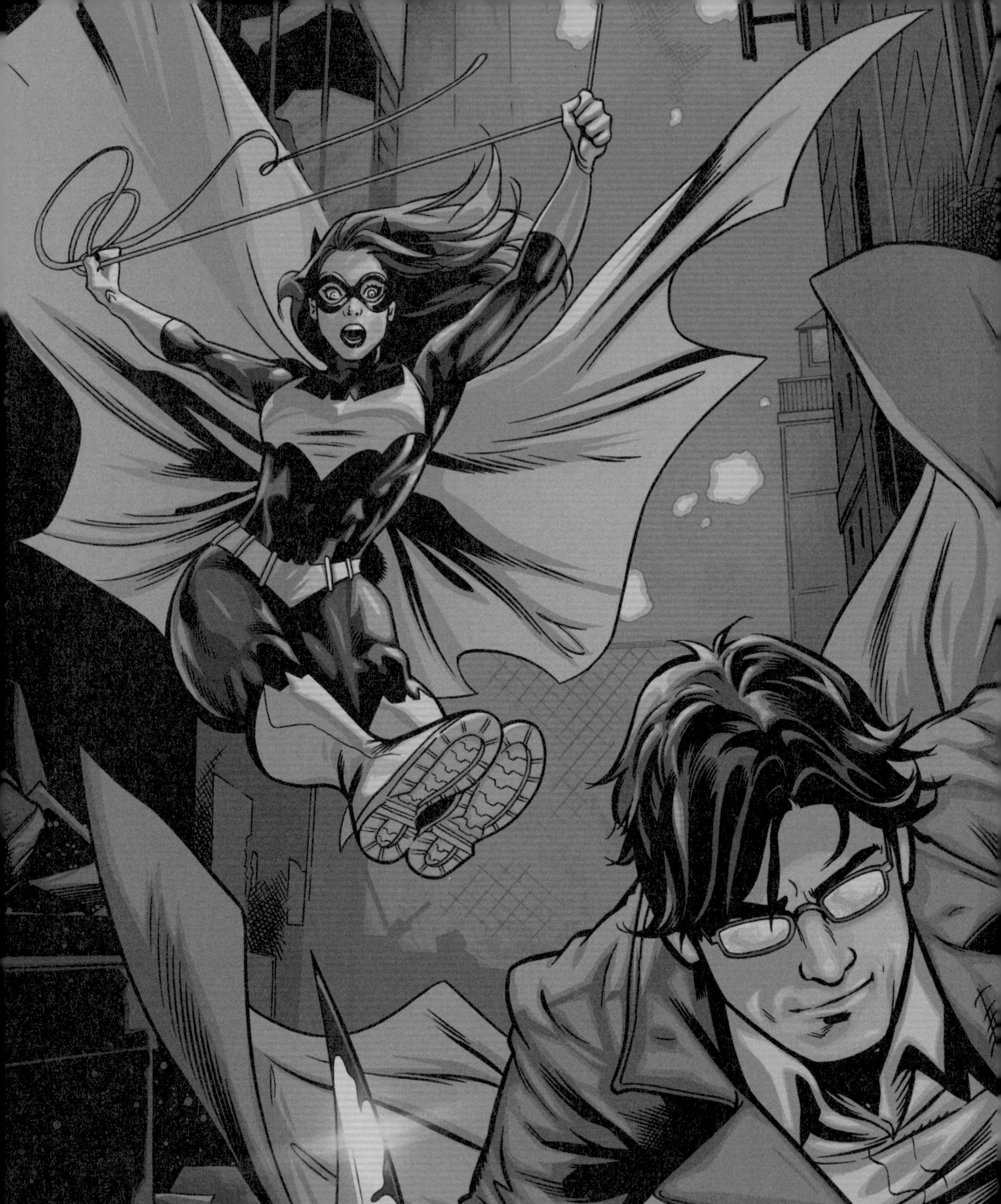

BATGIRL
#33

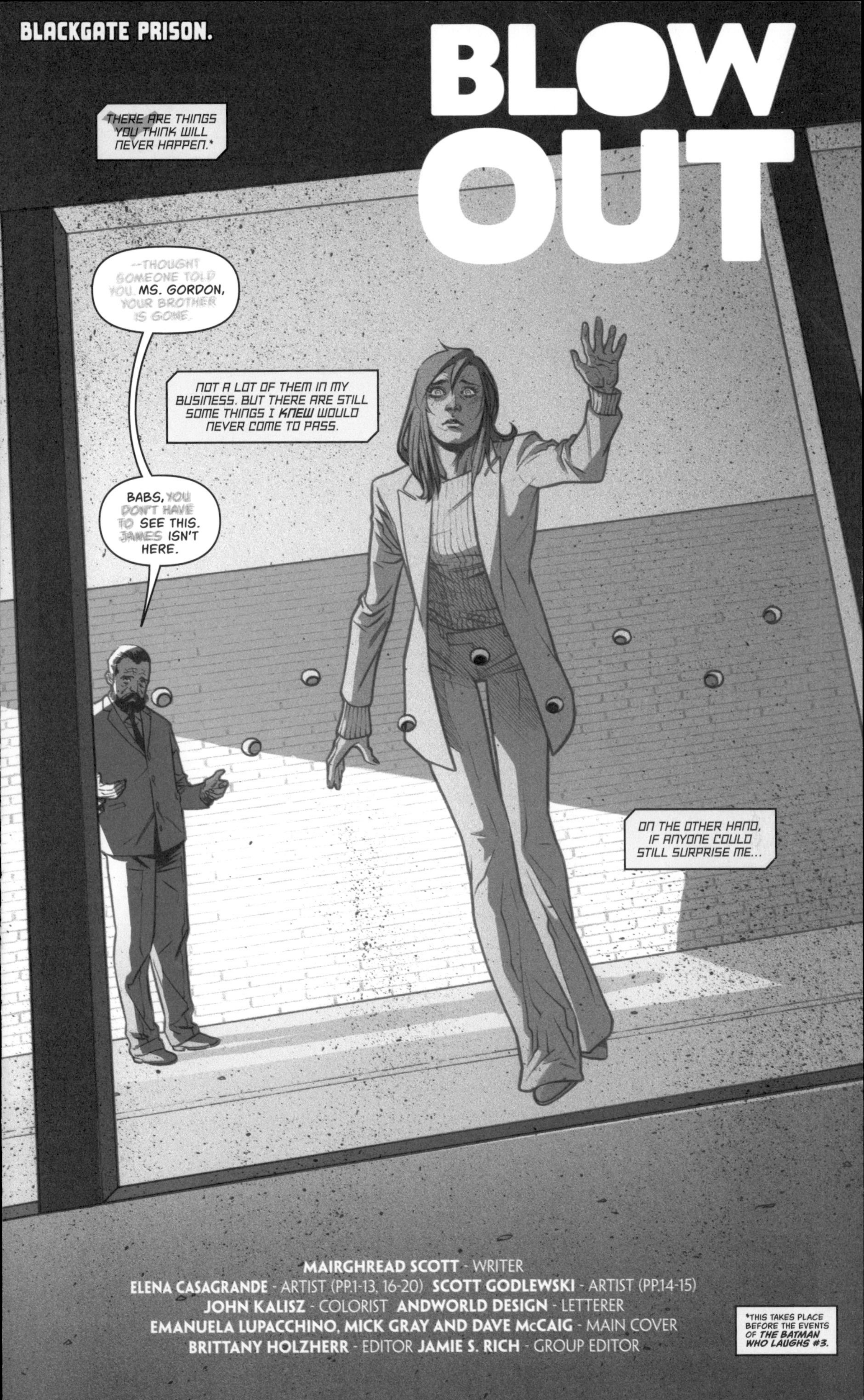
BLACKGATE PRISON.
BLOW OUT
THERE ARE THINGS YOU THINK WILL NEVER HAPPEN.*
--THOUGHT SOMEONE TOLD YOU, MS. GORDON, YOUR BROTHER IS GONE.
NOT A LOT OF THEM IN MY BUSINESS. BUT THERE ARE STILL SOME THINGS I KNEW WOULD NEVER COME TO PASS.
BABS, YOU DON'T HAVE TO SEE THIS. JAMES ISN'T HERE.
ON THE OTHER HAND, IF ANYONE COULD STILL SURPRISE ME...

MAIRGHREAD SCOTT - WRITER
ELENA CASAGRANDE - ARTIST (PP.1-13, 16-20) **SCOTT GODLEWSKI** - ARTIST (PP.14-15)
JOHN KALISZ - COLORIST **ANDWORLD DESIGN** - LETTERER
EMANUELA LUPACCHINO, MICK GRAY AND DAVE McCAIG - MAIN COVER
BRITTANY HOLZHERR - EDITOR **JAMIE S. RICH** - GROUP EDITOR

*THIS TAKES PLACE BEFORE THE EVENTS OF ***THE BATMAN WHO LAUGHS #3.***

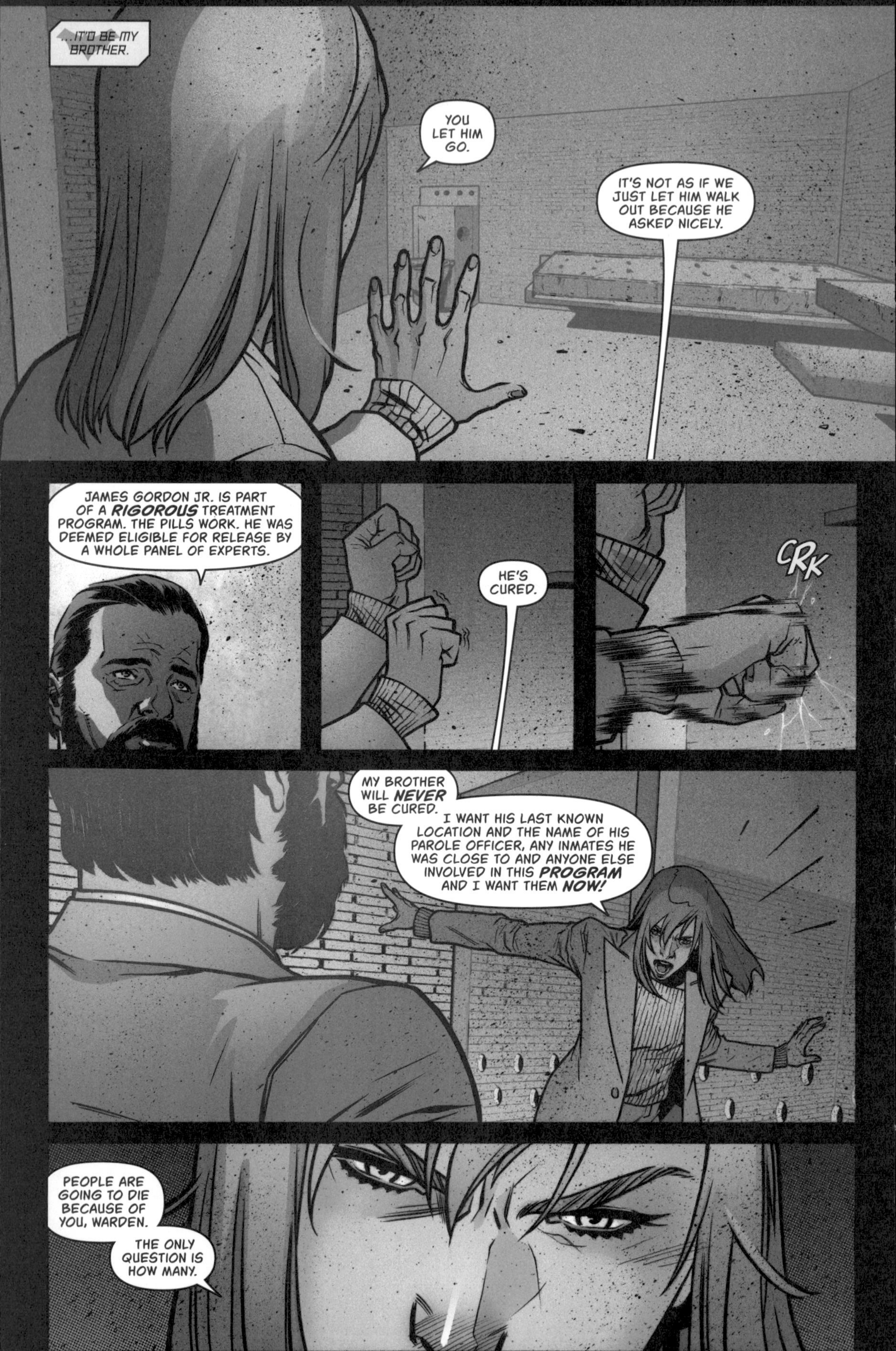

...IT'D BE MY BROTHER.
YOU LET HIM GO.
IT'S NOT AS IF WE JUST LET HIM WALK OUT BECAUSE HE ASKED NICELY.
JAMES GORDON JR. IS PART OF A RIGOROUS TREATMENT PROGRAM. THE PILLS WORK. HE WAS DEEMED ELIGIBLE FOR RELEASE BY A WHOLE PANEL OF EXPERTS.
HE'S CURED.
CRK
MY BROTHER WILL NEVER BE CURED.
I WANT HIS LAST KNOWN LOCATION AND THE NAME OF HIS PAROLE OFFICER, ANY INMATES HE WAS CLOSE TO AND ANYONE ELSE INVOLVED IN THIS PROGRAM AND I WANT THEM NOW!
PEOPLE ARE GOING TO DIE BECAUSE OF YOU, WARDEN.
THE ONLY QUESTION IS HOW MANY.

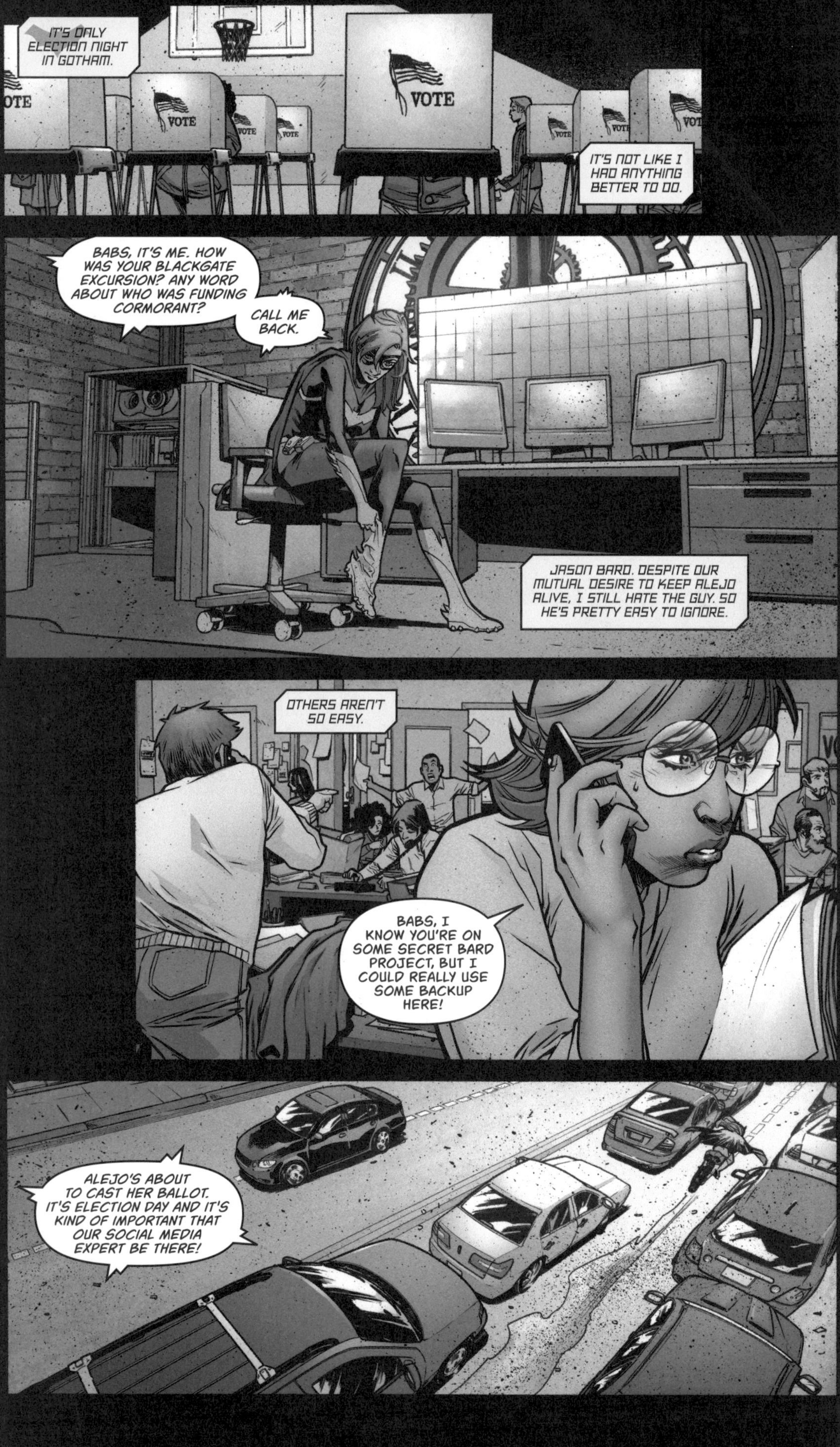
IT'S ONLY ELECTION NIGHT IN GOTHAM.
VOTE
IT'S NOT LIKE I HAD ANYTHING BETTER TO DO.
BABS, IT'S ME. HOW WAS YOUR BLACKGATE EXCURSION? ANY WORD ABOUT WHO WAS FUNDING CORMORANT?
CALL ME BACK.
JASON BARD. DESPITE OUR MUTUAL DESIRE TO KEEP ALEJO ALIVE, I STILL HATE THE GUY. SO HE'S PRETTY EASY TO IGNORE.
OTHERS AREN'T SO EASY.
BABS, I KNOW YOU'RE ON SOME SECRET BARD PROJECT, BUT I COULD REALLY USE SOME BACKUP HERE!
ALEJO'S ABOUT TO CAST HER BALLOT. IT'S ELECTION DAY AND IT'S KIND OF IMPORTANT THAT OUR SOCIAL MEDIA EXPERT BE THERE!

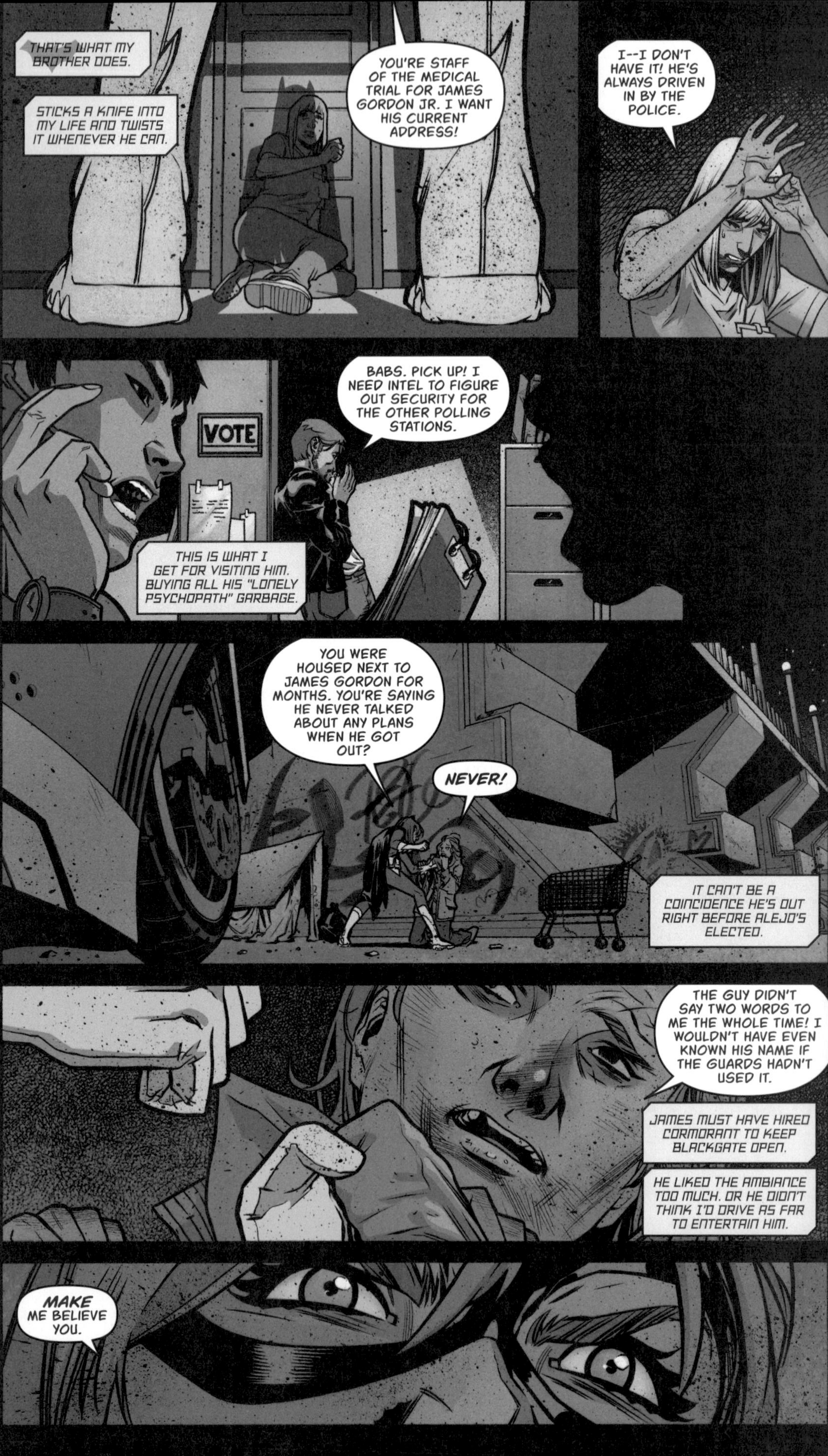
THAT'S WHAT MY BROTHER DOES.
STICKS A KNIFE INTO MY LIFE AND TWISTS IT WHENEVER HE CAN.
YOU'RE STAFF OF THE MEDICAL TRIAL FOR JAMES GORDON JR. I WANT HIS CURRENT ADDRESS!
I--I DON'T HAVE IT! HE'S ALWAYS DRIVEN IN BY THE POLICE.
BABS. PICK UP! I NEED INTEL TO FIGURE OUT SECURITY FOR THE OTHER POLLING STATIONS.
VOTE
THIS IS WHAT I GET FOR VISITING HIM. BUYING ALL HIS "LONELY PSYCHOPATH" GARBAGE.
YOU WERE HOUSED NEXT TO JAMES GORDON FOR MONTHS. YOU'RE SAYING HE NEVER TALKED ABOUT ANY PLANS WHEN HE GOT OUT?
NEVER!
IT CAN'T BE A COINCIDENCE HE'S OUT RIGHT BEFORE ALEJO'S ELECTED.
THE GUY DIDN'T SAY TWO WORDS TO ME THE WHOLE TIME! I WOULDN'T HAVE EVEN KNOWN HIS NAME IF THE GUARDS HADN'T USED IT.
JAMES MUST HAVE HIRED CORMORANT TO KEEP BLACKGATE OPEN.
HE LIKED THE AMBIANCE TOO MUCH. OR HE DIDN'T THINK I'D DRIVE AS FAR TO ENTERTAIN HIM.
MAKE ME BELIEVE YOU.

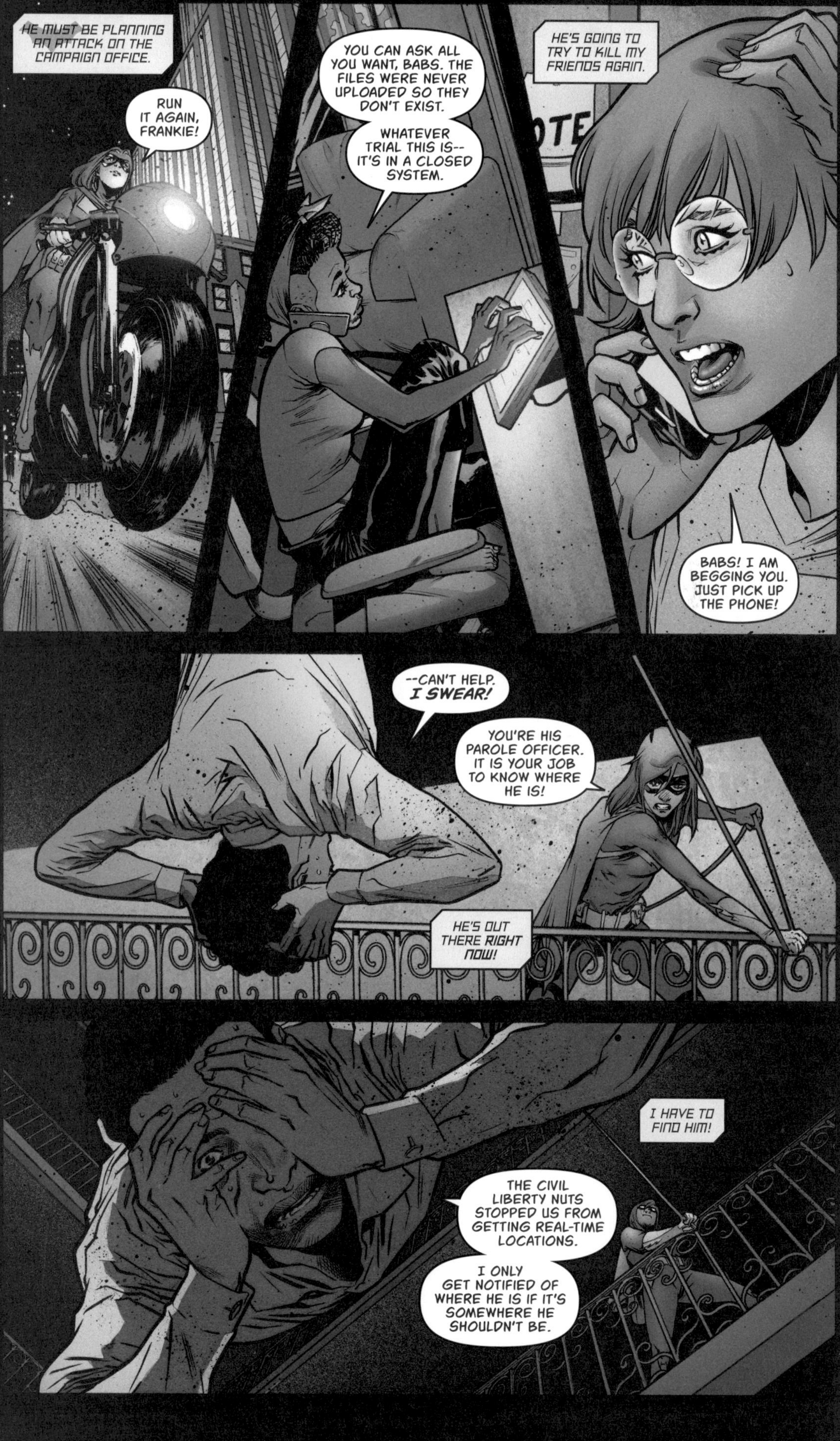
HE MUST BE PLANNING AN ATTACK ON THE CAMPAIGN OFFICE.
RUN IT AGAIN, FRANKIE!
YOU CAN ASK ALL YOU WANT, BABS. THE FILES WERE NEVER UPLOADED SO THEY DON'T EXIST.
WHATEVER TRIAL THIS IS--IT'S IN A CLOSED SYSTEM.
HE'S GOING TO TRY TO KILL MY FRIENDS AGAIN.
BABS! I AM BEGGING YOU. JUST PICK UP THE PHONE!
--CAN'T HELP. I SWEAR!
YOU'RE HIS PAROLE OFFICER. IT IS YOUR JOB TO KNOW WHERE HE IS!
HE'S OUT THERE RIGHT NOW!
I HAVE TO FIND HIM!
THE CIVIL LIBERTY NUTS STOPPED US FROM GETTING REAL-TIME LOCATIONS.
I ONLY GET NOTIFIED OF WHERE HE IS IF IT'S SOMEWHERE HE SHOULDN'T BE.

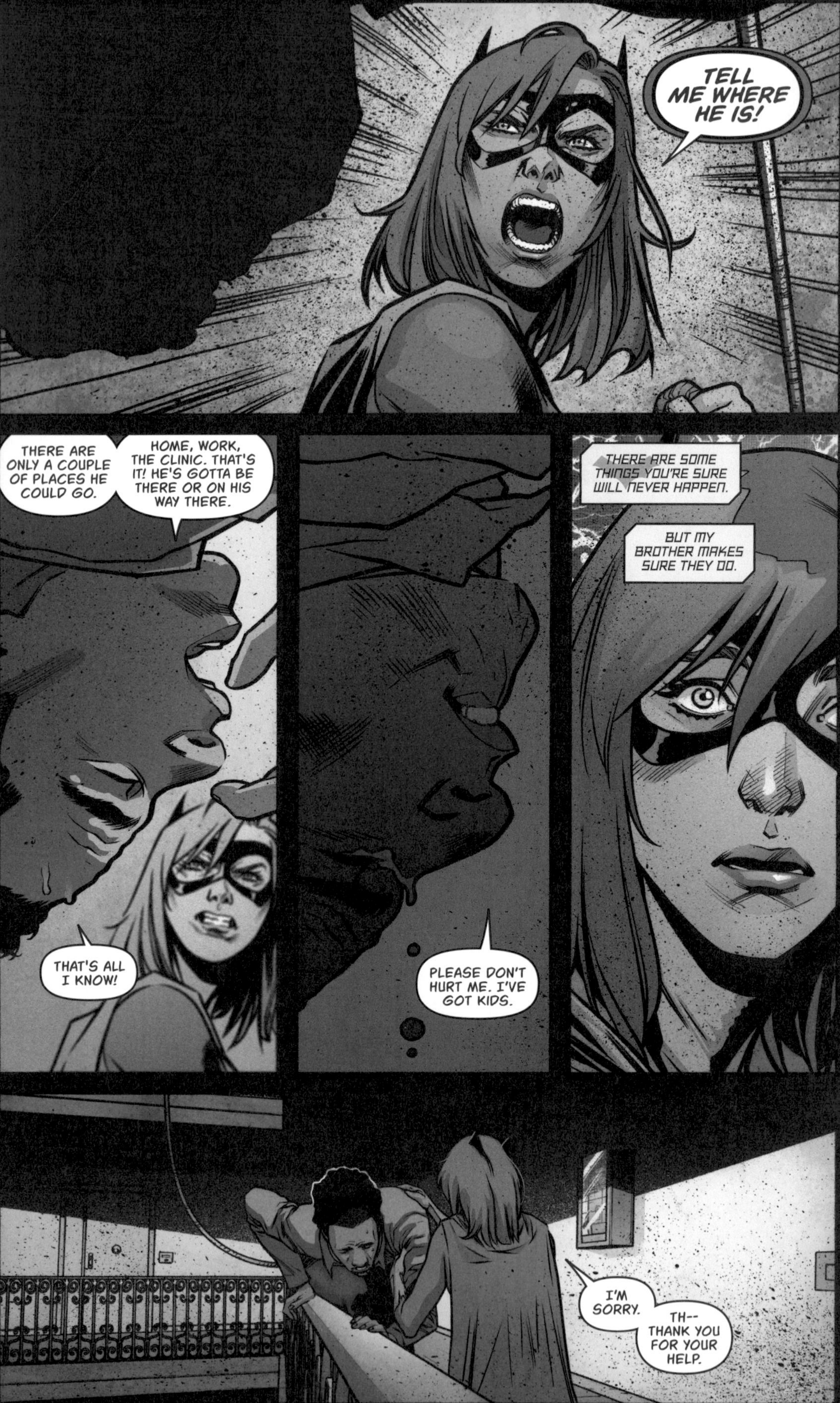
TELL ME WHERE HE IS!
THERE ARE ONLY A COUPLE OF PLACES HE COULD GO.
HOME, WORK, THE CLINIC. THAT'S IT! HE'S GOTTA BE THERE OR ON HIS WAY THERE.
THAT'S ALL I KNOW!
PLEASE DON'T HURT ME. I'VE GOT KIDS.
THERE ARE SOME THINGS YOU'RE SURE WILL NEVER HAPPEN.
BUT MY BROTHER MAKES SURE THEY DO.
I'M SORRY.
TH-- THANK YOU FOR YOUR HELP.

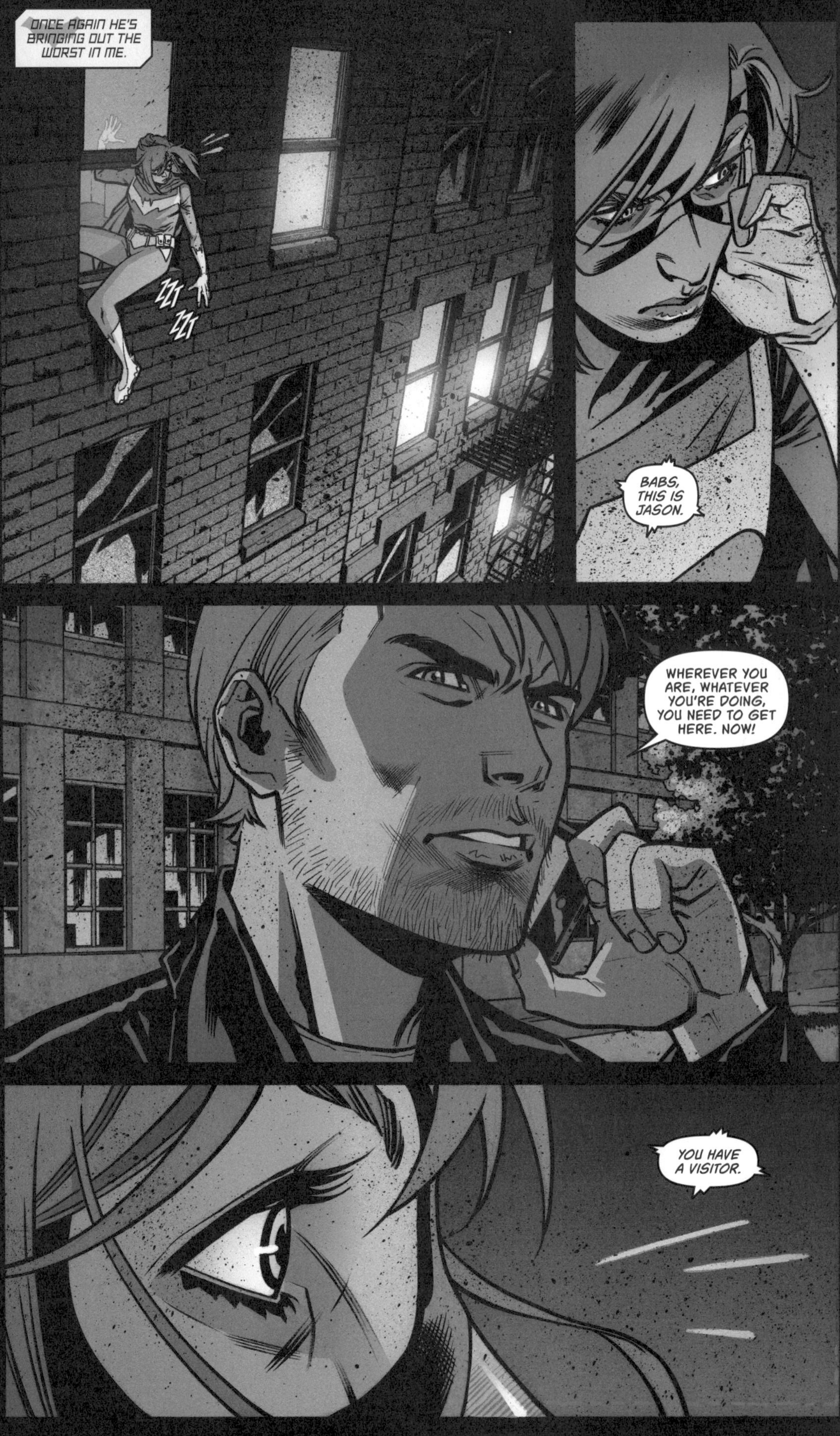
ONCE AGAIN HE'S BRINGING OUT THE WORST IN ME.
ZZT
ZZT
BABS, THIS IS JASON.
WHEREVER YOU ARE, WHATEVER YOU'RE DOING, YOU NEED TO GET HERE. NOW!
YOU HAVE A VISITOR.

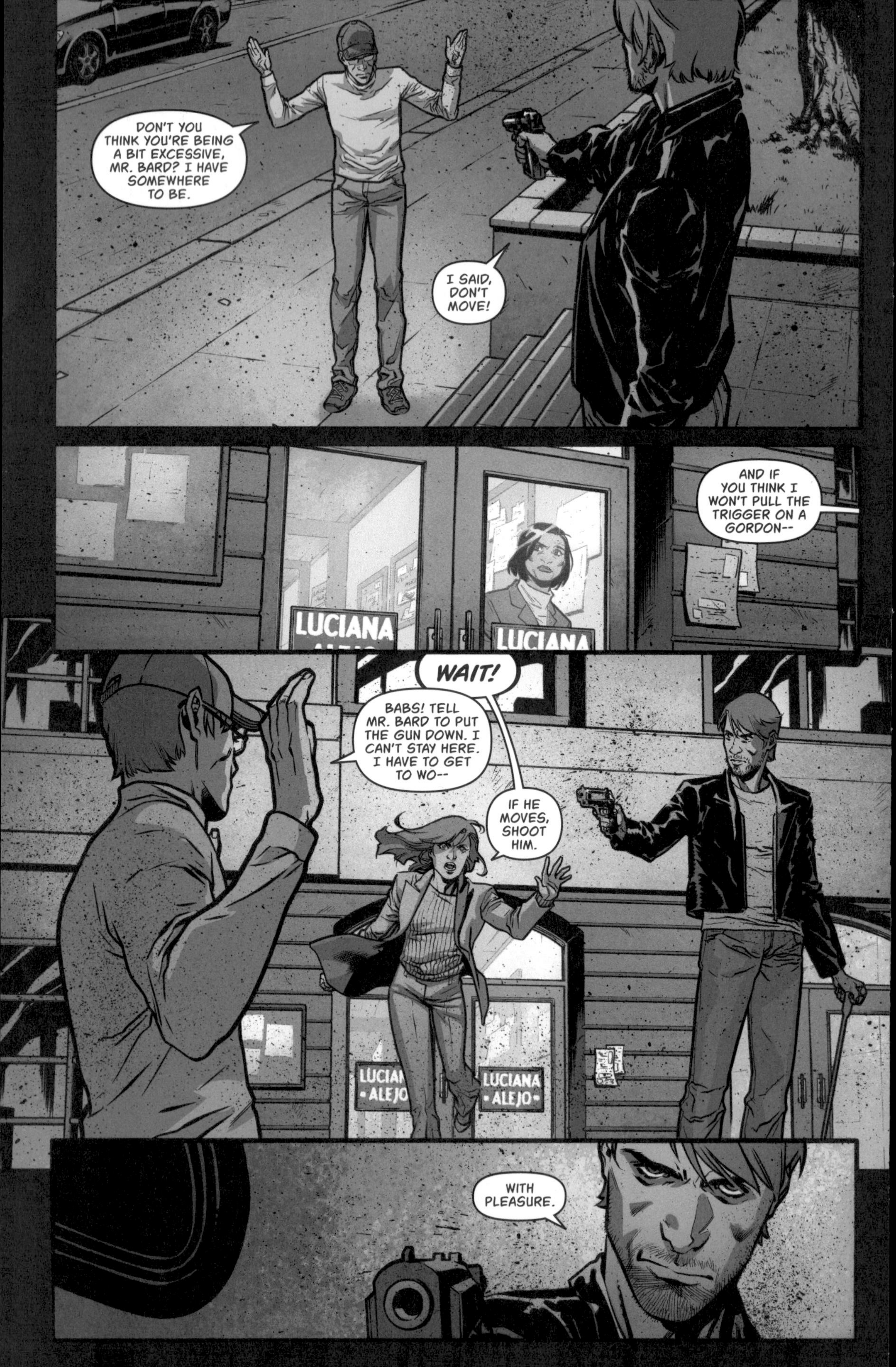

DON'T YOU THINK YOU'RE BEING A BIT EXCESSIVE, MR. BARD? I HAVE SOMEWHERE TO BE.
I SAID, DON'T MOVE!
AND IF YOU THINK I WON'T PULL THE TRIGGER ON A GORDON--
LUCIANA
LUCIANA
WAIT!
BABS! TELL MR. BARD TO PUT THE GUN DOWN. I CAN'T STAY HERE. I HAVE TO GET TO WO--
IF HE MOVES, SHOOT HIM.
LUCIANA ALEJO
LUCIANA ALEJO
WITH PLEASURE.

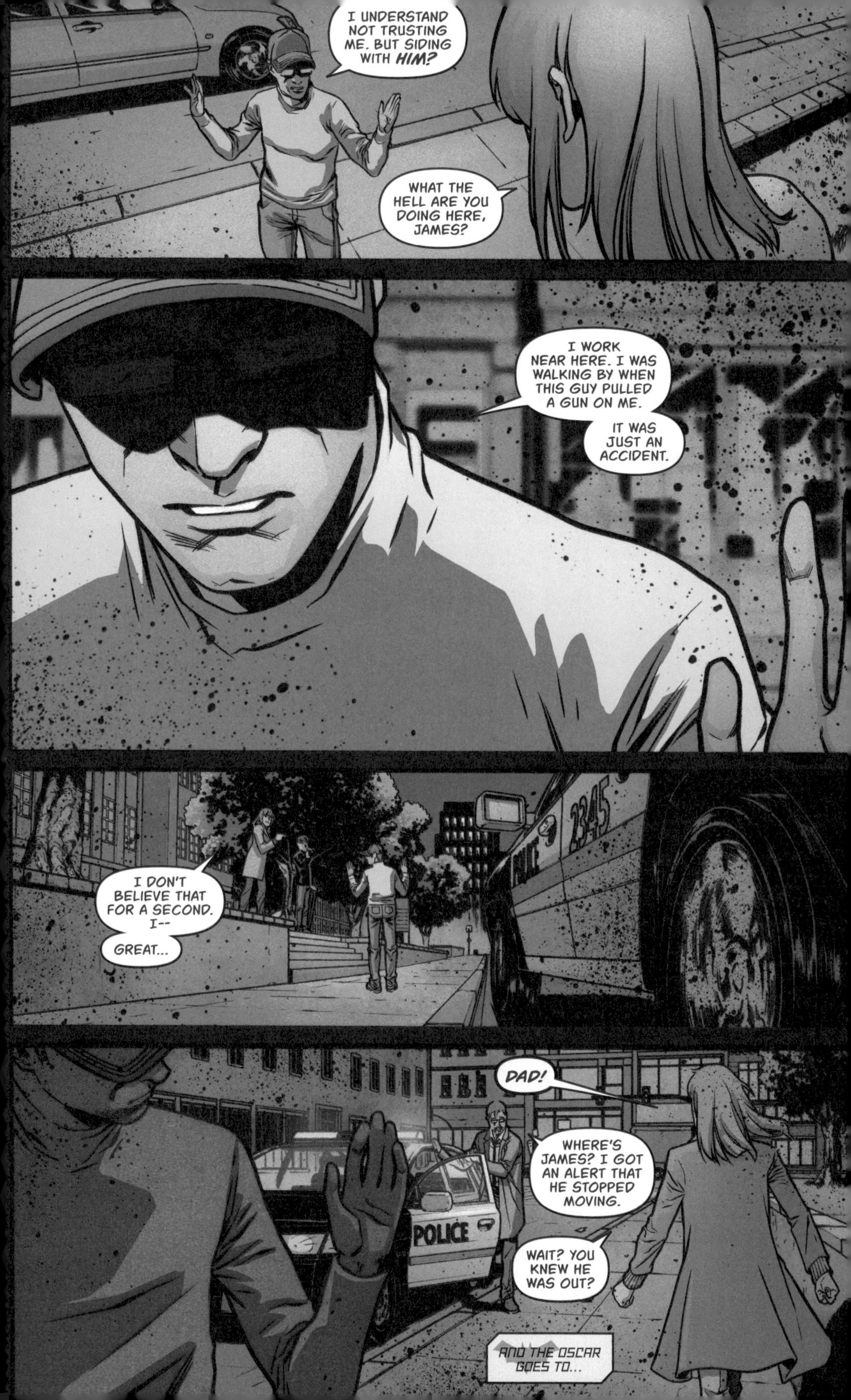
I UNDERSTAND NOT TRUSTING ME. BUT SIDING WITH HIM?
WHAT THE HELL ARE YOU DOING HERE, JAMES?
I WORK NEAR HERE. I WAS WALKING BY WHEN THIS GUY PULLED A GUN ON ME.
IT WAS JUST AN ACCIDENT.
I DON'T BELIEVE THAT FOR A SECOND. I--
GREAT...
POLICE
DAD!
WHERE'S JAMES? I GOT AN ALERT THAT HE STOPPED MOVING.
WAIT? YOU KNEW HE WAS OUT?
POLICE
AND THE OSCAR GOES TO...

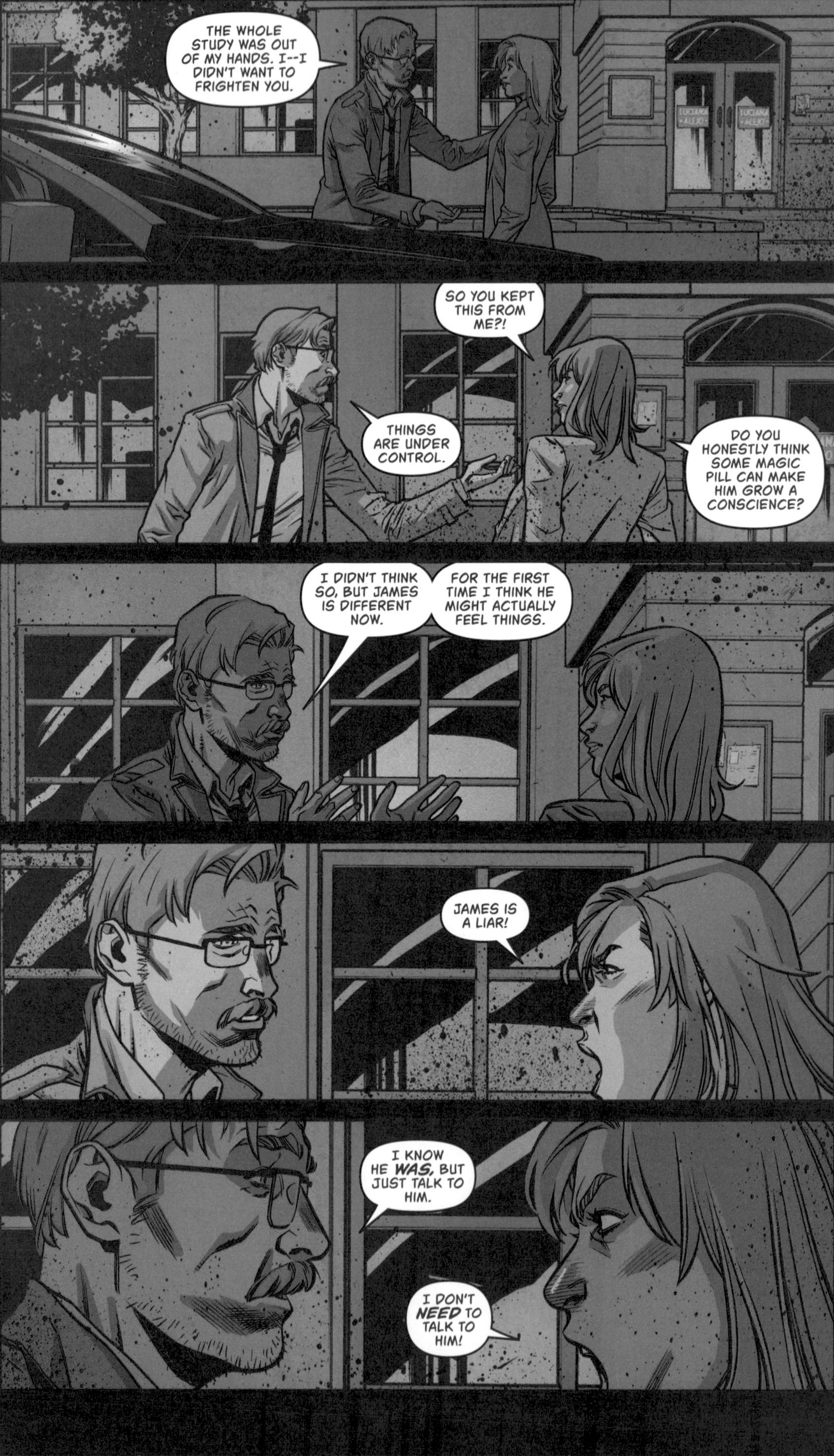
THE WHOLE STUDY WAS OUT OF MY HANDS. I--I DIDN'T WANT TO FRIGHTEN YOU.
SO YOU KEPT THIS FROM ME?!
THINGS ARE UNDER CONTROL.
DO YOU HONESTLY THINK SOME MAGIC PILL CAN MAKE HIM GROW A CONSCIENCE?
I DIDN'T THINK SO, BUT JAMES IS DIFFERENT NOW.
FOR THE FIRST TIME I THINK HE MIGHT ACTUALLY FEEL THINGS.
JAMES IS A LIAR!
I KNOW HE *WAS,* BUT JUST TALK TO HIM.
I DON'T *NEED* TO TALK TO HIM!

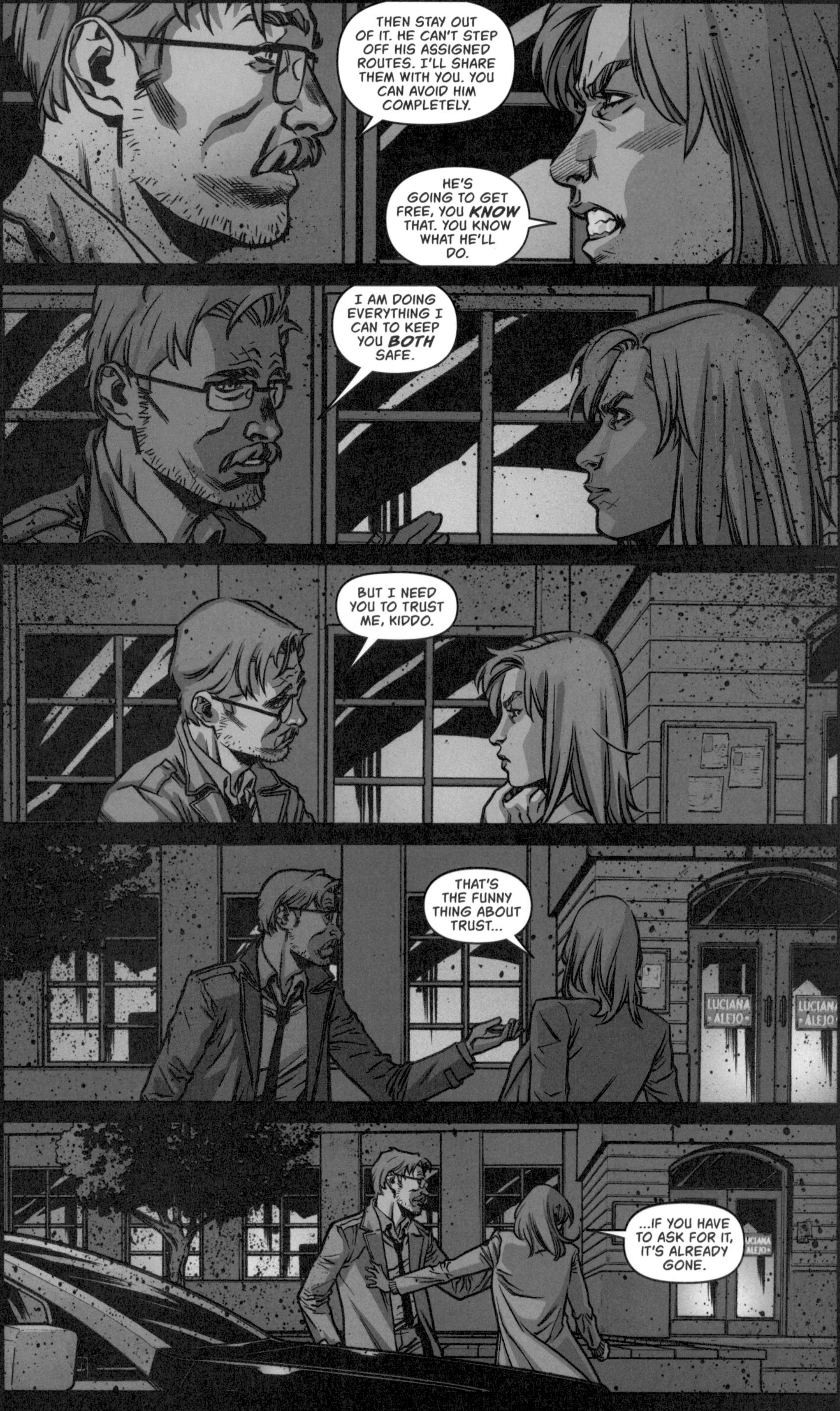
THEN STAY OUT OF IT. HE CAN'T STEP OFF HIS ASSIGNED ROUTES. I'LL SHARE THEM WITH YOU. YOU CAN AVOID HIM COMPLETELY.
HE'S GOING TO GET FREE, YOU KNOW THAT. YOU KNOW WHAT HE'LL DO.
I AM DOING EVERYTHING I CAN TO KEEP YOU BOTH SAFE.
BUT I NEED YOU TO TRUST ME, KIDDO.
THAT'S THE FUNNY THING ABOUT TRUST...
LUCIANA ALEJO
LUCIANA ALEJO
...IF YOU HAVE TO ASK FOR IT, IT'S ALREADY GONE.
LUCIANA ALEJO

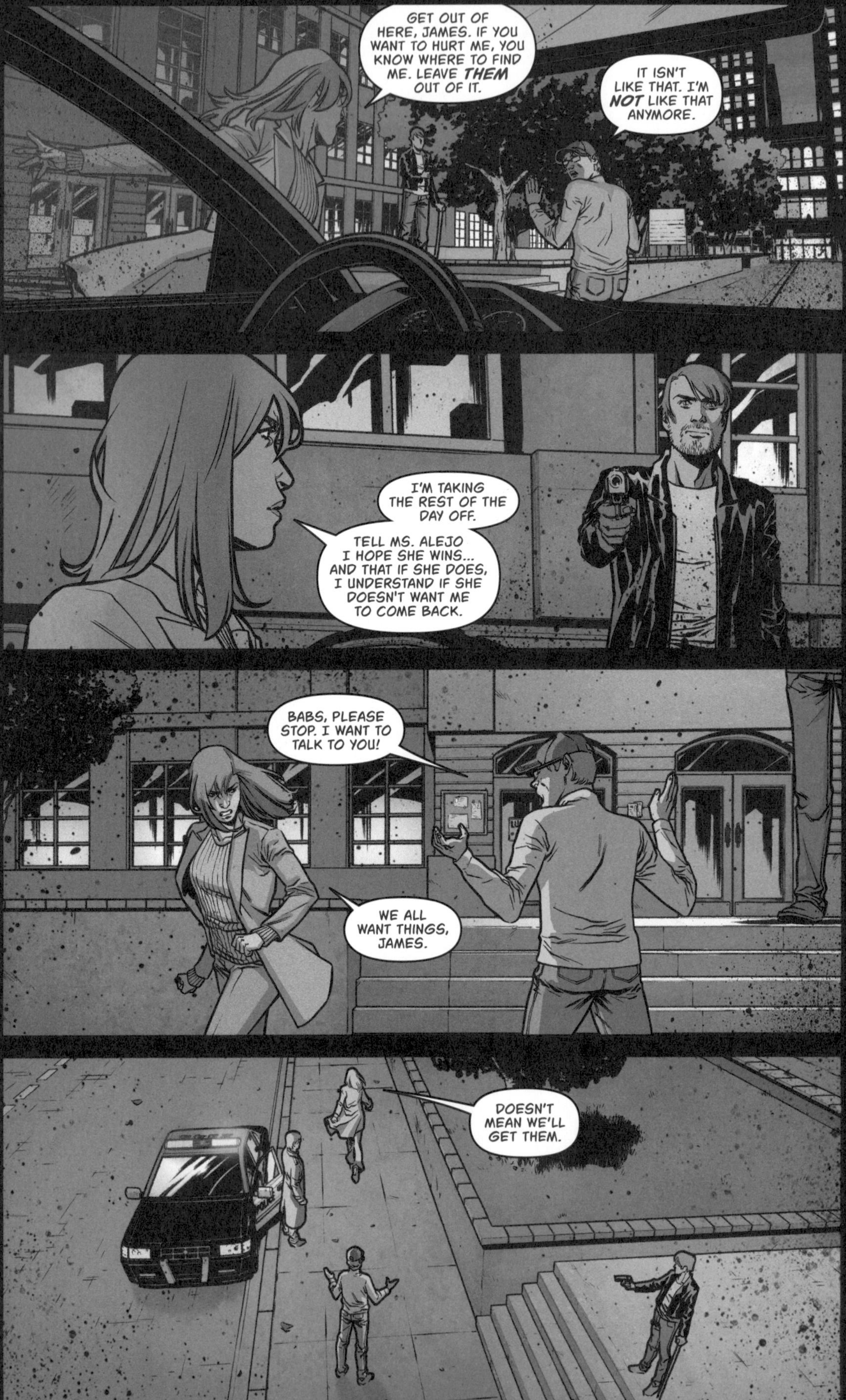
GET OUT OF HERE, JAMES. IF YOU WANT TO HURT ME, YOU KNOW WHERE TO FIND ME. LEAVE *THEM* OUT OF IT.
IT ISN'T LIKE THAT. I'M *NOT* LIKE THAT ANYMORE.
I'M TAKING THE REST OF THE DAY OFF.
TELL MS. ALEJO I HOPE SHE WINS... AND THAT IF SHE DOES, I UNDERSTAND IF SHE DOESN'T WANT ME TO COME BACK.
BABS, PLEASE STOP. I WANT TO TALK TO YOU!
WE ALL WANT THINGS, JAMES.
DOESN'T MEAN WE'LL GET THEM.

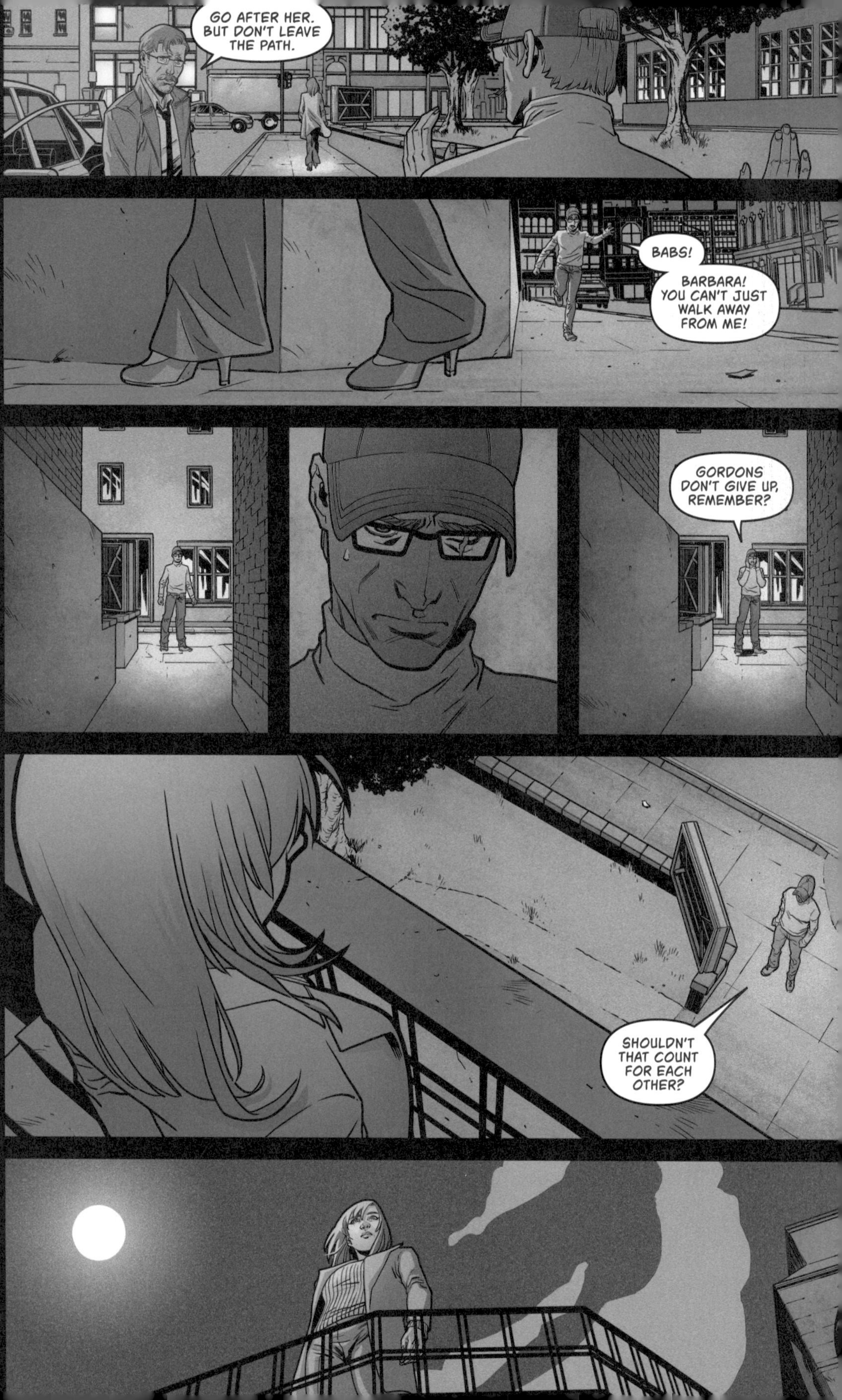
GO AFTER HER. BUT DON'T LEAVE THE PATH.
BABS!
BARBARA! YOU CAN'T JUST WALK AWAY FROM ME!
GORDONS DON'T GIVE UP, REMEMBER?
SHOULDN'T THAT COUNT FOR EACH OTHER?

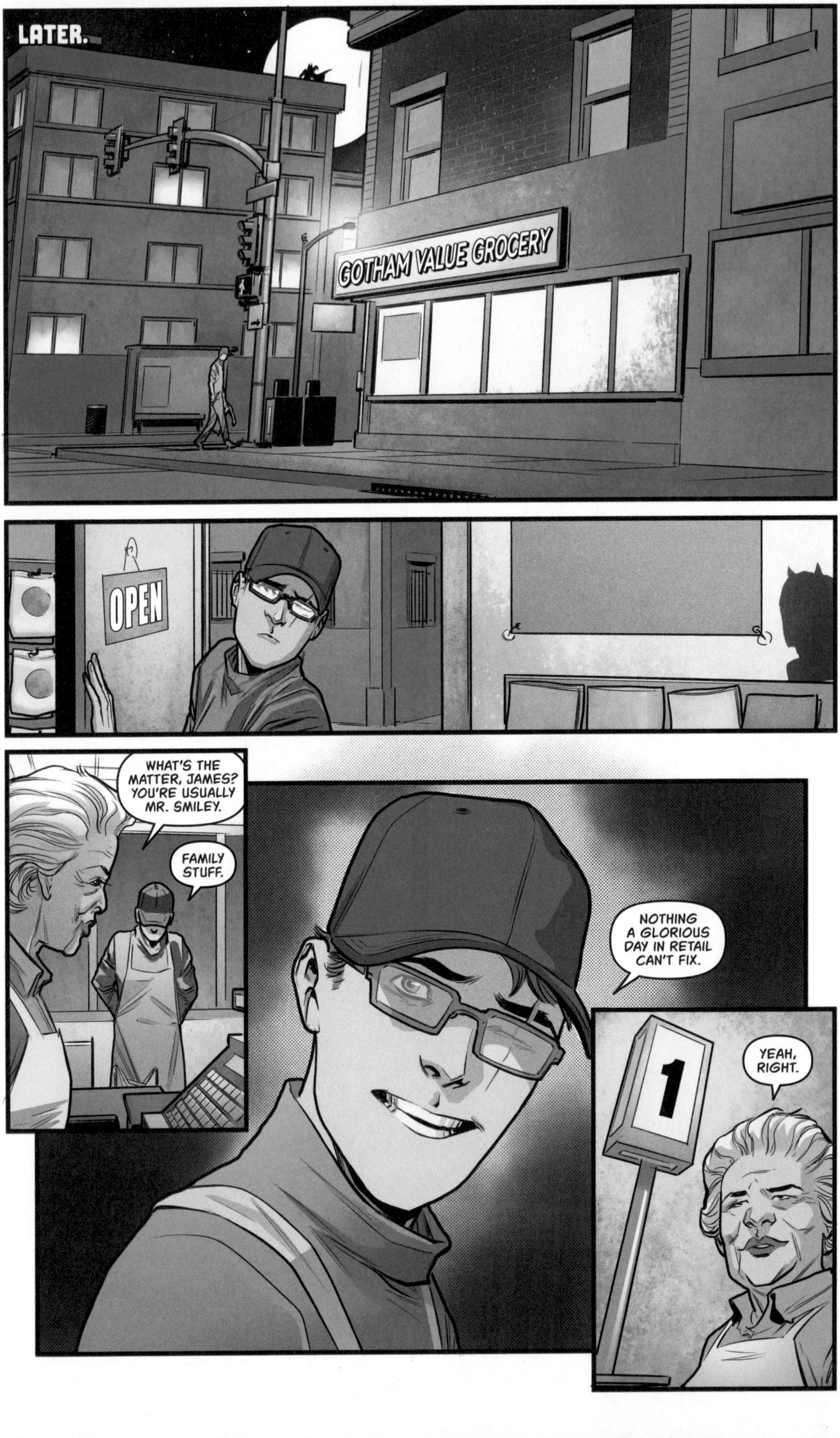
LATER.
GOTHAM VALUE GROCERY
OPEN
WHAT'S THE MATTER, JAMES? YOU'RE USUALLY MR. SMILEY.
FAMILY STUFF.
NOTHING A GLORIOUS DAY IN RETAIL CAN'T FIX.
1
YEAH, RIGHT.

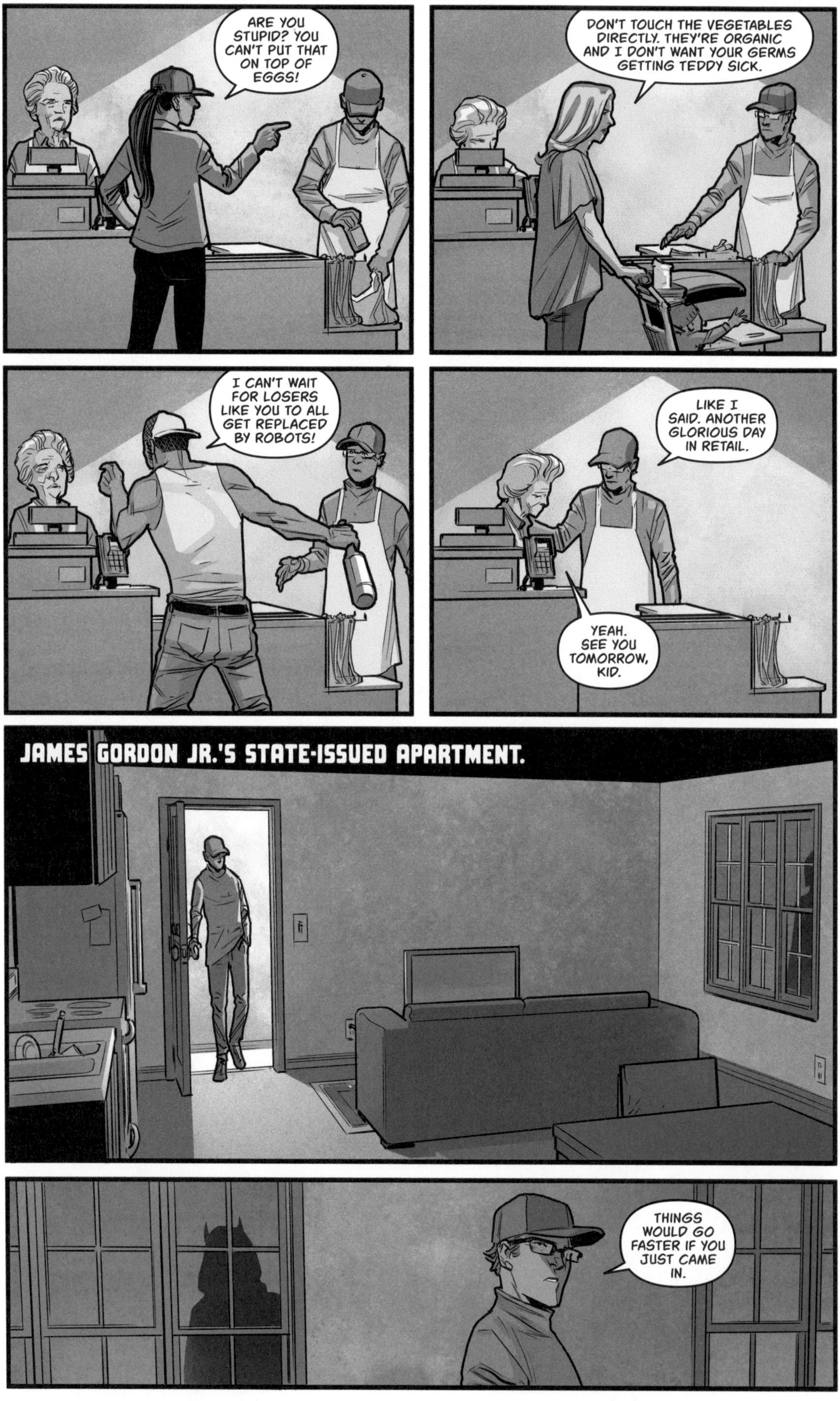
ARE YOU STUPID? YOU CAN'T PUT THAT ON TOP OF EGGS!
DON'T TOUCH THE VEGETABLES DIRECTLY. THEY'RE ORGANIC AND I DON'T WANT YOUR GERMS GETTING TEDDY SICK.
I CAN'T WAIT FOR LOSERS LIKE YOU TO ALL GET REPLACED BY ROBOTS!
LIKE I SAID. ANOTHER GLORIOUS DAY IN RETAIL.
YEAH. SEE YOU TOMORROW, KID.
JAMES GORDON JR.'S STATE-ISSUED APARTMENT.
THINGS WOULD GO FASTER IF YOU JUST CAME IN.

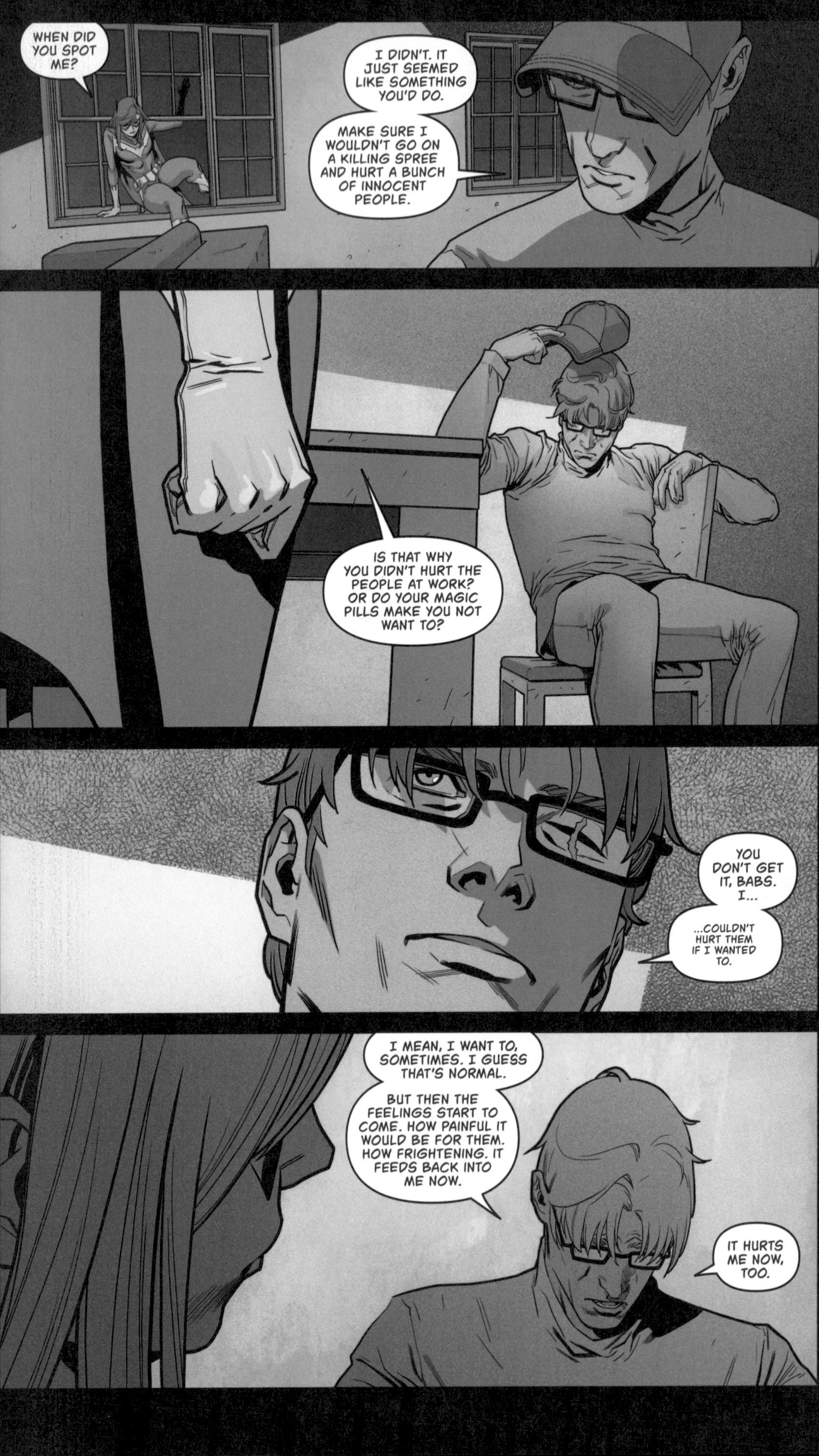
WHEN DID YOU SPOT ME?
I DIDN'T. IT JUST SEEMED LIKE SOMETHING YOU'D DO.
MAKE SURE I WOULDN'T GO ON A KILLING SPREE AND HURT A BUNCH OF INNOCENT PEOPLE.
IS THAT WHY YOU DIDN'T HURT THE PEOPLE AT WORK? OR DO YOUR MAGIC PILLS MAKE YOU NOT WANT TO?
YOU DON'T GET IT, BABS. I...
...COULDN'T HURT THEM IF I WANTED TO.
I MEAN, I WANT TO, SOMETIMES. I GUESS THAT'S NORMAL.
BUT THEN THE FEELINGS START TO COME. HOW PAINFUL IT WOULD BE FOR THEM. HOW FRIGHTENING. IT FEEDS BACK INTO ME NOW.
IT HURTS ME NOW, TOO.

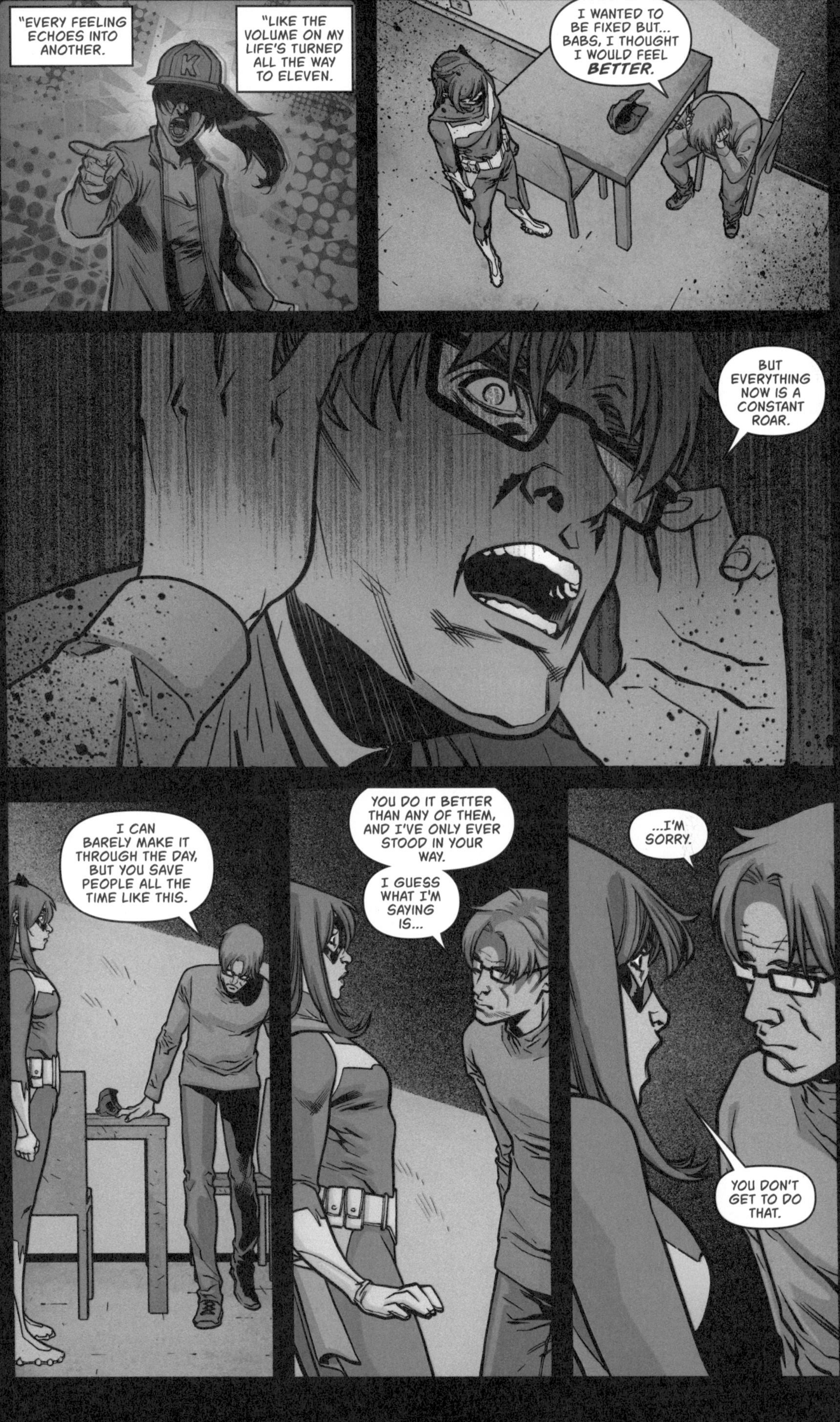
"EVERY FEELING ECHOES INTO ANOTHER.
"LIKE THE VOLUME ON MY LIFE'S TURNED ALL THE WAY TO ELEVEN.
I WANTED TO BE FIXED BUT... BABS, I THOUGHT I WOULD FEEL **BETTER**.
BUT EVERYTHING NOW IS A CONSTANT ROAR.
I CAN BARELY MAKE IT THROUGH THE DAY, BUT YOU SAVE PEOPLE ALL THE TIME LIKE THIS.
YOU DO IT BETTER THAN ANY OF THEM, AND I'VE ONLY EVER STOOD IN YOUR WAY.
I GUESS WHAT I'M SAYING IS...
...I'M SORRY.
YOU DON'T GET TO DO THAT.

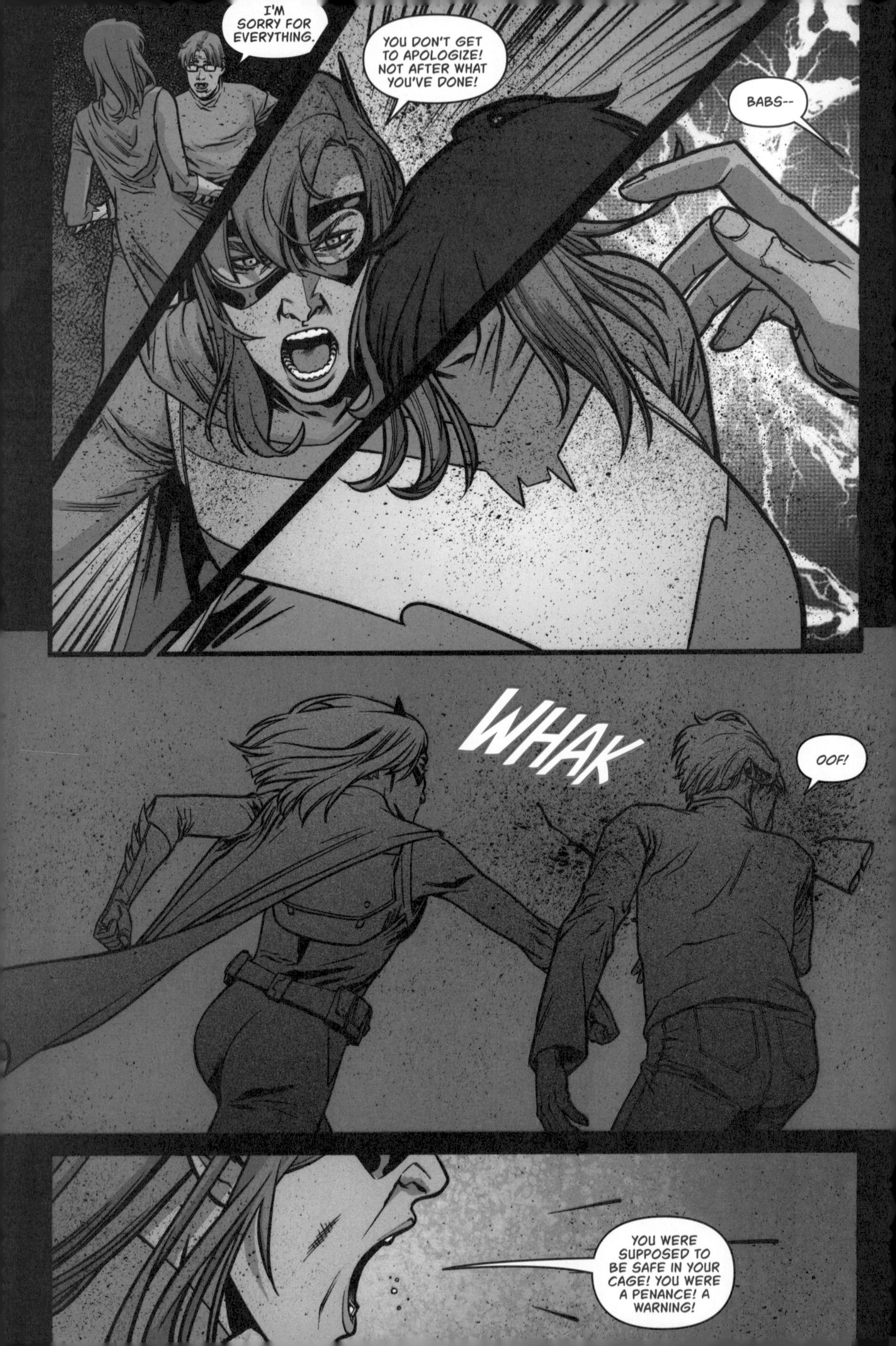
I'M SORRY FOR EVERYTHING.
YOU DON'T GET TO APOLOGIZE! NOT AFTER WHAT YOU'VE DONE!
BABS--
WHAK
OOF!
YOU WERE SUPPOSED TO BE SAFE IN YOUR CAGE! YOU WERE A PENANCE! A WARNING!

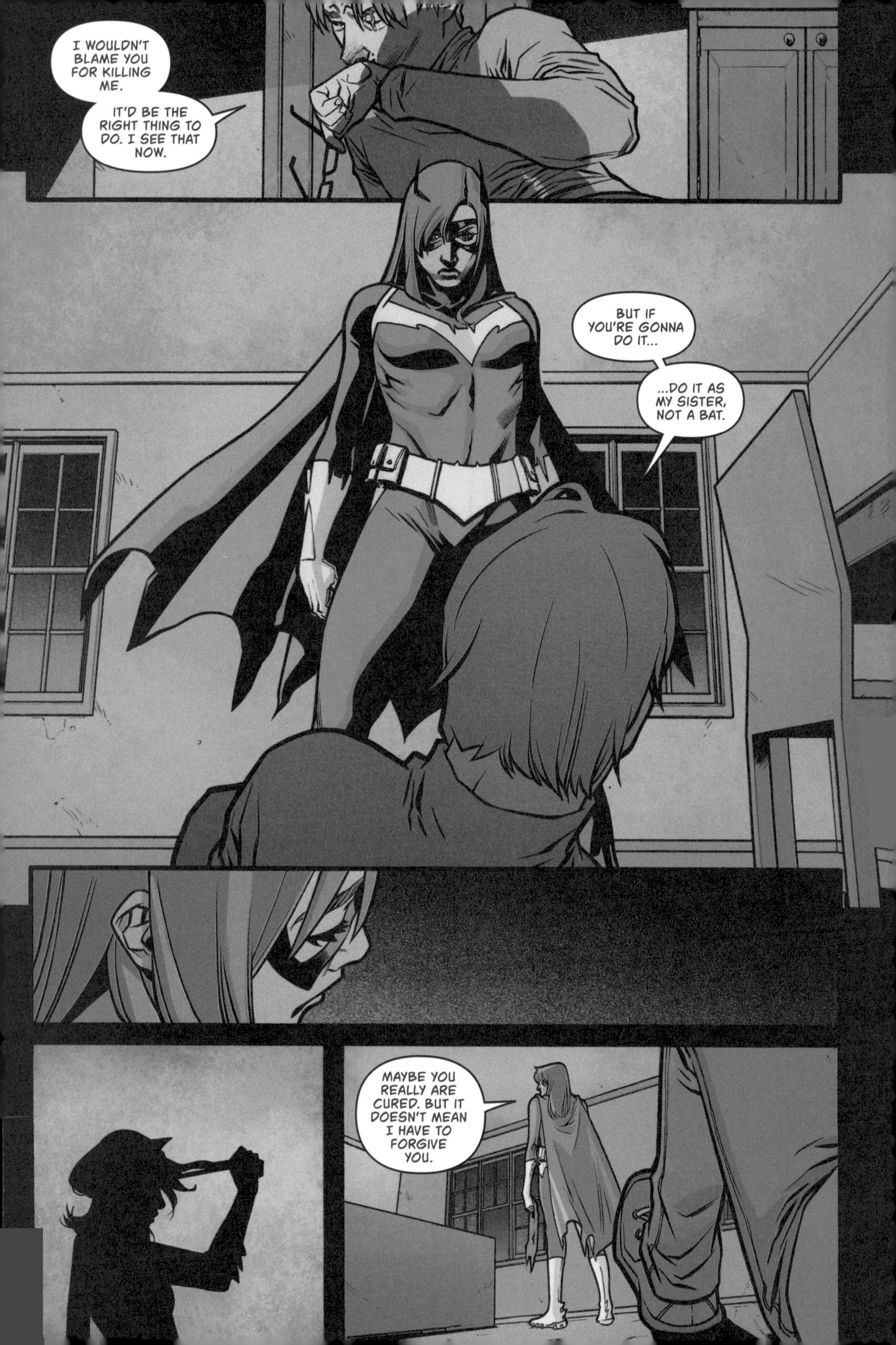
I WOULDN'T BLAME YOU FOR KILLING ME.
IT'D BE THE RIGHT THING TO DO. I SEE THAT NOW.
BUT IF YOU'RE GONNA DO IT...
...DO IT AS MY SISTER, NOT A BAT.
MAYBE YOU REALLY ARE CURED. BUT IT DOESN'T MEAN I HAVE TO FORGIVE YOU.

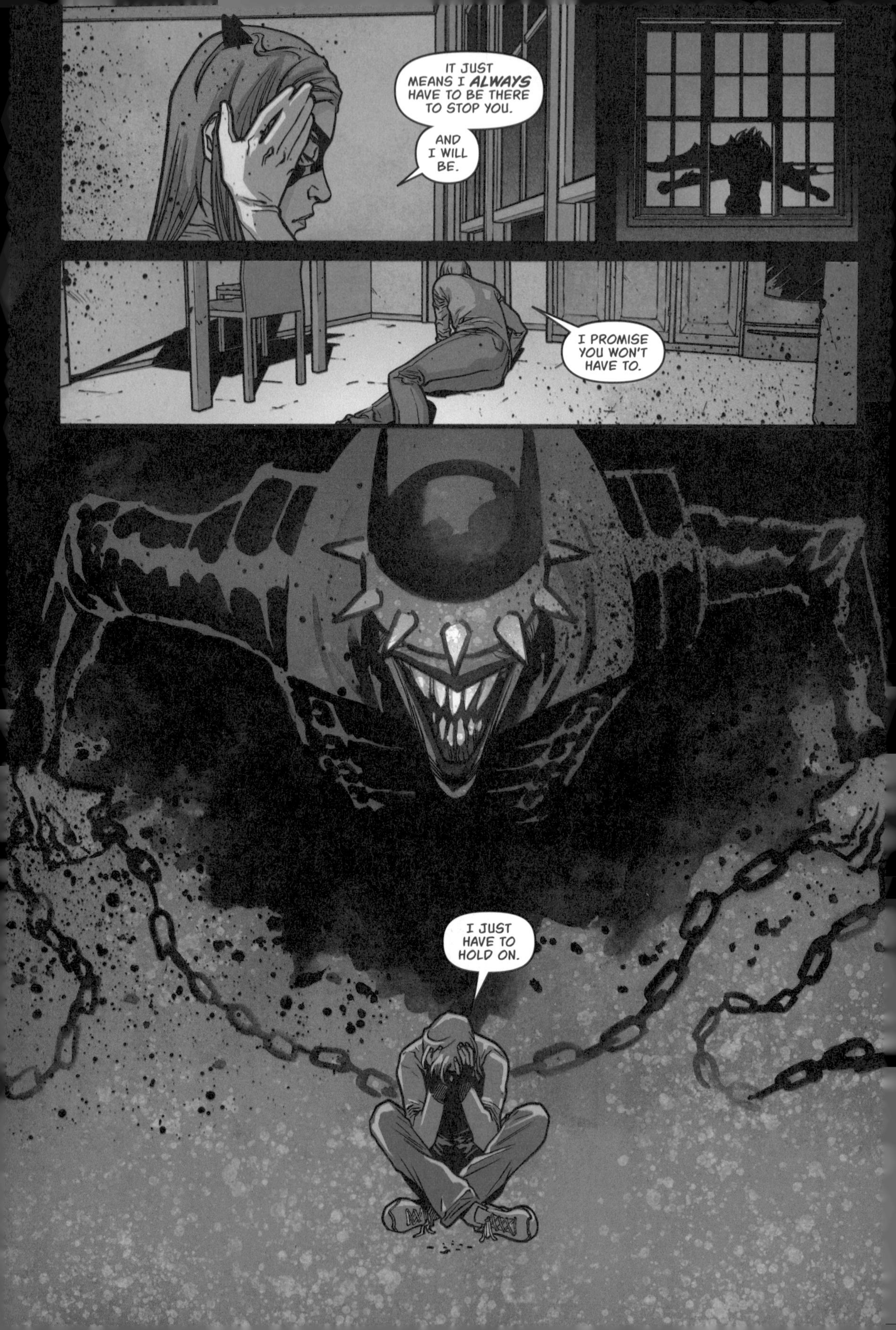
IT JUST MEANS I ALWAYS HAVE TO BE THERE TO STOP YOU.
AND I WILL BE.
I PROMISE YOU WON'T HAVE TO.
I JUST HAVE TO HOLD ON.

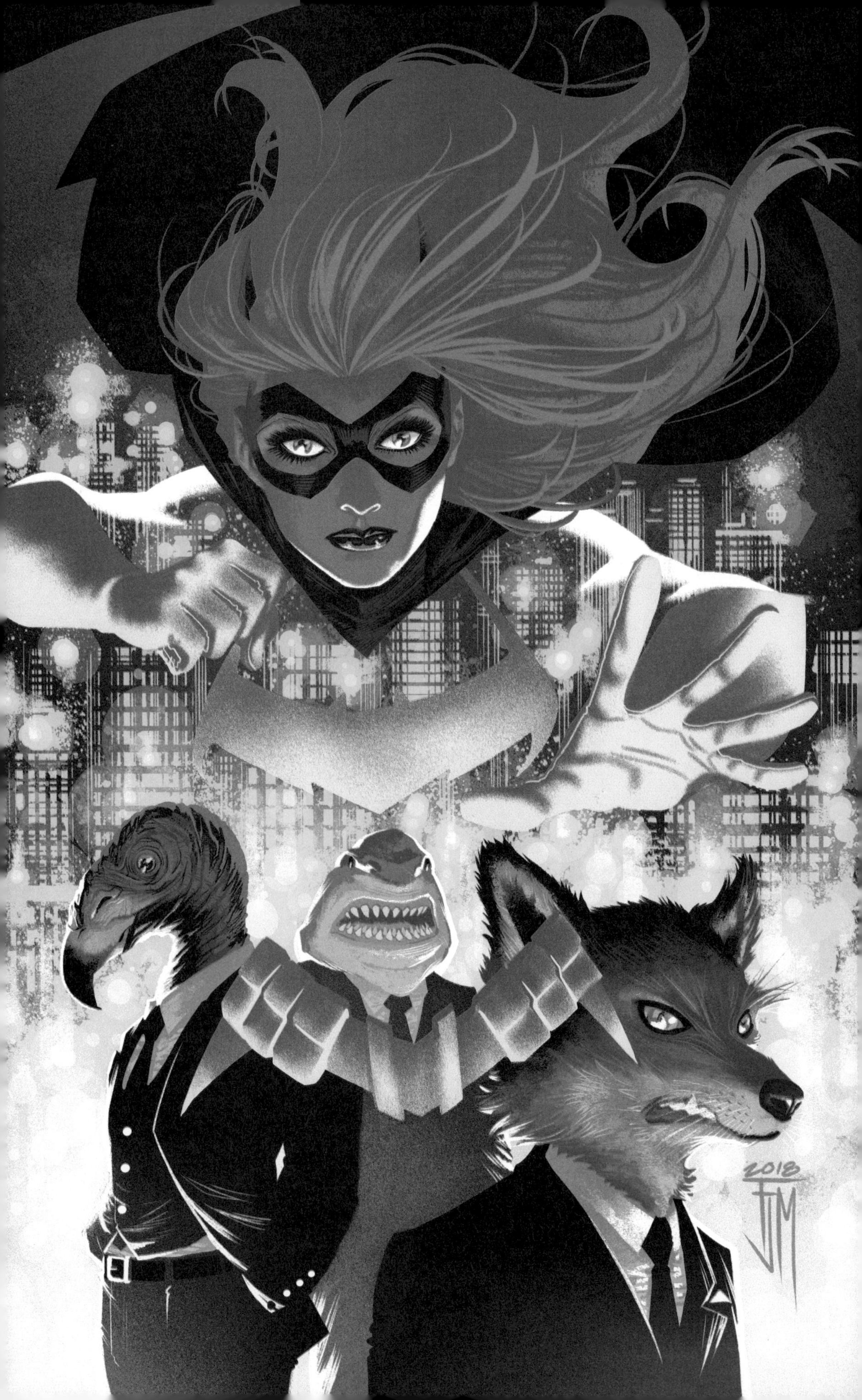

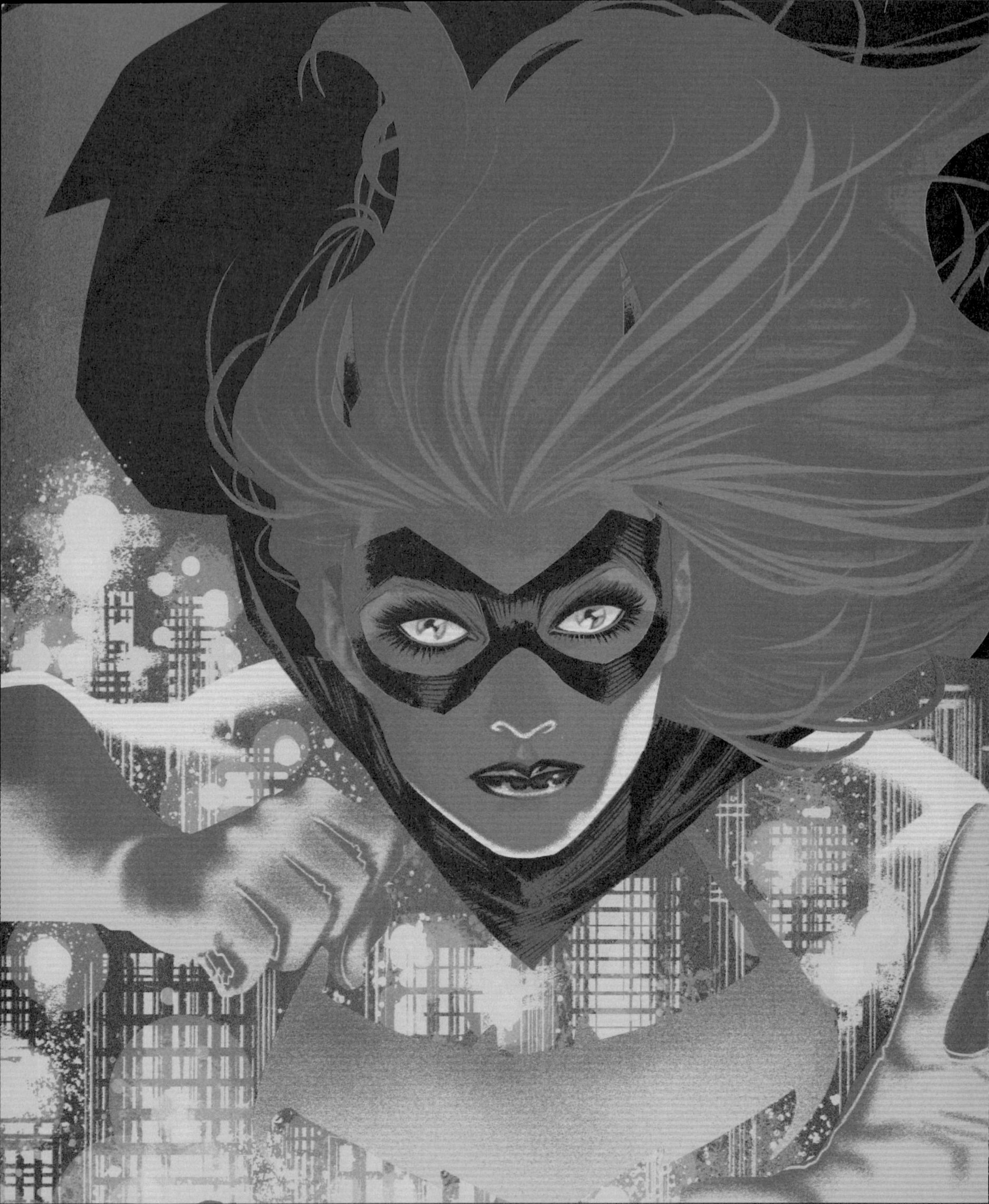

BATGIRL
#34

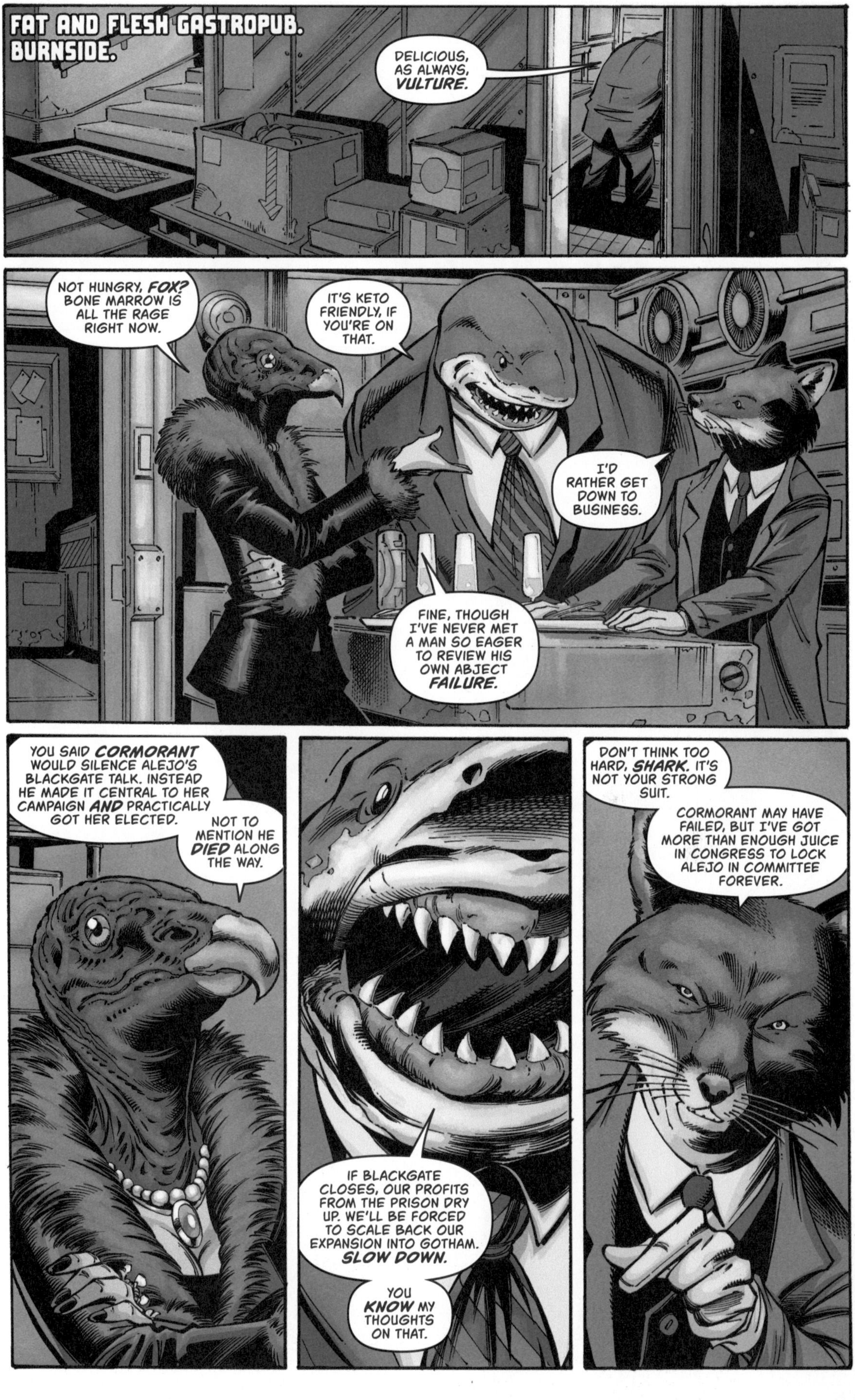
FAT AND FLESH GASTROPUB. BURNSIDE.
DELICIOUS, AS ALWAYS, VULTURE.
NOT HUNGRY, FOX? BONE MARROW IS ALL THE RAGE RIGHT NOW.
IT'S KETO FRIENDLY, IF YOU'RE ON THAT.
I'D RATHER GET DOWN TO BUSINESS.
FINE, THOUGH I'VE NEVER MET A MAN SO EAGER TO REVIEW HIS OWN ABJECT FAILURE.
YOU SAID CORMORANT WOULD SILENCE ALEJO'S BLACKGATE TALK. INSTEAD HE MADE IT CENTRAL TO HER CAMPAIGN AND PRACTICALLY GOT HER ELECTED.
NOT TO MENTION HE DIED ALONG THE WAY.
IF BLACKGATE CLOSES, OUR PROFITS FROM THE PRISON DRY UP. WE'LL BE FORCED TO SCALE BACK OUR EXPANSION INTO GOTHAM. SLOW DOWN.
YOU KNOW MY THOUGHTS ON THAT.
DON'T THINK TOO HARD, SHARK. IT'S NOT YOUR STRONG SUIT.
CORMORANT MAY HAVE FAILED, BUT I'VE GOT MORE THAN ENOUGH JUICE IN CONGRESS TO LOCK ALEJO IN COMMITTEE FOREVER.

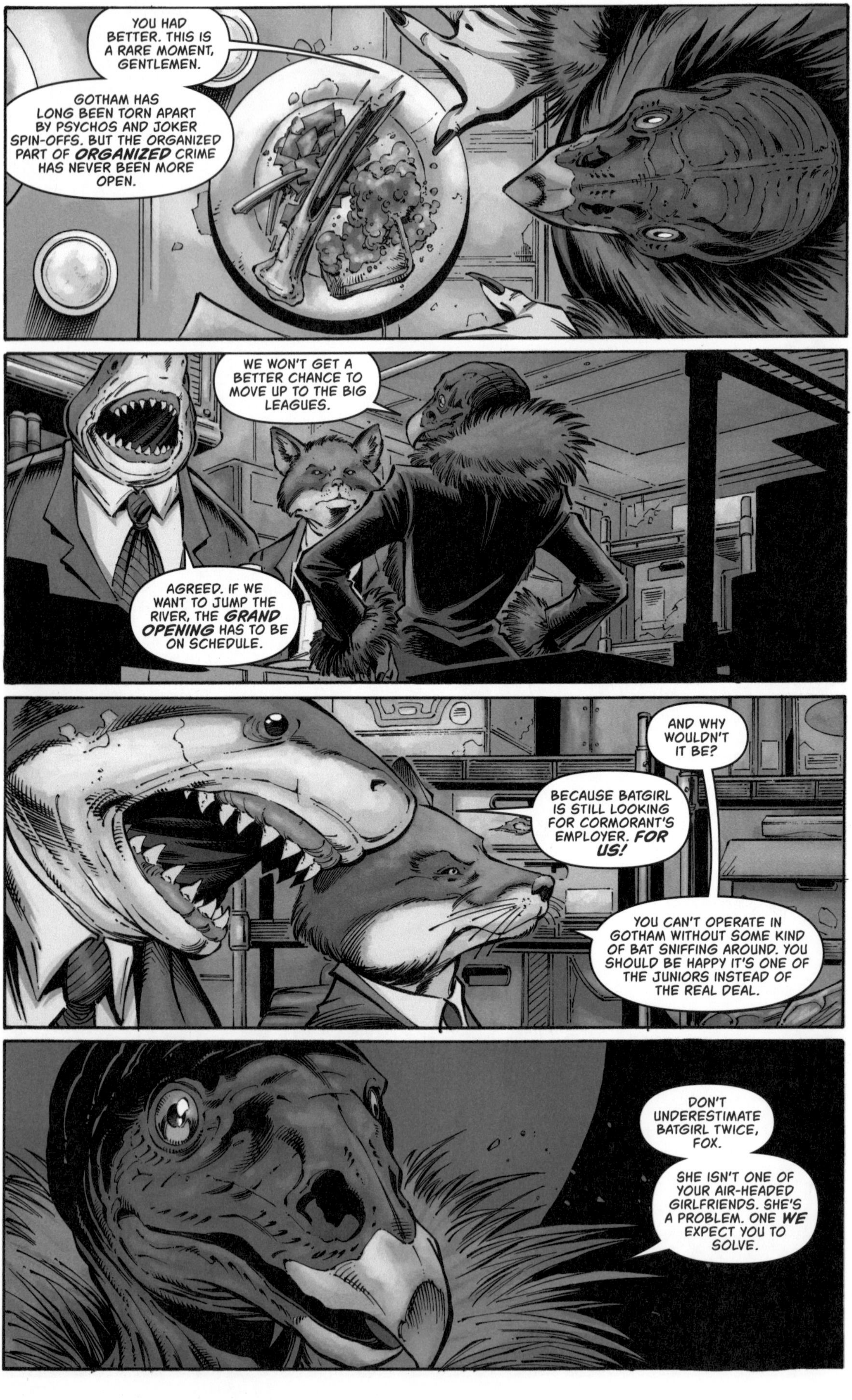
YOU HAD BETTER. THIS IS A RARE MOMENT, GENTLEMEN.
GOTHAM HAS LONG BEEN TORN APART BY PSYCHOS AND JOKER SPIN-OFFS. BUT THE ORGANIZED PART OF ORGANIZED CRIME HAS NEVER BEEN MORE OPEN.
WE WON'T GET A BETTER CHANCE TO MOVE UP TO THE BIG LEAGUES.
AGREED. IF WE WANT TO JUMP THE RIVER, THE GRAND OPENING HAS TO BE ON SCHEDULE.
AND WHY WOULDN'T IT BE?
BECAUSE BATGIRL IS STILL LOOKING FOR CORMORANT'S EMPLOYER. FOR US!
YOU CAN'T OPERATE IN GOTHAM WITHOUT SOME KIND OF BAT SNIFFING AROUND. YOU SHOULD BE HAPPY IT'S ONE OF THE JUNIORS INSTEAD OF THE REAL DEAL.
DON'T UNDERESTIMATE BATGIRL TWICE, FOX.
SHE ISN'T ONE OF YOUR AIR-HEADED GIRLFRIENDS. SHE'S A PROBLEM. ONE WE EXPECT YOU TO SOLVE.

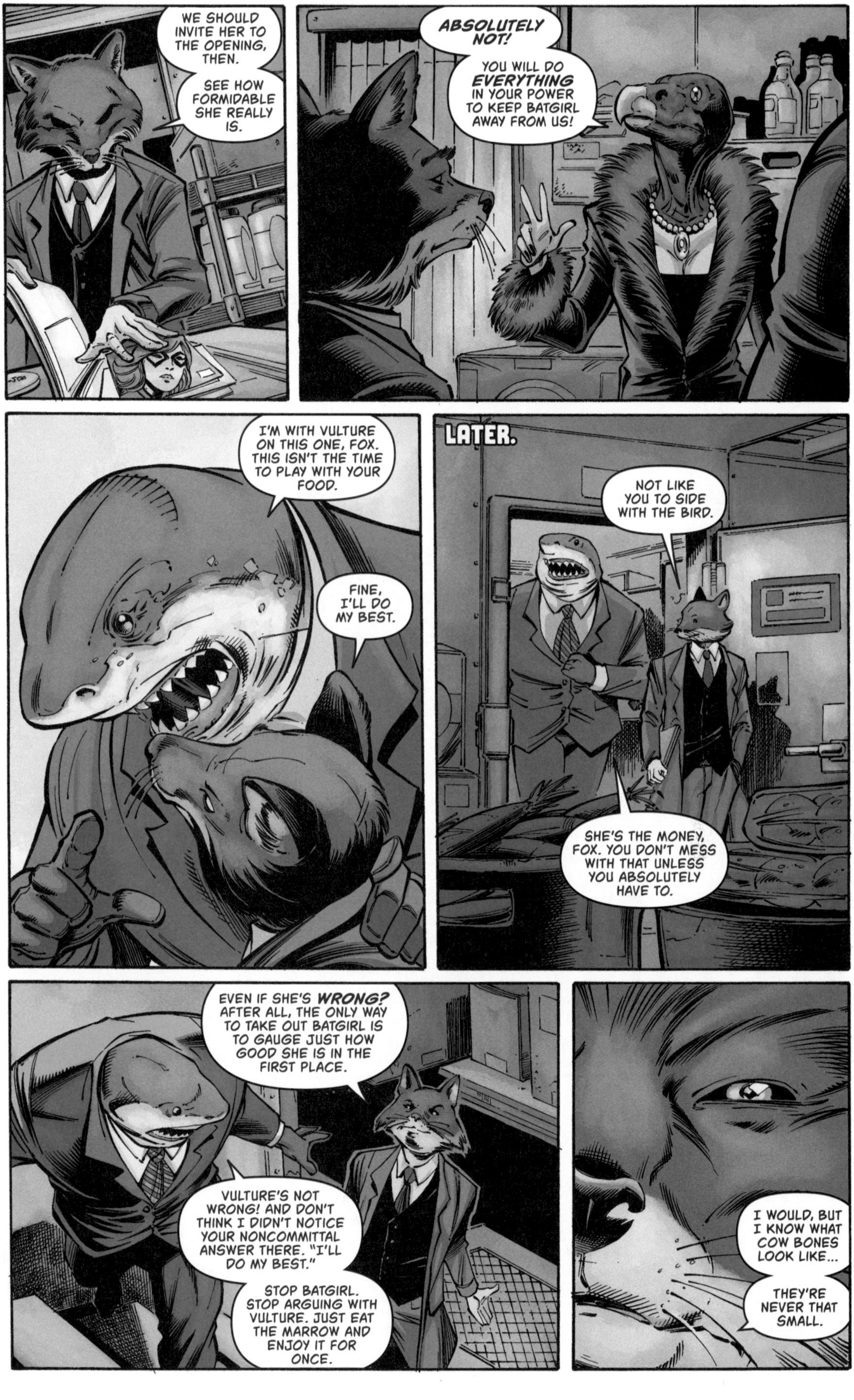
WE SHOULD INVITE HER TO THE OPENING, THEN.
SEE HOW FORMIDABLE SHE REALLY IS.
ABSOLUTELY NOT!
YOU WILL DO EVERYTHING IN YOUR POWER TO KEEP BATGIRL AWAY FROM US!
I'M WITH VULTURE ON THIS ONE, FOX. THIS ISN'T THE TIME TO PLAY WITH YOUR FOOD.
FINE, I'LL DO MY BEST.
LATER.
NOT LIKE YOU TO SIDE WITH THE BIRD.
SHE'S THE MONEY, FOX. YOU DON'T MESS WITH THAT UNLESS YOU ABSOLUTELY HAVE TO.
EVEN IF SHE'S WRONG? AFTER ALL, THE ONLY WAY TO TAKE OUT BATGIRL IS TO GAUGE JUST HOW GOOD SHE IS IN THE FIRST PLACE.
VULTURE'S NOT WRONG! AND DON'T THINK I DIDN'T NOTICE YOUR NONCOMMITTAL ANSWER THERE. "I'LL DO MY BEST."
STOP BATGIRL. STOP ARGUING WITH VULTURE. JUST EAT THE MARROW AND ENJOY IT FOR ONCE.
I WOULD, BUT I KNOW WHAT COW BONES LOOK LIKE...
THEY'RE NEVER THAT SMALL.

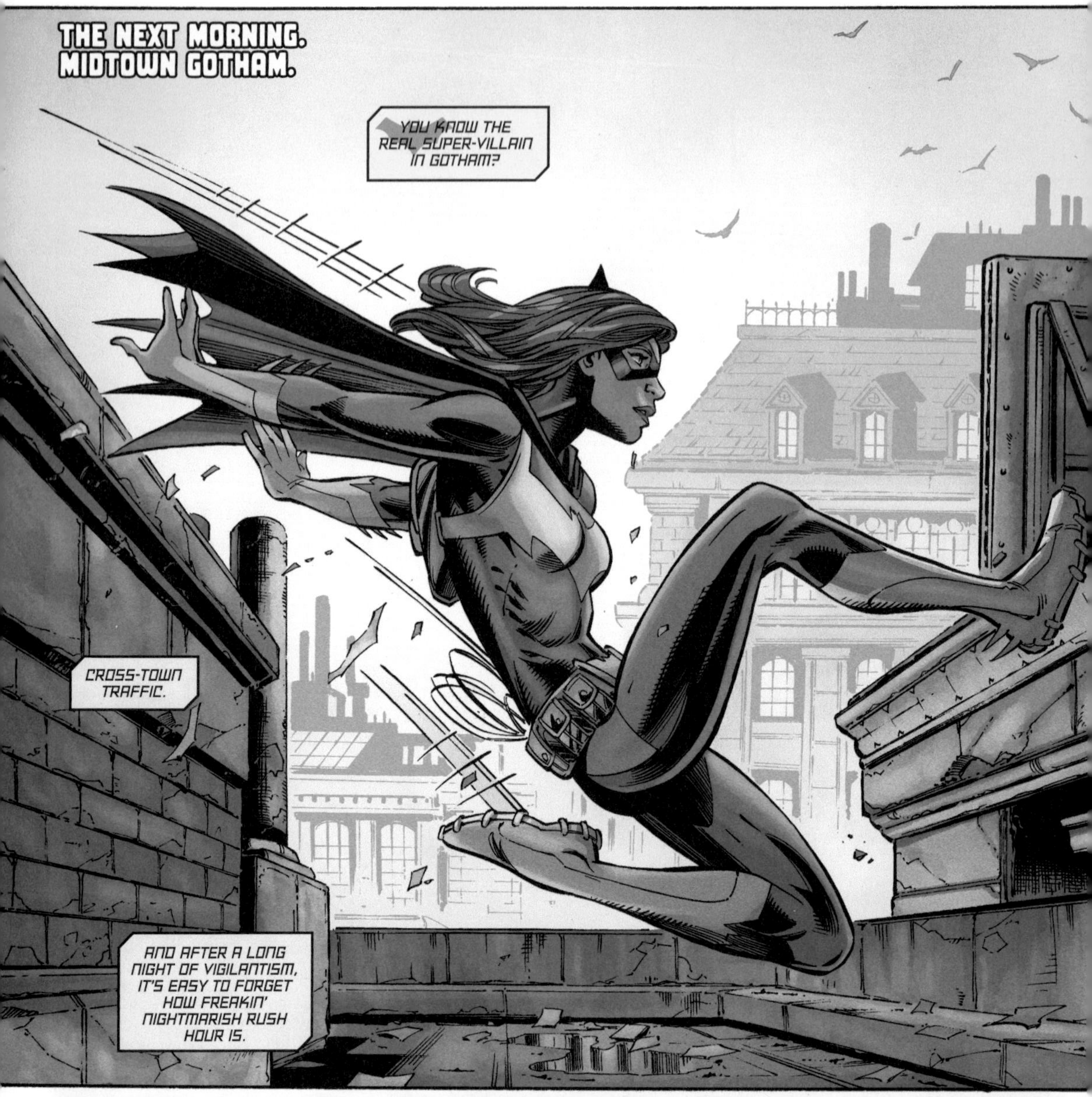
THE NEXT MORNING. MIDTOWN GOTHAM.
YOU KNOW THE REAL SUPER-VILLAIN IN GOTHAM?
CROSS-TOWN TRAFFIC.
AND AFTER A LONG NIGHT OF VIGILANTISM, IT'S EASY TO FORGET HOW FREAKIN' NIGHTMARISH RUSH HOUR IS.

TERRIBLE PART 1 OF 3

Mairghread Scott writer Paul Pelletier penciller Norm Rapmund inker
Jordie Bellaire colorist AndWorld Design letterer
Brittany Holzherr editor Brian Cunningham group editor

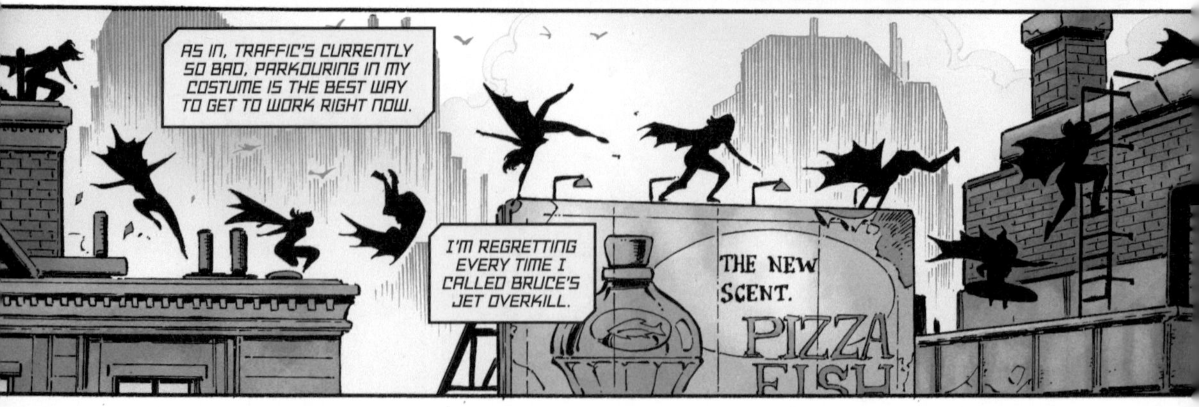
AS IN, TRAFFIC'S CURRENTLY SO BAD, PARKOURING IN MY COSTUME IS THE BEST WAY TO GET TO WORK RIGHT NOW.
I'M REGRETTING EVERY TIME I CALLED BRUCE'S JET OVERKILL.
THE NEW SCENT.
PIZZA

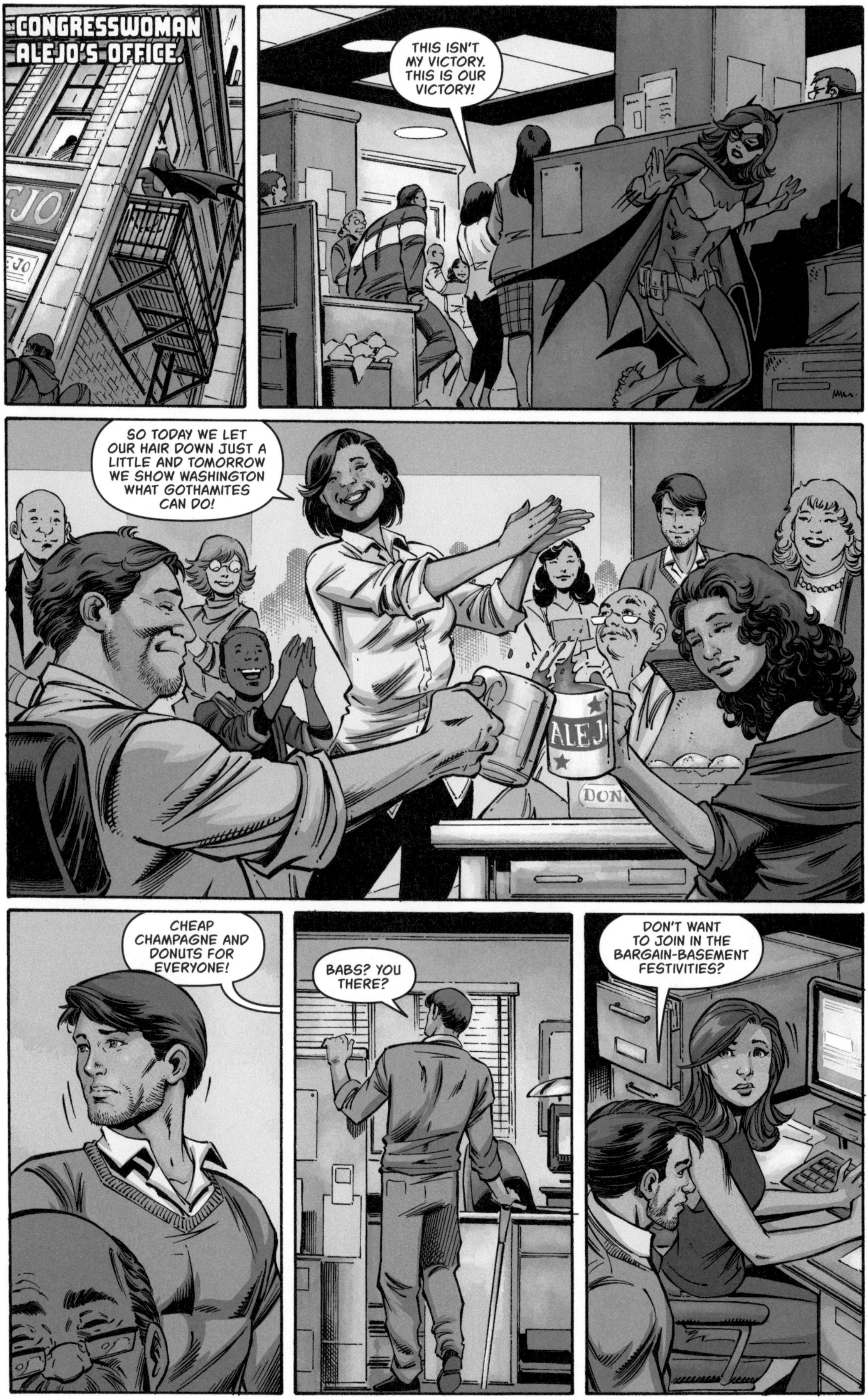
CONGRESSWOMAN ALEJO'S OFFICE.
FJO
EJO
THIS ISN'T MY VICTORY. THIS IS OUR VICTORY!
SO TODAY WE LET OUR HAIR DOWN JUST A LITTLE AND TOMORROW WE SHOW WASHINGTON WHAT GOTHAMITES CAN DO!
ALEJ
DON
CHEAP CHAMPAGNE AND DONUTS FOR EVERYONE!
BABS? YOU THERE?
DON'T WANT TO JOIN IN THE BARGAIN-BASEMENT FESTIVITIES?

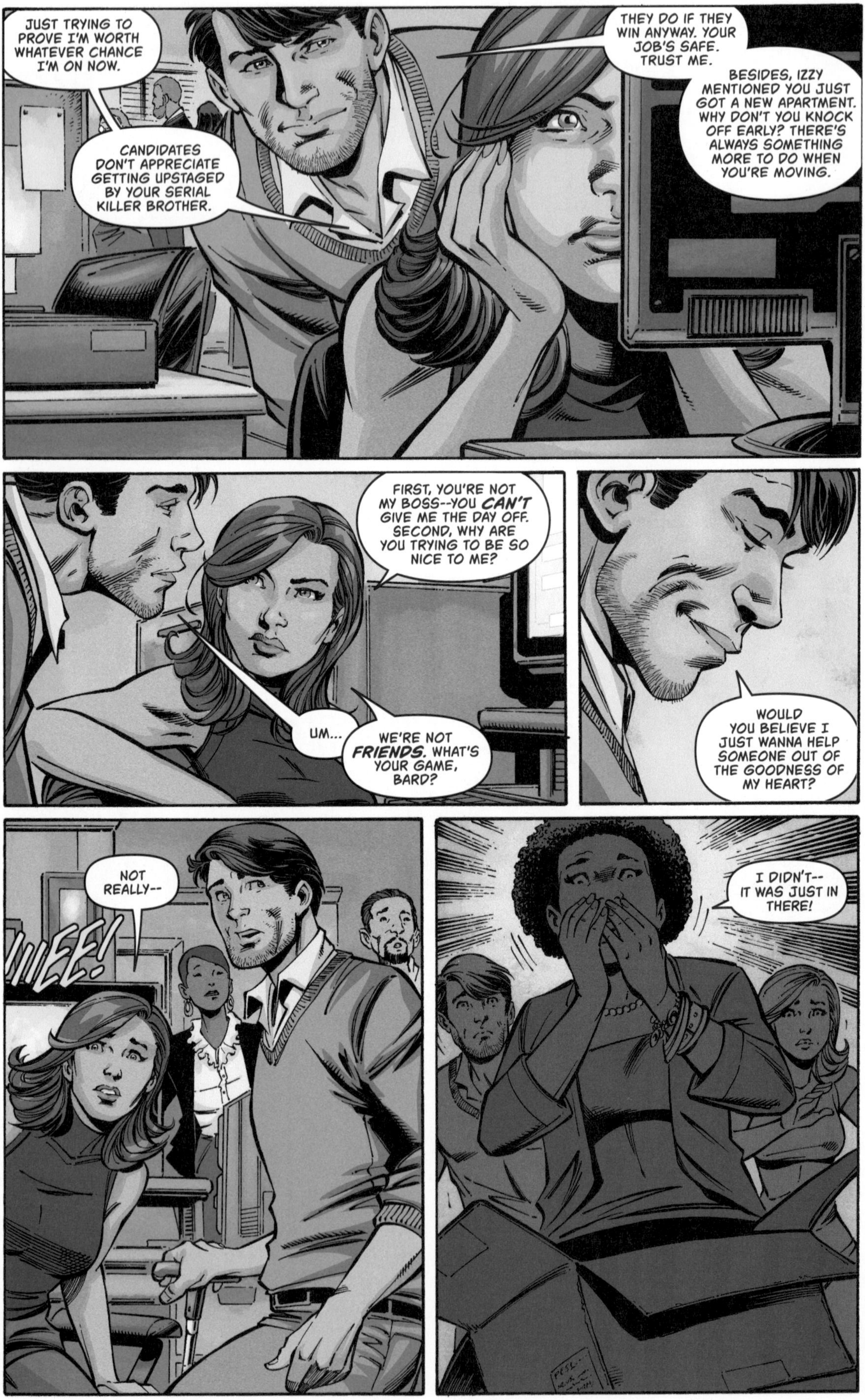
JUST TRYING TO PROVE I'M WORTH WHATEVER CHANCE I'M ON NOW.
CANDIDATES DON'T APPRECIATE GETTING UPSTAGED BY YOUR SERIAL KILLER BROTHER.
THEY DO IF THEY WIN ANYWAY. YOUR JOB'S SAFE. TRUST ME.
BESIDES, IZZY MENTIONED YOU JUST GOT A NEW APARTMENT. WHY DON'T YOU KNOCK OFF EARLY? THERE'S ALWAYS SOMETHING MORE TO DO WHEN YOU'RE MOVING.
FIRST, YOU'RE NOT MY BOSS--YOU ***CAN'T*** GIVE ME THE DAY OFF. SECOND, WHY ARE YOU TRYING TO BE SO NICE TO ME?
UM...
WE'RE NOT ***FRIENDS.*** WHAT'S YOUR GAME, BARD?
WOULD YOU BELIEVE I JUST WANNA HELP SOMEONE OUT OF THE GOODNESS OF MY HEART?
NOT REALLY--
IIIEE!
I DIDN'T-- IT WAS JUST IN THERE!

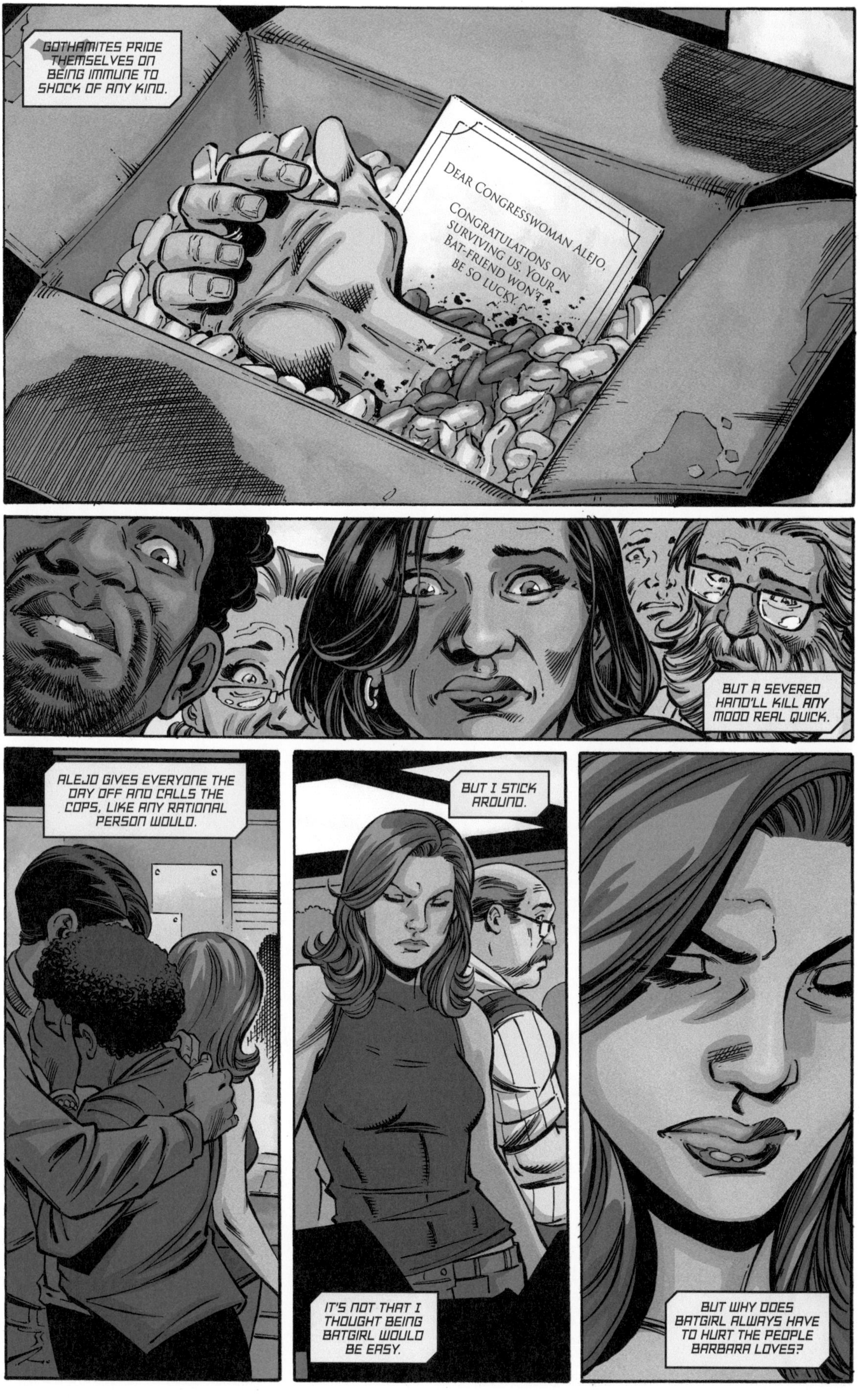
GOTHAMITES PRIDE THEMSELVES ON BEING IMMUNE TO SHOCK OF ANY KIND.
Dear Congresswoman Alejo,
Congratulations on surviving us. Your Bat-friend won't be so lucky.
BUT A SEVERED HAND'LL KILL ANY MOOD REAL QUICK.
ALEJO GIVES EVERYONE THE DAY OFF AND CALLS THE COPS, LIKE ANY RATIONAL PERSON WOULD.
BUT I STICK AROUND.
IT'S NOT THAT I THOUGHT BEING BATGIRL WOULD BE EASY.
BUT WHY DOES BATGIRL ALWAYS HAVE TO HURT THE PEOPLE BARBARA LOVES?

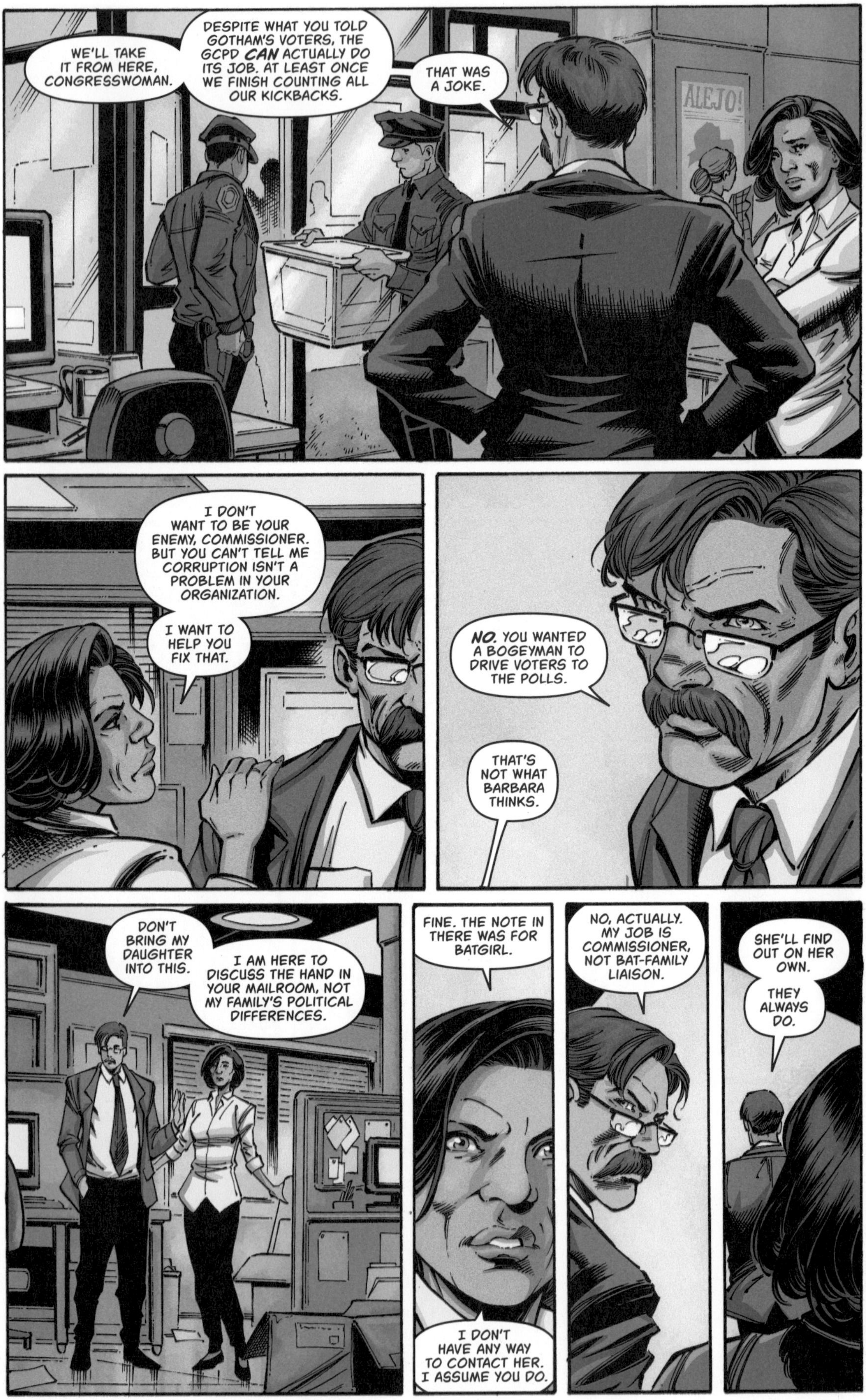
WE'LL TAKE IT FROM HERE, CONGRESSWOMAN.
DESPITE WHAT YOU TOLD GOTHAM'S VOTERS, THE GCPD **CAN** ACTUALLY DO ITS JOB. AT LEAST ONCE WE FINISH COUNTING ALL OUR KICKBACKS.
THAT WAS A JOKE.
ALEJO!
I DON'T WANT TO BE YOUR ENEMY, COMMISSIONER. BUT YOU CAN'T TELL ME CORRUPTION ISN'T A PROBLEM IN YOUR ORGANIZATION.
I WANT TO HELP YOU FIX THAT.
NO. YOU WANTED A BOGEYMAN TO DRIVE VOTERS TO THE POLLS.
THAT'S NOT WHAT BARBARA THINKS.
DON'T BRING MY DAUGHTER INTO THIS.
I AM HERE TO DISCUSS THE HAND IN YOUR MAILROOM, NOT MY FAMILY'S POLITICAL DIFFERENCES.
FINE. THE NOTE IN THERE WAS FOR BATGIRL.
I DON'T HAVE ANY WAY TO CONTACT HER. I ASSUME YOU DO.
NO, ACTUALLY. MY JOB IS COMMISSIONER, NOT BAT-FAMILY LIAISON.
SHE'LL FIND OUT ON HER OWN.
THEY ALWAYS DO.

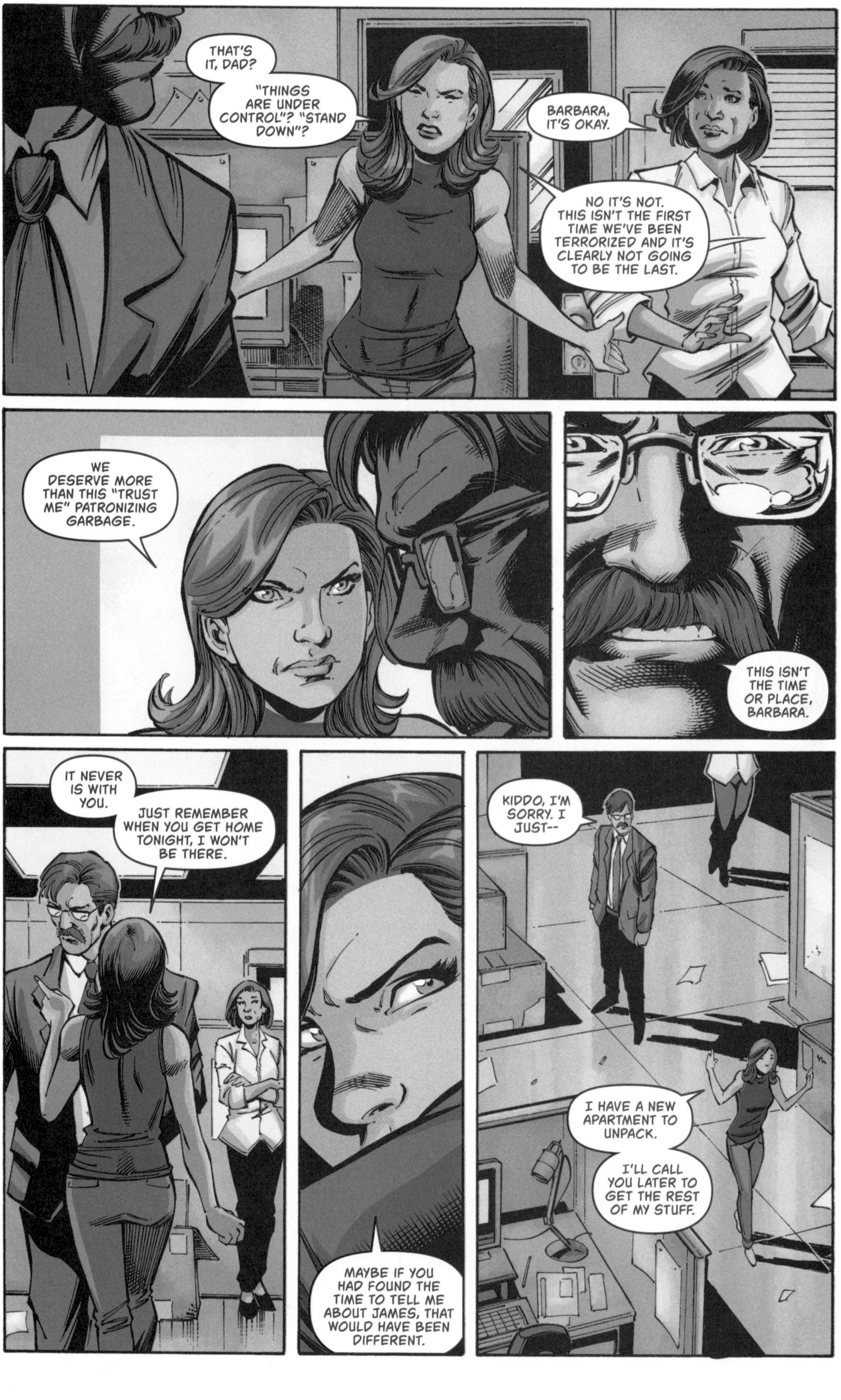
THAT'S IT, DAD?
"THINGS ARE UNDER CONTROL"? "STAND DOWN"?
BARBARA, IT'S OKAY.
NO IT'S NOT. THIS ISN'T THE FIRST TIME WE'VE BEEN TERRORIZED AND IT'S CLEARLY NOT GOING TO BE THE LAST.
WE DESERVE MORE THAN THIS "TRUST ME" PATRONIZING GARBAGE.
THIS ISN'T THE TIME OR PLACE, BARBARA.
IT NEVER IS WITH YOU.
JUST REMEMBER WHEN YOU GET HOME TONIGHT, I WON'T BE THERE.
MAYBE IF YOU HAD FOUND THE TIME TO TELL ME ABOUT JAMES, THAT WOULD HAVE BEEN DIFFERENT.
KIDDO, I'M SORRY. I JUST--
I HAVE A NEW APARTMENT TO UNPACK.
I'LL CALL YOU LATER TO GET THE REST OF MY STUFF.

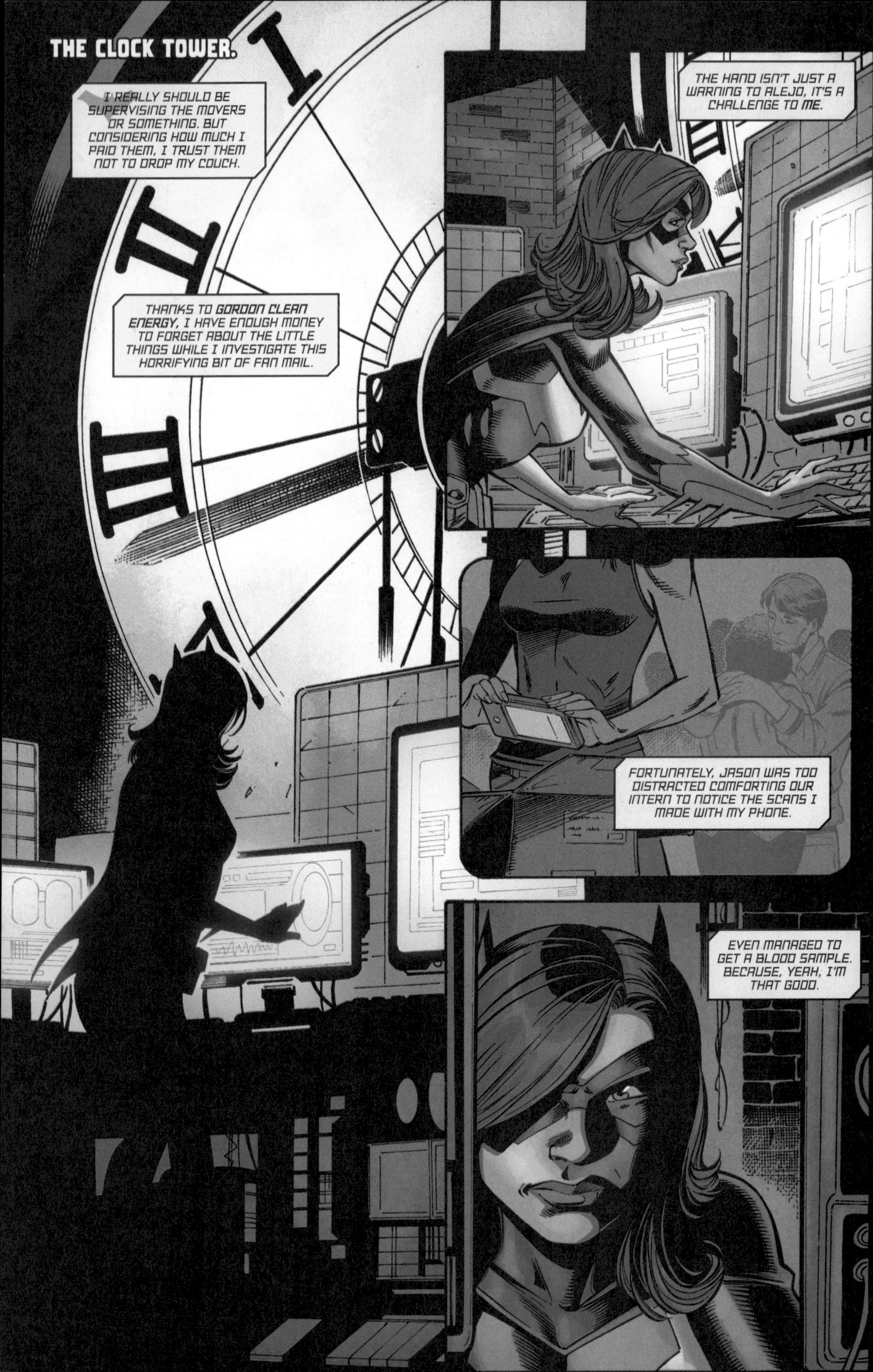
THE CLOCK TOWER.
I REALLY SHOULD BE SUPERVISING THE MOVERS OR SOMETHING. BUT CONSIDERING HOW MUCH I PAID THEM, I TRUST THEM NOT TO DROP MY COUCH.
THANKS TO GORDON CLEAN ENERGY, I HAVE ENOUGH MONEY TO FORGET ABOUT THE LITTLE THINGS WHILE I INVESTIGATE THIS HORRIFYING BIT OF FAN MAIL.
THE HAND ISN'T JUST A WARNING TO ALEJO, IT'S A CHALLENGE TO ME.
FORTUNATELY, JASON WAS TOO DISTRACTED COMFORTING OUR INTERN TO NOTICE THE SCANS I MADE WITH MY PHONE.
EVEN MANAGED TO GET A BLOOD SAMPLE. BECAUSE, YEAH, I'M THAT GOOD.

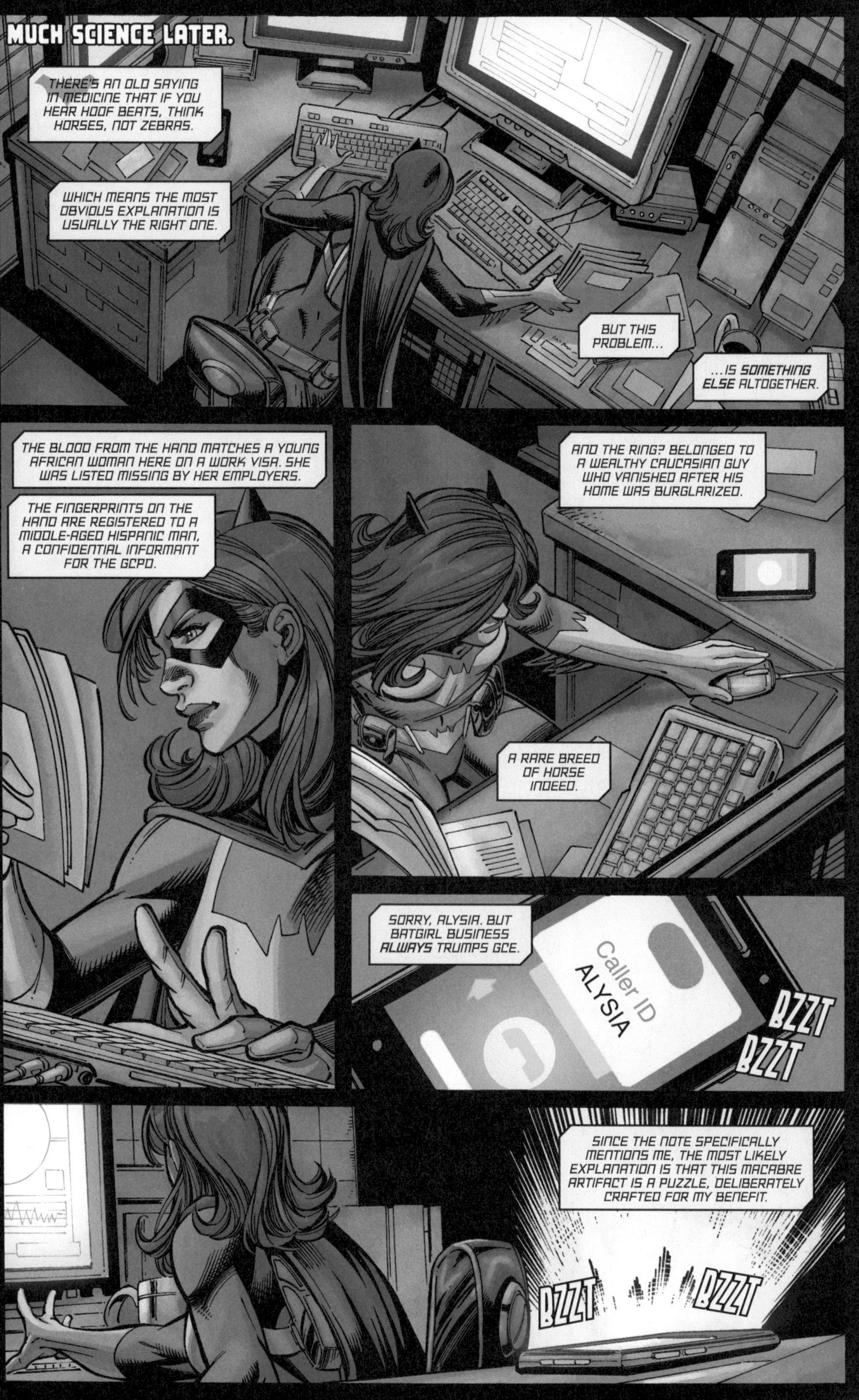
MUCH SCIENCE LATER.
THERE'S AN OLD SAYING IN MEDICINE THAT IF YOU HEAR HOOF BEATS, THINK HORSES, NOT ZEBRAS.
WHICH MEANS THE MOST OBVIOUS EXPLANATION IS USUALLY THE RIGHT ONE.
BUT THIS PROBLEM...
...IS SOMETHING ELSE ALTOGETHER.
THE BLOOD FROM THE HAND MATCHES A YOUNG AFRICAN WOMAN HERE ON A WORK VISA. SHE WAS LISTED MISSING BY HER EMPLOYERS.
THE FINGERPRINTS ON THE HAND ARE REGISTERED TO A MIDDLE-AGED HISPANIC MAN, A CONFIDENTIAL INFORMANT FOR THE GCPD.
AND THE RING? BELONGED TO A WEALTHY CAUCASIAN GUY WHO VANISHED AFTER HIS HOME WAS BURGLARIZED.
A RARE BREED OF HORSE INDEED.
SORRY, ALYSIA. BUT BATGIRL BUSINESS ALWAYS TRUMPS GCE.
Caller ID
ALYSIA
BZZT
BZZT
SINCE THE NOTE SPECIFICALLY MENTIONS ME, THE MOST LIKELY EXPLANATION IS THAT THIS MACABRE ARTIFACT IS A PUZZLE, DELIBERATELY CRAFTED FOR MY BENEFIT.
BZZT
BZZT

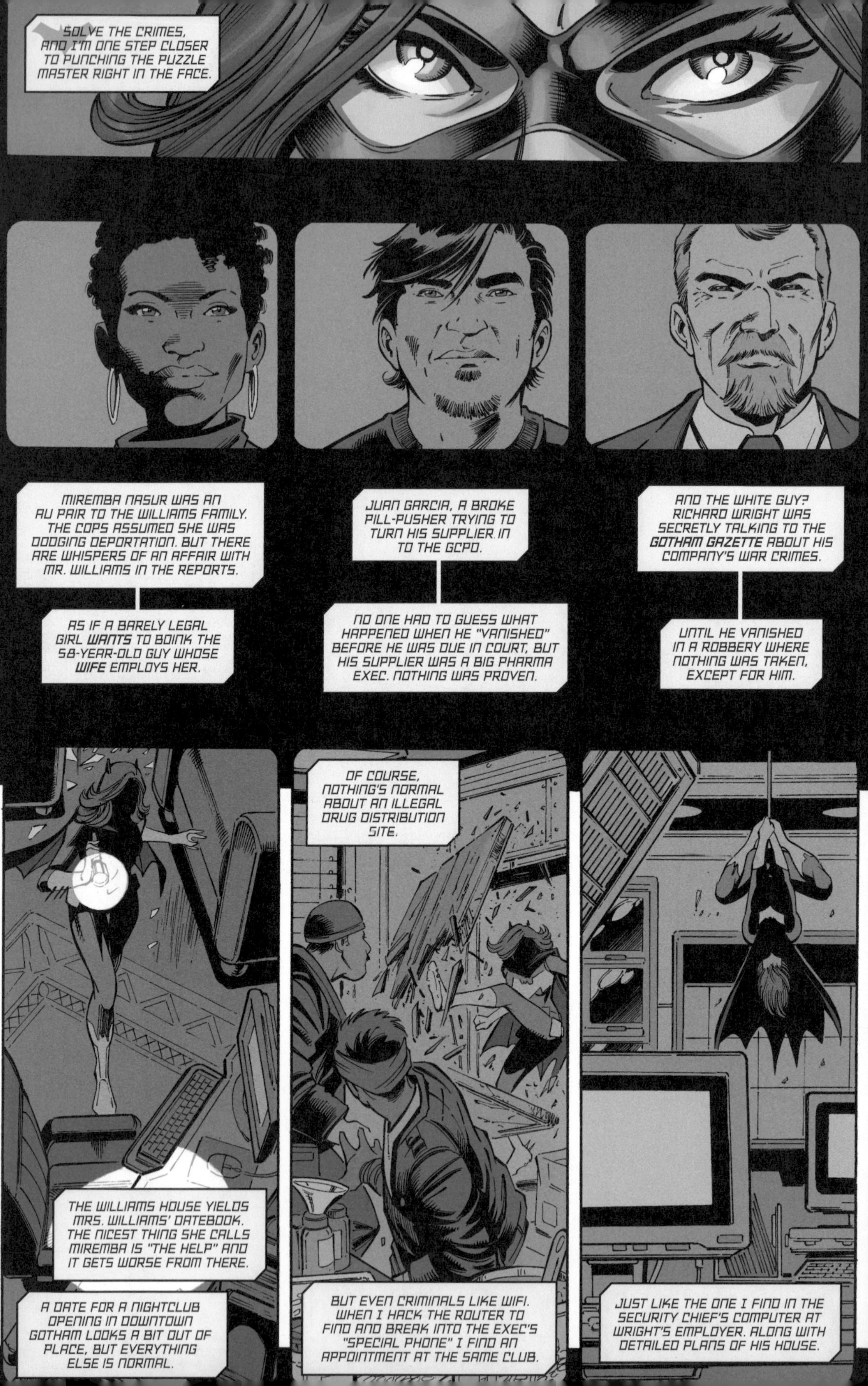
SOLVE THE CRIMES, AND I'M ONE STEP CLOSER TO PUNCHING THE PUZZLE MASTER RIGHT IN THE FACE.
MIREMBA NASUR WAS AN AU PAIR TO THE WILLIAMS FAMILY. THE COPS ASSUMED SHE WAS DODGING DEPORTATION. BUT THERE ARE WHISPERS OF AN AFFAIR WITH MR. WILLIAMS IN THE REPORTS.
AS IF A BARELY LEGAL GIRL **WANTS** TO BOINK THE 58-YEAR-OLD GUY WHOSE **WIFE** EMPLOYS HER.
JUAN GARCIA, A BROKE PILL-PUSHER TRYING TO TURN HIS SUPPLIER IN TO THE GCPD.
NO ONE HAD TO GUESS WHAT HAPPENED WHEN HE "VANISHED" BEFORE HE WAS DUE IN COURT, BUT HIS SUPPLIER WAS A BIG PHARMA EXEC. NOTHING WAS PROVEN.
AND THE WHITE GUY? RICHARD WRIGHT WAS SECRETLY TALKING TO THE ***GOTHAM GAZETTE*** ABOUT HIS COMPANY'S WAR CRIMES.
UNTIL HE VANISHED IN A ROBBERY WHERE NOTHING WAS TAKEN, EXCEPT FOR HIM.
THE WILLIAMS HOUSE YIELDS MRS. WILLIAMS' DATEBOOK. THE NICEST THING SHE CALLS MIREMBA IS "THE HELP" AND IT GETS WORSE FROM THERE.
A DATE FOR A NIGHTCLUB OPENING IN DOWNTOWN GOTHAM LOOKS A BIT OUT OF PLACE, BUT EVERYTHING ELSE IS NORMAL.
OF COURSE, NOTHING'S NORMAL ABOUT AN ILLEGAL DRUG DISTRIBUTION SITE.
BUT EVEN CRIMINALS LIKE WIFI. WHEN I HACK THE ROUTER TO FIND AND BREAK INTO THE EXEC'S "SPECIAL PHONE" I FIND AN APPOINTMENT AT THE SAME CLUB.
JUST LIKE THE ONE I FIND IN THE SECURITY CHIEF'S COMPUTER AT WRIGHT'S EMPLOYER. ALONG WITH DETAILED PLANS OF HIS HOUSE.

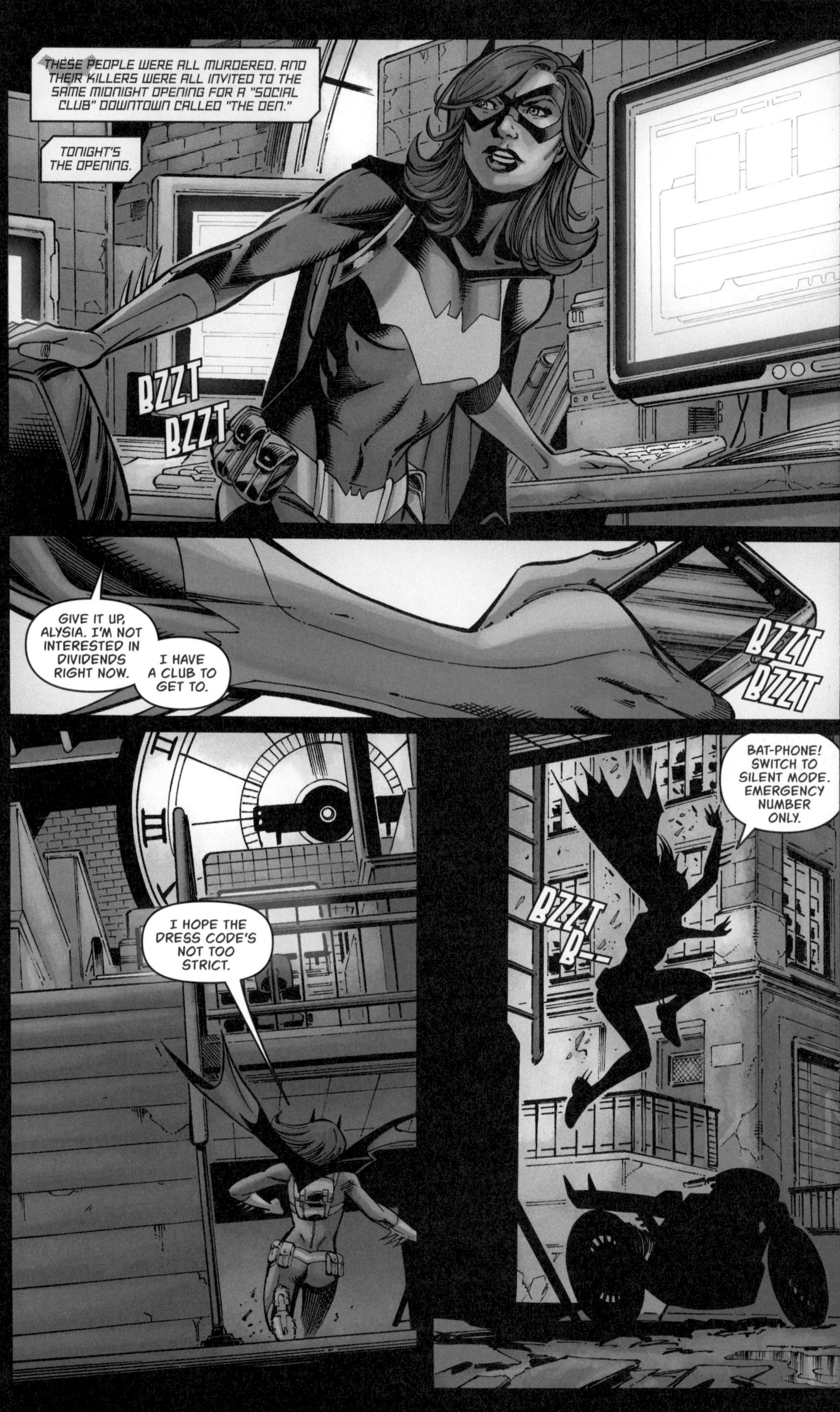
THESE PEOPLE WERE ALL MURDERED. AND THEIR KILLERS WERE ALL INVITED TO THE SAME MIDNIGHT OPENING FOR A "SOCIAL CLUB" DOWNTOWN CALLED "THE DEN."
TONIGHT'S THE OPENING.
BZZT BZZT
GIVE IT UP, ALYSIA. I'M NOT INTERESTED IN DIVIDENDS RIGHT NOW.
I HAVE A CLUB TO GET TO.
BZZT BZZT
I HOPE THE DRESS CODE'S NOT TOO STRICT.
BAT-PHONE! SWITCH TO SILENT MODE. EMERGENCY NUMBER ONLY.
BZZT B--

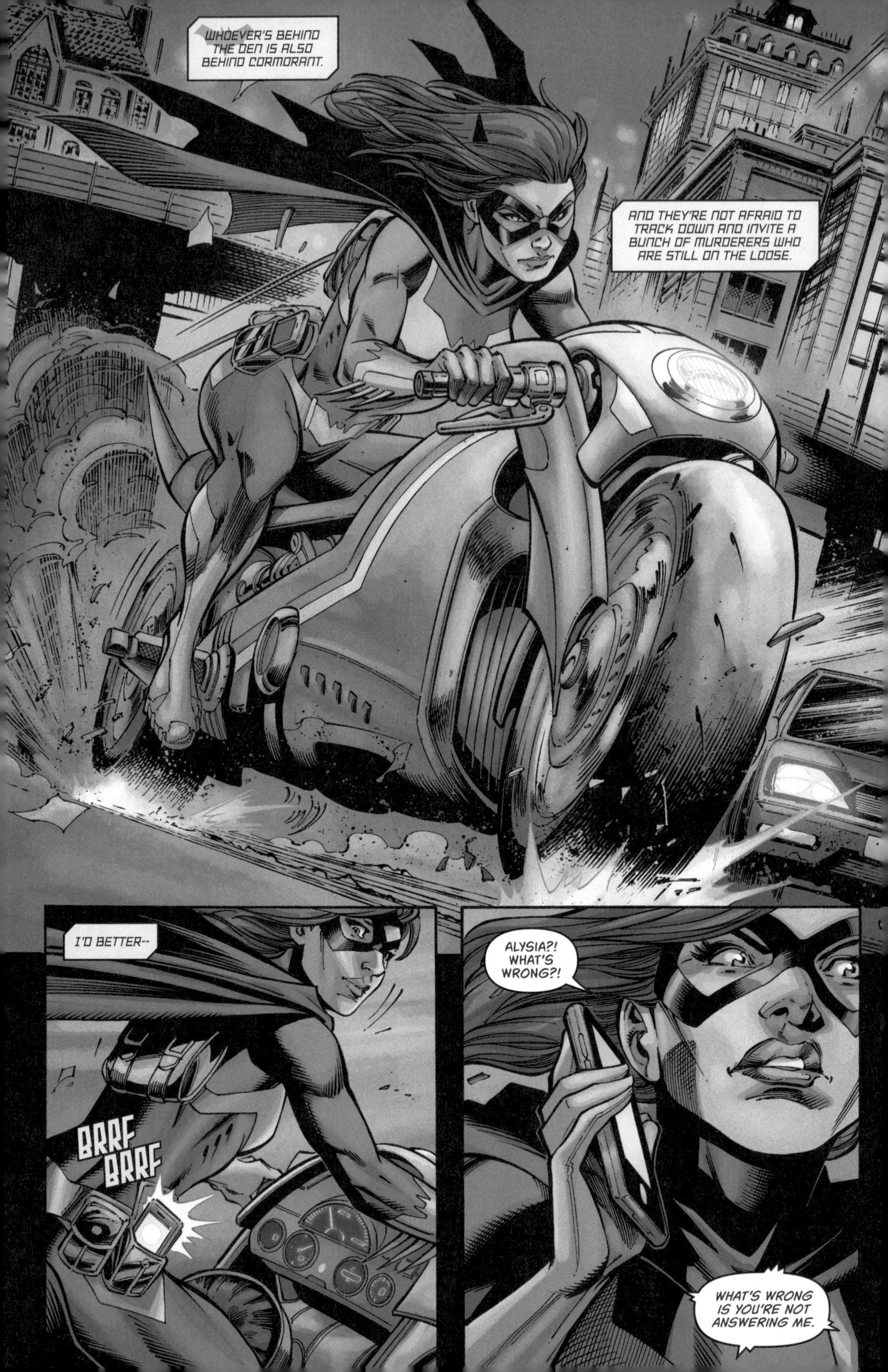
WHOEVER'S BEHIND THE DEN IS ALSO BEHIND CORMORANT.
AND THEY'RE NOT AFRAID TO TRACK DOWN AND INVITE A BUNCH OF MURDERERS WHO ARE STILL ON THE LOOSE.
I'D BETTER--
BRRF BRRF
ALYSIA?! WHAT'S WRONG?!
WHAT'S WRONG IS YOU'RE NOT ANSWERING ME.

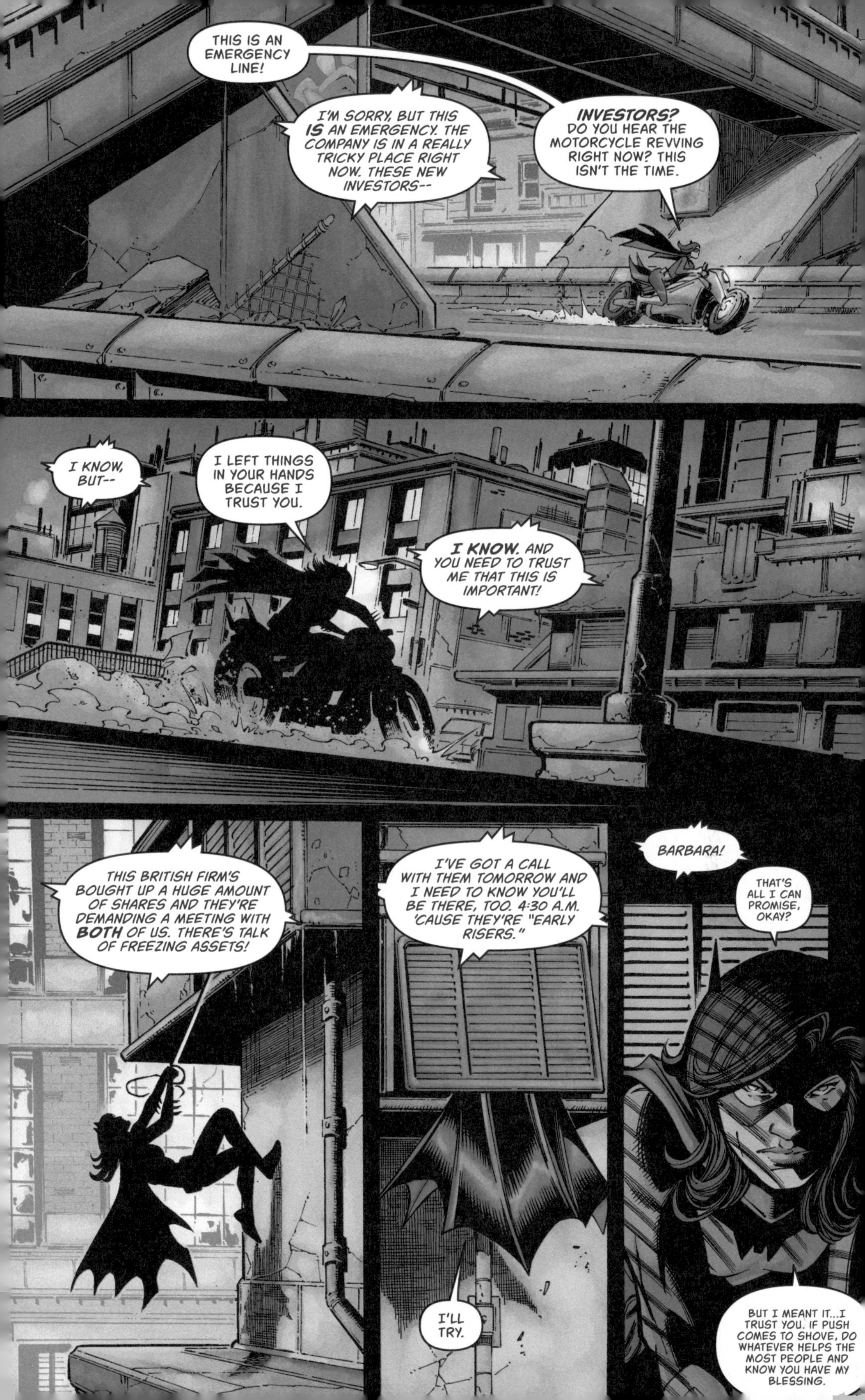
THIS IS AN EMERGENCY LINE!
I'M SORRY, BUT THIS IS AN EMERGENCY. THE COMPANY IS IN A REALLY TRICKY PLACE RIGHT NOW. THESE NEW INVESTORS--
INVESTORS? DO YOU HEAR THE MOTORCYCLE REVVING RIGHT NOW? THIS ISN'T THE TIME.
I KNOW, BUT--
I LEFT THINGS IN YOUR HANDS BECAUSE I TRUST YOU.
I KNOW. AND YOU NEED TO TRUST ME THAT THIS IS IMPORTANT!
THIS BRITISH FIRM'S BOUGHT UP A HUGE AMOUNT OF SHARES AND THEY'RE DEMANDING A MEETING WITH BOTH OF US. THERE'S TALK OF FREEZING ASSETS!
I'VE GOT A CALL WITH THEM TOMORROW AND I NEED TO KNOW YOU'LL BE THERE, TOO. 4:30 A.M. 'CAUSE THEY'RE "EARLY RISERS."
I'LL TRY.
BARBARA!
THAT'S ALL I CAN PROMISE, OKAY?
BUT I MEANT IT...I TRUST YOU. IF PUSH COMES TO SHOVE, DO WHATEVER HELPS THE MOST PEOPLE AND KNOW YOU HAVE MY BLESSING.

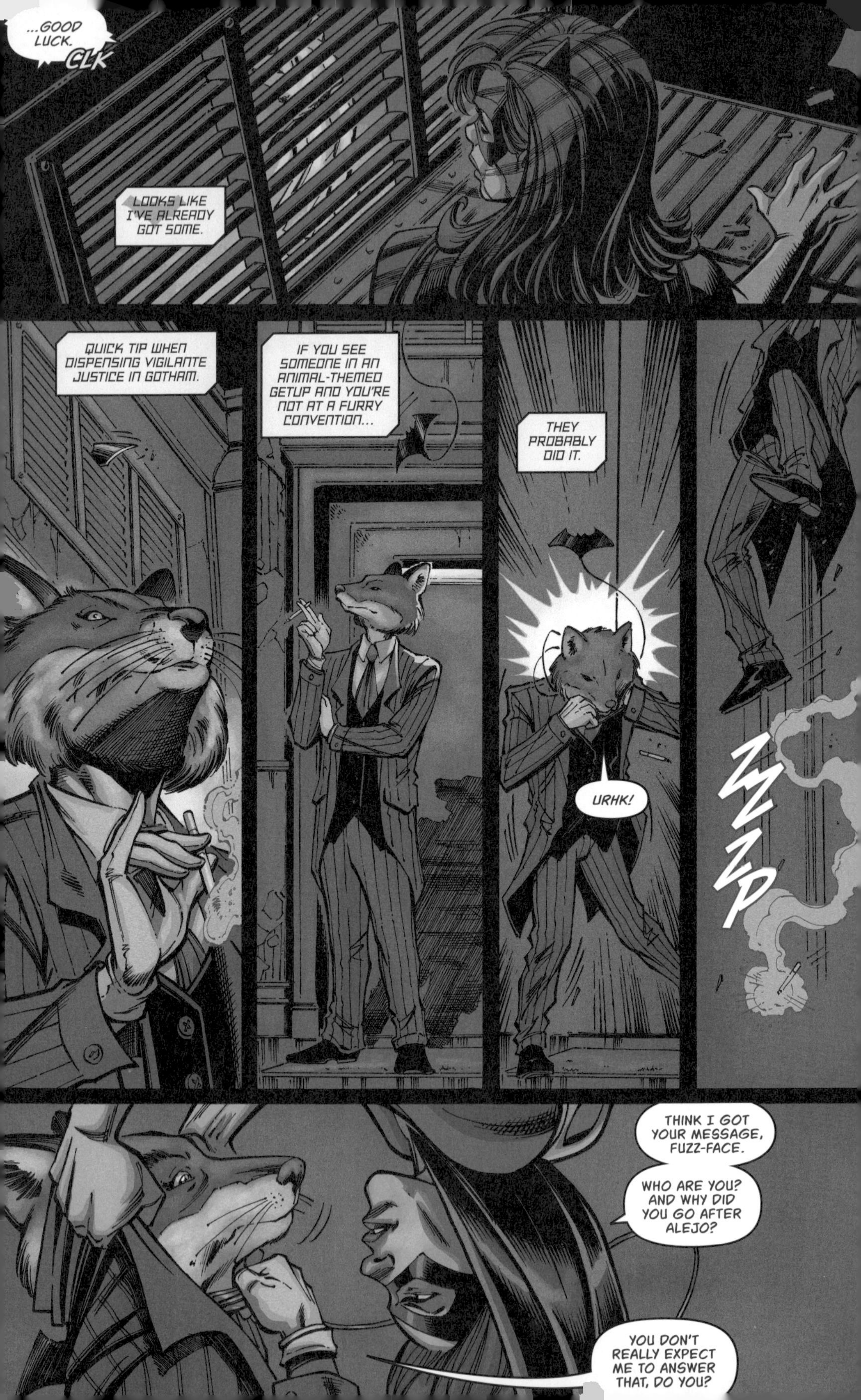
...GOOD LUCK.
CLK
LOOKS LIKE I'VE ALREADY GOT SOME.
QUICK TIP WHEN DISPENSING VIGILANTE JUSTICE IN GOTHAM.
IF YOU SEE SOMEONE IN AN ANIMAL-THEMED GETUP AND YOU'RE NOT AT A FURRY CONVENTION...
THEY PROBABLY DID IT.
URHK!
ZZZP
THINK I GOT YOUR MESSAGE, FUZZ-FACE.
WHO ARE YOU? AND WHY DID YOU GO AFTER ALEJO?
YOU DON'T REALLY EXPECT ME TO ANSWER THAT, DO YOU?

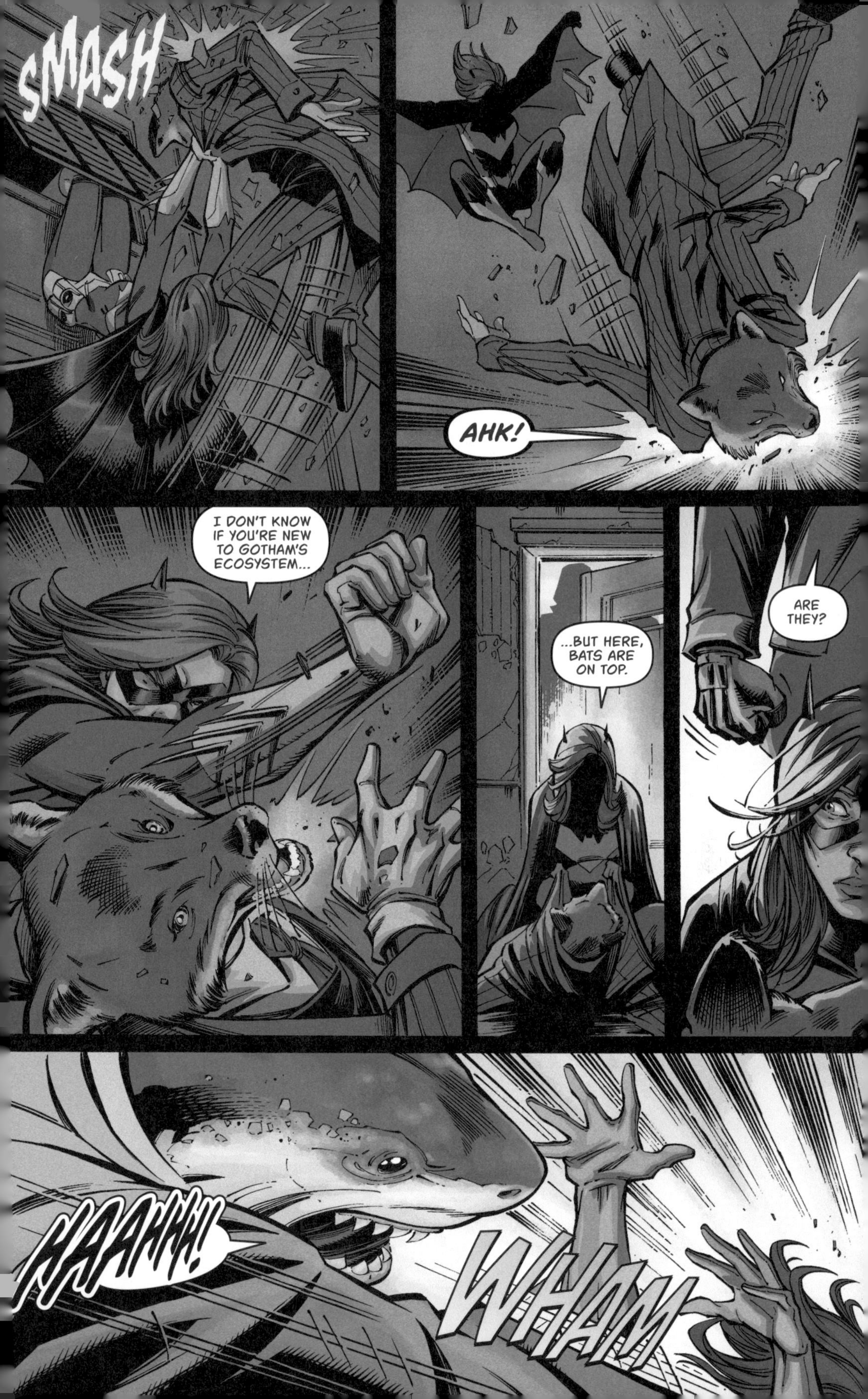
SMASH
AHK!
I DON'T KNOW IF YOU'RE NEW TO GOTHAM'S ECOSYSTEM...
...BUT HERE, BATS ARE ON TOP.
ARE THEY?
HAAAHHH!
WHAM

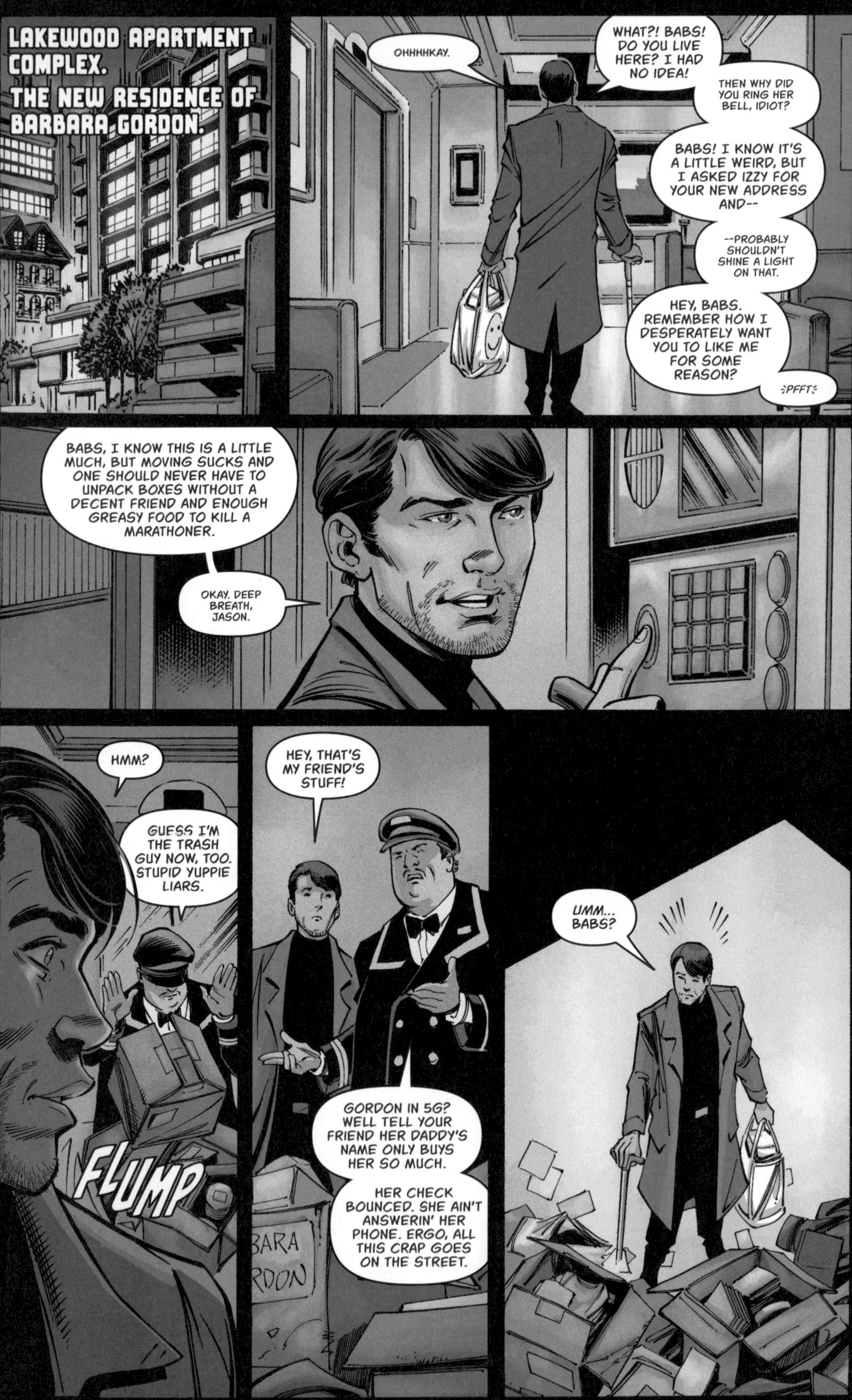
LAKEWOOD APARTMENT COMPLEX.
THE NEW RESIDENCE OF BARBARA GORDON.
OHHHHKAY.
WHAT?! BABS! DO YOU LIVE HERE? I HAD NO IDEA!
THEN WHY DID YOU RING HER BELL, IDIOT?
BABS! I KNOW IT'S A LITTLE WEIRD, BUT I ASKED IZZY FOR YOUR NEW ADDRESS AND--
--PROBABLY SHOULDN'T SHINE A LIGHT ON THAT.
HEY, BABS. REMEMBER HOW I DESPERATELY WANT YOU TO LIKE ME FOR SOME REASON?
PFFT
BABS, I KNOW THIS IS A LITTLE MUCH, BUT MOVING SUCKS AND ONE SHOULD NEVER HAVE TO UNPACK BOXES WITHOUT A DECENT FRIEND AND ENOUGH GREASY FOOD TO KILL A MARATHONER.
OKAY. DEEP BREATH, JASON.
HMM?
GUESS I'M THE TRASH GUY NOW, TOO. STUPID YUPPIE LIARS.
FLUMP
HEY, THAT'S MY FRIEND'S STUFF!
GORDON IN 5G? WELL TELL YOUR FRIEND HER DADDY'S NAME ONLY BUYS HER SO MUCH.
HER CHECK BOUNCED. SHE AIN'T ANSWERIN' HER PHONE. ERGO, ALL THIS CRAP GOES ON THE STREET.
UMM... BABS?

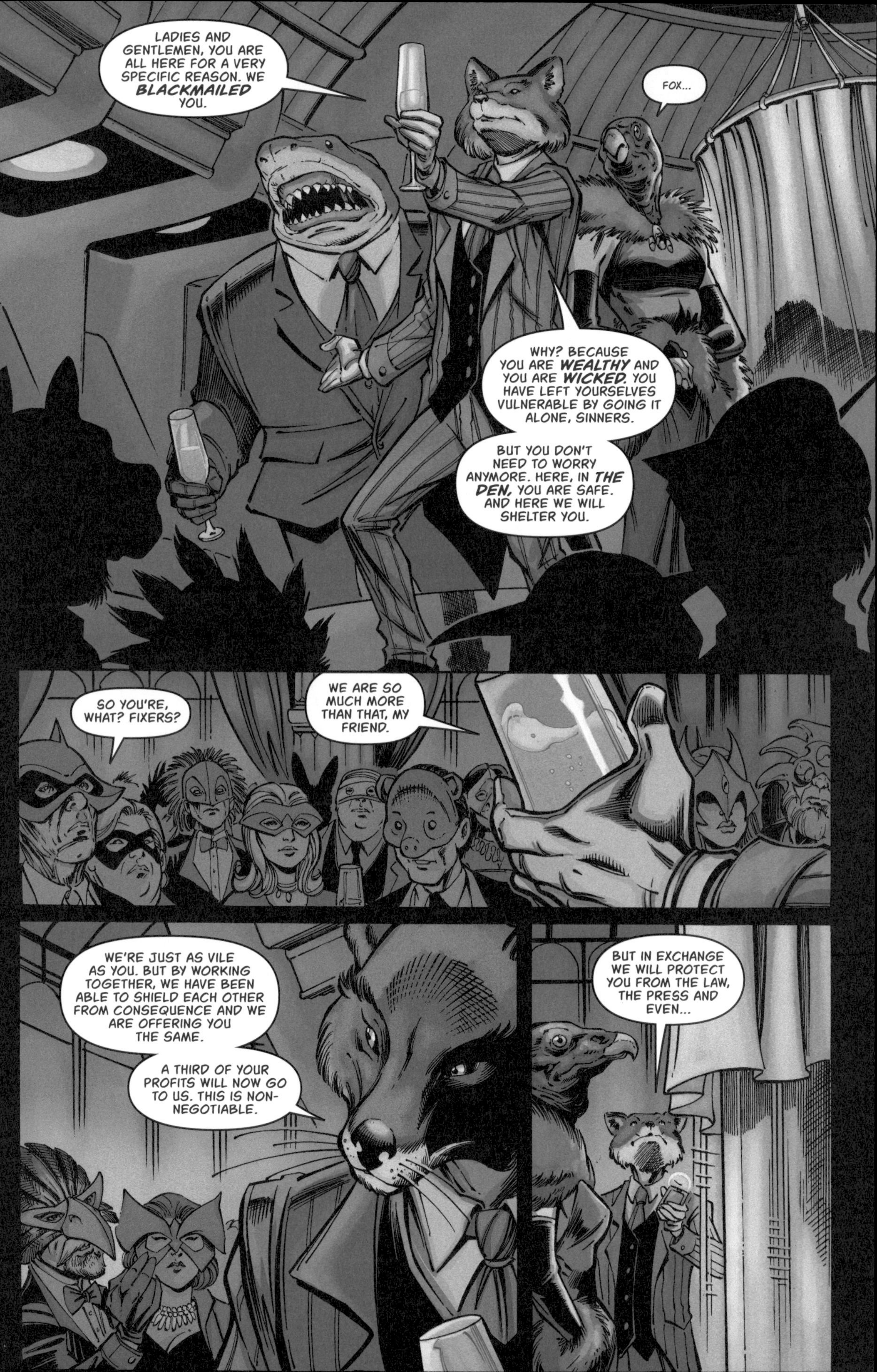
LADIES AND GENTLEMEN, YOU ARE ALL HERE FOR A VERY SPECIFIC REASON. WE BLACKMAILED YOU.
FOX...
WHY? BECAUSE YOU ARE WEALTHY AND YOU ARE WICKED. YOU HAVE LEFT YOURSELVES VULNERABLE BY GOING IT ALONE, SINNERS.
BUT YOU DON'T NEED TO WORRY ANYMORE. HERE, IN THE DEN, YOU ARE SAFE. AND HERE WE WILL SHELTER YOU.
SO YOU'RE, WHAT? FIXERS?
WE ARE SO MUCH MORE THAN THAT, MY FRIEND.
WE'RE JUST AS VILE AS YOU. BUT BY WORKING TOGETHER, WE HAVE BEEN ABLE TO SHIELD EACH OTHER FROM CONSEQUENCE AND WE ARE OFFERING YOU THE SAME.
A THIRD OF YOUR PROFITS WILL NOW GO TO US. THIS IS NON-NEGOTIABLE.
BUT IN EXCHANGE WE WILL PROTECT YOU FROM THE LAW, THE PRESS AND EVEN...

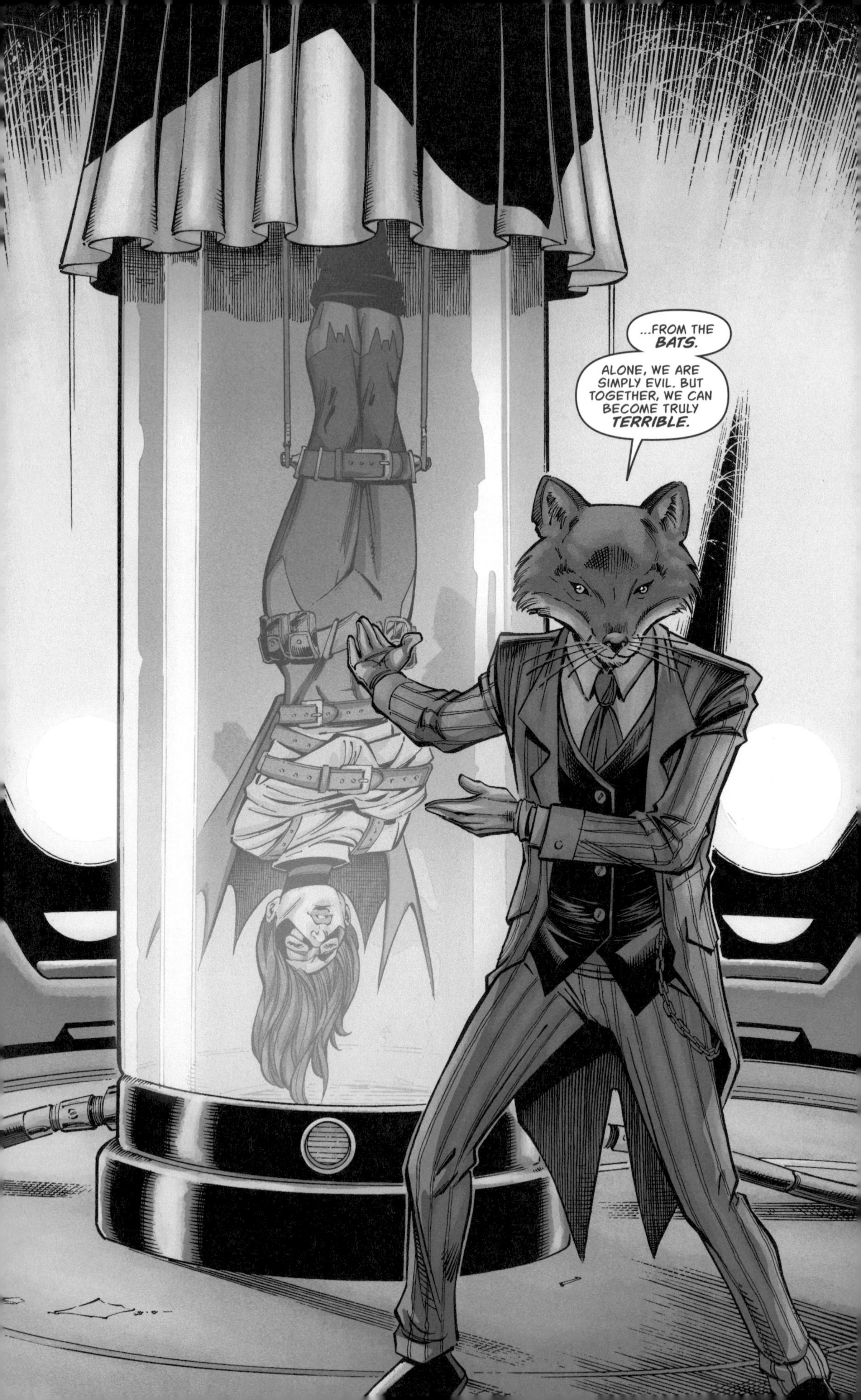
...FROM THE BATS.
ALONE, WE ARE SIMPLY EVIL. BUT TOGETHER, WE CAN BECOME TRULY TERRIBLE.

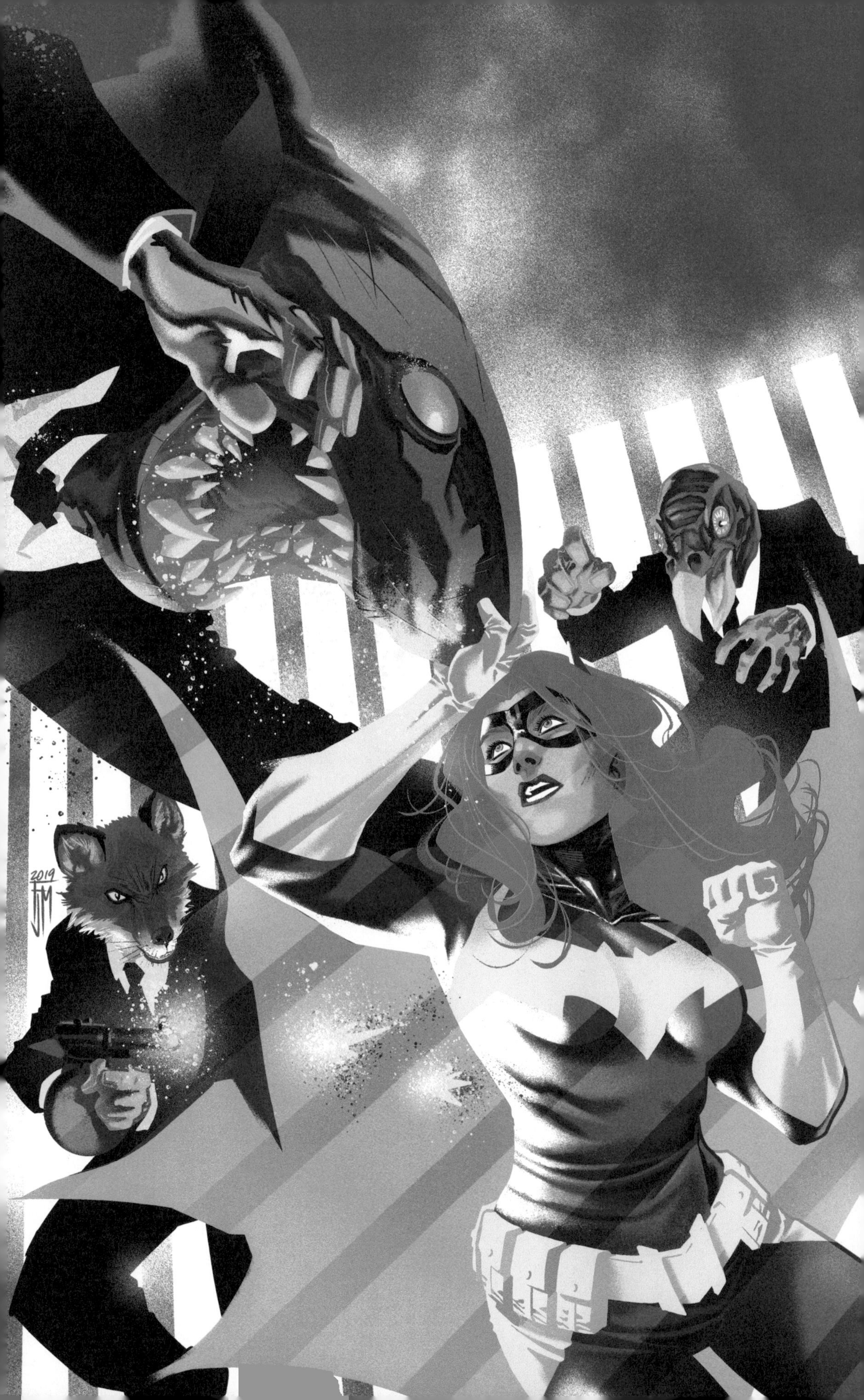
2019

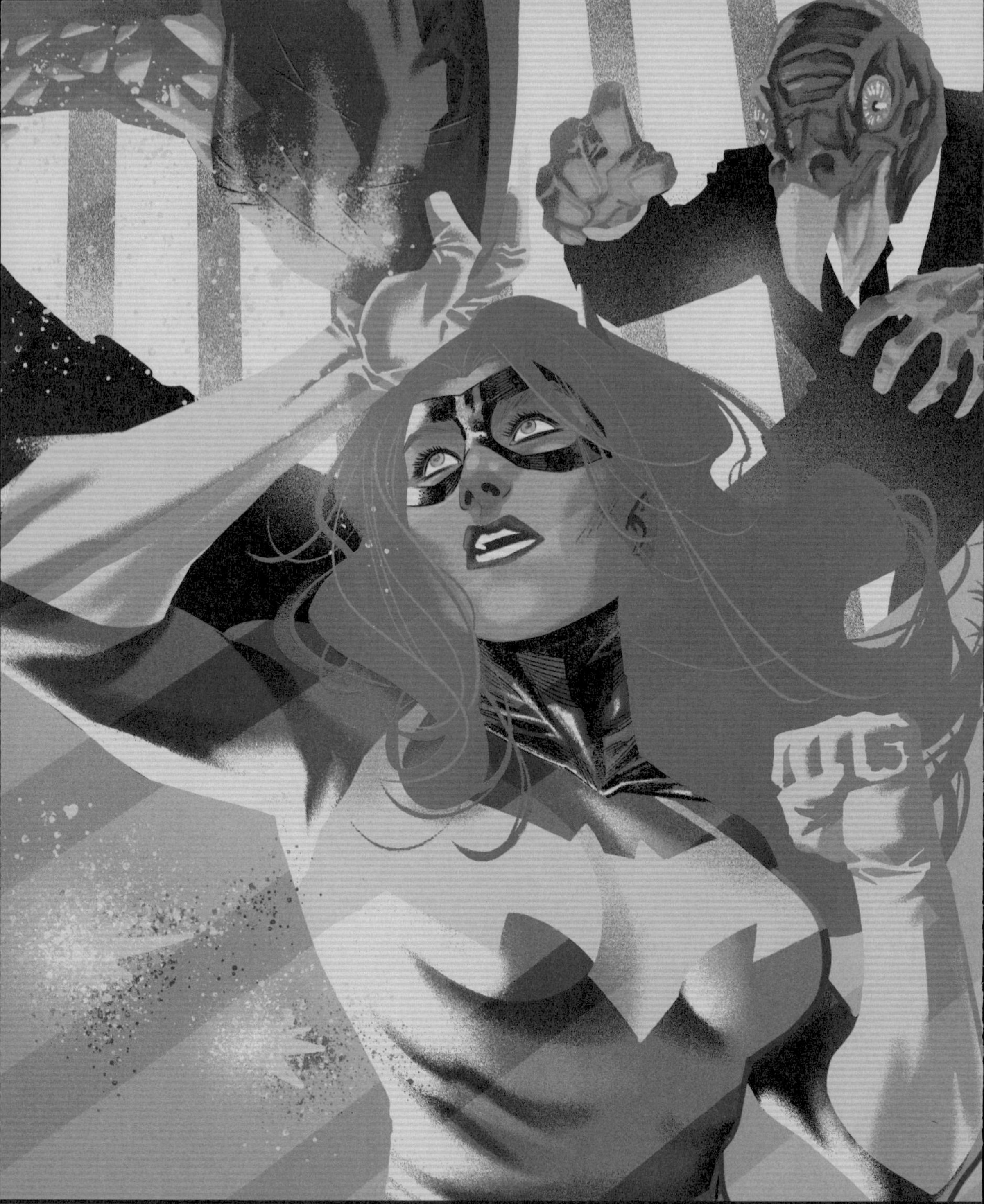

BATGIRL
#35

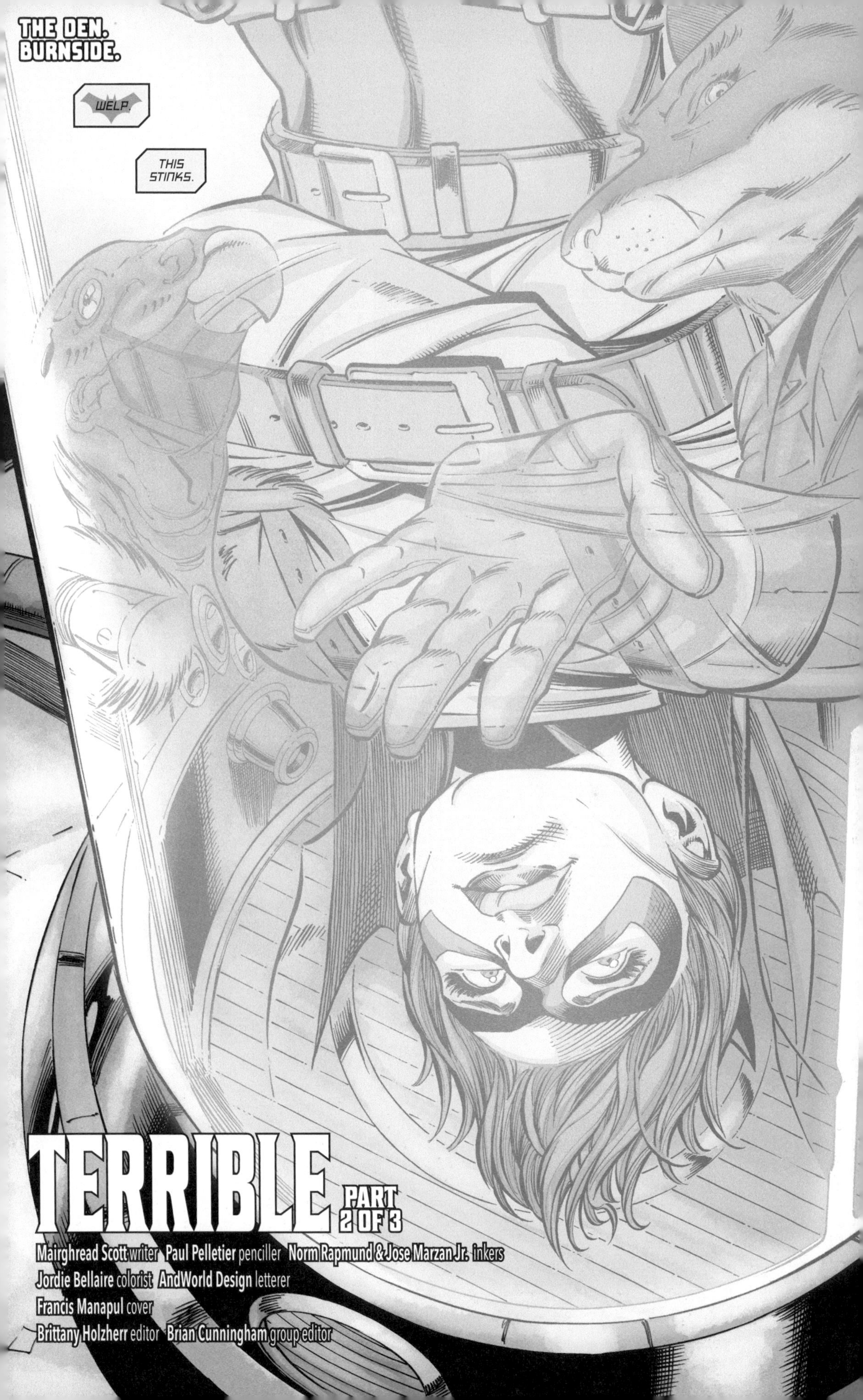
THE DEN. BURNSIDE.
WELP.
THIS STINKS.
TERRIBLE PART 2 OF 3
Mairghread Scott writer Paul Pelletier penciller Norm Rapmund & Jose Marzan Jr. inkers
Jordie Bellaire colorist AndWorld Design letterer
Francis Manapul cover
Brittany Holzherr editor Brian Cunningham group editor

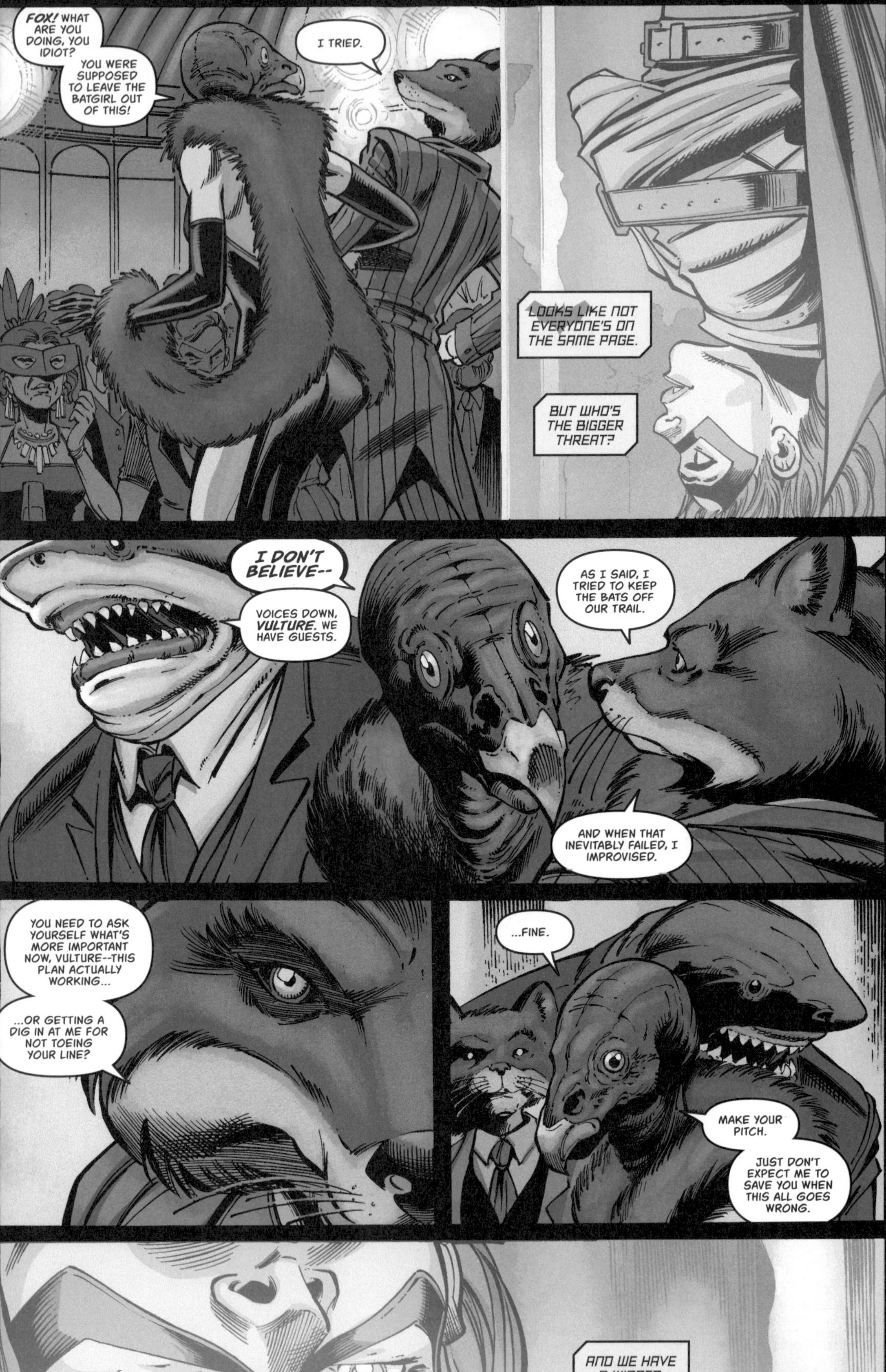
FOX! WHAT ARE YOU DOING, YOU IDIOT?
YOU WERE SUPPOSED TO LEAVE THE BATGIRL OUT OF THIS!
I TRIED.
LOOKS LIKE NOT EVERYONE'S ON THE SAME PAGE.
BUT WHO'S THE BIGGER THREAT?
I DON'T BELIEVE--
VOICES DOWN, VULTURE. WE HAVE GUESTS.
AS I SAID, I TRIED TO KEEP THE BATS OFF OUR TRAIL.
AND WHEN THAT INEVITABLY FAILED, I IMPROVISED.
YOU NEED TO ASK YOURSELF WHAT'S MORE IMPORTANT NOW, VULTURE--THIS PLAN ACTUALLY WORKING...
...OR GETTING A DIG IN AT ME FOR NOT TOEING YOUR LINE?
...FINE.
MAKE YOUR PITCH.
JUST DON'T EXPECT ME TO SAVE YOU WHEN THIS ALL GOES WRONG.
AND WE HAVE A WINNER.

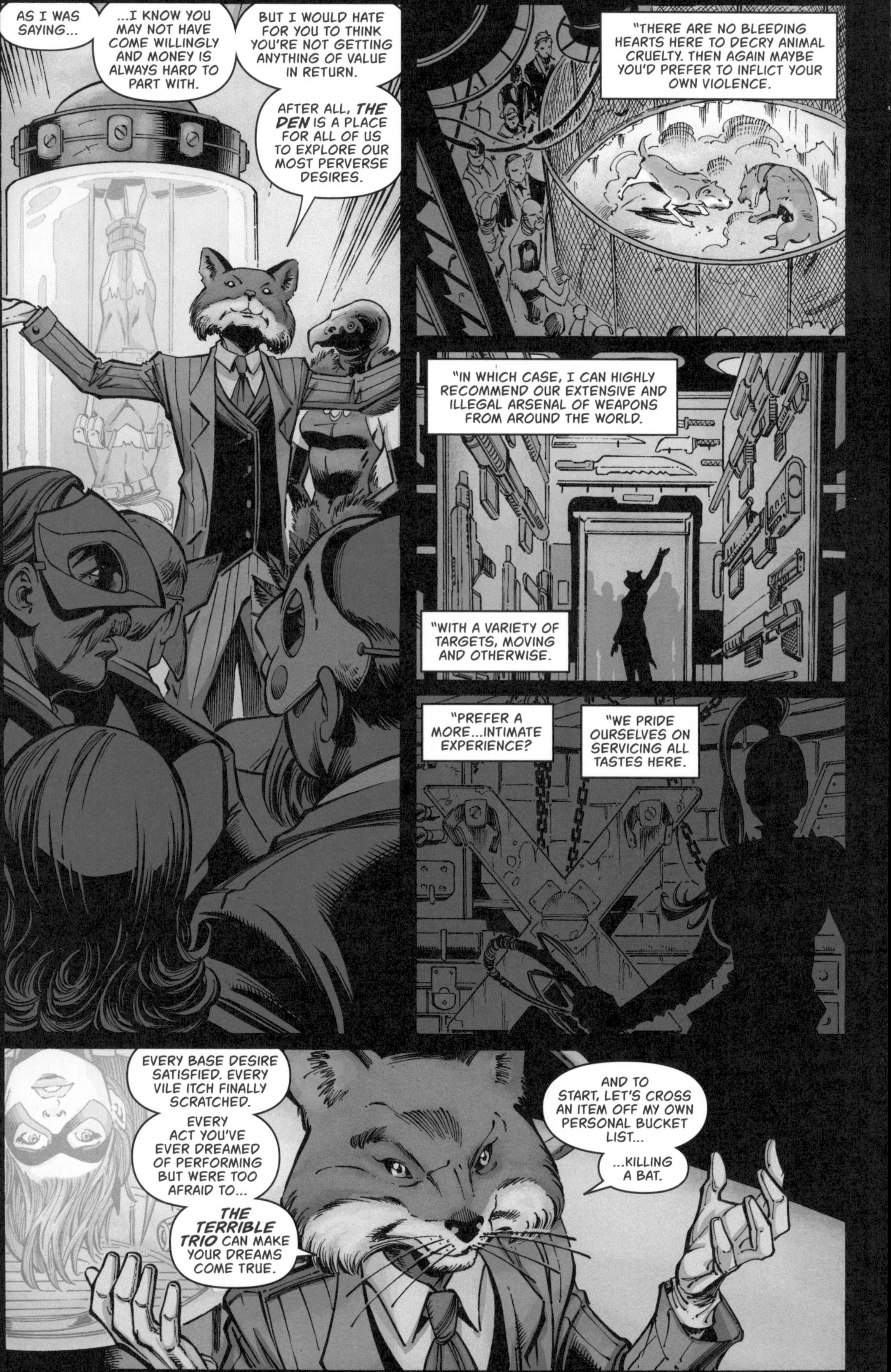

AS I WAS SAYING...
...I KNOW YOU MAY NOT HAVE COME WILLINGLY AND MONEY IS ALWAYS HARD TO PART WITH.
BUT I WOULD HATE FOR YOU TO THINK YOU'RE NOT GETTING ANYTHING OF VALUE IN RETURN.
AFTER ALL, THE DEN IS A PLACE FOR ALL OF US TO EXPLORE OUR MOST PERVERSE DESIRES.
"THERE ARE NO BLEEDING HEARTS HERE TO DECRY ANIMAL CRUELTY. THEN AGAIN MAYBE YOU'D PREFER TO INFLICT YOUR OWN VIOLENCE.
"IN WHICH CASE, I CAN HIGHLY RECOMMEND OUR EXTENSIVE AND ILLEGAL ARSENAL OF WEAPONS FROM AROUND THE WORLD.
"WITH A VARIETY OF TARGETS, MOVING AND OTHERWISE.
"PREFER A MORE...INTIMATE EXPERIENCE?
"WE PRIDE OURSELVES ON SERVICING ALL TASTES HERE.
EVERY BASE DESIRE SATISFIED. EVERY VILE ITCH FINALLY SCRATCHED.
EVERY ACT YOU'VE EVER DREAMED OF PERFORMING BUT WERE TOO AFRAID TO...
THE TERRIBLE TRIO CAN MAKE YOUR DREAMS COME TRUE.
AND TO START, LET'S CROSS AN ITEM OFF MY OWN PERSONAL BUCKET LIST...
...KILLING A BAT.

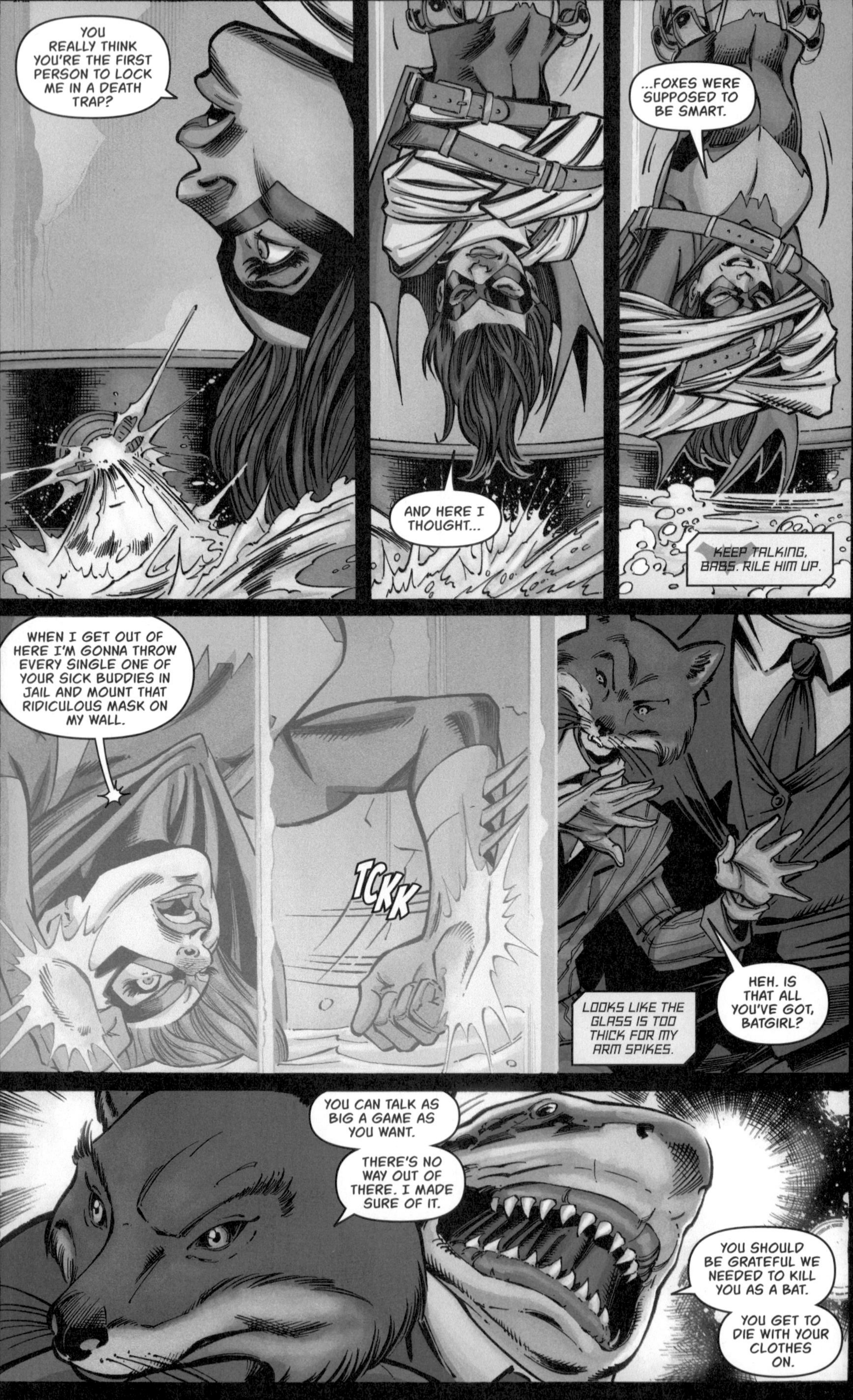
YOU REALLY THINK YOU'RE THE FIRST PERSON TO LOCK ME IN A DEATH TRAP?
AND HERE I THOUGHT...
...FOXES WERE SUPPOSED TO BE SMART.
KEEP TALKING, BABS. RILE HIM UP.
WHEN I GET OUT OF HERE I'M GONNA THROW EVERY SINGLE ONE OF YOUR SICK BUDDIES IN JAIL AND MOUNT THAT RIDICULOUS MASK ON MY WALL.
TCKK
LOOKS LIKE THE GLASS IS TOO THICK FOR MY ARM SPIKES.
HEH. IS THAT ALL YOU'VE GOT, BATGIRL?
YOU CAN TALK AS BIG A GAME AS YOU WANT.
THERE'S NO WAY OUT OF THERE. I MADE SURE OF IT.
YOU SHOULD BE GRATEFUL WE NEEDED TO KILL YOU AS A BAT.
YOU GET TO DIE WITH YOUR CLOTHES ON.

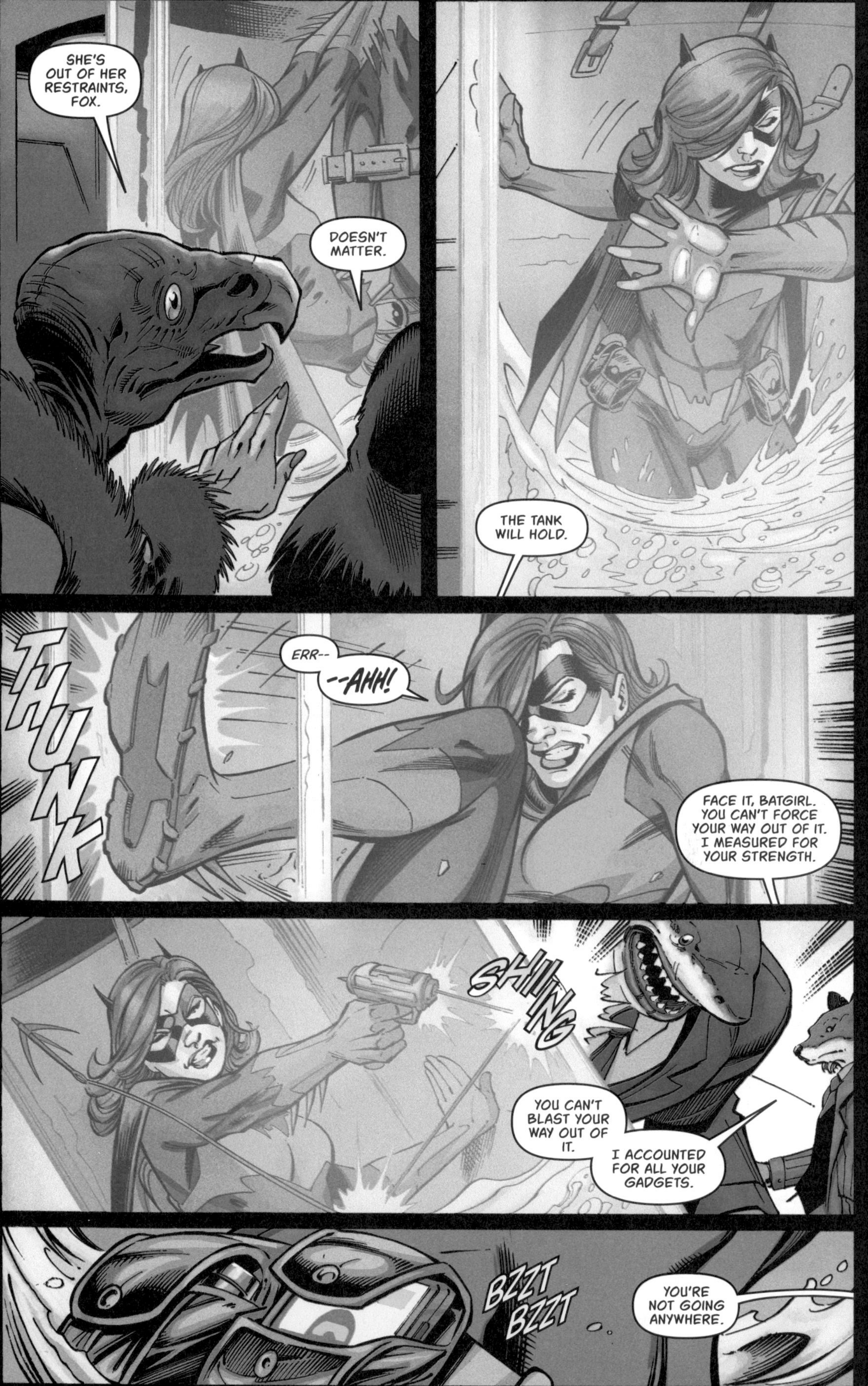
SHE'S OUT OF HER RESTRAINTS, FOX.
DOESN'T MATTER.
THE TANK WILL HOLD.
THUNK
ERR--
--AHH!
FACE IT, BATGIRL. YOU CAN'T FORCE YOUR WAY OUT OF IT. I MEASURED FOR YOUR STRENGTH.
SHIIING
YOU CAN'T BLAST YOUR WAY OUT OF IT.
I ACCOUNTED FOR ALL YOUR GADGETS.
BZZT BZZT
YOU'RE NOT GOING ANYWHERE.

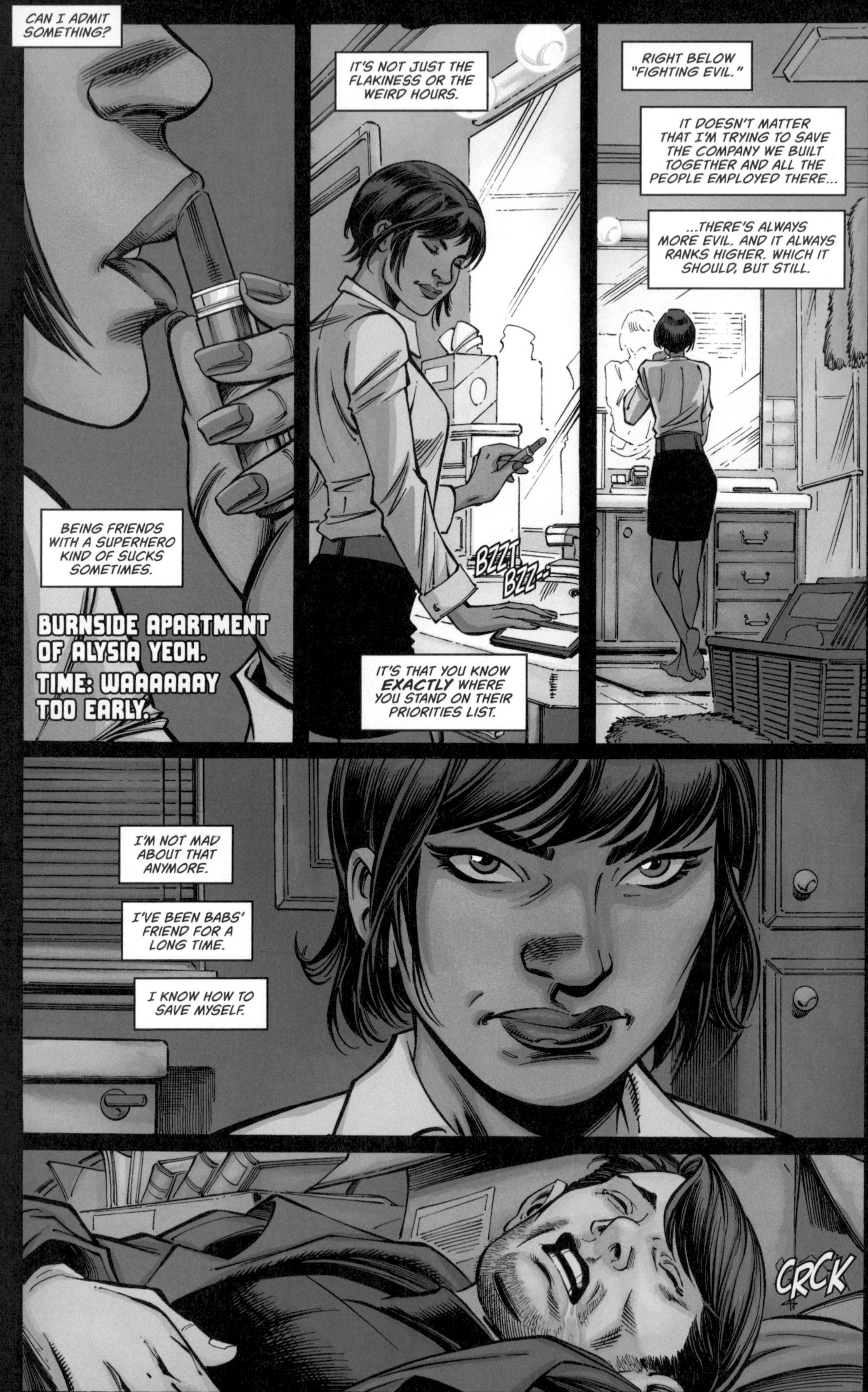

CAN I ADMIT SOMETHING?
BEING FRIENDS WITH A SUPERHERO KIND OF SUCKS SOMETIMES.
BURNSIDE APARTMENT OF ALYSIA YEOH.
TIME: WAAAAAAY TOO EARLY.
IT'S NOT JUST THE FLAKINESS OR THE WEIRD HOURS.
BZZT. BZZ--
IT'S THAT YOU KNOW EXACTLY WHERE YOU STAND ON THEIR PRIORITIES LIST.
RIGHT BELOW "FIGHTING EVIL."
IT DOESN'T MATTER THAT I'M TRYING TO SAVE THE COMPANY WE BUILT TOGETHER AND ALL THE PEOPLE EMPLOYED THERE...
...THERE'S ALWAYS MORE EVIL. AND IT ALWAYS RANKS HIGHER. WHICH IT SHOULD, BUT STILL.
I'M NOT MAD ABOUT THAT ANYMORE.
I'VE BEEN BABS' FRIEND FOR A LONG TIME.
I KNOW HOW TO SAVE MYSELF.
CRCK

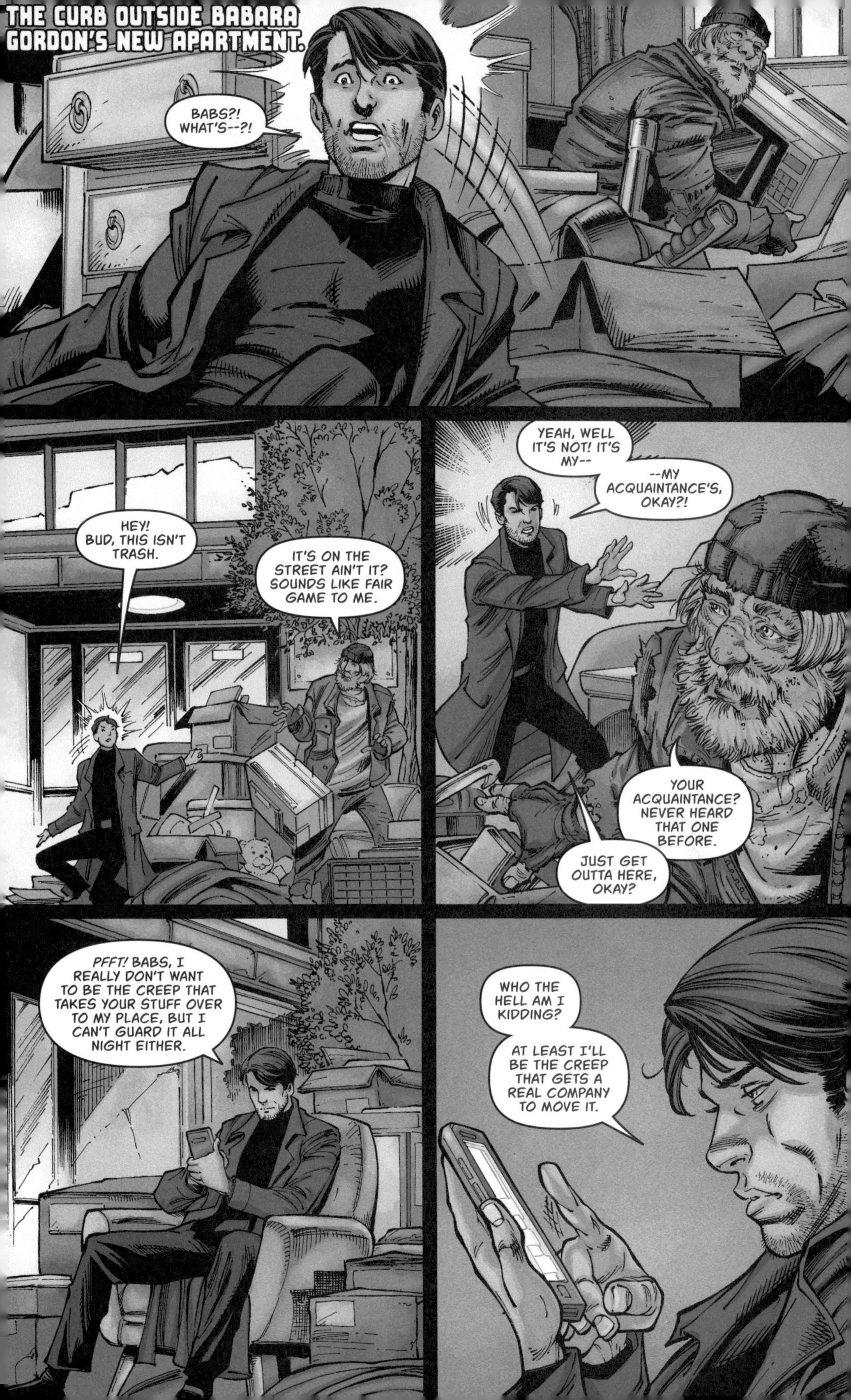
THE CURB OUTSIDE BABARA GORDON'S NEW APARTMENT.
BABS?! WHAT'S--?!
HEY! BUD, THIS ISN'T TRASH.
IT'S ON THE STREET AIN'T IT? SOUNDS LIKE FAIR GAME TO ME.
YEAH, WELL IT'S NOT! IT'S MY--
--MY ACQUAINTANCE'S, OKAY?!
YOUR ACQUAINTANCE? NEVER HEARD THAT ONE BEFORE.
JUST GET OUTTA HERE, OKAY?
PFFT! BABS, I REALLY DON'T WANT TO BE THE CREEP THAT TAKES YOUR STUFF OVER TO MY PLACE, BUT I CAN'T GUARD IT ALL NIGHT EITHER.
WHO THE HELL AM I KIDDING?
AT LEAST I'LL BE THE CREEP THAT GETS A REAL COMPANY TO MOVE IT.

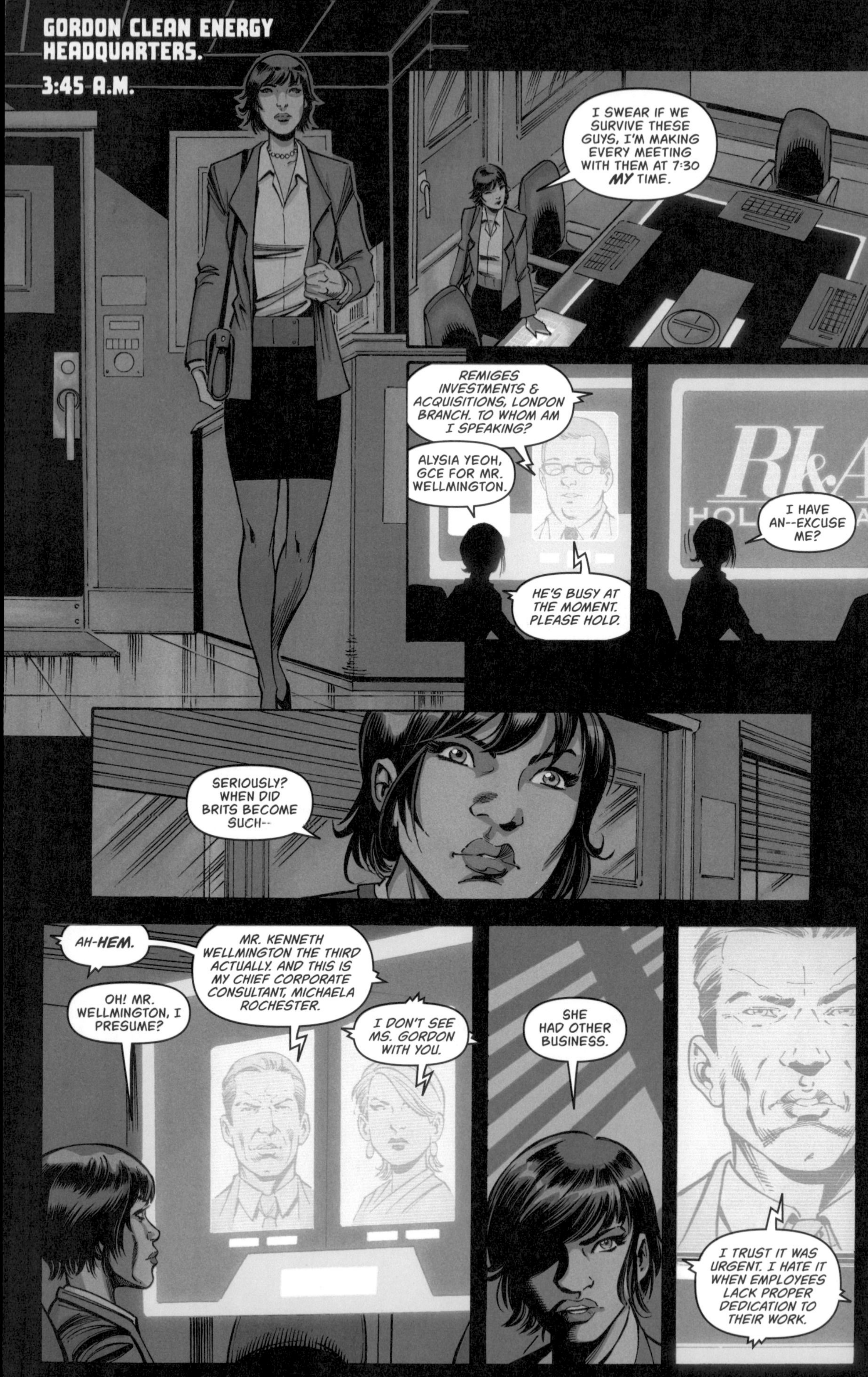

GORDON CLEAN ENERGY HEADQUARTERS.
3:45 A.M.
I SWEAR IF WE SURVIVE THESE GUYS, I'M MAKING EVERY MEETING WITH THEM AT 7:30 MY TIME.
REMIGES INVESTMENTS & ACQUISITIONS, LONDON BRANCH. TO WHOM AM I SPEAKING?
ALYSIA YEOH, GCE FOR MR. WELLMINGTON.
HE'S BUSY AT THE MOMENT. PLEASE HOLD.
I HAVE AN--EXCUSE ME?
SERIOUSLY? WHEN DID BRITS BECOME SUCH--
AH-HEM.
MR. KENNETH WELLMINGTON THE THIRD ACTUALLY. AND THIS IS MY CHIEF CORPORATE CONSULTANT, MICHAELA ROCHESTER.
OH! MR. WELLMINGTON, I PRESUME?
I DON'T SEE MS. GORDON WITH YOU.
SHE HAD OTHER BUSINESS.
I TRUST IT WAS URGENT. I HATE IT WHEN EMPLOYEES LACK PROPER DEDICATION TO THEIR WORK.

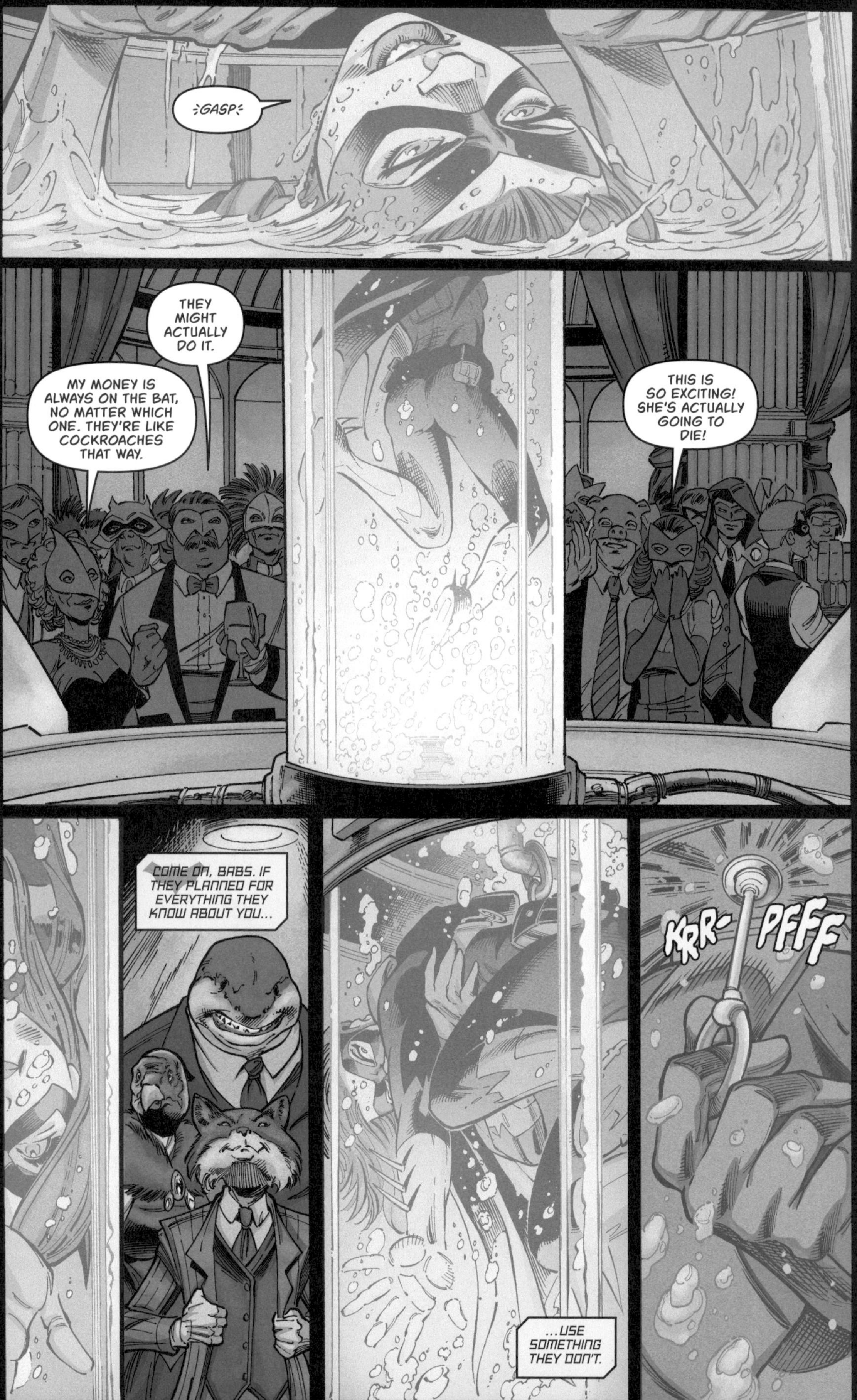

GASP
THEY MIGHT ACTUALLY DO IT.
MY MONEY IS ALWAYS ON THE BAT, NO MATTER WHICH ONE. THEY'RE LIKE COCKROACHES THAT WAY.
THIS IS SO EXCITING! SHE'S ACTUALLY GOING TO DIE!
COME ON, BABS. IF THEY PLANNED FOR EVERYTHING THEY KNOW ABOUT YOU...
...USE SOMETHING THEY DON'T.
KRR- PFFF

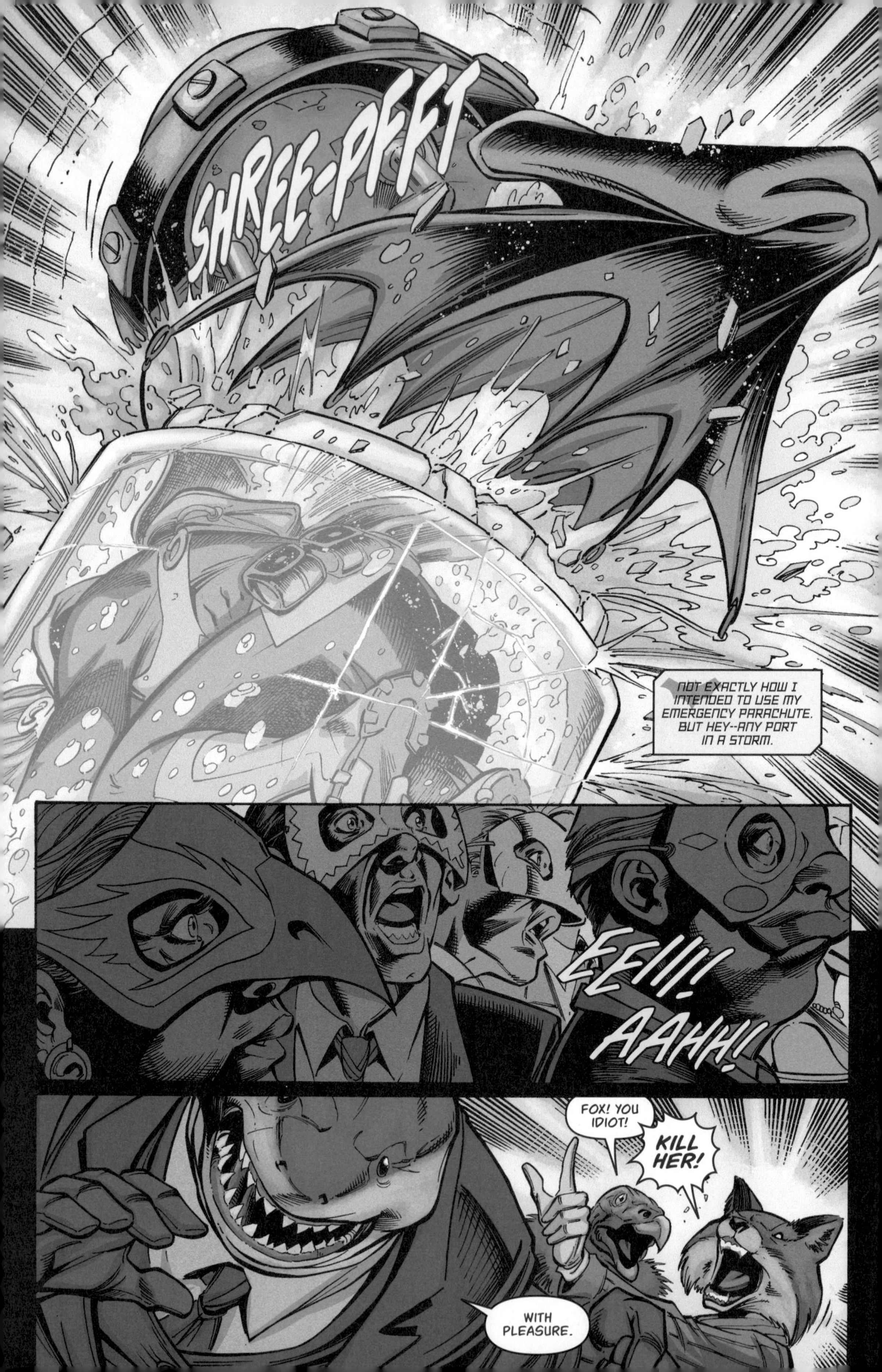
SHREE-PFFT
NOT EXACTLY HOW I INTENDED TO USE MY EMERGENCY PARACHUTE. BUT HEY--ANY PORT IN A STORM.
EEIII! AAHH!
FOX! YOU IDIOT!
KILL HER!
WITH PLEASURE.

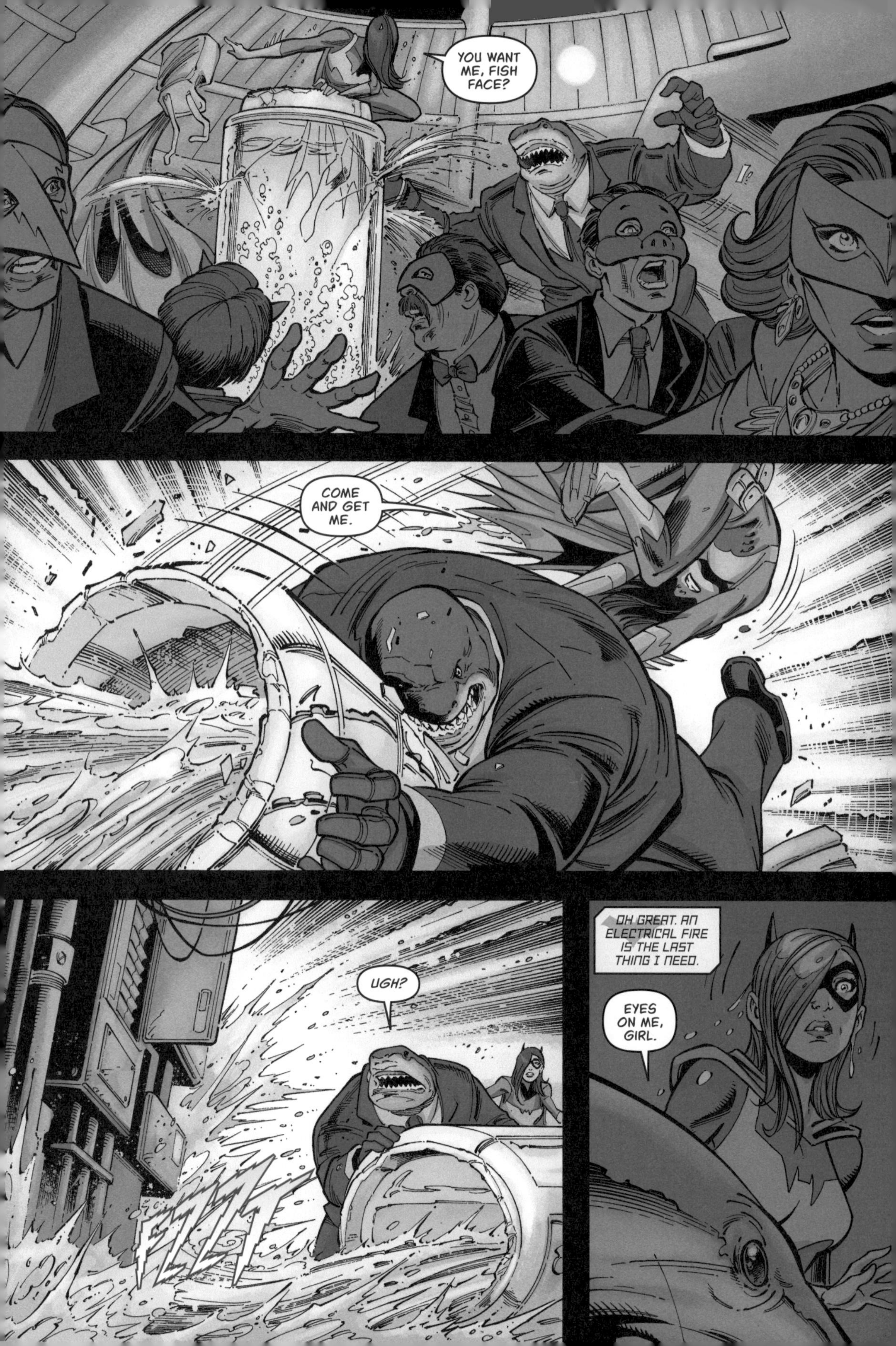
YOU WANT ME, FISH FACE?
!
COME AND GET ME.
UGH?
FZZT
OH GREAT. AN ELECTRICAL FIRE IS THE LAST THING I NEED.
EYES ON ME, GIRL.

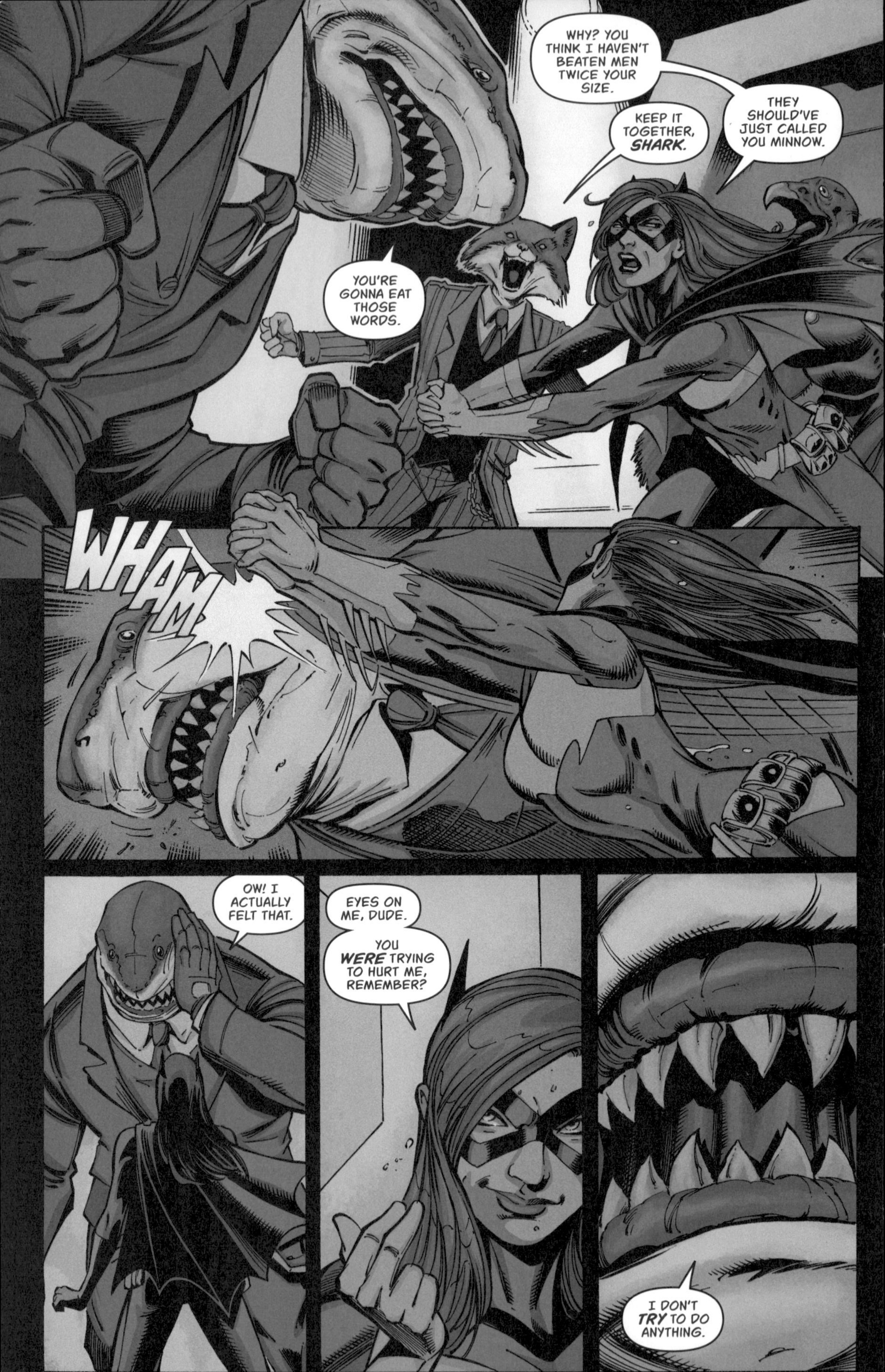
WHY? YOU THINK I HAVEN'T BEATEN MEN TWICE YOUR SIZE.
KEEP IT TOGETHER, SHARK.
THEY SHOULD'VE JUST CALLED YOU MINNOW.
YOU'RE GONNA EAT THOSE WORDS.
WHAM
OW! I ACTUALLY FELT THAT.
EYES ON ME, DUDE.
YOU WERE TRYING TO HURT ME, REMEMBER?
I DON'T TRY TO DO ANYTHING.

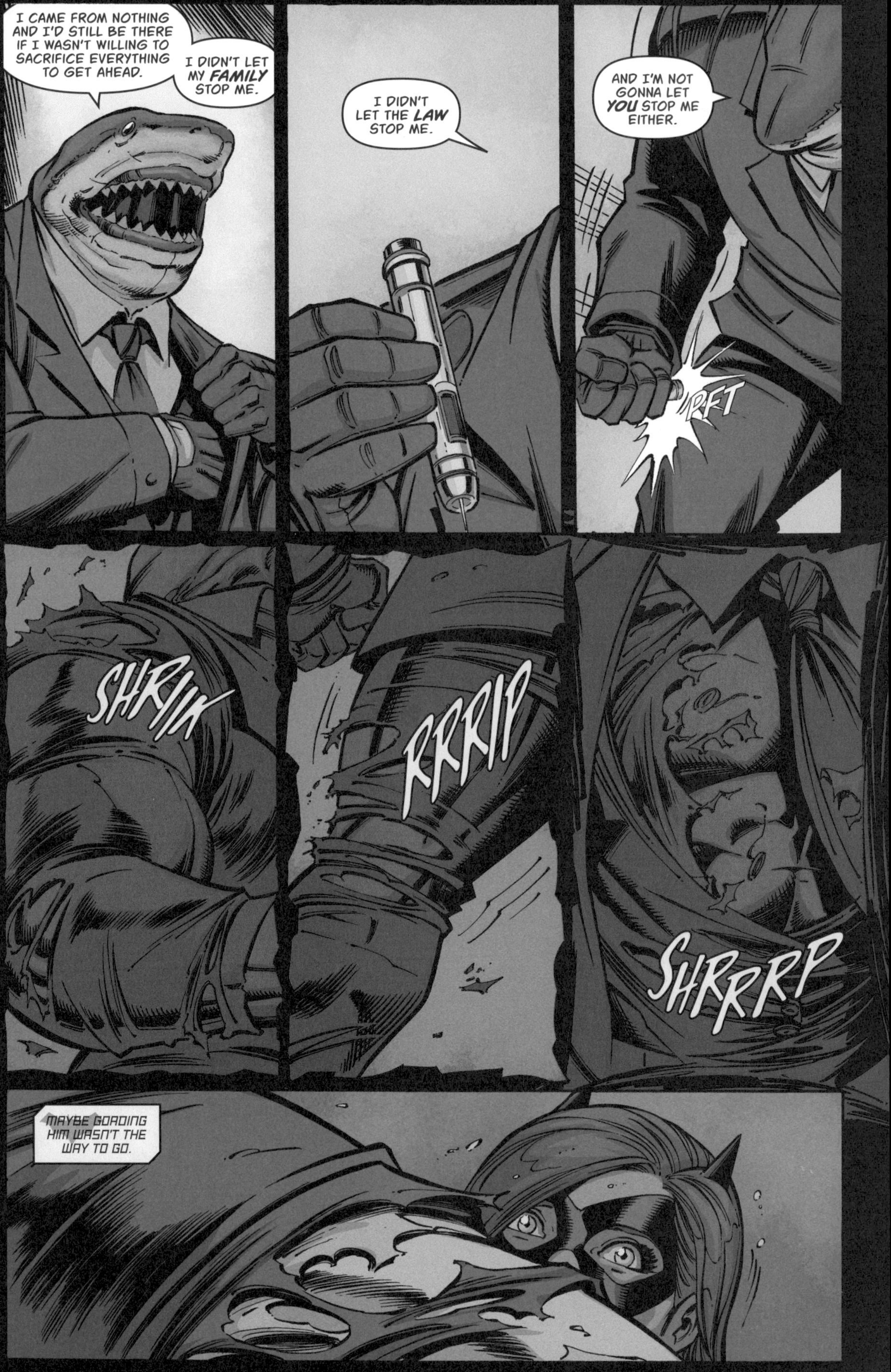

I CAME FROM NOTHING AND I'D STILL BE THERE IF I WASN'T WILLING TO SACRIFICE EVERYTHING TO GET AHEAD.
I DIDN'T LET MY FAMILY STOP ME.
I DIDN'T LET THE LAW STOP ME.
AND I'M NOT GONNA LET YOU STOP ME EITHER.
PFFT
SHRIIK
RRRIP
SHRRRP
MAYBE GOADING HIM WASN'T THE WAY TO GO.

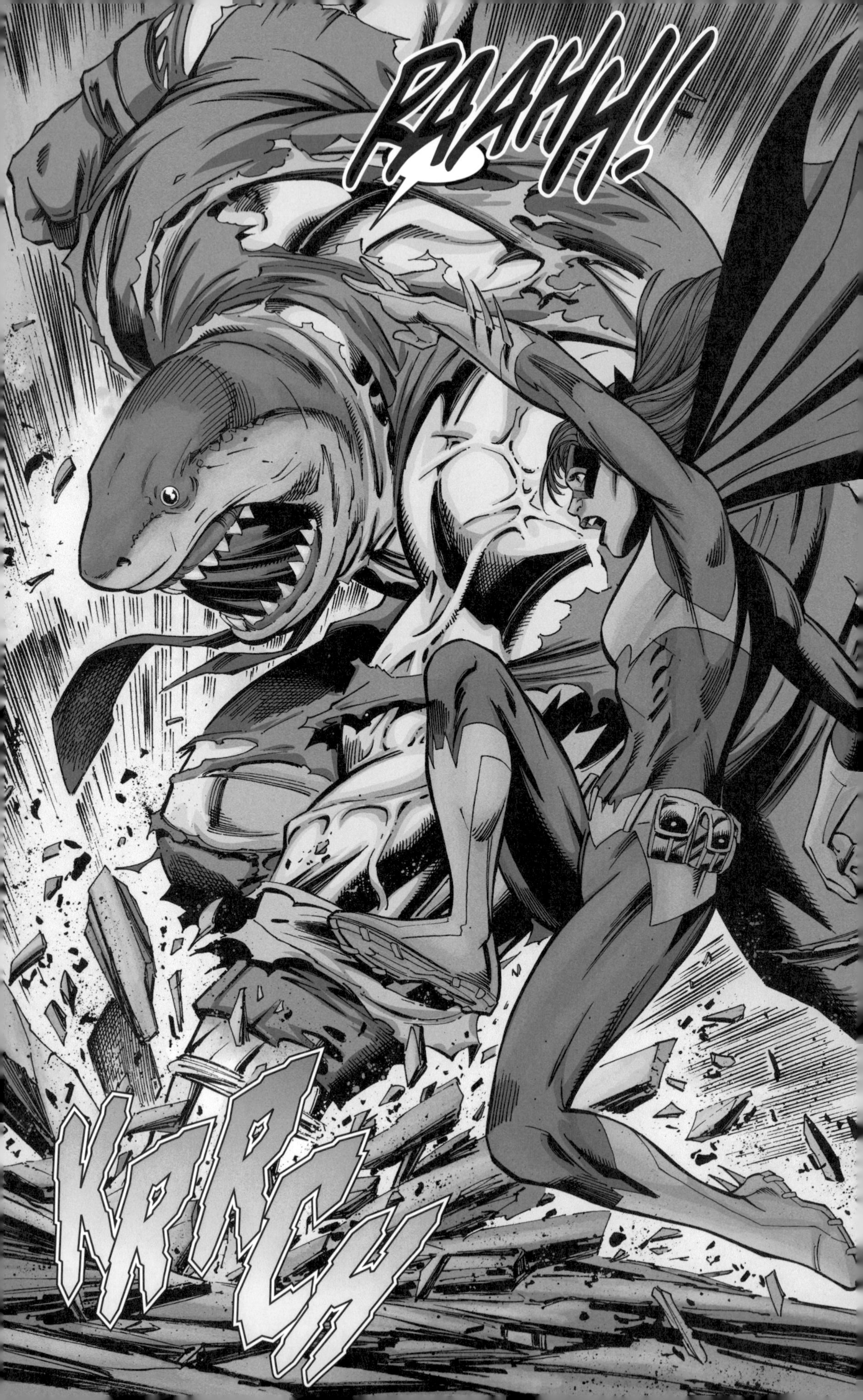
RAAHH!
KRRCH

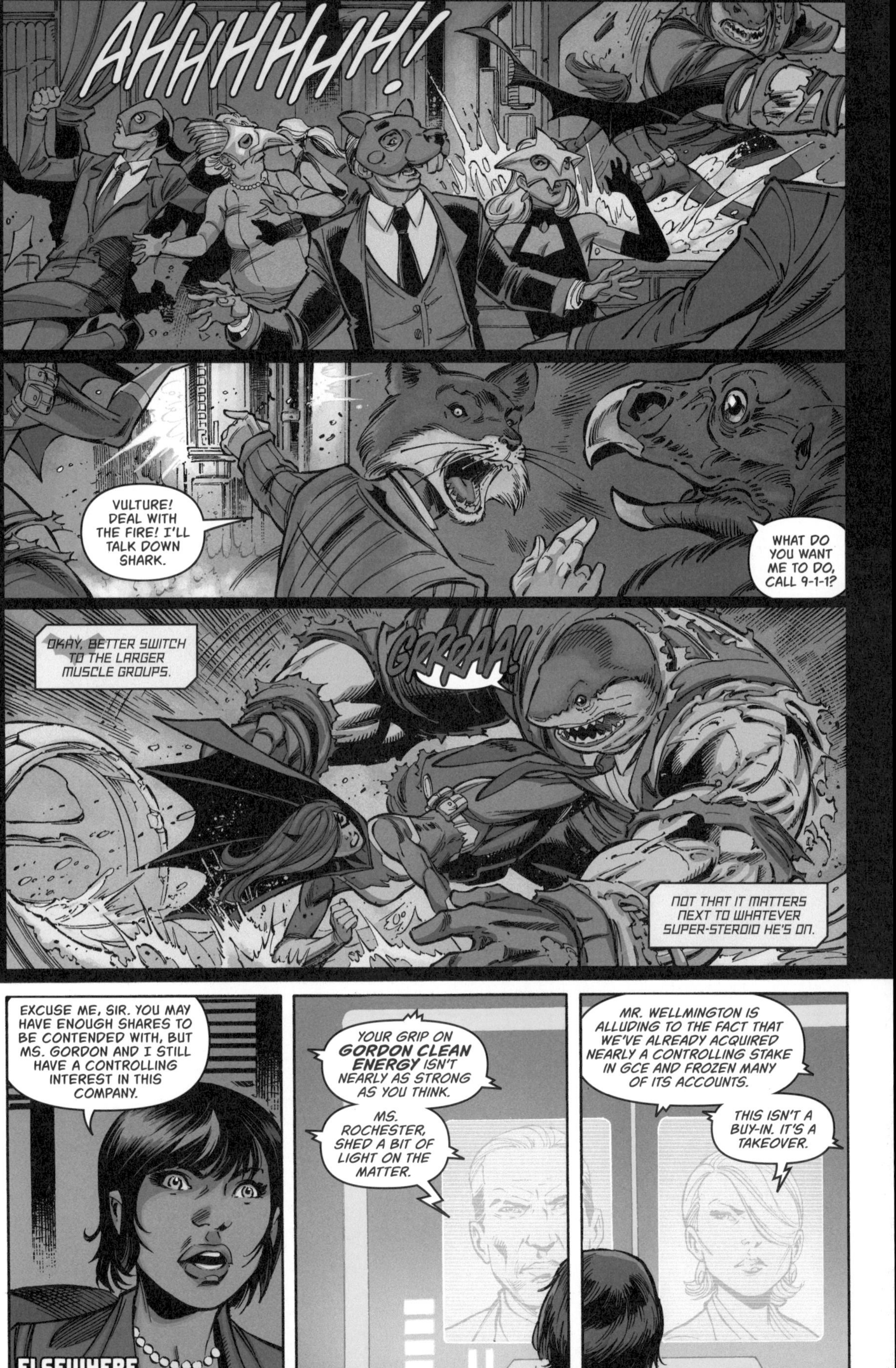

AHHHHHH!
VULTURE! DEAL WITH THE FIRE! I'LL TALK DOWN SHARK.
WHAT DO YOU WANT ME TO DO, CALL 9-1-1?
OKAY, BETTER SWITCH TO THE LARGER MUSCLE GROUPS.
GRRRAA!
NOT THAT IT MATTERS NEXT TO WHATEVER SUPER-STEROID HE'S ON.
ELSEWHERE.
EXCUSE ME, SIR. YOU MAY HAVE ENOUGH SHARES TO BE CONTENDED WITH, BUT MS. GORDON AND I STILL HAVE A CONTROLLING INTEREST IN THIS COMPANY.
YOUR GRIP ON GORDON CLEAN ENERGY ISN'T NEARLY AS STRONG AS YOU THINK.
MS. ROCHESTER, SHED A BIT OF LIGHT ON THE MATTER.
MR. WELLMINGTON IS ALLUDING TO THE FACT THAT WE'VE ALREADY ACQUIRED NEARLY A CONTROLLING STAKE IN GCE AND FROZEN MANY OF ITS ACCOUNTS.
THIS ISN'T A BUY-IN. IT'S A TAKEOVER.

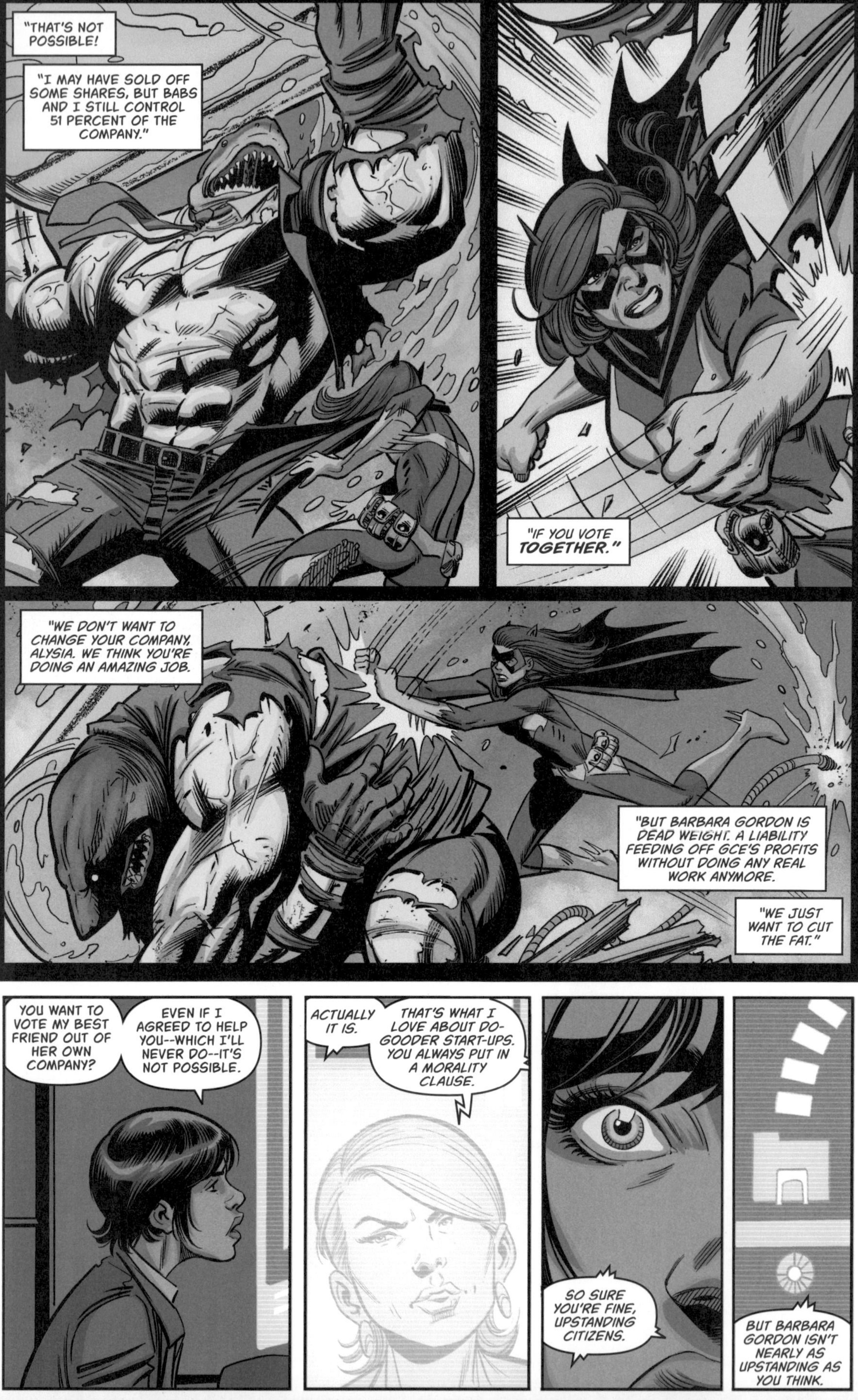
"THAT'S NOT POSSIBLE!
"I MAY HAVE SOLD OFF SOME SHARES, BUT BABS AND I STILL CONTROL 51 PERCENT OF THE COMPANY."
"IF YOU VOTE TOGETHER."
"WE DON'T WANT TO CHANGE YOUR COMPANY, ALYSIA. WE THINK YOU'RE DOING AN AMAZING JOB.
"BUT BARBARA GORDON IS DEAD WEIGHT. A LIABILITY FEEDING OFF GCE'S PROFITS WITHOUT DOING ANY REAL WORK ANYMORE.
"WE JUST WANT TO CUT THE FAT."
YOU WANT TO VOTE MY BEST FRIEND OUT OF HER OWN COMPANY?
EVEN IF I AGREED TO HELP YOU--WHICH I'LL NEVER DO--IT'S NOT POSSIBLE.
ACTUALLY IT IS.
THAT'S WHAT I LOVE ABOUT DO-GOODER START-UPS. YOU ALWAYS PUT IN A MORALITY CLAUSE.
SO SURE YOU'RE FINE, UPSTANDING CITIZENS.
BUT BARBARA GORDON ISN'T NEARLY AS UPSTANDING AS YOU THINK.

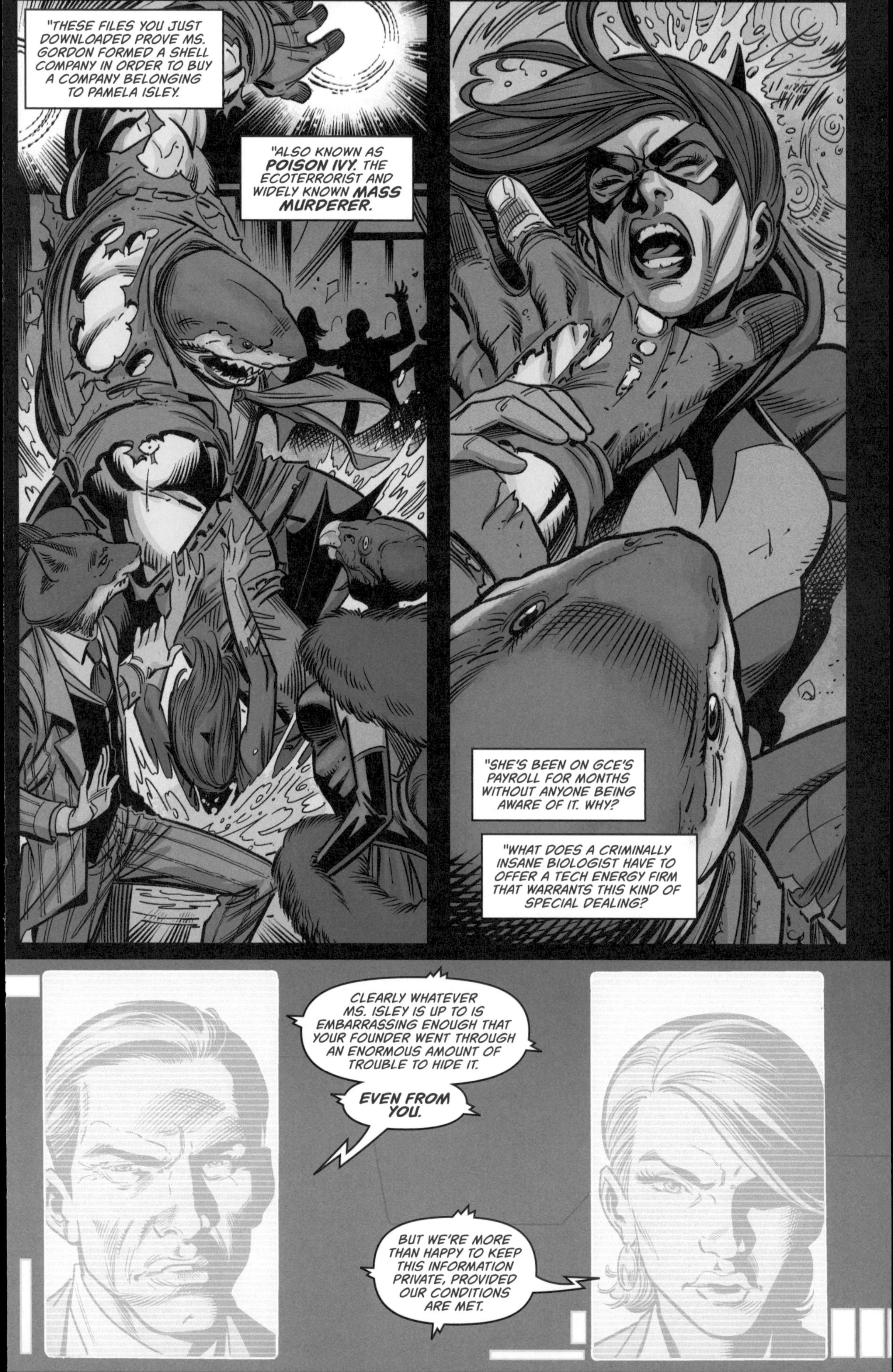
"THESE FILES YOU JUST DOWNLOADED PROVE MS. GORDON FORMED A SHELL COMPANY IN ORDER TO BUY A COMPANY BELONGING TO PAMELA ISLEY.
"ALSO KNOWN AS POISON IVY. THE ECOTERRORIST AND WIDELY KNOWN MASS MURDERER.
"SHE'S BEEN ON GCE'S PAYROLL FOR MONTHS WITHOUT ANYONE BEING AWARE OF IT. WHY?
"WHAT DOES A CRIMINALLY INSANE BIOLOGIST HAVE TO OFFER A TECH ENERGY FIRM THAT WARRANTS THIS KIND OF SPECIAL DEALING?
CLEARLY WHATEVER MS. ISLEY IS UP TO IS EMBARRASSING ENOUGH THAT YOUR FOUNDER WENT THROUGH AN ENORMOUS AMOUNT OF TROUBLE TO HIDE IT.
EVEN FROM YOU.
BUT WE'RE MORE THAN HAPPY TO KEEP THIS INFORMATION PRIVATE, PROVIDED OUR CONDITIONS ARE MET.

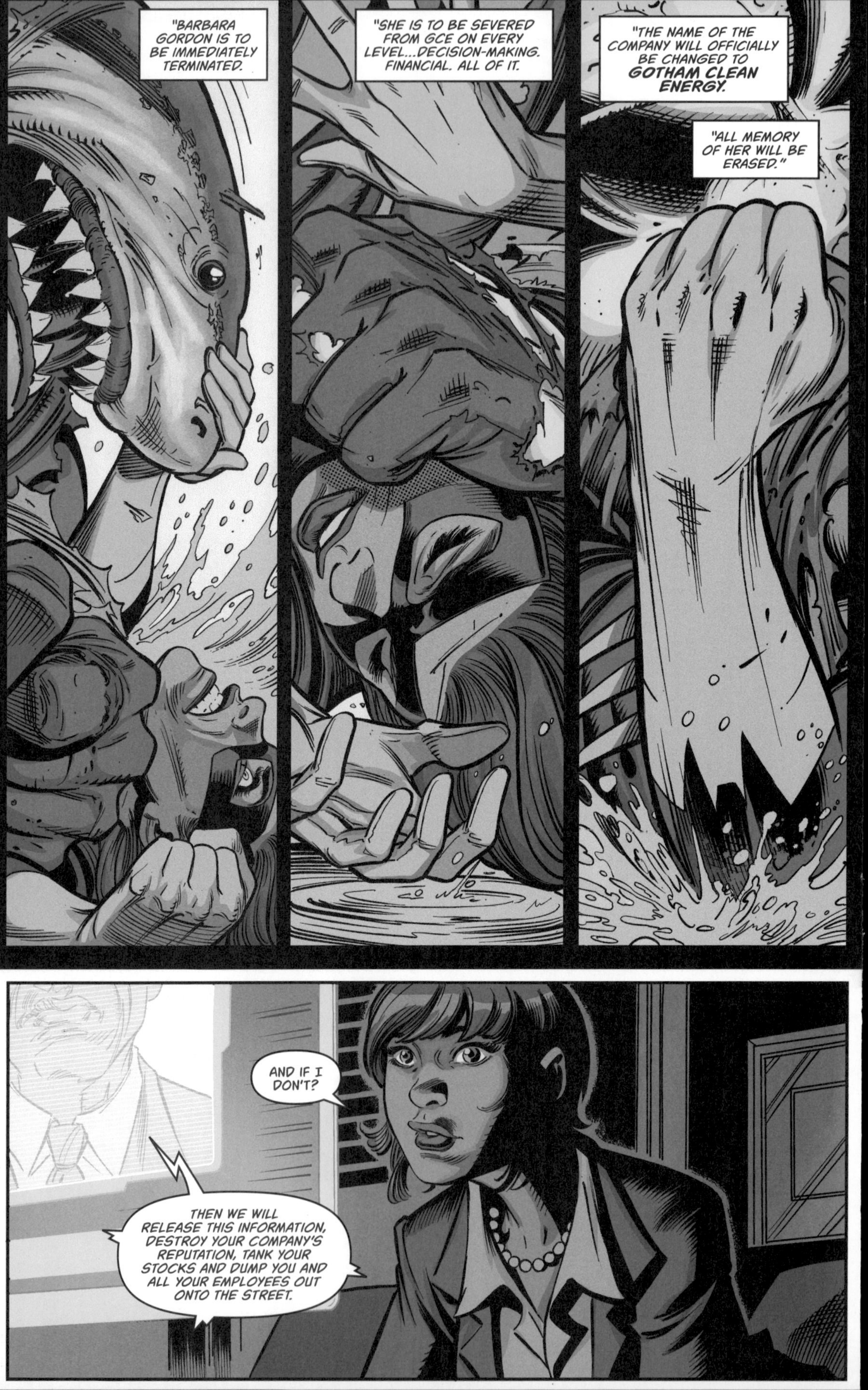
"BARBARA GORDON IS TO BE IMMEDIATELY TERMINATED.
"SHE IS TO BE SEVERED FROM GCE ON EVERY LEVEL...DECISION-MAKING. FINANCIAL. ALL OF IT.
"THE NAME OF THE COMPANY WILL OFFICIALLY BE CHANGED TO GOTHAM CLEAN ENERGY.
"ALL MEMORY OF HER WILL BE ERASED."
AND IF I DON'T?
THEN WE WILL RELEASE THIS INFORMATION, DESTROY YOUR COMPANY'S REPUTATION, TANK YOUR STOCKS AND DUMP YOU AND ALL YOUR EMPLOYEES OUT ONTO THE STREET.

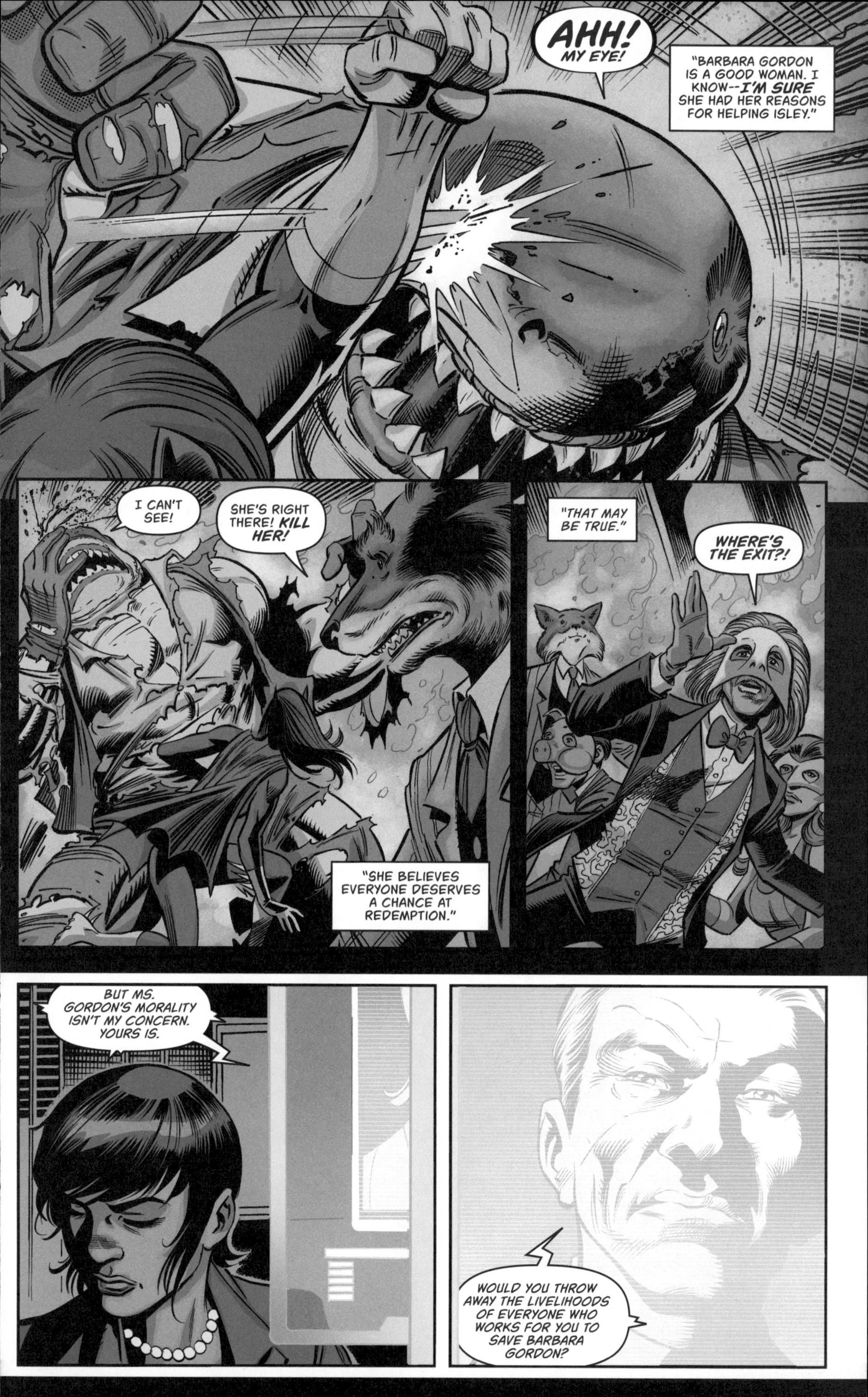
AHH! MY EYE!
"BARBARA GORDON IS A GOOD WOMAN. I KNOW--I'M SURE SHE HAD HER REASONS FOR HELPING ISLEY."
I CAN'T SEE!
SHE'S RIGHT THERE! KILL HER!
"SHE BELIEVES EVERYONE DESERVES A CHANCE AT REDEMPTION."
"THAT MAY BE TRUE."
WHERE'S THE EXIT?!
BUT MS. GORDON'S MORALITY ISN'T MY CONCERN. YOURS IS.
WOULD YOU THROW AWAY THE LIVELIHOODS OF EVERYONE WHO WORKS FOR YOU TO SAVE BARBARA GORDON?

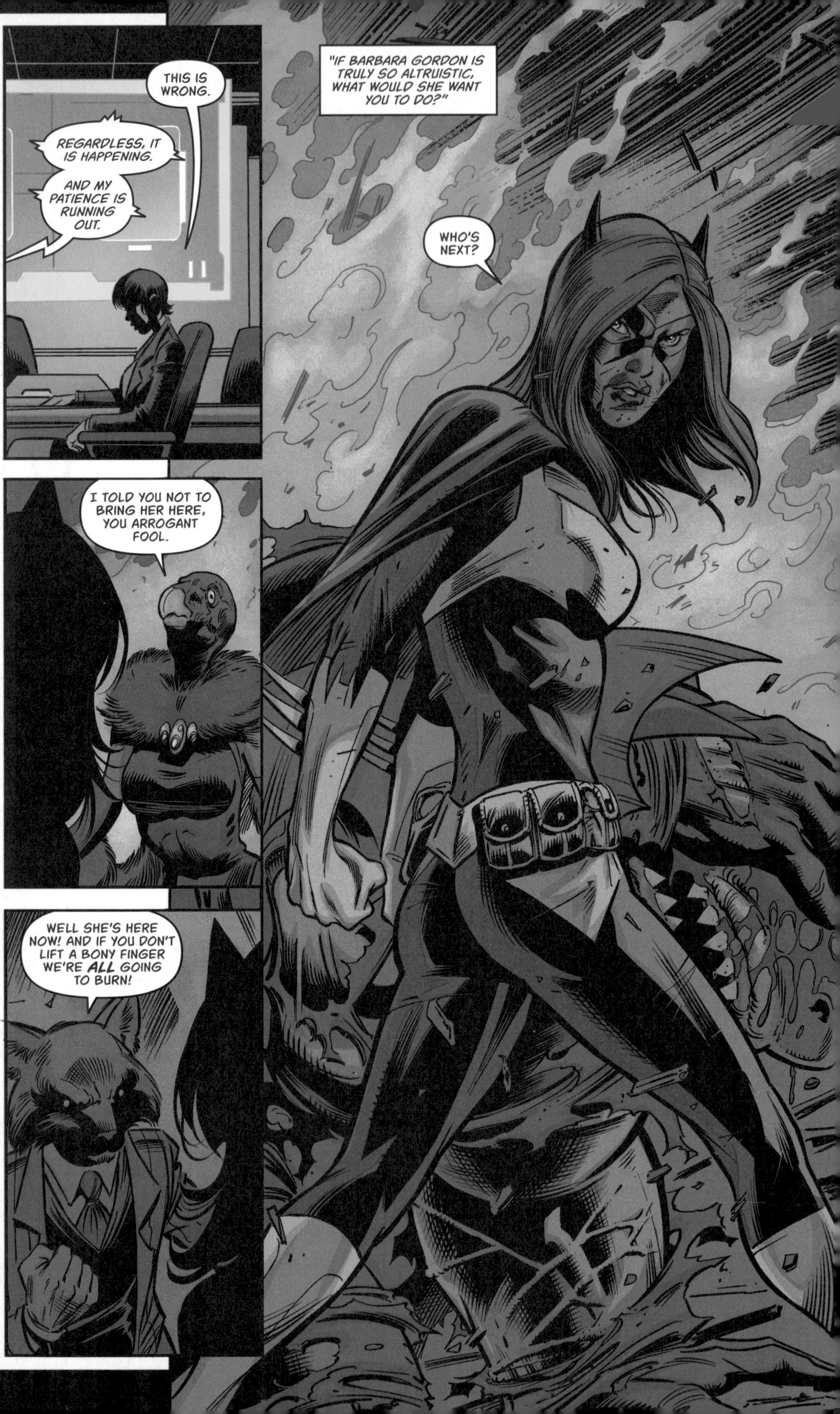
THIS IS WRONG.
REGARDLESS, IT IS HAPPENING.
AND MY PATIENCE IS RUNNING OUT.
"IF BARBARA GORDON IS TRULY SO ALTRUISTIC, WHAT WOULD SHE WANT YOU TO DO?"
WHO'S NEXT?
I TOLD YOU NOT TO BRING HER HERE, YOU ARROGANT FOOL.
WELL SHE'S HERE NOW! AND IF YOU DON'T LIFT A BONY FINGER WE'RE ALL GOING TO BURN!

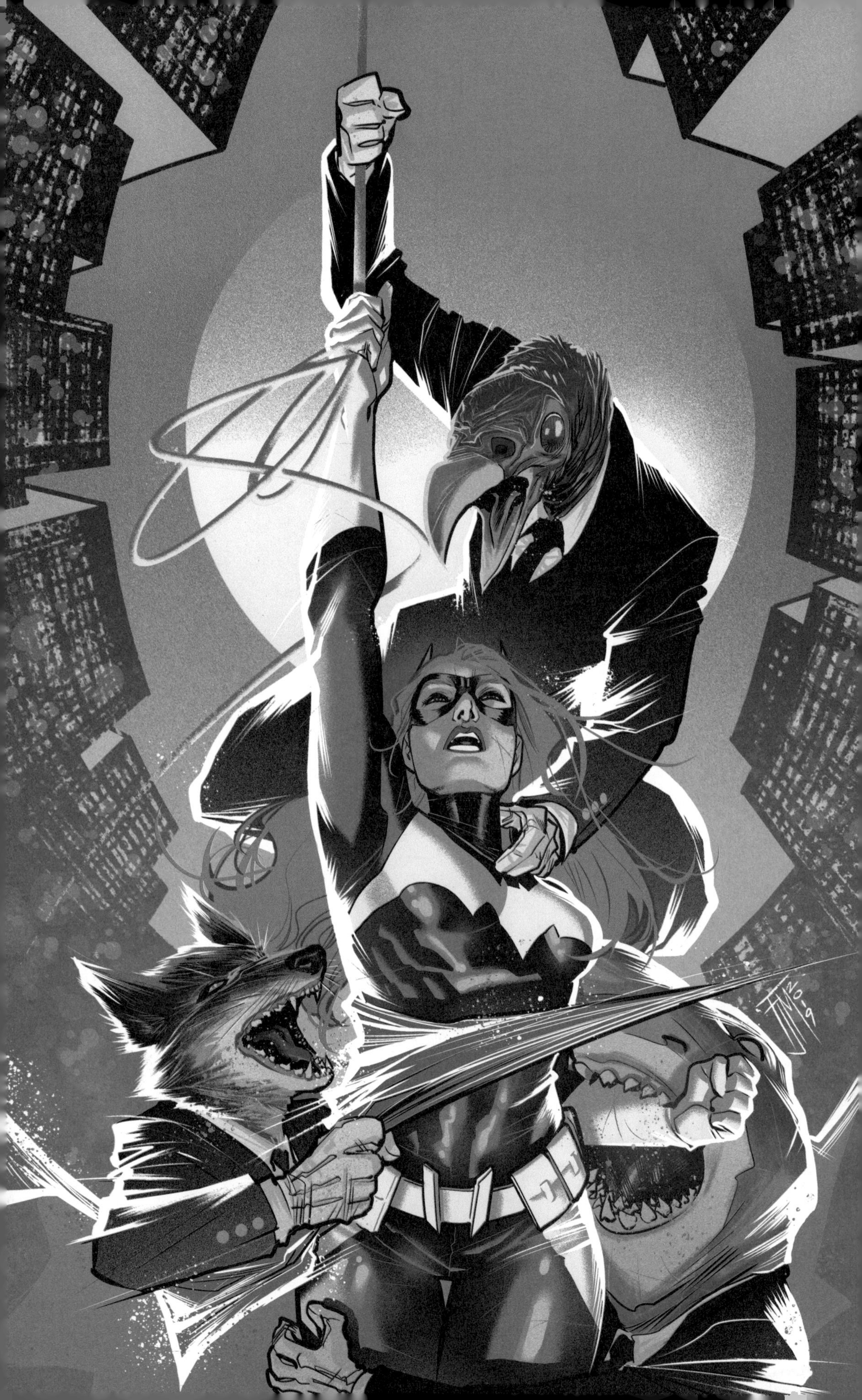

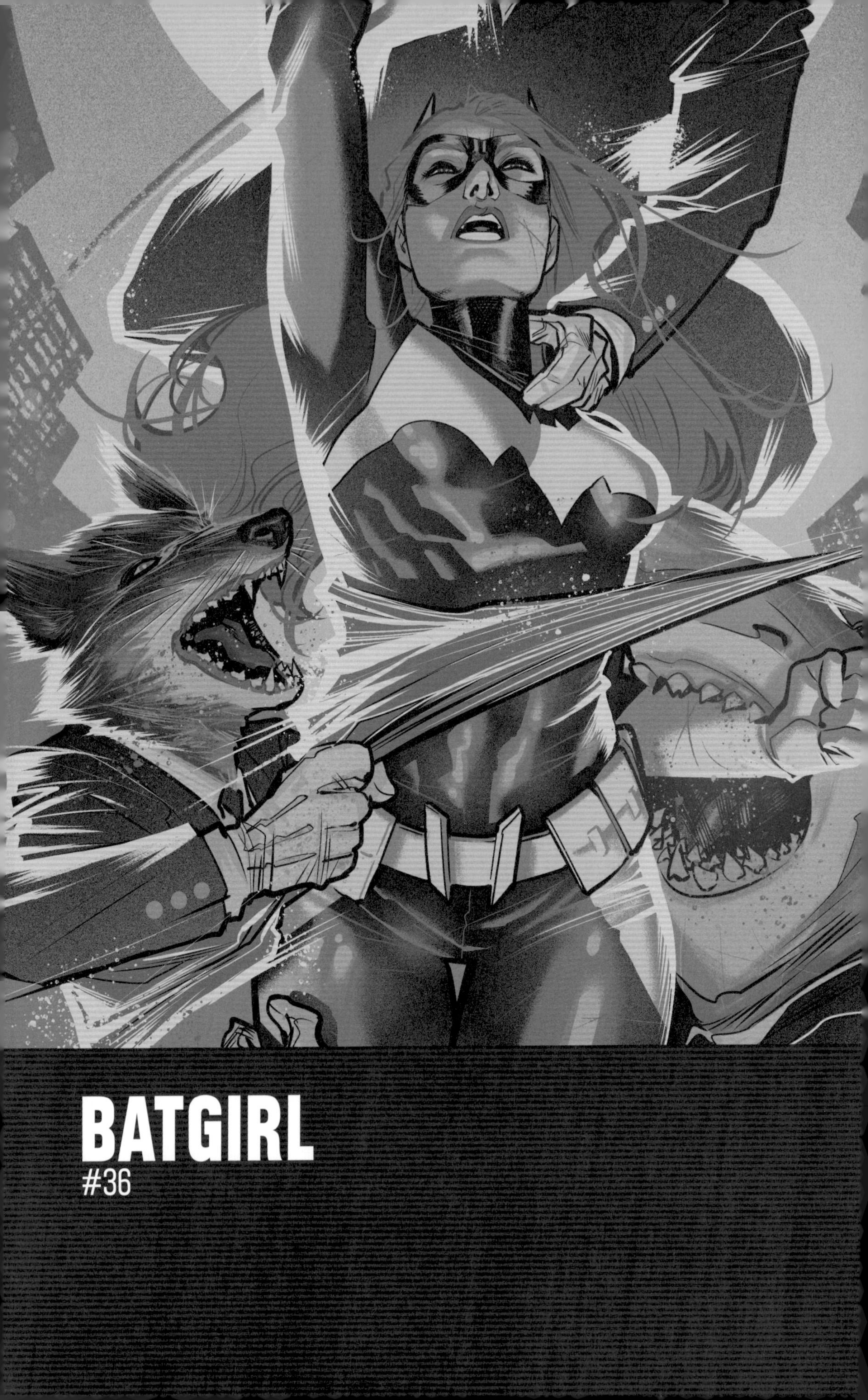

BATGIRL
#36

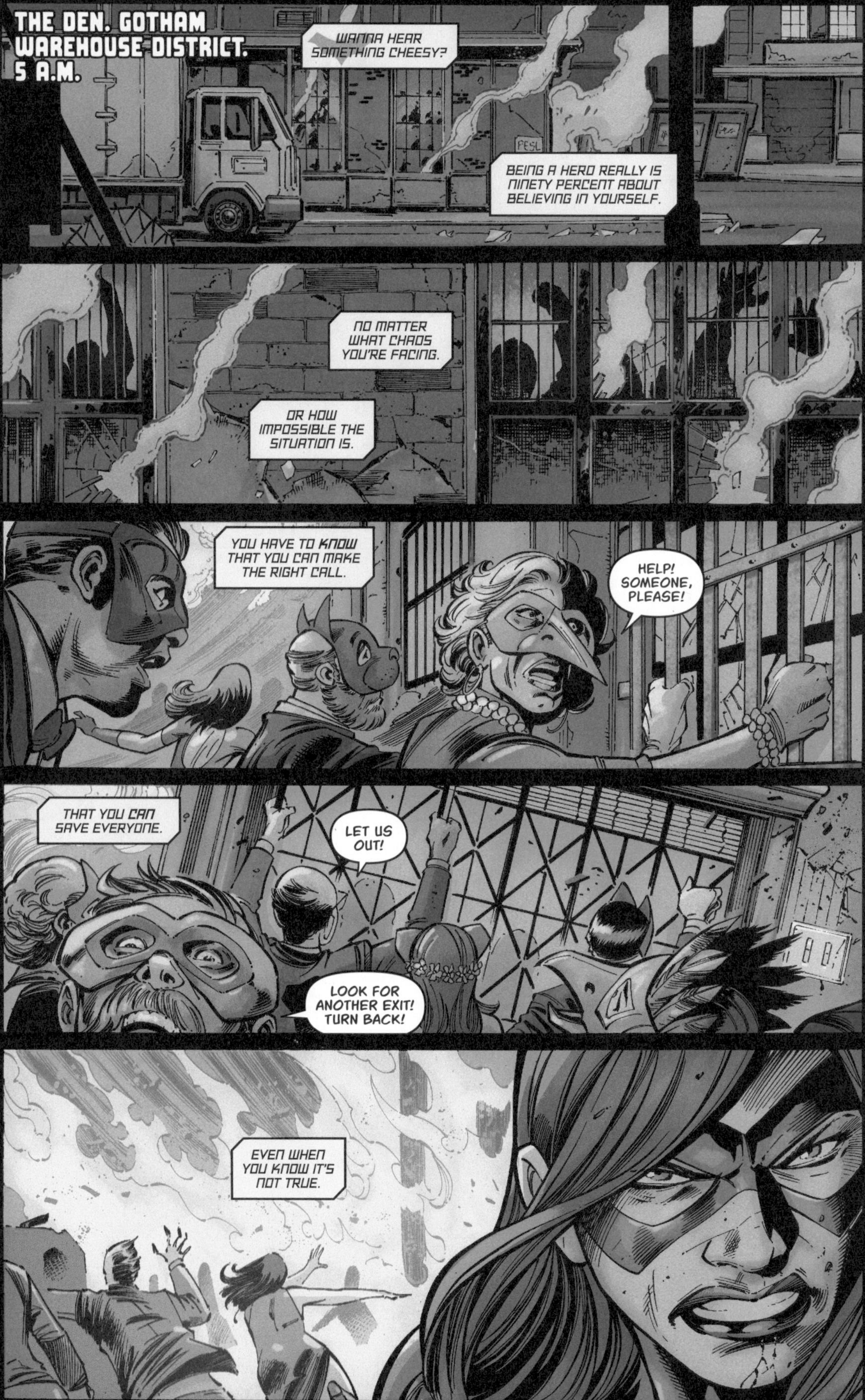
THE DEN. GOTHAM WAREHOUSE DISTRICT. 5 A.M.
WANNA HEAR SOMETHING CHEESY?
BEING A HERO REALLY IS NINETY PERCENT ABOUT BELIEVING IN YOURSELF.
NO MATTER WHAT CHAOS YOU'RE FACING.
OR HOW IMPOSSIBLE THE SITUATION IS.
YOU HAVE TO KNOW THAT YOU CAN MAKE THE RIGHT CALL.
HELP! SOMEONE, PLEASE!
THAT YOU CAN SAVE EVERYONE.
LET US OUT!
LOOK FOR ANOTHER EXIT! TURN BACK!
EVEN WHEN YOU KNOW IT'S NOT TRUE.

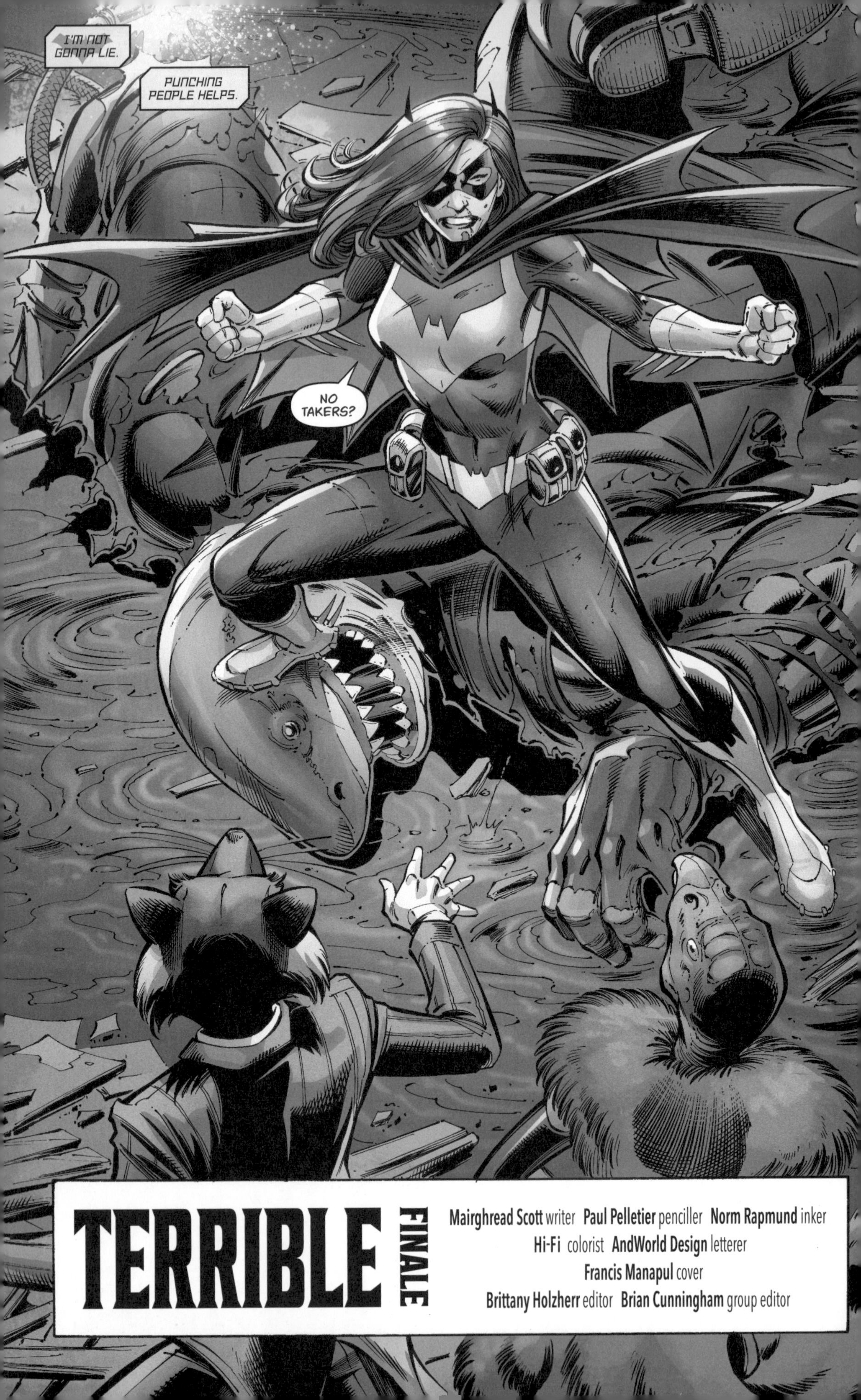
I'M NOT GONNA LIE.
PUNCHING PEOPLE HELPS.
NO TAKERS?
TERRIBLE
FINALE
Mairghread Scott writer Paul Pelletier penciller Norm Rapmund inker
Hi-Fi colorist AndWorld Design letterer
Francis Manapul cover
Brittany Holzherr editor Brian Cunningham group editor

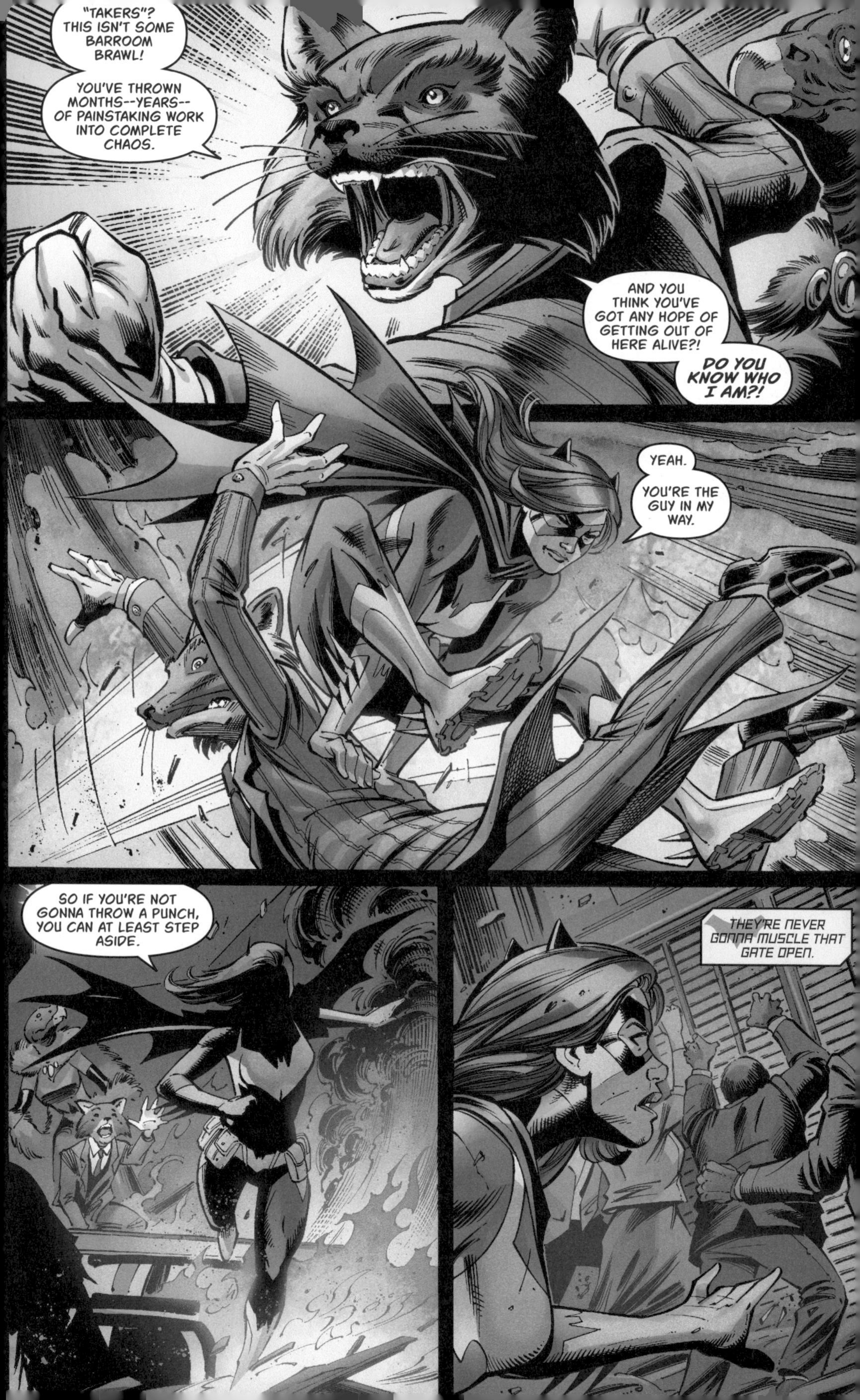
"TAKERS"? THIS ISN'T SOME BARROOM BRAWL!
YOU'VE THROWN MONTHS--YEARS--OF PAINSTAKING WORK INTO COMPLETE CHAOS.
AND YOU THINK YOU'VE GOT ANY HOPE OF GETTING OUT OF HERE ALIVE?!
DO YOU KNOW WHO I AM?!
YEAH.
YOU'RE THE GUY IN MY WAY.
SO IF YOU'RE NOT GONNA THROW A PUNCH, YOU CAN AT LEAST STEP ASIDE.
THEY'RE NEVER GONNA MUSCLE THAT GATE OPEN.

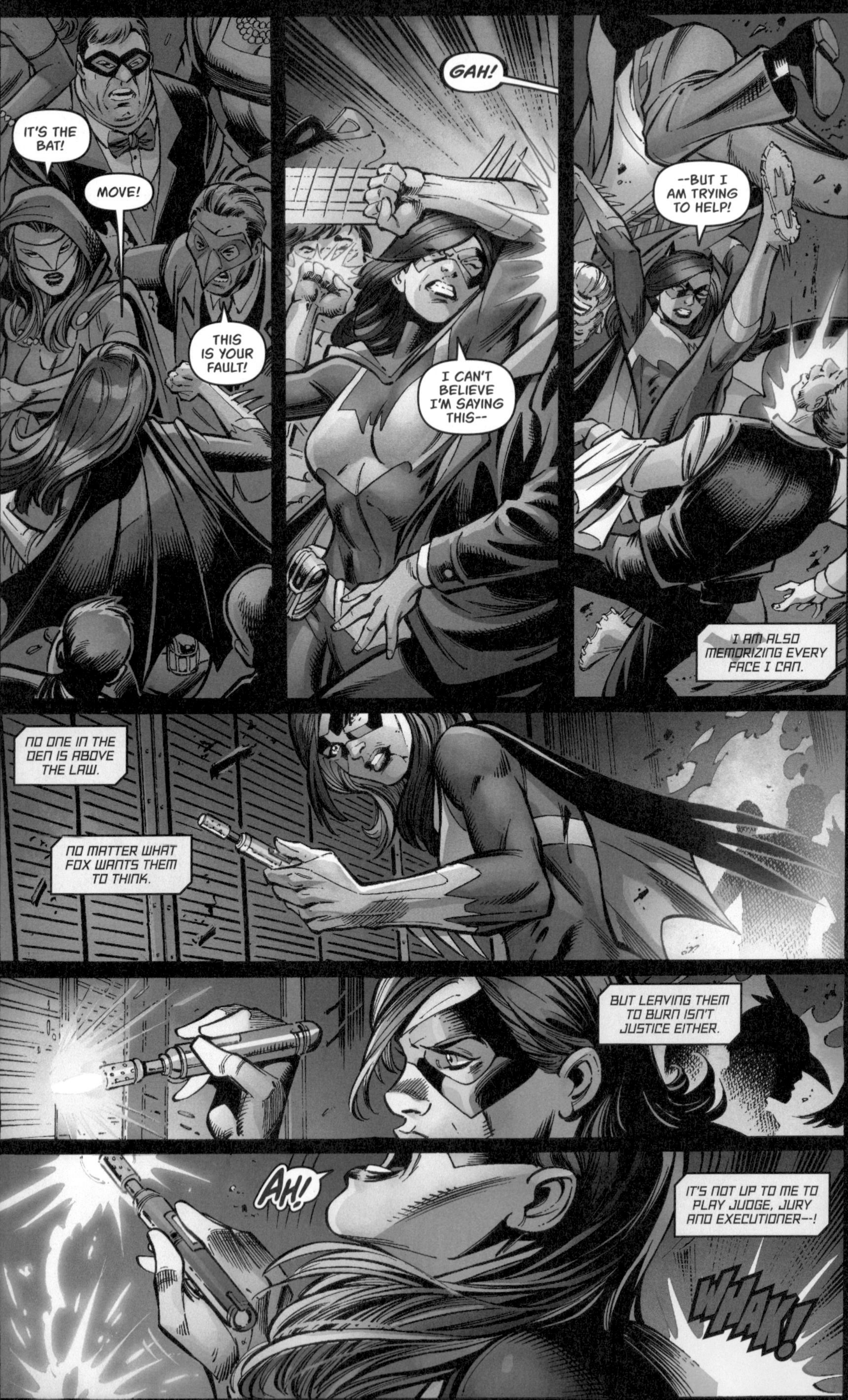
IT'S THE BAT!
MOVE!
THIS IS YOUR FAULT!
GAH!
I CAN'T BELIEVE I'M SAYING THIS--
--BUT I AM TRYING TO HELP!
I AM ALSO MEMORIZING EVERY FACE I CAN.
NO ONE IN THE DEN IS ABOVE THE LAW.
NO MATTER WHAT FOX WANTS THEM TO THINK.
BUT LEAVING THEM TO BURN ISN'T JUSTICE EITHER.
AH!
IT'S NOT UP TO ME TO PLAY JUDGE, JURY AND EXECUTIONER--!
WHAK!

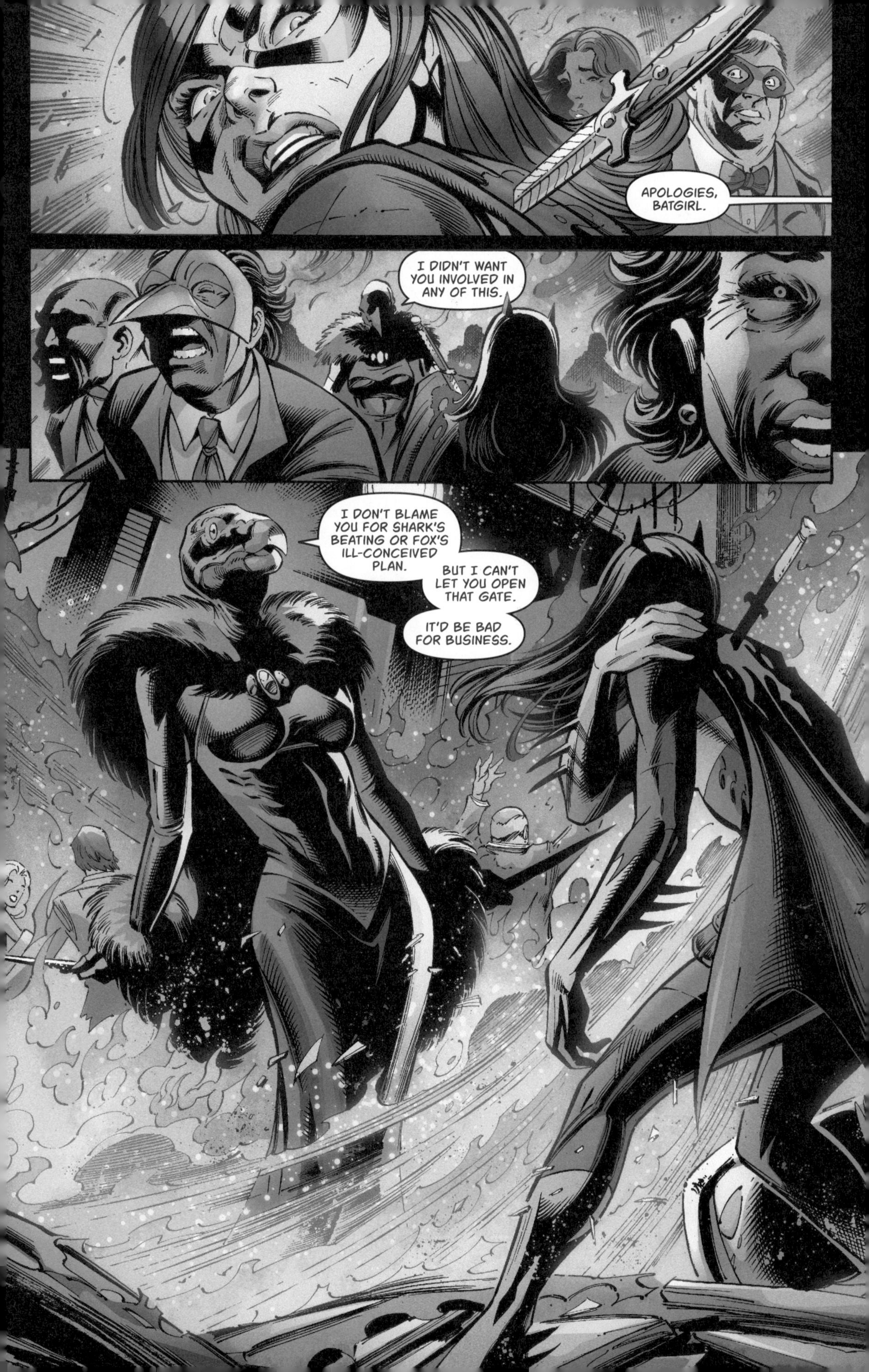
APOLOGIES, BATGIRL.
I DIDN'T WANT YOU INVOLVED IN ANY OF THIS.
I DON'T BLAME YOU FOR SHARK'S BEATING OR FOX'S ILL-CONCEIVED PLAN.
BUT I CAN'T LET YOU OPEN THAT GATE.
IT'D BE BAD FOR BUSINESS.

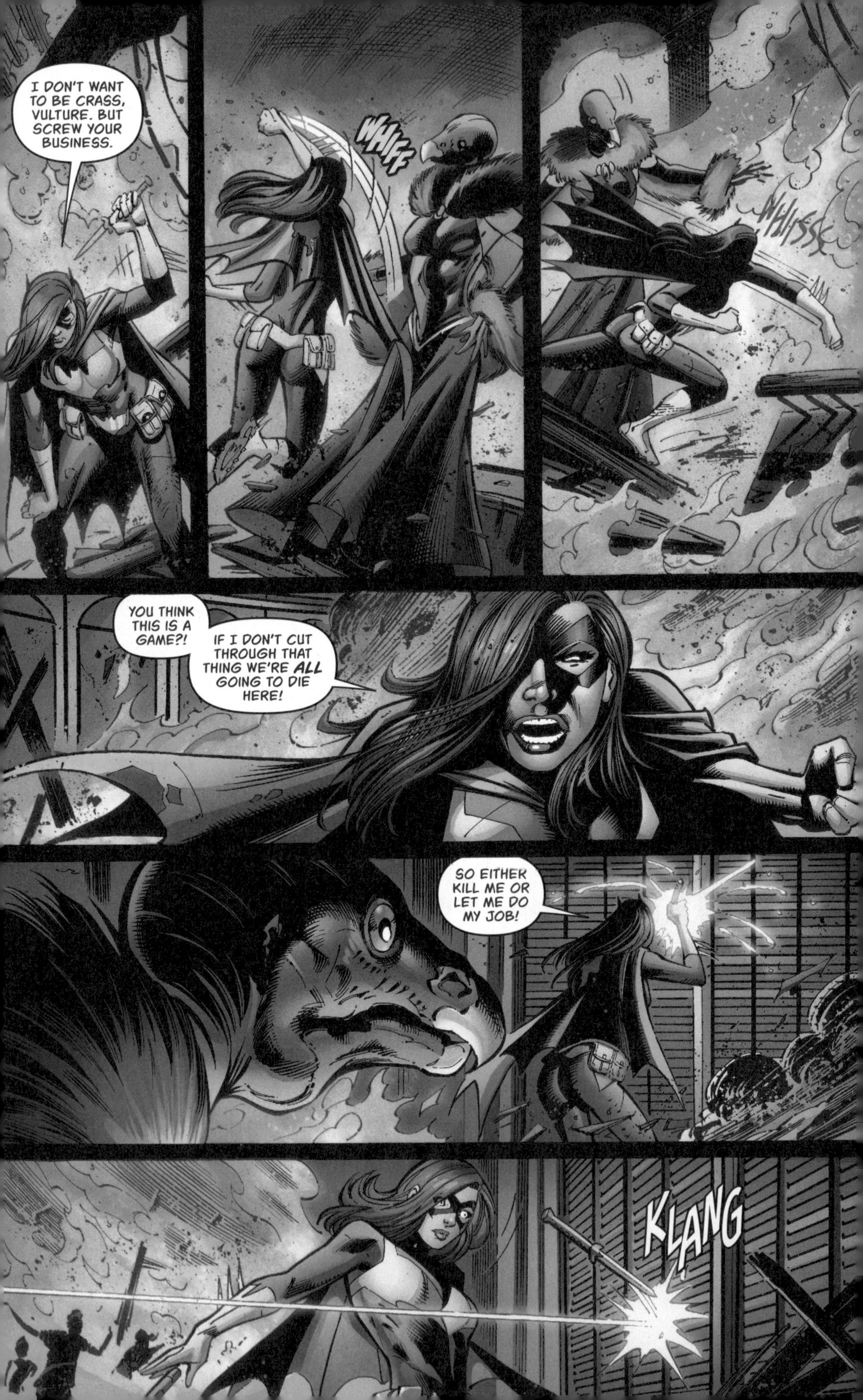
I DON'T WANT TO BE CRASS, VULTURE. BUT SCREW YOUR BUSINESS.
WHIFF
WHISSK
YOU THINK THIS IS A GAME?!
IF I DON'T CUT THROUGH THAT THING WE'RE ALL GOING TO DIE HERE!
SO EITHER KILL ME OR LET ME DO MY JOB!
KLANG

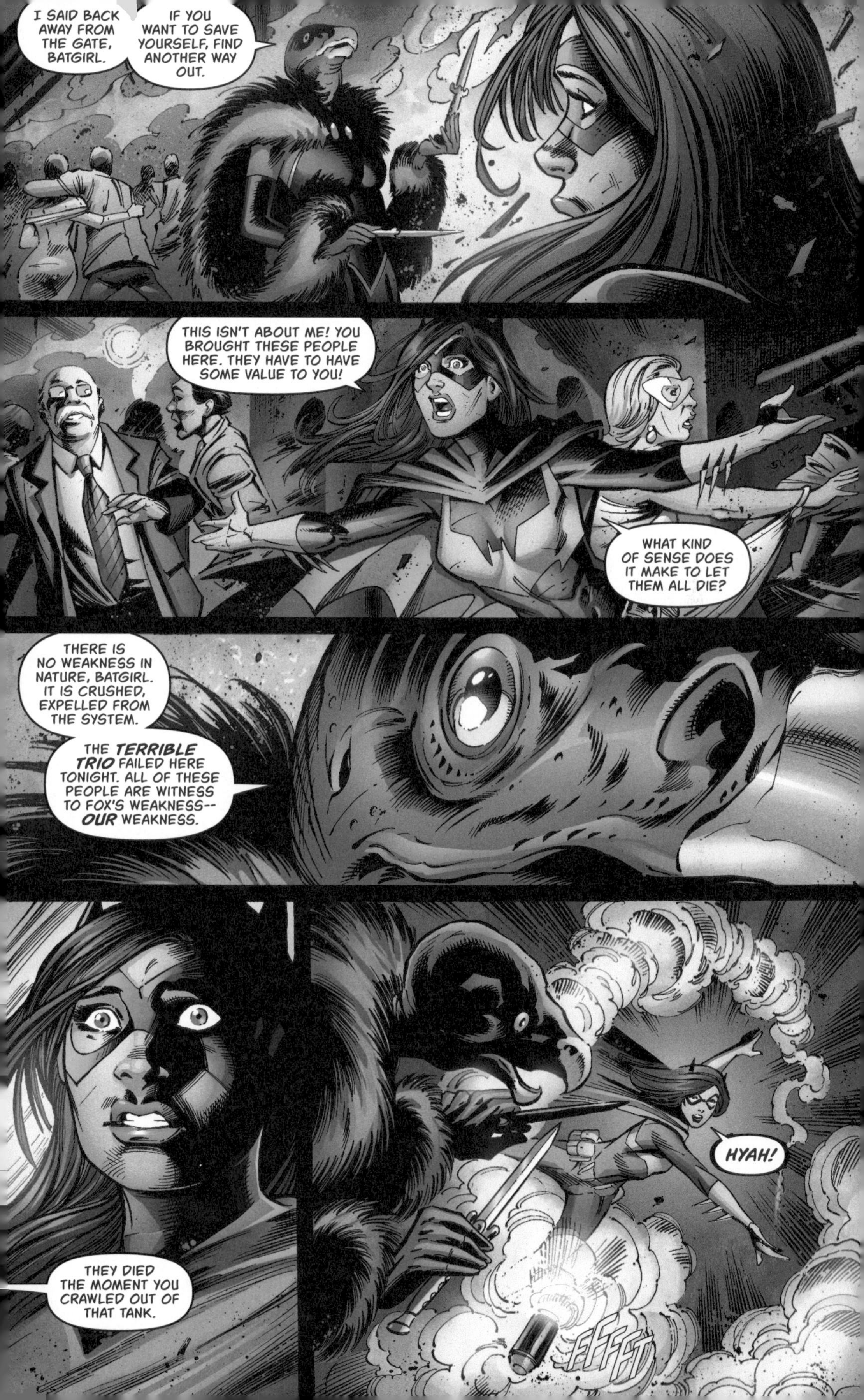
I SAID BACK AWAY FROM THE GATE, BATGIRL.
IF YOU WANT TO SAVE YOURSELF, FIND ANOTHER WAY OUT.
THIS ISN'T ABOUT ME! YOU BROUGHT THESE PEOPLE HERE. THEY HAVE TO HAVE SOME VALUE TO YOU!
WHAT KIND OF SENSE DOES IT MAKE TO LET THEM ALL DIE?
THERE IS NO WEAKNESS IN NATURE, BATGIRL. IT IS CRUSHED, EXPELLED FROM THE SYSTEM.
THE TERRIBLE TRIO FAILED HERE TONIGHT. ALL OF THESE PEOPLE ARE WITNESS TO FOX'S WEAKNESS-- OUR WEAKNESS.
THEY DIED THE MOMENT YOU CRAWLED OUT OF THAT TANK.
HYAH!
FFFFFT

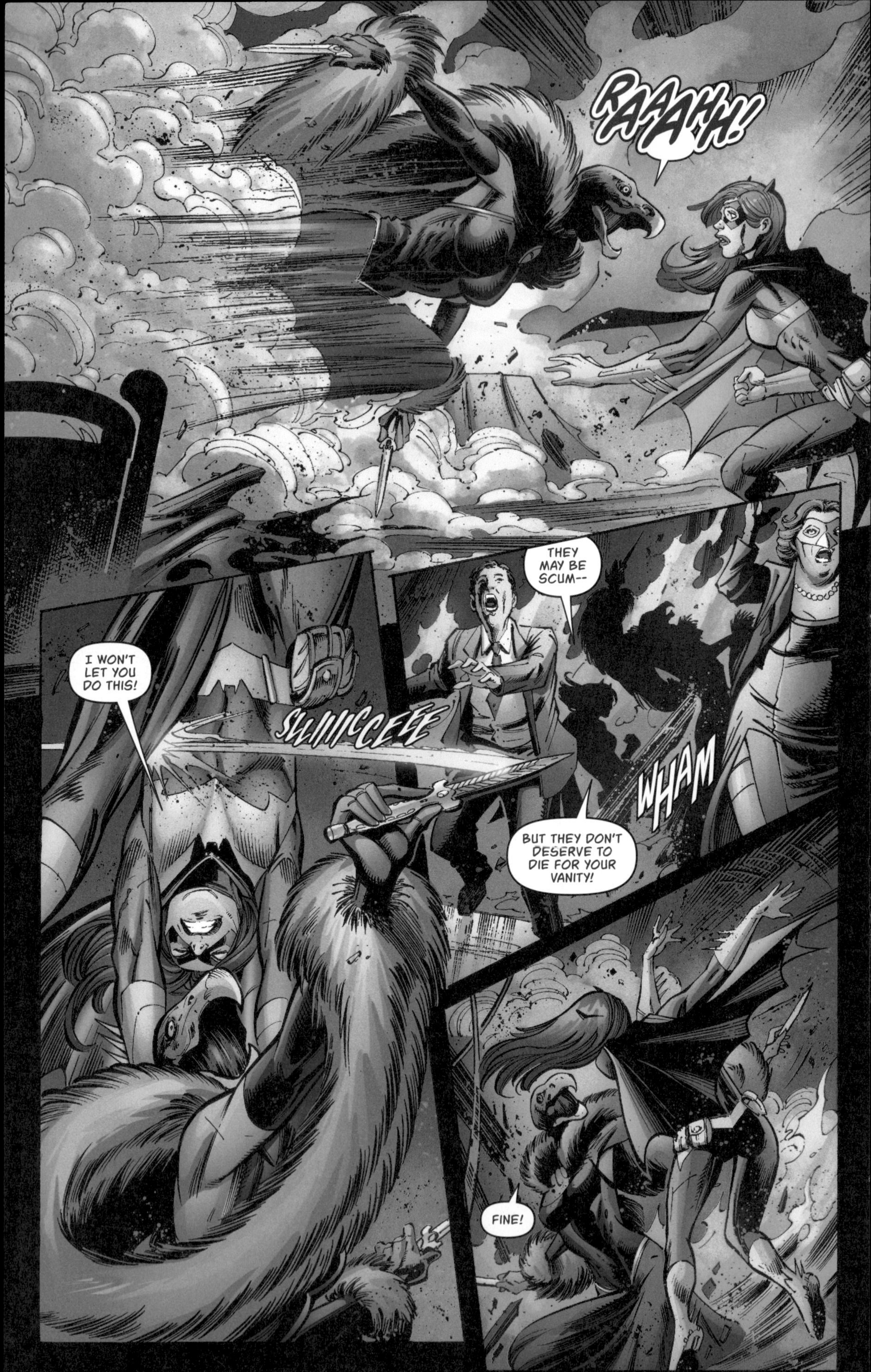
RAAAHH!
THEY MAY BE SCUM--
I WON'T LET YOU DO THIS!
SLLIIIICCEEE
WHAM
BUT THEY DON'T DESERVE TO DIE FOR YOUR VANITY!
FINE!

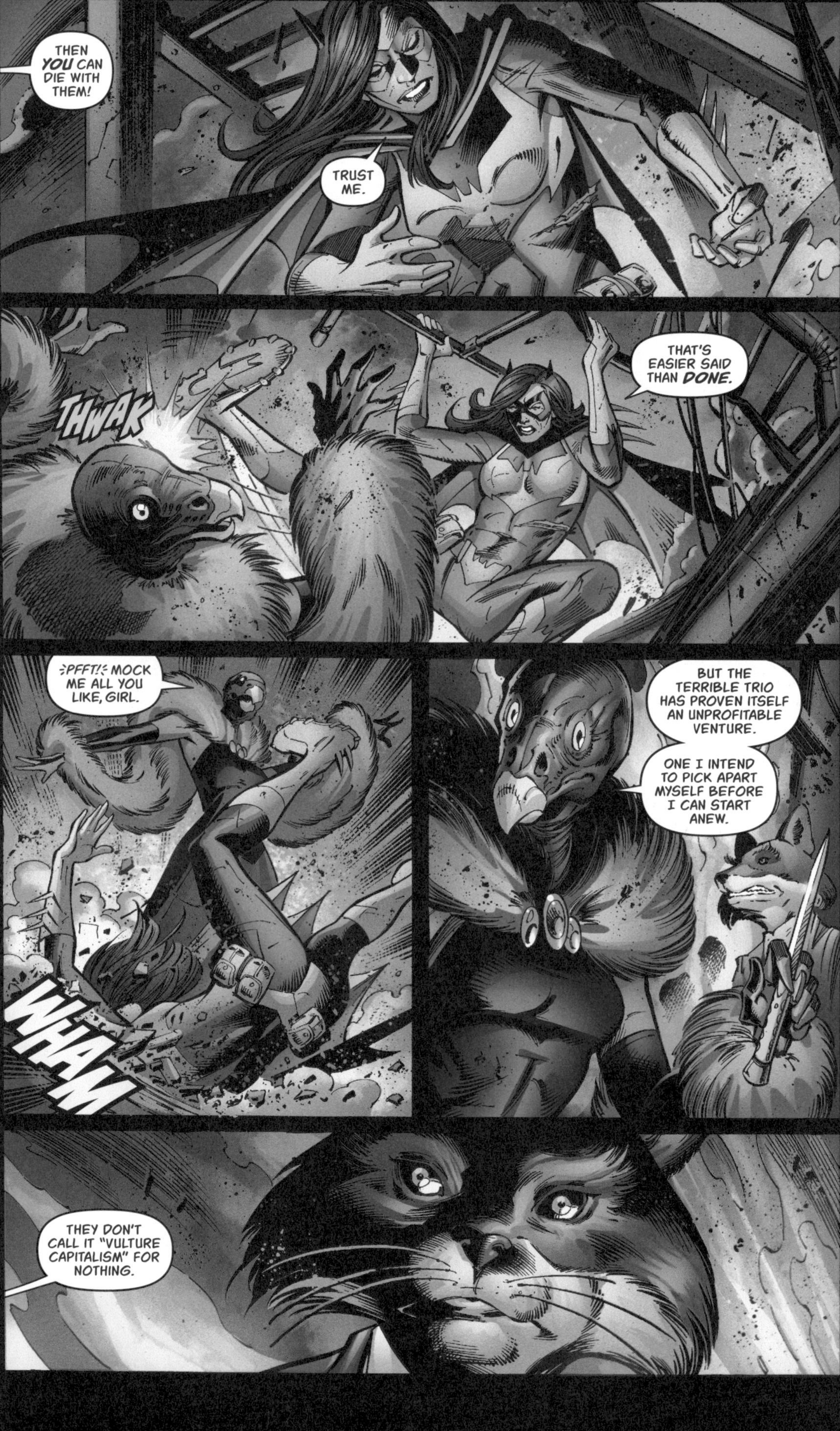
THEN YOU CAN DIE WITH THEM!
TRUST ME.
THWAK
THAT'S EASIER SAID THAN DONE.
PFFT! MOCK ME ALL YOU LIKE, GIRL.
WHAM
BUT THE TERRIBLE TRIO HAS PROVEN ITSELF AN UNPROFITABLE VENTURE.
ONE I INTEND TO PICK APART MYSELF BEFORE I CAN START ANEW.
THEY DON'T CALL IT "VULTURE CAPITALISM" FOR NOTHING.

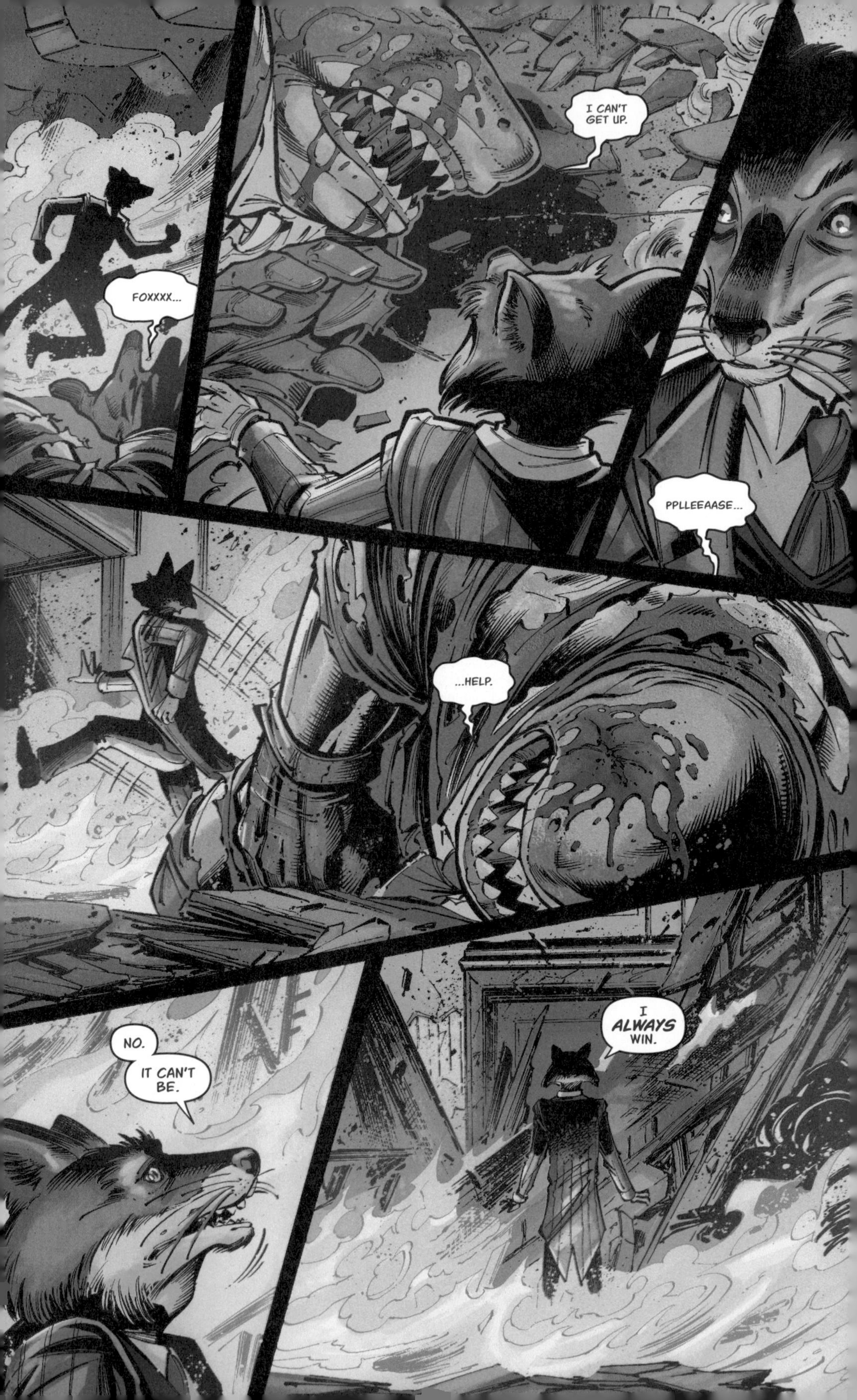
FOXXXX...
I CAN'T GET UP.
PPLLEEAASE...
...HELP.
NO.
IT CAN'T BE.
I *ALWAYS* WIN.

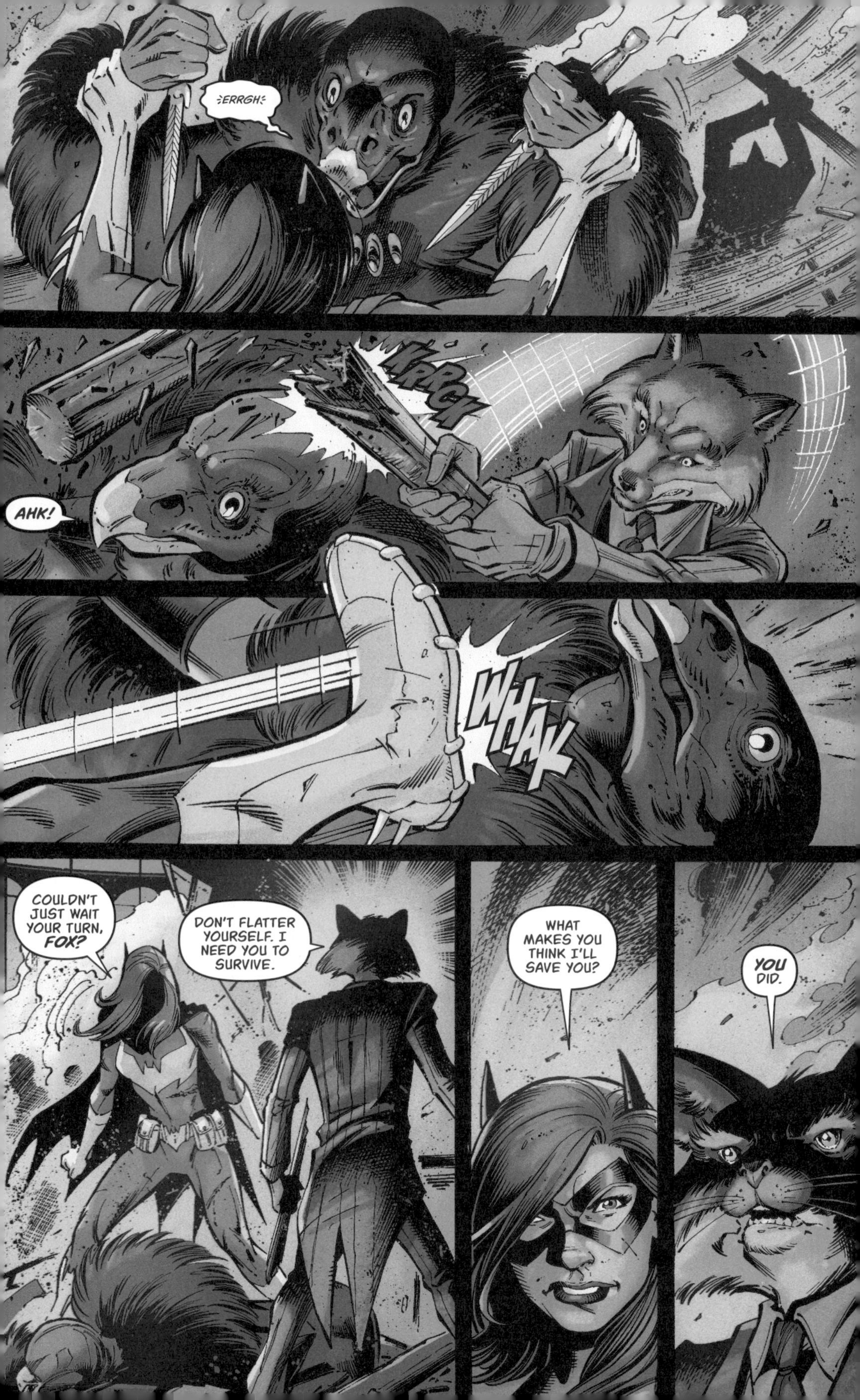

ERRGH
KRRCK
AHK!
WHAK
COULDN'T JUST WAIT YOUR TURN, FOX?
DON'T FLATTER YOURSELF. I NEED YOU TO SURVIVE.
WHAT MAKES YOU THINK I'LL SAVE YOU?
YOU DID.

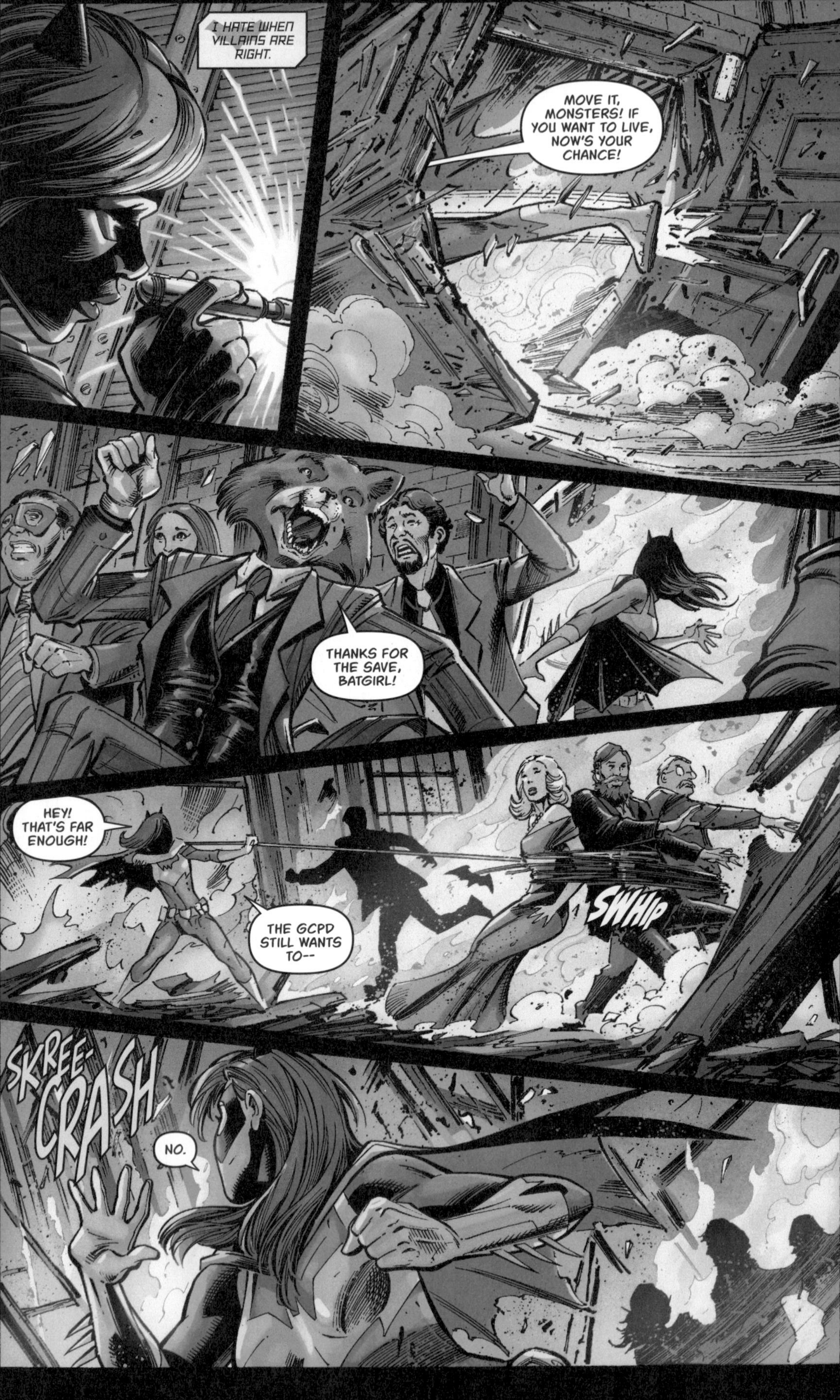
I HATE WHEN VILLAINS ARE RIGHT.
MOVE IT, MONSTERS! IF YOU WANT TO LIVE, NOW'S YOUR CHANCE!
THANKS FOR THE SAVE, BATGIRL!
HEY! THAT'S FAR ENOUGH!
THE GCPD STILL WANTS TO--
SWHIP
SKREE-CRASH
NO.

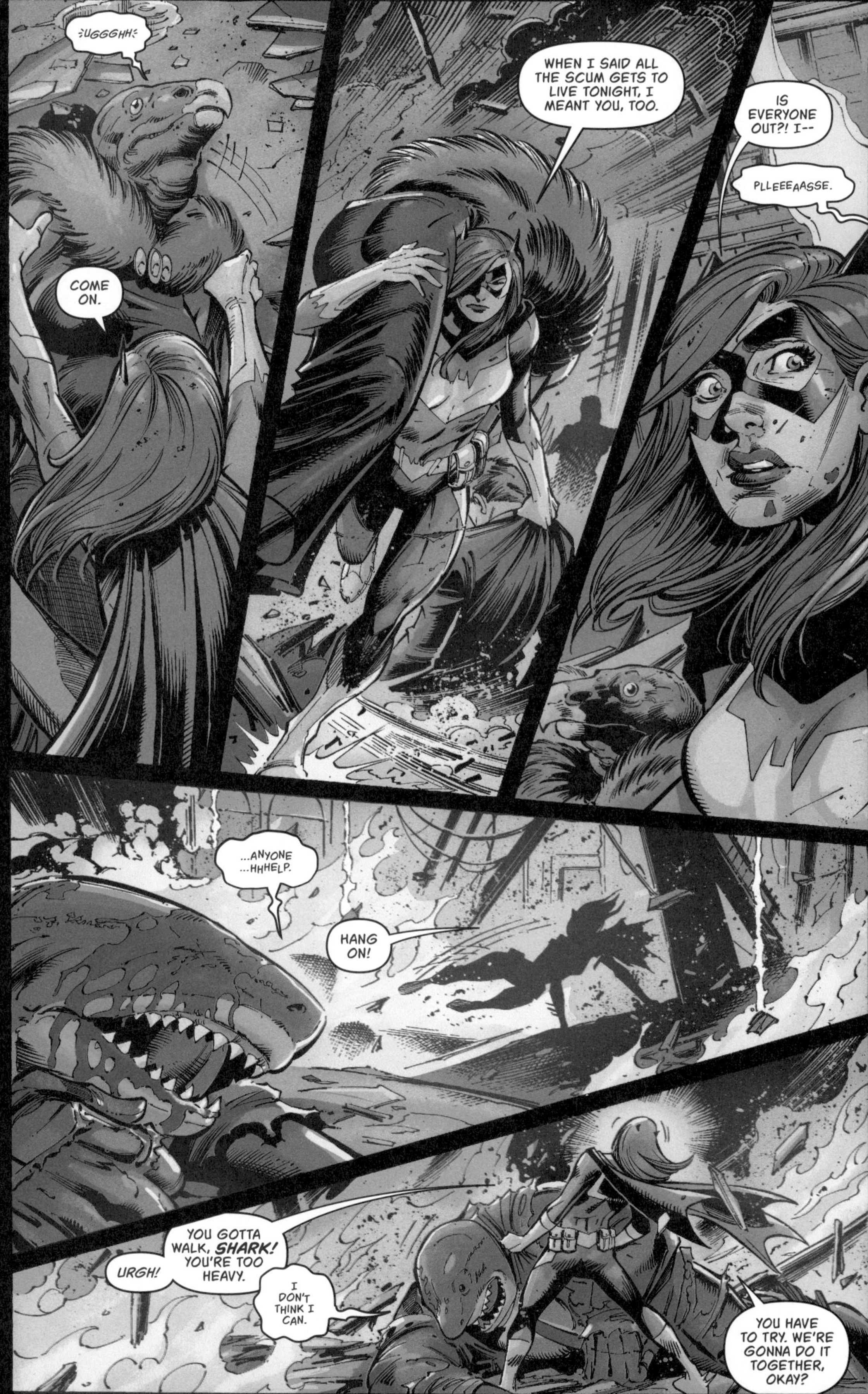
UGGGHH
COME ON.
WHEN I SAID ALL THE SCUM GETS TO LIVE TONIGHT, I MEANT YOU, TOO.
IS EVERYONE OUT?! I--
PLLEEEAASSE.
...ANYONE ...HHHELP.
HANG ON!
URGH!
YOU GOTTA WALK, SHARK! YOU'RE TOO HEAVY.
I DON'T THINK I CAN.
YOU HAVE TO TRY. WE'RE GONNA DO IT TOGETHER, OKAY?

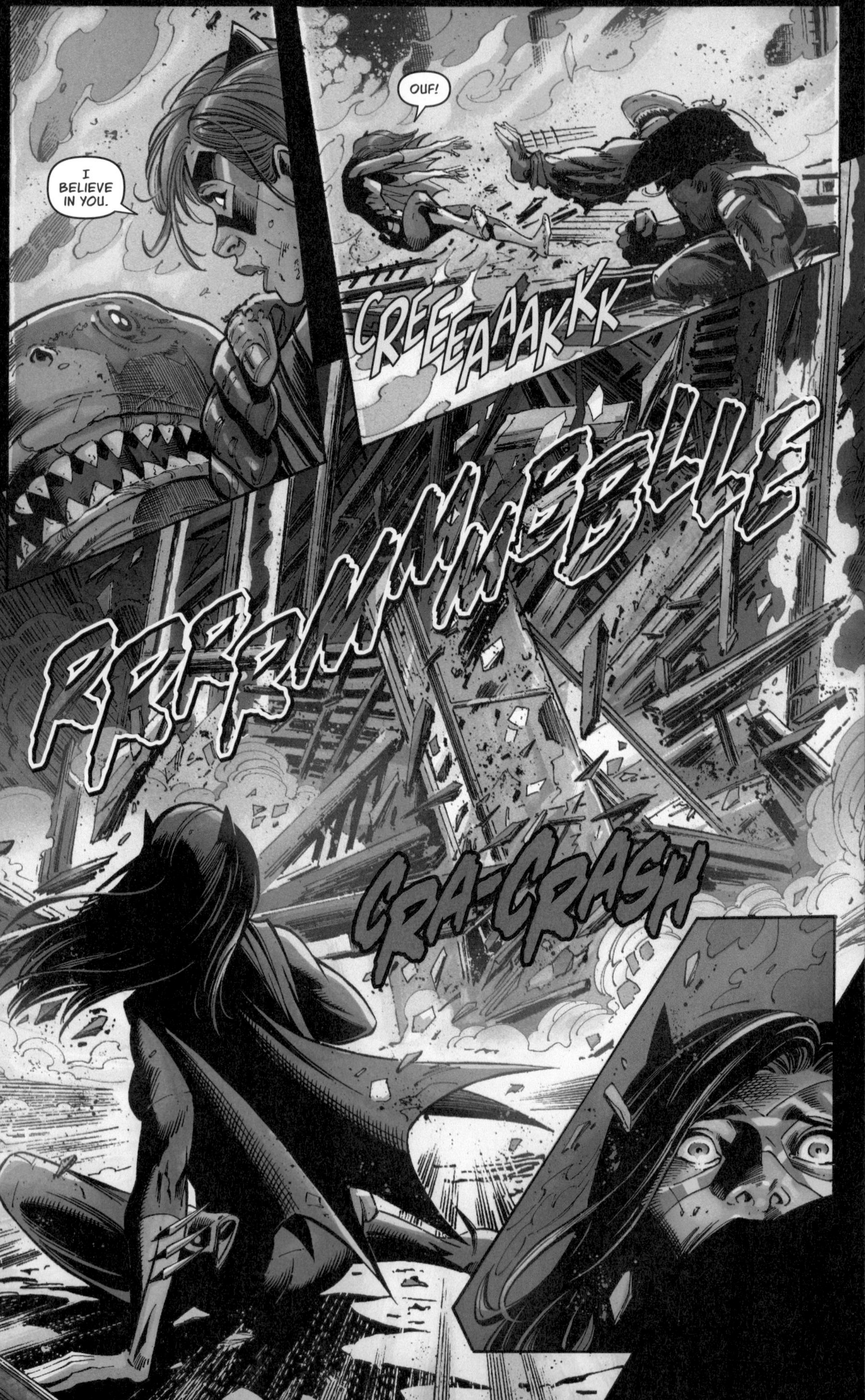
I BELIEVE IN YOU.
OUF!
CREEEAAAKKK
RRRRUMMMBBLLE
CRA-CRASH

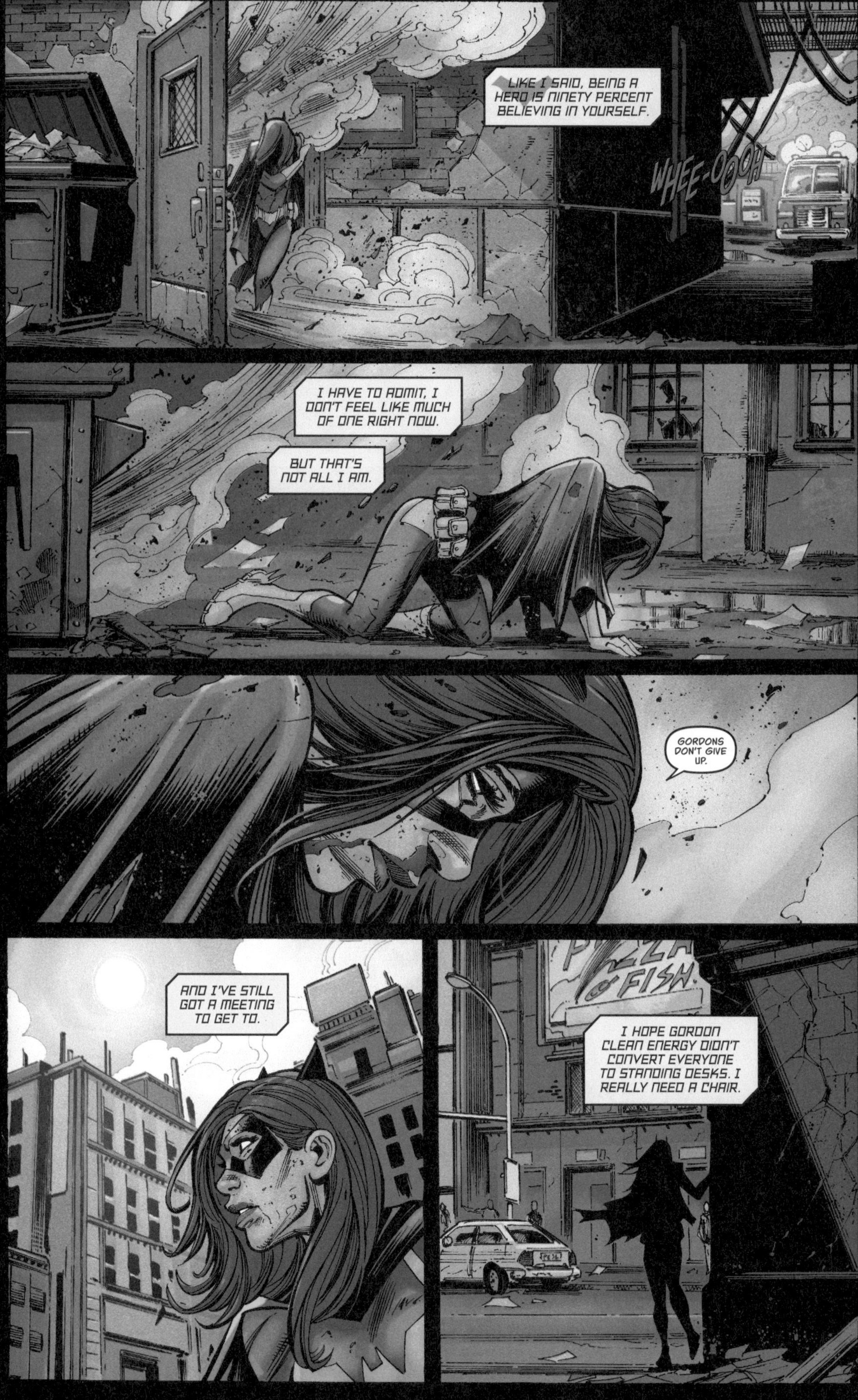
LIKE I SAID, BEING A HERO IS NINETY PERCENT BELIEVING IN YOURSELF.
WHEE-OOOH
I HAVE TO ADMIT, I DON'T FEEL LIKE MUCH OF ONE RIGHT NOW.
BUT THAT'S NOT ALL I AM.
GORDONS DON'T GIVE UP.
AND I'VE STILL GOT A MEETING TO GET TO.
I HOPE GORDON CLEAN ENERGY DIDN'T CONVERT EVERYONE TO STANDING DESKS. I REALLY NEED A CHAIR.

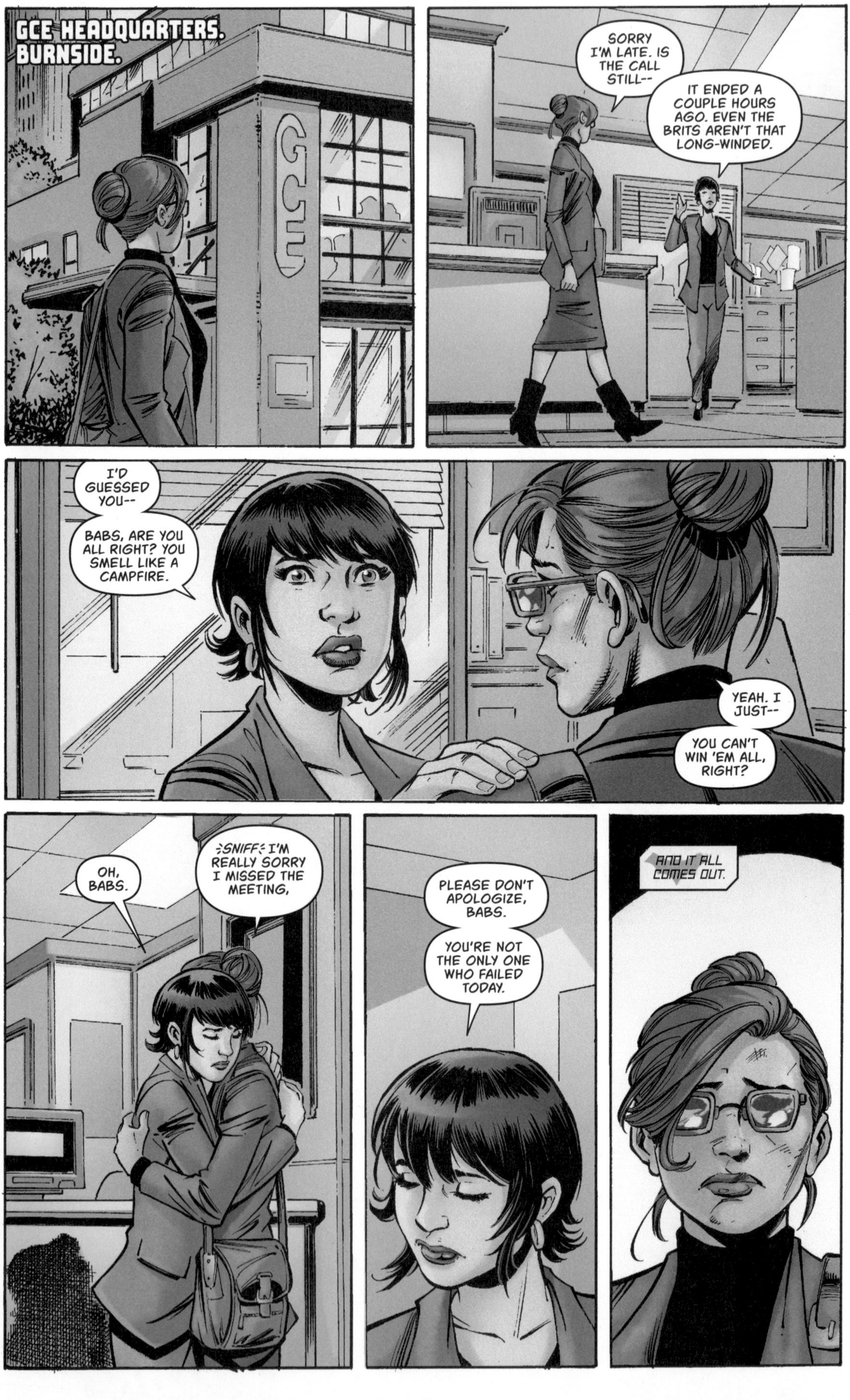
GCE HEADQUARTERS. BURNSIDE.
SORRY I'M LATE. IS THE CALL STILL--
IT ENDED A COUPLE HOURS AGO. EVEN THE BRITS AREN'T THAT LONG-WINDED.
I'D GUESSED YOU--
BABS, ARE YOU ALL RIGHT? YOU SMELL LIKE A CAMPFIRE.
YEAH. I JUST--
YOU CAN'T WIN 'EM ALL, RIGHT?
OH, BABS.
SNIFF I'M REALLY SORRY I MISSED THE MEETING,
PLEASE DON'T APOLOGIZE, BABS.
YOU'RE NOT THE ONLY ONE WHO FAILED TODAY.
AND IT ALL COMES OUT.

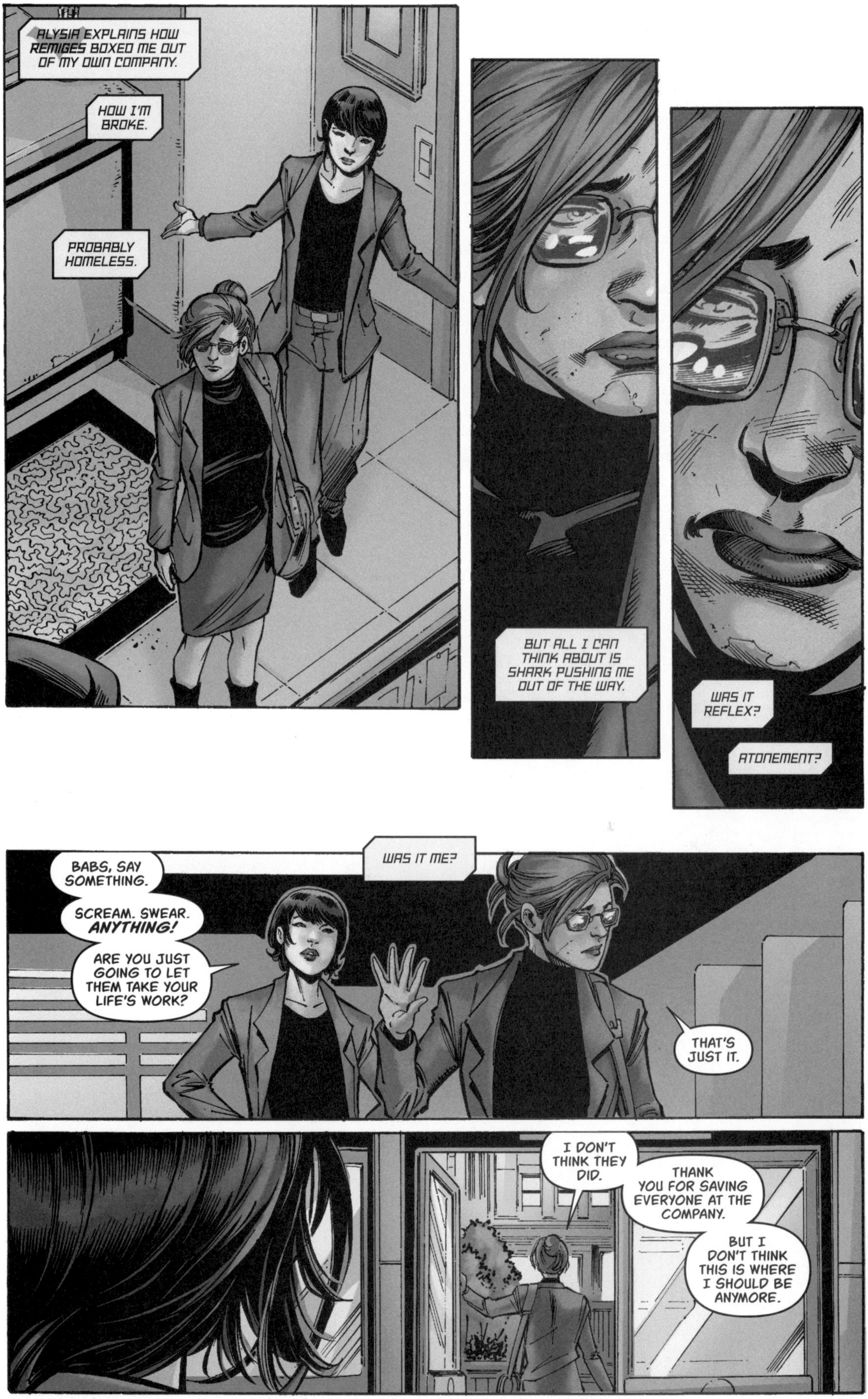
ALYSIA EXPLAINS HOW REMIGES BOXED ME OUT OF MY OWN COMPANY.
HOW I'M BROKE.
PROBABLY HOMELESS.
BUT ALL I CAN THINK ABOUT IS SHARK PUSHING ME OUT OF THE WAY.
WAS IT REFLEX?
ATONEMENT?
WAS IT ME?
BABS, SAY SOMETHING.
SCREAM. SWEAR. ANYTHING!
ARE YOU JUST GOING TO LET THEM TAKE YOUR LIFE'S WORK?
THAT'S JUST IT.
I DON'T THINK THEY DID.
THANK YOU FOR SAVING EVERYONE AT THE COMPANY.
BUT I DON'T THINK THIS IS WHERE I SHOULD BE ANYMORE.

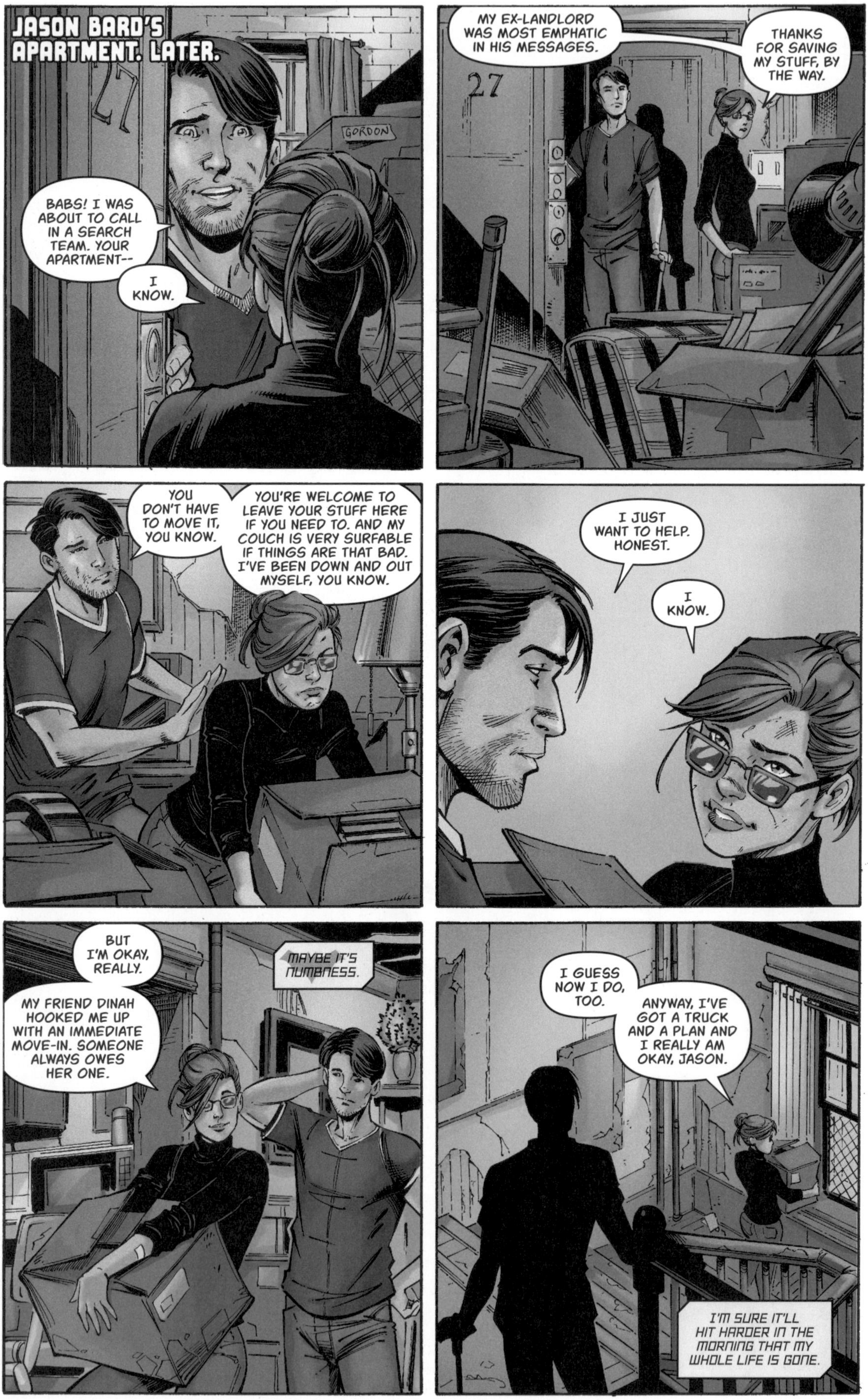
JASON BARD'S APARTMENT. LATER.
BABS! I WAS ABOUT TO CALL IN A SEARCH TEAM. YOUR APARTMENT--
I KNOW.
GORDON
MY EX-LANDLORD WAS MOST EMPHATIC IN HIS MESSAGES.
THANKS FOR SAVING MY STUFF, BY THE WAY.
27
YOU DON'T HAVE TO MOVE IT, YOU KNOW.
YOU'RE WELCOME TO LEAVE YOUR STUFF HERE IF YOU NEED TO. AND MY COUCH IS VERY SURFABLE IF THINGS ARE THAT BAD. I'VE BEEN DOWN AND OUT MYSELF, YOU KNOW.
I JUST WANT TO HELP. HONEST.
I KNOW.
BUT I'M OKAY, REALLY.
MAYBE IT'S NUMBNESS.
MY FRIEND DINAH HOOKED ME UP WITH AN IMMEDIATE MOVE-IN. SOMEONE ALWAYS OWES HER ONE.
I GUESS NOW I DO, TOO.
ANYWAY, I'VE GOT A TRUCK AND A PLAN AND I REALLY AM OKAY, JASON.
I'M SURE IT'LL HIT HARDER IN THE MORNING THAT MY WHOLE LIFE IS GONE.

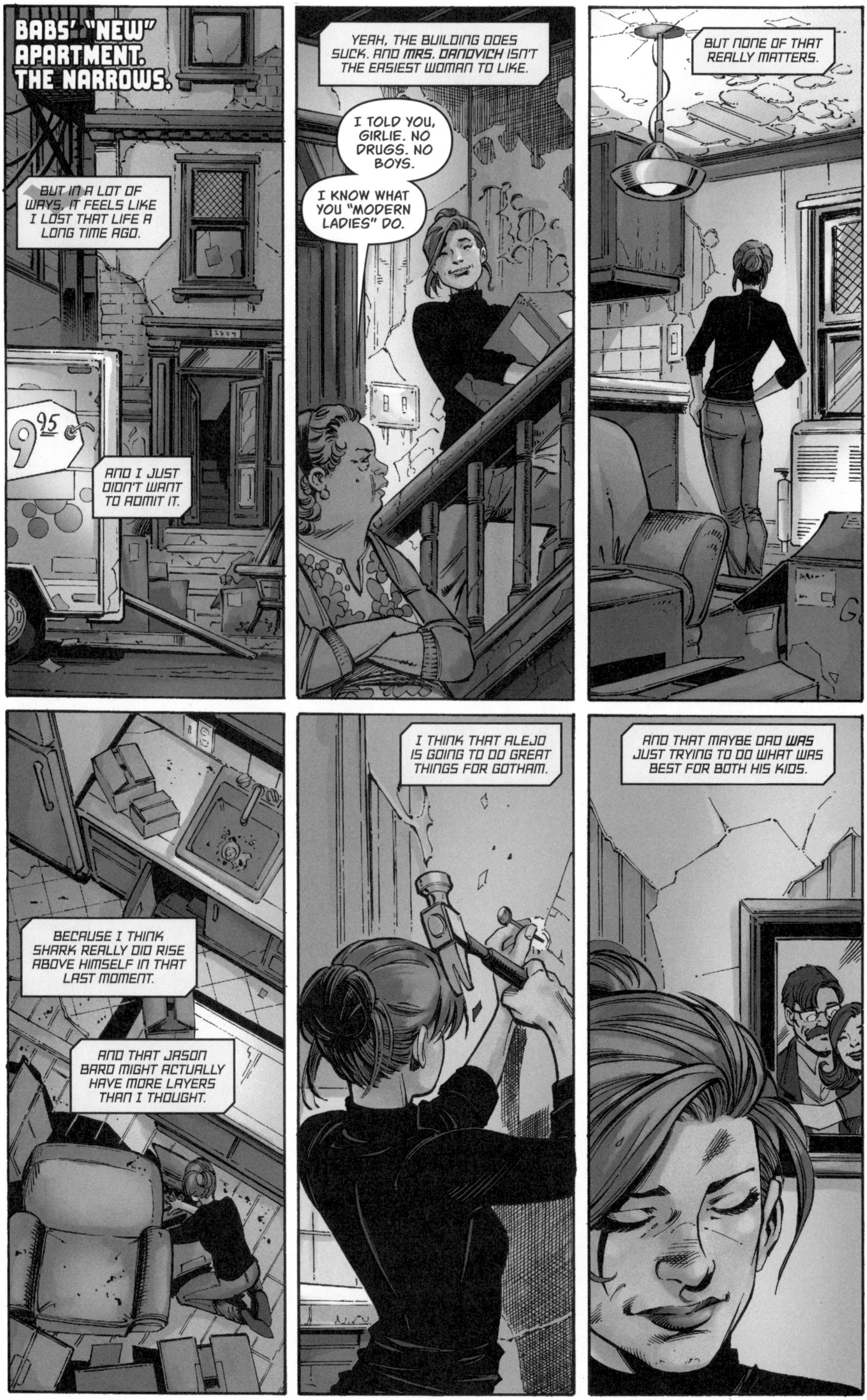
BABS' "NEW" APARTMENT. THE NARROWS.
BUT IN A LOT OF WAYS, IT FEELS LIKE I LOST THAT LIFE A LONG TIME AGO.
9.95
AND I JUST DIDN'T WANT TO ADMIT IT.
YEAH, THE BUILDING DOES SUCK. AND MRS. DANOVICH ISN'T THE EASIEST WOMAN TO LIKE.
I TOLD YOU, GIRLIE. NO DRUGS. NO BOYS.
I KNOW WHAT YOU "MODERN LADIES" DO.
BUT NONE OF THAT REALLY MATTERS.
BECAUSE I THINK SHARK REALLY DID RISE ABOVE HIMSELF IN THAT LAST MOMENT.
AND THAT JASON BARD MIGHT ACTUALLY HAVE MORE LAYERS THAN I THOUGHT.
I THINK THAT ALEJO IS GOING TO DO GREAT THINGS FOR GOTHAM.
AND THAT MAYBE DAD WAS JUST TRYING TO DO WHAT WAS BEST FOR BOTH HIS KIDS.

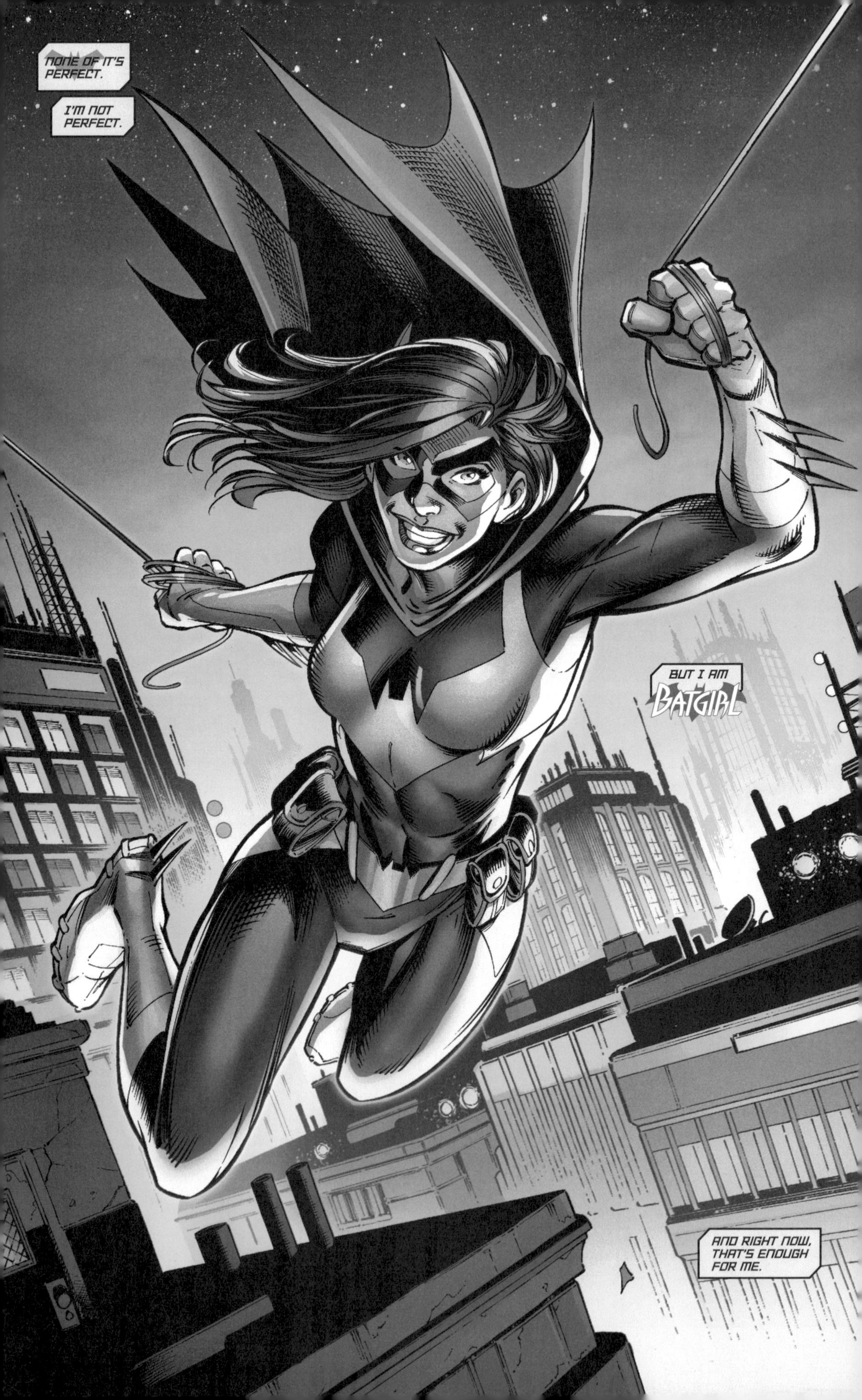
NONE OF IT'S PERFECT.
I'M NOT PERFECT.
BUT I AM BATGIRL
AND RIGHT NOW, THAT'S ENOUGH FOR ME.

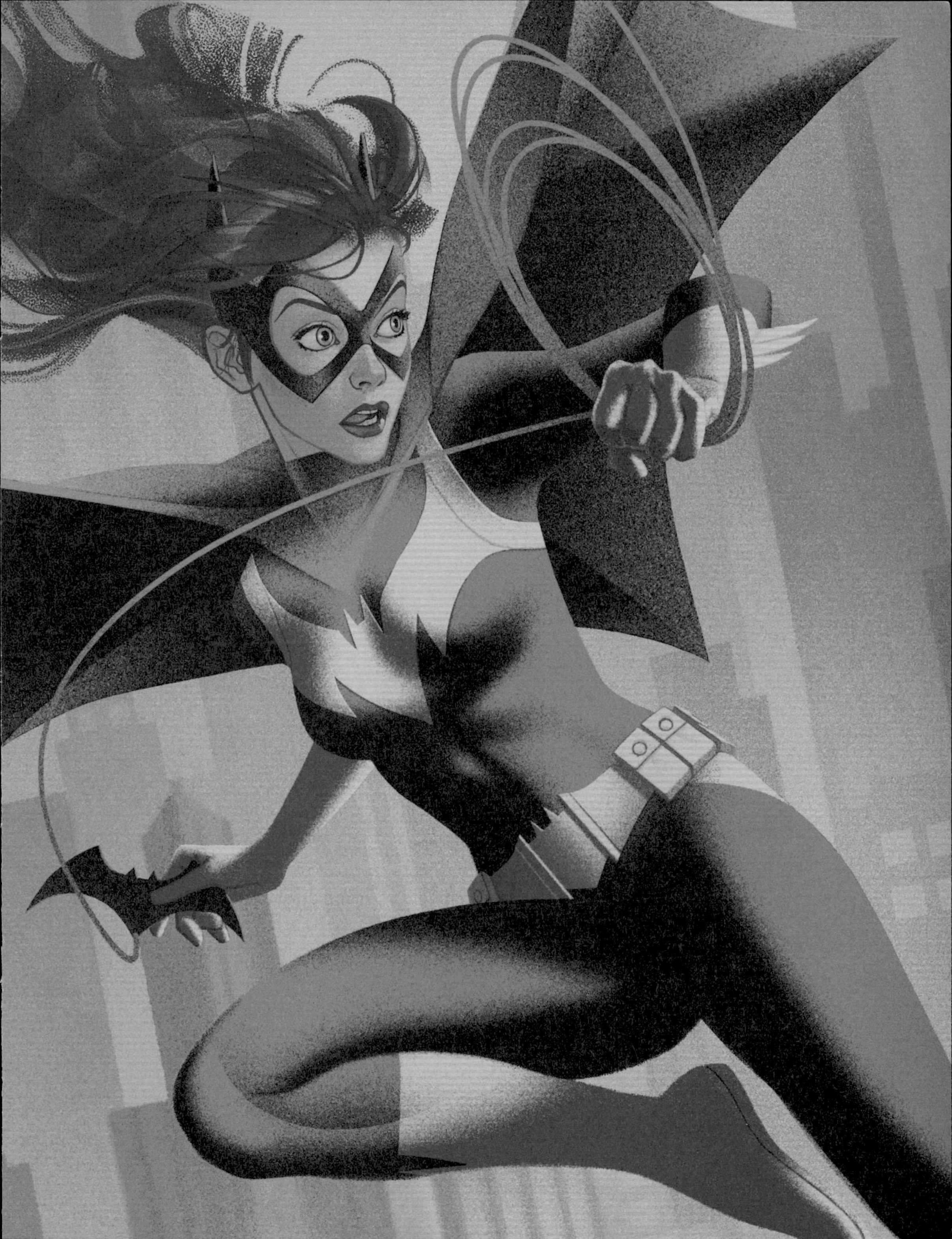

VARIANT COVER GALLERY

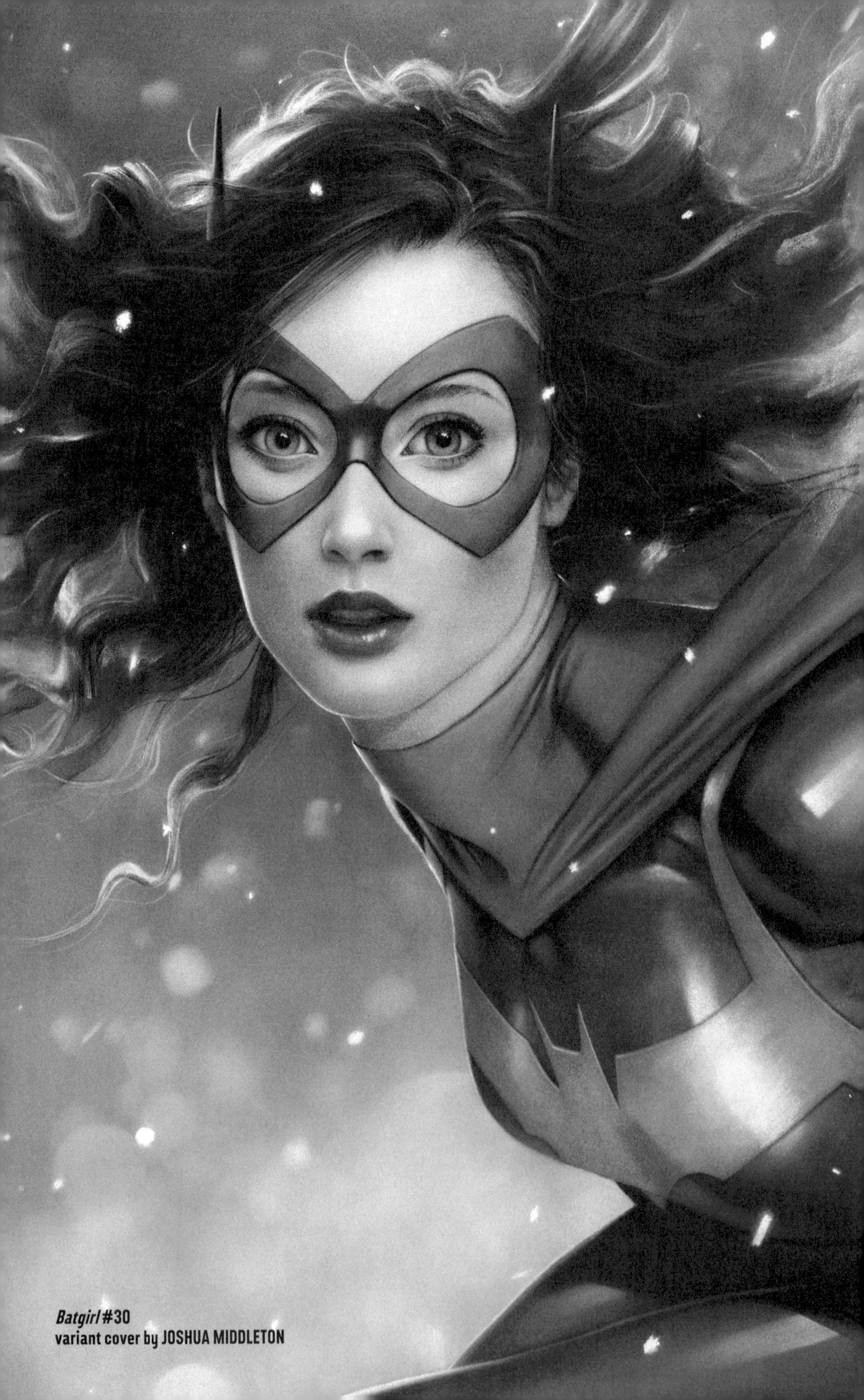

Batgirl #30
variant cover by JOSHUA MIDDLETON

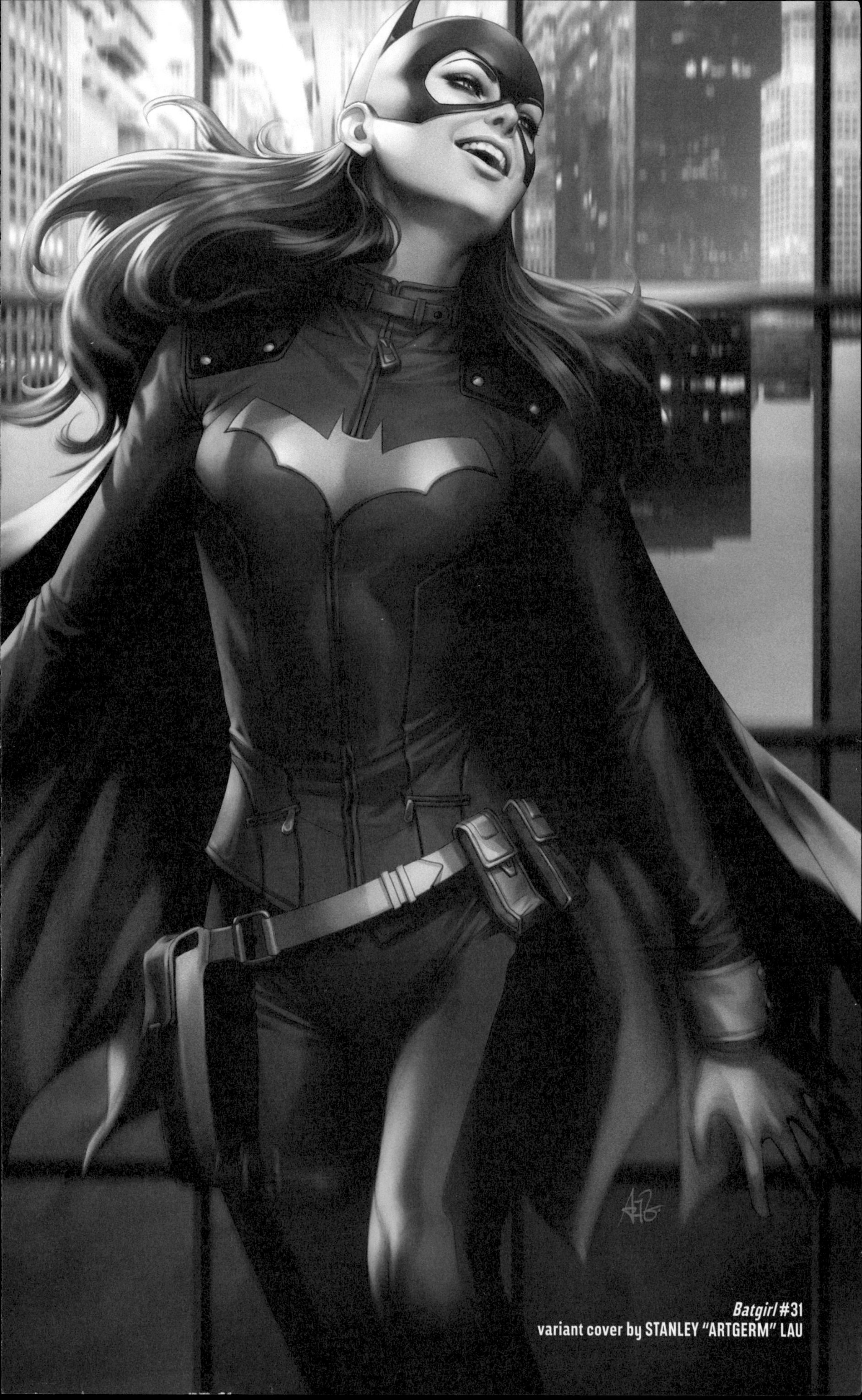

Batgirl #31
variant cover by STANLEY "ARTGERM" LAU

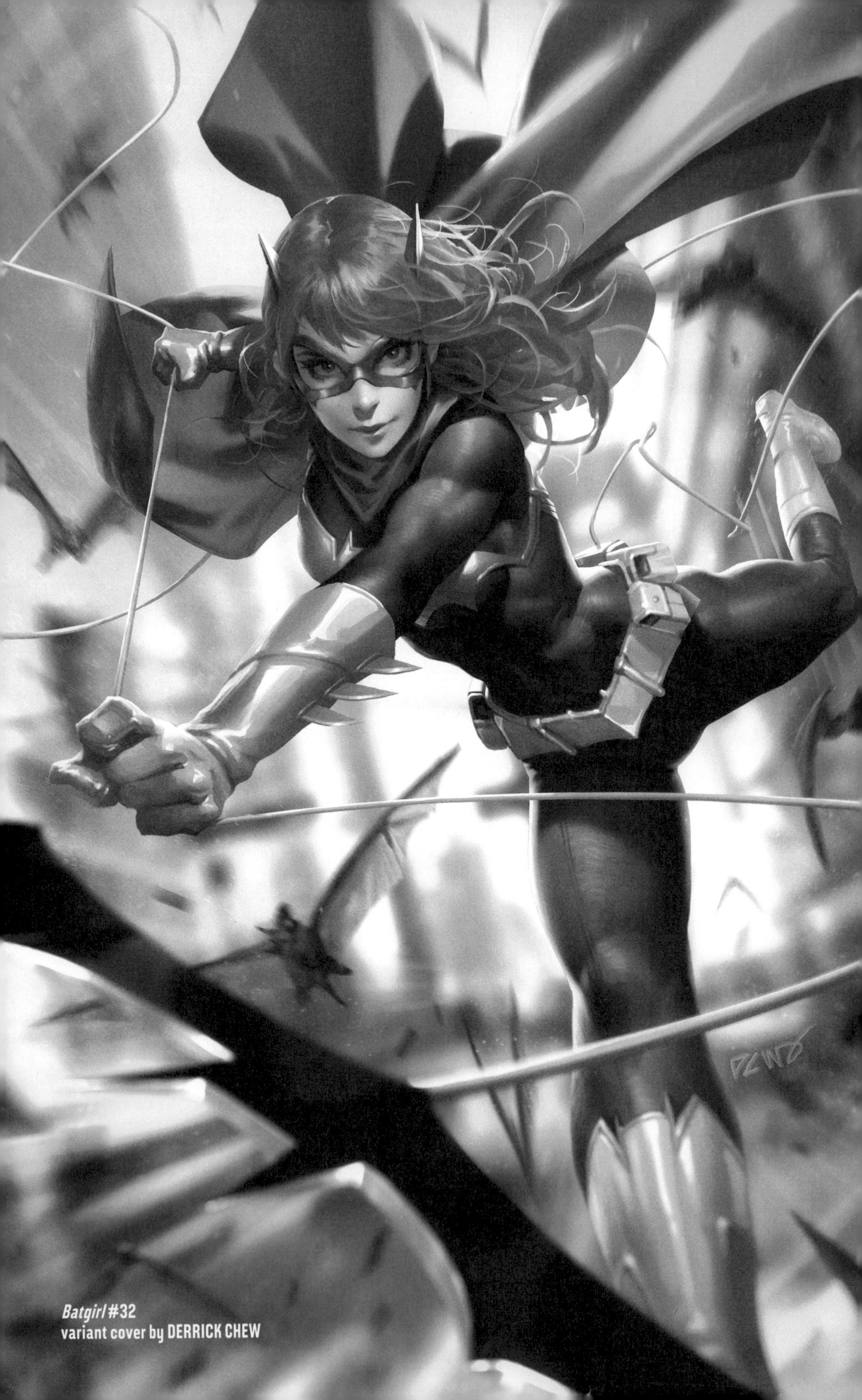

Batgirl #32
variant cover by DERRICK CHEW

Batgirl #33
variant cover by YASMINE PUTRI

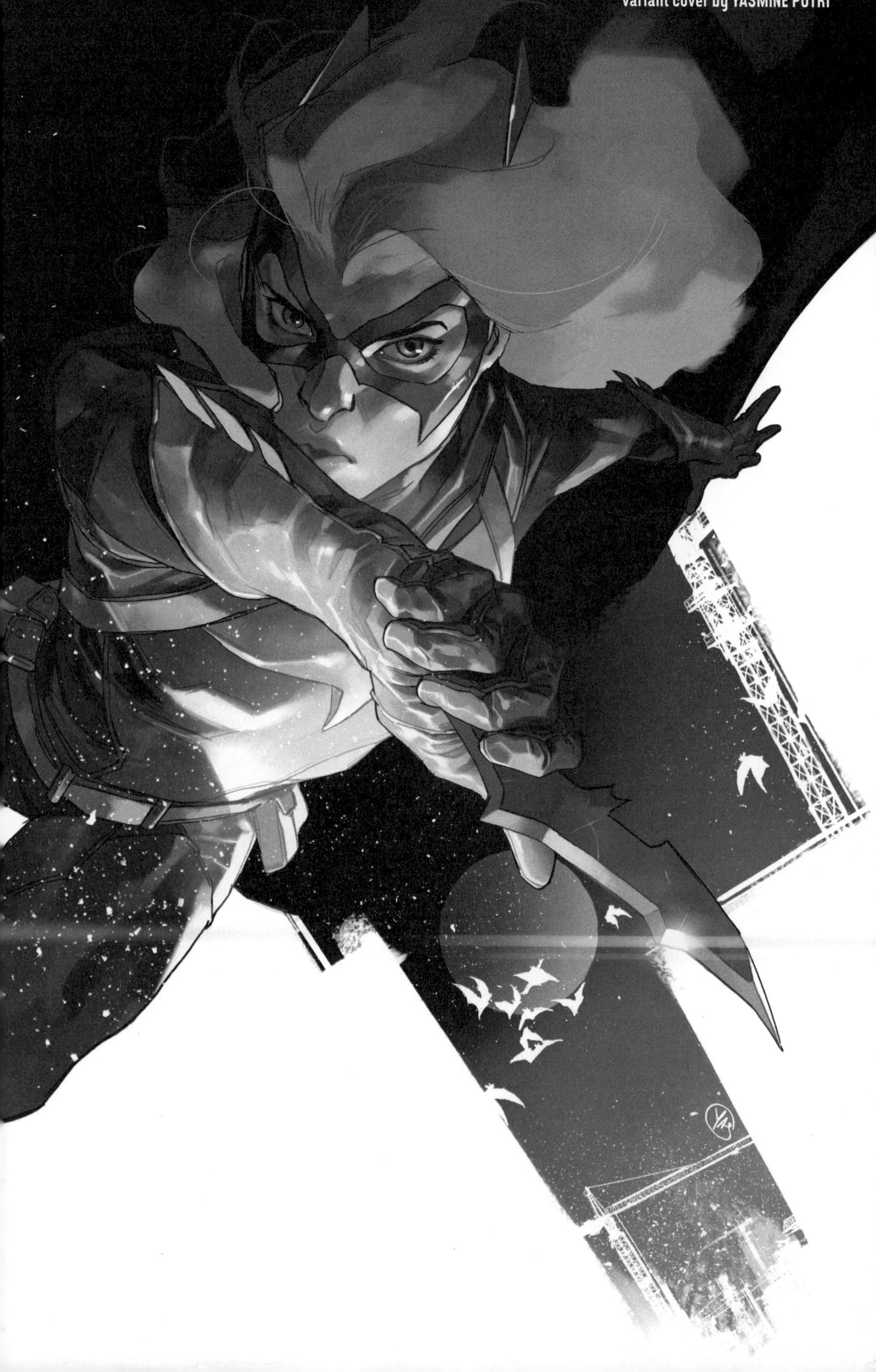

Batgirl #34
variant cover by JOSHUA MIDDLETON

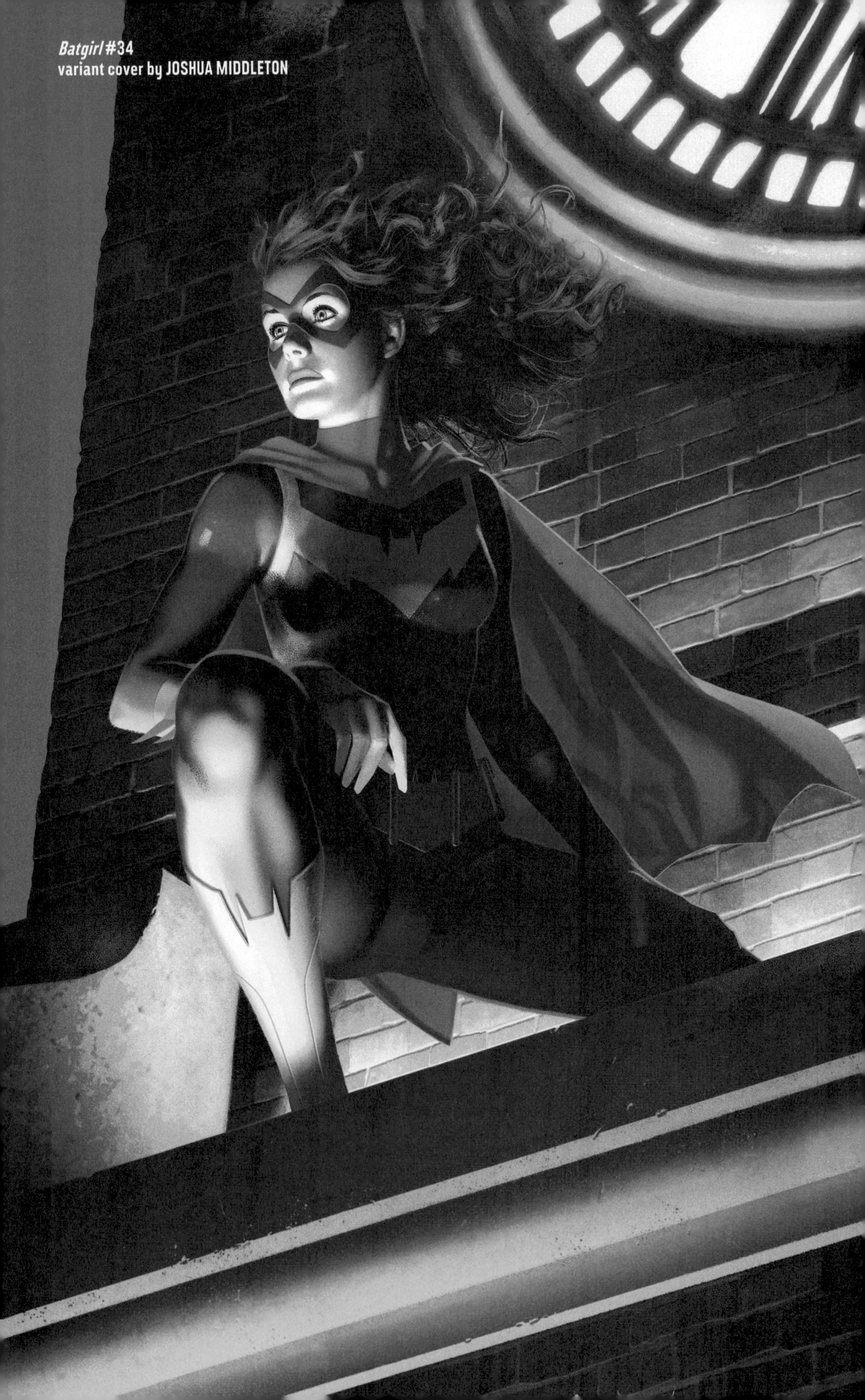

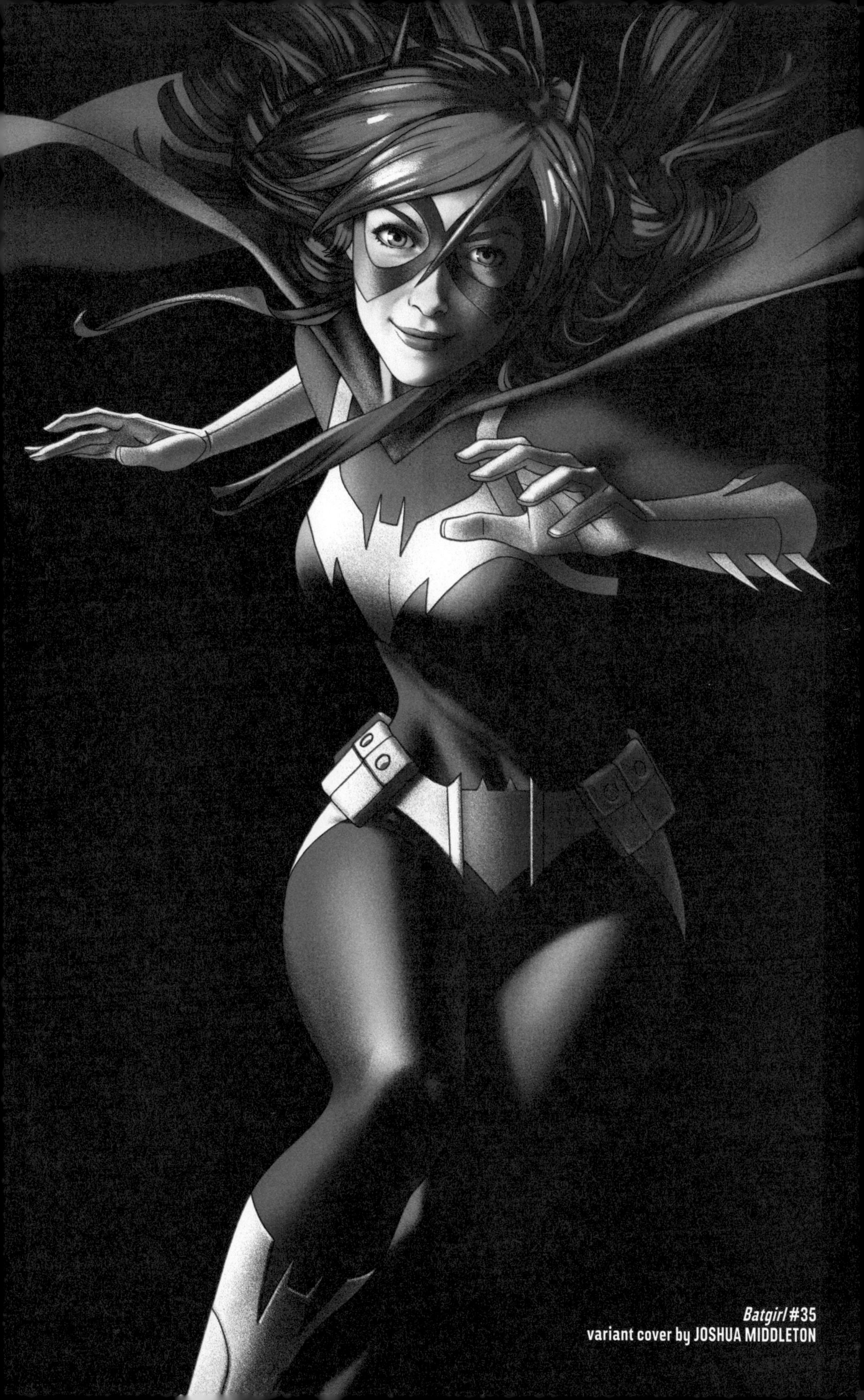

Batgirl #35
variant cover by JOSHUA MIDDLETON

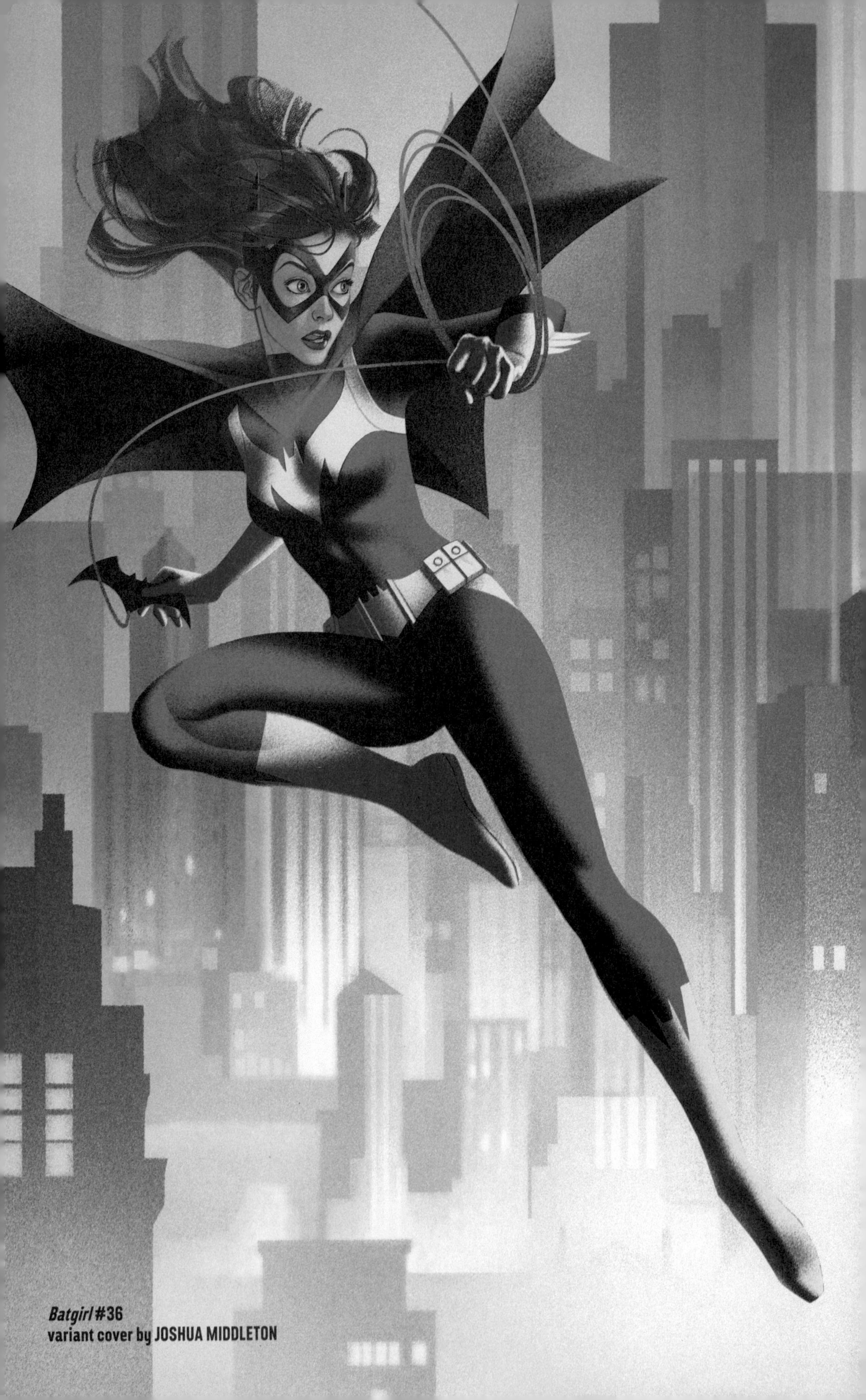

Batgirl #36
variant cover by JOSHUA MIDDLETON

Batgirl #34 and #36
cover sketches by FRANCIS MANAPUL

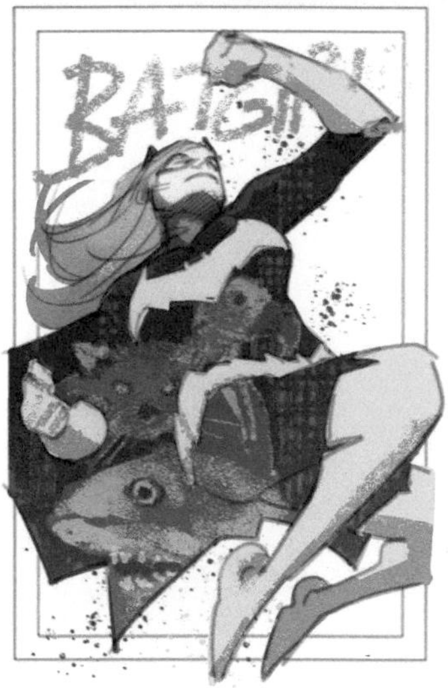

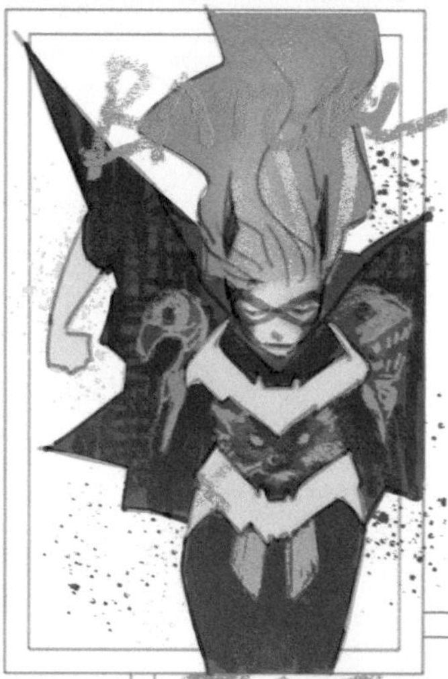

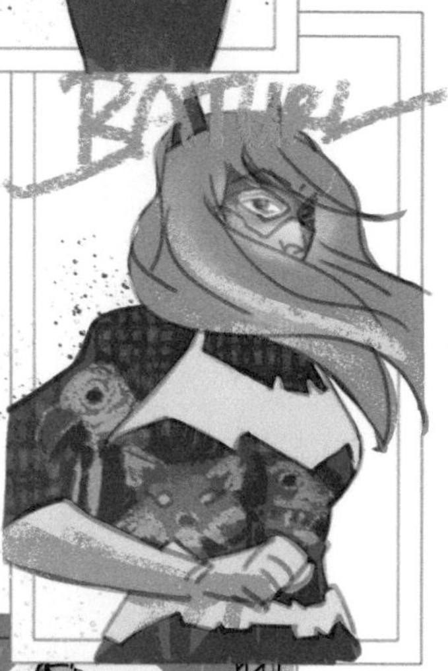

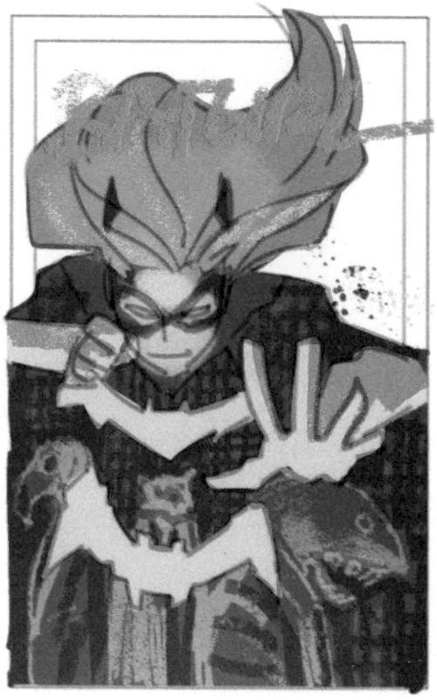

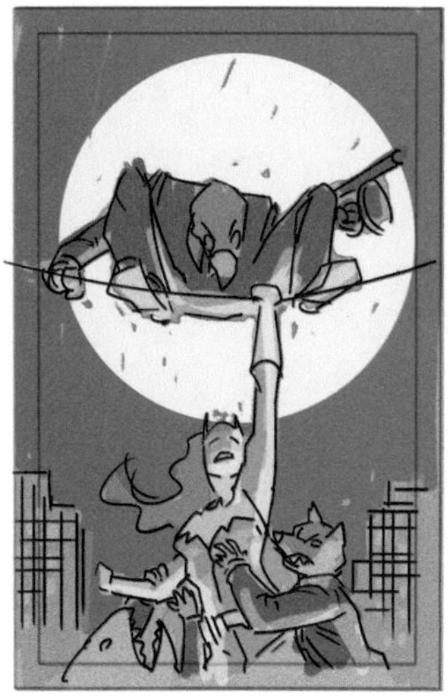

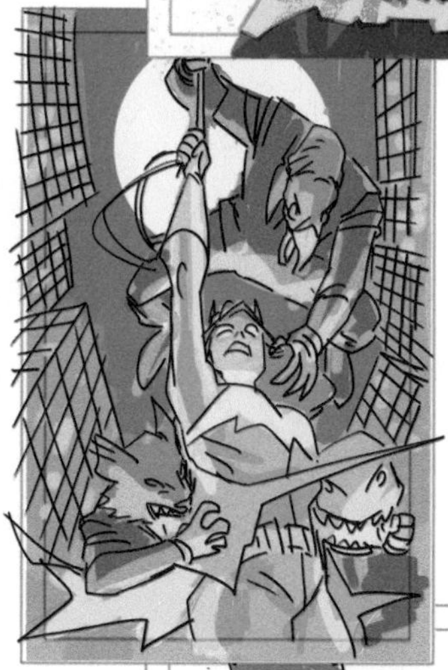

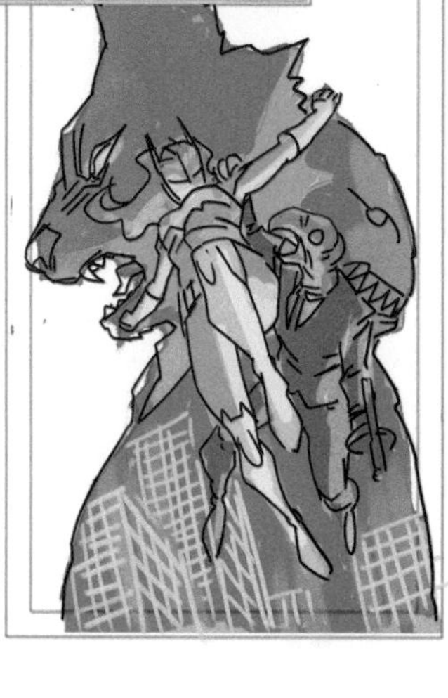

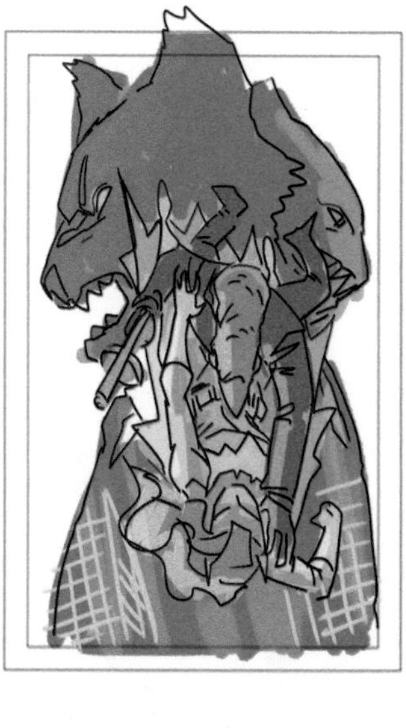

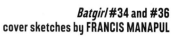

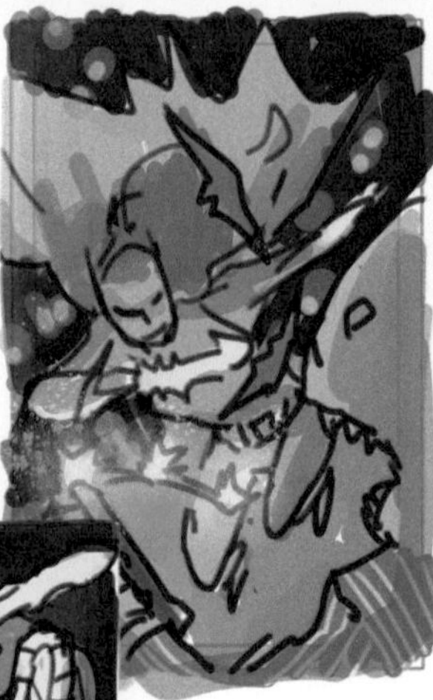
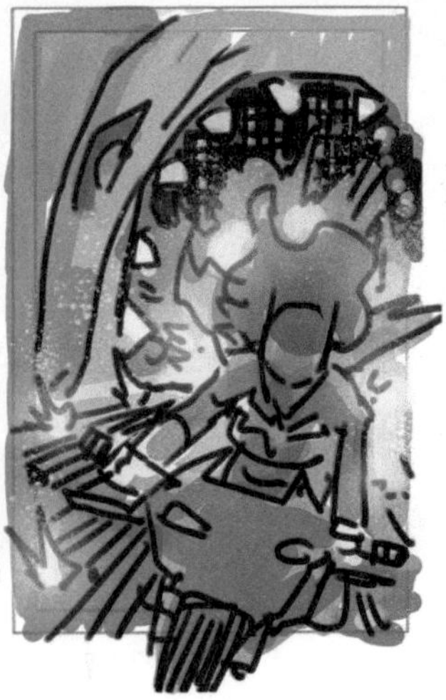
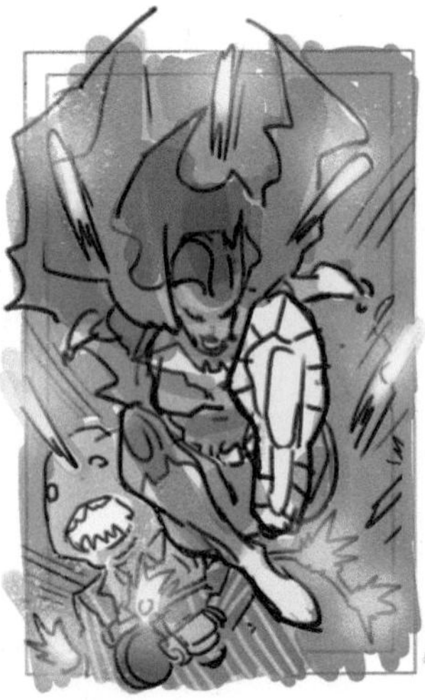
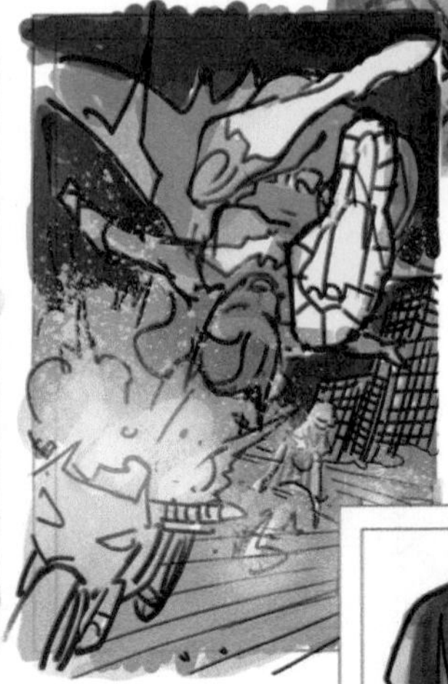
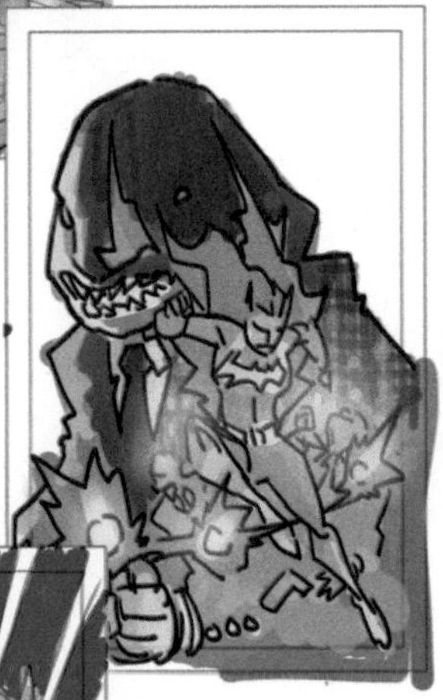
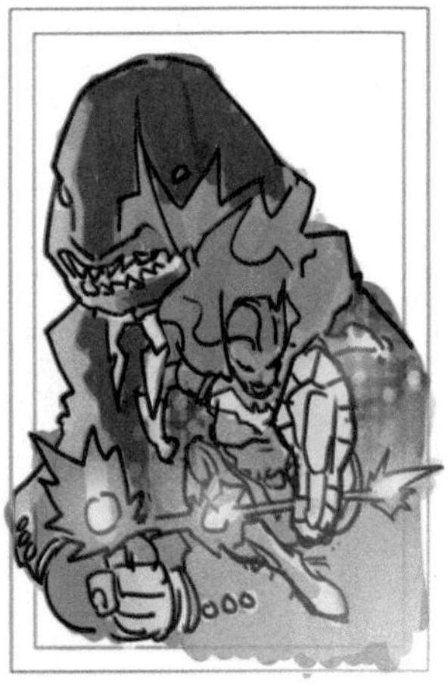
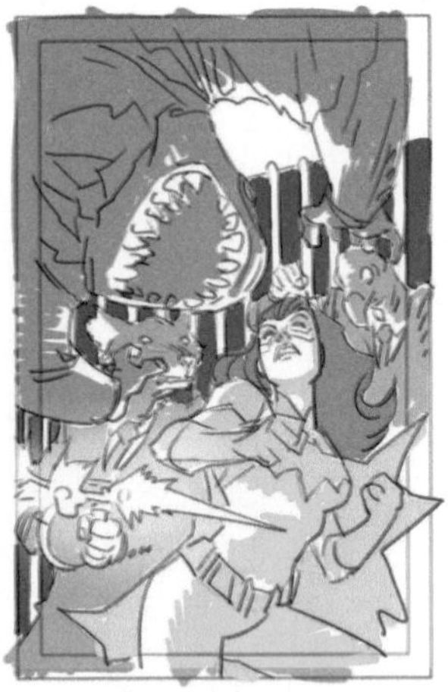
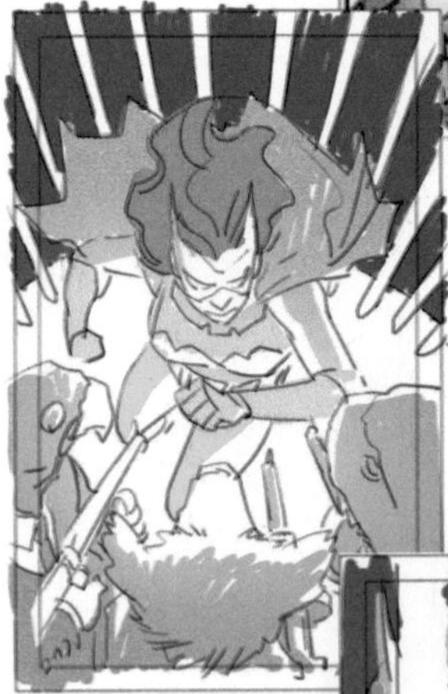
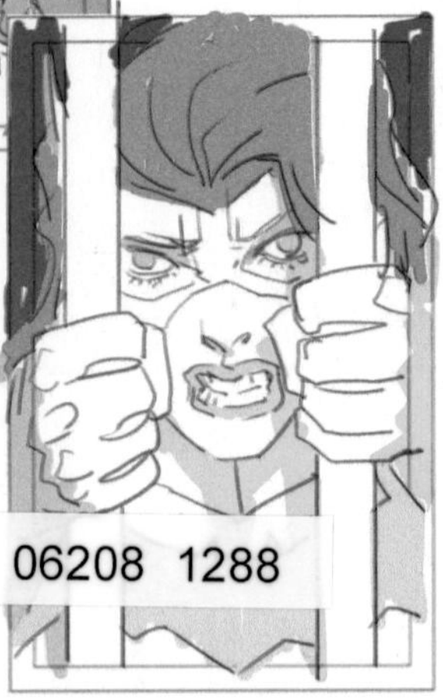
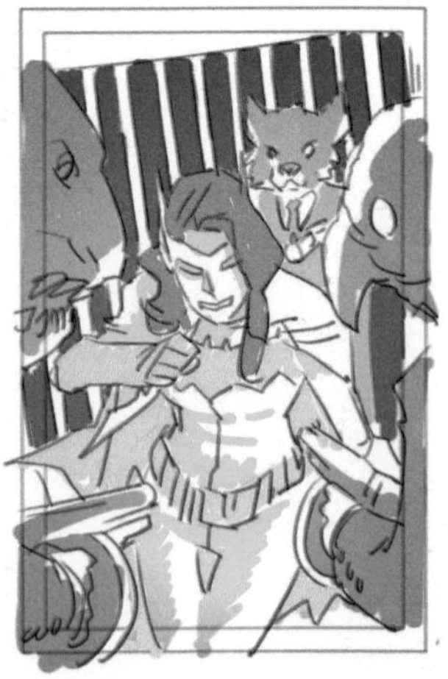

Batgirl #35
cover sketches by FRANCIS MANAPUL